Norbert Elias and Modern Sociology

# Advance Praise for Norbert Elias and Modern Sociology: Knowledge, Interdependence, Power, Process

This is an engagingly written book by two of the world's leading experts on the work of Norbert Elias. Focusing on Elias's sociology of knowledge they show how this might bring sociologists nearer to a cumulative theoretical and empirical science of human social relations. Indispensable.
– Ian Burkitt, Reader in Social Science, University of Bradford, UK

A state-of-the-art assessment of the significance of Norbert Elias's contribution to sociological knowledge and thought.
– Professor Johan Goudsblom, University of Amsterdam, The Netherlands

Given the recent importance afforded to Norbert Elias's work in sociology there has been surprisingly little written on him. This book certainly fills that void. Dunning and Hughes provide a powerful and original overview of Elias's work that is written in a jargon-free, fluent, and clear style.
– Steven Loyal, University College Dublin, Ireland

In an era when sociology has lost its way, Dunning and Hughes have produced an accessible and stimulating analysis of contemporary disciplinary and societal crises that provides an invaluable explication and development of the writings of the last great classical sociologist of our time, Norbert Elias.
– Professor Chris Shilling, Director of Graduate Studies (Research), University of Kent, UK

Eric Dunning and Jason Hughes manage admirably to demonstrate the key ideas – and their origins – of this great sociologist, and to locate them in the context of contemporary discourse. Written in a clear, but never oversimplified language, the book helps us to better understand how Elias's theories enable us to overcome the paradigmatic fragmentation of today's many sociologies.
– Helmut Kuzmics, Professor of Sociology, University of Graz, Austria

By using Elias's sociology of knowledge to contextualize the current 'crisis' in sociology, Dunning and Hughes bring a freshness and contemporary relevance to a familiar – but often misunderstood – theoretical perspective. Their ultimate goal is even more ambitious: to reinvigorate sociology to meet the challenges of the twenty-first century. Consequently, Norbert Elias and Modern Sociology is a must read for Elias's devotees and detractors alike.
– Dominic Malcolm, Senior Lecturer, Loughborough University, UK

# Norbert Elias and Modern Sociology
## Knowledge, Interdependence, Power, Process

Eric Dunning

Jason Hughes

BLOOMSBURY
LONDON • NEW DELHI • NEW YORK • SYDNEY

Bloomsbury Academic
An imprint of Bloomsbury Publishing Plc

| 50 Bedford Square | 175 Fifth Avenue |
| London | New York |
| WC1B 3DP | NY 10010 |
| UK | USA |

www.bloomsbury.com
First published 2013
© Eric Dunning and Jason Hughes, 2013

This work is published subject to a Creative Commons Attribution Non-Commercial Licence. You may share this work for non-commercial purposes only, provided you give attribution to the copyright holder and the publisher. For permission to publish commercial versions please contact Bloomsbury Academic.

CIP records for this book are available from the British Library and the Library of Congress

ISBN: HB: 978-1-78093-225-5
PB: 978-1-78093-226-2

*For Florence, James and Sophia*

while the unknown world – or, expressed differently, the ocean of people's ignorance – like the universe itself may not be finite, the island of reliable knowledge of the universe built into the limitless ocean of our ignorance can be made to grow.

Norbert Elias (2009c: 179),
'The Creed of a Nominalist: Observations on Popper's
*The Logic of Scientific Discovery*',
University College Dublin Press.

# Contents

Acknowledgements xi

Introduction: Sociology and its Discontents 1

1  Working with Elias 17

2  Some Basic Concepts of Figurational Sociology 50

3  Elias's 'Central Theory' 76

4  The Development of Knowledge and the Sciences as Social Processes 112

5  Problems of Method and Values in the Development of Sociological Knowledge 136

6  Elias and 'The Habits of Good Sociology' 162

Conclusion: A Relational 'Turn'? The Future Prospects of Figurational Sociology 201

Notes 208
Bibliography 219
Index 231

# Acknowledgements

The Authors and Publishers would like to thank the Norbert Elias Foundation for kind permission to reprint three diagrams in this book:

Figure 2.1: Some of the stages of integration as they can be presented today from Norbert Elias, *Involvement and Detachment* (Dublin: UCD Press, 2007 (Collected Works, vol. 8)), p. 208.

Figure 2.2: Basic pattern of the egocentric view of society from Norbert Elias, *What is Sociology?* (Dublin: UCD Press, 2012 (Collected Works, vol. 5)), p. 8.

Figure 2.3: A figuration of interdependent individuals ('family', 'state', 'group', 'society', etc.), from Norbert Elias, *What is Sociology?* (Dublin: UCD Press, 2012 (Collected Works, vol. 5)), p. 9.

The Foundation also kindly granted permission to reprint extracts from Elias's personal correspondence and documentation held at the Deutsches Literaturarchiv, Marbach am Neckar.

We would like to thank the following people for their valuable comments, constructive criticism and advice on earlier drafts of this manuscript: Stephen Mennell, Richard Kilminster, Derek Layder, Chris Rojek. We would also like to acknowledge the tremendous support provided by John Goodwin, Henrietta O'Connor, Susan Walker, Ken Sheard, Patrick Murphy, Ivan Waddington, Joe Maguire, Jennifer Maguire, Günther Lüschen, John Loy, Bero Rigauer, Alan Bairner, Katie Liston, Louise Mansfield, Margaret Milsom, Liz Pike, Cas Wouters, Joop Goudsblom, Jon Fletcher, and Hermann Korte. This book was many years in the making, it would not have been possible without the unfailing love and support of Beata Hughes, Allan Hughes, Elisabeth Hughes, Michael Dunning, Rachel Dunning, Kahryn Hughes, Colette Hughes, and Jo-Ann Hughes.

# Introduction
## Sociology and its discontents

A number of excellent introductory texts on the work of Norbert Elias have already been published. Central among them are Stephen Mennell's seminal *Norbert Elias: an Introduction* (1998); Richard Kilminster's pathbreaking *The Sociological Revolution* (1998) and *Norbert Elias: Post-Philosophical Sociology* (2007); Johan Goudsblom's pioneering *Sociology in the Balance* (1977); Robert van Krieken's insightful *Norbert Elias* (1998); Jonathan Fletcher's highly original *Violence and Civilization* (1997); and Cas Wouters's excellent *Informalization: Manners and Emotions Since 1890* (2007). To these must be added two outstanding German texts: Hermann Korte's *Über Norbert Elias: Das Werden eines Menschenwissenschaftlers* (*About Norbert Elias: Becoming a Human Scientist*) (1988) and Helmut Kuzmics's *Der Preis der Zivilisation: Die Zwänge der Moderne im theoretischen Vergleich* (1989) (*The Costs of Civilization: The Pressures of Modernity in Theoretical Comparison*); and Marc Joly's *Devenir Norbert Elias* (*Becoming Norbert Elias*) (2012). While our aim in the present book is not to provide a wholly comprehensive account of Elias's work, we share with the authors of all these texts three central endeavours – 1) that of bringing the sociology of Elias to a new and wider audience; 2) that of providing an explication of some of his key ideas; and 3) finally, that of exploring the implications of his work for sociology more generally.

The distinctive features of our book are threefold. The first is that a central focus of the text is upon Elias's sociology of knowledge. We explore, in particular, Elias's vision of how sociology might proceed in a more 'scientific' manner, with a focus on the principal conceptual reorientations he sought to advance in relation to this undertaking.[1] The second is that we have attempted to position our discussion of Elias's approach within the context of a more general 'crisis', both of sociology as a subject and of the human world at large. Thirdly, and in relation to these other undertakings, we have endeavoured throughout this book, sometimes explicitly, sometimes implicitly or more *sotto voce*, to advance a central line of argument concerning these twin 'human' and 'sociological' crises on the back of our exposition of Elias's work.

In essence, our central argument is that, since social relations form an often unrecognised, frequently misunderstood, and variably important part of everything humans are and do, sociology – the study of these relations – is a discipline which is potentially of significance for and benefit to humankind. There resides in this statement a set of assumptions concerning the role of sociological knowledge which obviously require considerable qualification and clarification. We shall explore such issues at some length in the chapters that follow. For the moment, it is enough to say that sociology, along with humanity itself since its earliest times, has faced a series of recurring 'crises'. In the case of sociology, such crises appear in the longer term to have escalated. Our contention is that Elias's 'figurational' or 'process-sociological' approach, his distinctive model of sociological practice, and many of his key concepts – interdependence, interdependency chains, power balances, figurational dynamics, changing we-I balances, the triad of basic controls, blind processes, 'civilising' and 'decivilising' processes, double-bind figurations – offer considerable potential utility for combating the two-levelled, simultaneously practical and academic crises we humans have thus far faced, and are still currently facing. While, as we shall show, there remain aspects of Elias's approach that require development, extension, and revision – and as he himself recognised, at the most his work constitutes a hopeful 'starting point', not a 'finished' or in any sense 'finalised' paradigm – his work enshrines a model of the sociological endeavour that, we shall argue, potentially offers the basis for what we might call a 'relational turn' within the discipline. Such a 'turn', we suggest, would involve a programme of conjoined theory and research that could serve as a more adequate means of orientation towards the recurrent human crises we have alluded to above, and would indeed constitute a move beyond the current sociological crisis.

## The sociological 'crisis'

The term 'crisis' has a series of connotations, some useful, some less so for the purposes of our present discussion. Etymologically, the word derives from the Greek noun, *krisis*, literally meaning 'decision', and in turn from the verb *krinein*, 'to decide'. It was used by medical philosophers such as Galen and Hippocrates to refer to the 'turning point' of a disease, and, in relation to these origins, has come since the seventeenth century to mean a 'decisive point' (OED 2005). Within intellectual circles, the term has become increasingly politicised. In sociological usage, talk of a 'crisis' might variously refer to: a society on the precipice of rapid change or 'collapse'; social conditions *in need* of urgent and radical transformation; an intransigent social or political phase that, through its own immanent dynamics, is set to become transformed at some point in the future; times of intense social upheaval, change, or volatility; and periods of 'rupture', 'break', and historical discontinuity. In using the term, we wish to avoid some of these connotations, in particular the overtones of historical staccato, and the tendency to think about humans as a species and sociology as a discipline, in a 'hodiecentric' (Goudsblom 1977), that is, present-centred manner. Indeed, as will shortly be discussed, successive waves of sociologists have declared the discipline to be facing a 'crisis'; and similarly, generations of humans have variously proclaimed their societies to be facing rapid and critical decline, characteristically calling for a return to an imagined 'golden age' that is or was considered to reside somewhere in the distant past (Elias 1987a: 357). At all costs, we wish to avoid the impression that we consider the 'crises' to which we are referring in this book as representing the 'culmination' of long lines of development which somehow 'finish' dramatically in the present and, at that, with hitherto unparalleled problems and difficulties. That said, where the term crisis is rather more useful for our purposes lies in its invoking of a sense of urgency. More specifically, its connotation of a need for change is intended here to convey our view that there needs to be some reconsideration of how the sociological enterprise is conceived, particularly in relation to how sociological knowledge might be developed and utilised, specifically to help avert some aspects of the 'human crisis'.[2] Also, in a rather pragmatic sense, the term crisis provides us with a means for considering the development of sociology as a discipline in conjunction with a number of specific social developments. It thus allows us to explore the inter-relationships between social problems and paradigmatic problems within the discipline.

In 1970, a highly influential book by Alvin Gouldner was published with the title, *The Coming Crisis of Western Sociology*. Gouldner's central thesis in that book was that America was then in the throes of a multi-layered rebellion in which the black civil rights movement, the women's movement, and protest against the Vietnam War were central. It was a rebellion mainly of younger people which spread widely through the West, with university campuses forming major sites of resistance to the *status quo*. In such a context, Gouldner argued rhetorically that:

> Social theorists today work within a crumbling social matrix of paralyzed urban centers and battered campuses. Some may put cotton in their ears, but their bodies still feel the shock waves. It is no exaggeration to say that we theorize today within the sound of guns. The old order has the picks of a hundred rebellions thrust into its hide. (Gouldner 1970: vii)

In such a context, Gouldner maintained, sociologists were becoming increasingly drawn into 'the coalescing military-industrial-welfare complex' with the consequence that it was becoming 'unthinkingly evident that sociology has become dangerously dependent on the very world it has pledged to study objectively' (1970: 511). In short, sociologists were being increasingly incorporated into the *status quo* and used as instruments of management and social control. They were, Gouldner proposed, producing 'interested' accounts of the social world and, in that way, becoming both part of the problem and of the forthcoming sociological crisis as Gouldner envisaged it. His solution was to call for the development of a 'radical' and 'reflexive' sociology practised by self-aware and critical sociologists dedicated to gathering knowledge which could be used in ushering in a new era.[3]

The Western world and its universities have, indeed, changed in fundamental ways since Gouldner wrote, but the changes have not necessarily followed the lines he envisaged. With his partly Marxist leanings, he seems to have expected – and he was by no means alone in this – a series of broadly egalitarian social changes to occur both within Western countries and between the West and 'the rest' (Hall 1992). Instead, at least until the banking crisis of 2008, the agents of corporate capital have increased their national and international control; neo-liberal economics have, albeit through new iterations, arguably become increasingly hegemonic globally; the gap between developing countries and the West has tended, with notable exceptions such as China, India and Brazil, to widen and, as part of this, the former Soviet Union has collapsed and lost control over its former satellites in Eastern Europe. Some of these, especially the Czech Republic, Slovakia, Hungary and Poland, have subsequently become more integrated with the West. To this must be added the growing significance of Christian-Moslem and Moslem-Jewish, and Moslem-Moslem tensions, including, in recent years, internal tensions culminating in the wave of uprisings in the Middle East commonly referred to as the 'Arab Spring'. All of this, of course, is to say nothing of the problems connected with the largely anthropogenic processes of 'global warming' and 'climate change', of which people have become increasingly aware in recent years.

In our view, the challenge to sociology produced in this situation is best understood in the context of this more general crisis. Both the changes in the 1960s and 1970s which worried Gouldner and about which he wrote so eloquently and with relative optimism – and the changes in the 1980s, 90s and early 2000s we have just discussed – can be seen as having occurred primarily as part of a process of accelerating and increasingly global social change which can be traced to the interconnected 'scientific', 'industrial' and 'democratic' 'revolutions'[4] which gathered momentum in Europe in the seventeenth, eighteenth, nineteenth, and twentieth centuries. An increasingly secular and 'fact'-orientated approach to the understanding of these processes and their social origins and ramifications grew up as part of them. In short, in a period of accelerating social change and the uncertainties that it engendered, specific groups of intellectuals, at first outside the universities (for example, Comte and Marx), and later within them (for example, Durkheim and Weber), began to take humans and the societies they form as objects of 'scientific' reflection and research. In that way and in that sense, the 'social sciences' were 'born'.

In order to explore how the work of Elias constituted an attempt to deal with and overcome the gathering sociological crisis, it is first necessary to outline some of its major characteristics. As we see it, 'sociology' began to emerge as part of this overall social process. A crucial early stage was marked by the invention of the term 'sociology' itself by Auguste Comte in 1835. He (and others such as his collaborator, St Simon) had previously used the term 'social physics' but, in 1835, Adolphe Quetelet, a Belgian statistician, published a book which he called *On Man and the Development of Human Faculties: An Essay in Social Physics* (1835). This was anathema to Comte for two main reasons: first, he objected to Quetelet's vision of 'social physics' as a primarily statistical subject; and second, he objected to what he regarded as Quetelet's utopian and, in Comte's view, scientifically unwarranted egalitarianism (Coser 1971). Comte did not believe in the possibility of 'perfect equality' and he saw sociology as a science which, through a combination of observation and reasoning, would enable people to make a better life for themselves by transcending both the unrealistic dreams offered by 'theological' and 'metaphysical' thinking, and the 'wild', equally unrealistic terrors generated by what Comte regarded as these 'primitive' anthropomorphic and anthropocentric forms of thinking.

Another term coined by Comte was 'positivism'. The chief 'positive' method – a method liable to yield 'positive' results – that he recommended for use in sociology was the method of historical comparison. Even though the meaning of 'positivism' has changed (see our discussion in Chapters 4 and 5) such that it has now become something of a pejorative term referring to the inappropriate use of natural science methods in studies in the social field, a struggle between sociologists who advocate comparative-historical methods and those who advocate statistics has been built into our subject since its early days.[5] Paraphrasing Dahrendorf's (1959) description of the 'new middle class' in capitalist societies, sociology can be said to have been 'born decomposed', that is, with differences, conflicts and tensions built into its core. Indeed, one might describe the subject as having been inherently 'crisis-ridden' from the outset.

These early sociological conflicts were fiercely fought. However, the conflicts between the proponents of opposing paradigms that surfaced in the 1960s and that continue through to today – which were manifestations, as we suggested earlier, of what Alvin Gouldner labelled in 1970 'the coming crisis' – are fiercer and more intense than past conflicts. For some twenty years following the end of the Second World War, advocates of functional and non-Comtean (that is, ahistorical and even anti-historical) 'positivist' sociology, many of them from, or émigrés to, the United States, reigned supreme.[6] Then, for a variety of sociological and extra-sociological reasons, the functionalist-empiricist/functionalist-'positivist' hegemony collapsed and sociology, the subject which had been born 'decomposed', became multiply fractured and 'crisis-ridden' at its core. The sociological reasons for this process of decomposition included, among other things, the difficulties encountered by functionalists, especially Parsons and his followers, in dealing with issues such as conflict, power, and change.[7] The extra-sociological reasons included the effects on a younger generation of sociologists whose adult identities and stances towards the subject were being forged in a context influenced by powerful events which included: the Vietnam war and the protest against it; the 'civil rights' struggle by 'blacks' in the USA; the rise of 'second-wave' feminism; the campus rebellions which broke out in North America and many countries in Western Europe in the late 1960s; the growth of the 'sexual revolution' and 'informalisation' or 'permissiveness' as it was popularly called (Wouters 1977); and the power shift towards the younger generation propelled by technological change, egalitarian ideologies, and the increasing child-centeredness of parents. Sociologists who received their training in the late 1960s and early 1970s differed from their predecessors. The former worried less about the dangers of the 'Cold War' and the prospect of nuclear annihilation and focused more on struggling against capitalism which, for most Marxists and near-Marxists, was seen as the principal cause of most iniquities and global conflicts. Perhaps because fewer of them had directly experienced the Second World War, they were more inclined to take peace for granted.

The events in France in May 1968 are often cited as a crucial 'turning point' in the development of contemporary sociology. The dramatic student uprisings, factory occupations, and workers' general strike that took place then have been referred to as the '... last major revolutionary uprising in the Western world' (Kellner 2002: xvi). There remains considerable debate, though, concerning the precise significance of these events. On the one hand, they are seen by some to mark a watershed of 1960s cultural change that extended considerably beyond the French national context – marking a 'near revolution': namely the culmination and ascendancy of strengthening opposition to Western capitalism. Indeed, the 'explosions' of 1968 contained antisystemic elements that were repeated worldwide (Wallerstein 2004: 469). On the other hand, however, the events were and are for some also the source of great disappointment, symbolising 'the revolution that never came' and a victory for the French state led by its premier, Charles de Gaulle, who successfully anticipated and countered the insurrection, ultimately containing it, and in so doing demonstrating once and for all that the capitalist establishment could resist and absorb almost any form of opposition (Kellner 2002: xv-xvii). While Marxists such as Herbert Marcuse and Henri Lefèbvre found in the uprisings only confirmation of their core beliefs, for others who were involved in the protests – such as Michel Foucault, Jean Baudrillard, Jean Francois Lyotard, Jacques Derrida, and Julia Kristeva – the lack of revolutionary success demonstrated, or further reinforced, the need for fundamentally new forms of revolutionary thought; and with this the foundations of the poststructuralist movement were consolidated (Kellner 2002: xvii). As we shall endeavour to show towards the end of this book, Foucault and Elias each knew of the other's work and were to some extent influenced by it.

Poststructuralist and postmodernist writers variously called into question some of the most fundamental aspects of sociology as a discipline. In particular, these writers came to question aspects of what they considered to be the 'modernist project' of 'privileging' scientific knowledge as a basis for 'truth claims'. More fundamentally, they rejected the supposedly modernist 'faith' in human rationality, which they suggested at once constituted both the 'subject' and the 'object' of knowledge in the human sciences. In other words, they highlighted the paradox that human self-reflection is at once the condition for, and the limit of, knowledge about the social world, and as such, these writers rejected the very enterprise of 'social science' since this involved a fallacious cycle of proceeding '... from that which is given to representation to that which renders representation possible, but which is still representation' (Foucault 2002: 364). Thus the poststructuralist 'movement' – and the term is problematic, because it did/does not constitute a coherent or homogeneous school of thought as such – led *via* various different avenues of thought to a radical scepticism, not only about whether it was meaningful to talk about 'the real world', but of whether such a 'reality' was even amenable to human 'scientific' reasoning, or even 'existed' in any independent or literal sense. Against this backdrop, classical sociological writers such as Comte, Marx, Durkheim and Weber came by a number of influential scholars to be regarded as outmoded, as having their roots in the Enlightenment, and indeed as forming part of the rational scientific impetus that so characterised the 'modernism' against which postmodernist and poststructuralist writers sought to rally.

Part of the legacy of poststructuralism was ever greater paradigmatic diversification. Since the 1960s, rather than conciliation and paradigmatic resolution, or even ground-clearing, there has been on offer in sociology an increasing array of paradigms, albeit that some have now fallen from vogue. These include – and this is by no means an exhaustive list – various forms of functionalism (for example, 'neo', 'normative' and 'general', 'soft' and 'hard'); social systems theory; Marxism (for example, 'humanist' and 'structuralist'); feminist sociology (for example, 'liberal', 'socialist', 'Marxist', 'post-' and 'cultural'); critical sociology; conflict theory; Weberian theory; rational choice theory; ethnomethodology; symbolic interactionism; structuralism; post-structuralism (of which there are too many variants to list); postmodernist sociology; actor-network theory; critical realism; reflexive sociology; structuration theory; and figurational (also 'developmental' or 'process') sociology. Among other things, these paradigms differ regarding the positions taken by their advocates in relation to: (i) epistemological/methodological issues, that is how knowledge is obtained and how we can know what we think we know; and (ii) ontological/factual issues, that is how the universe and, as part of it, our world and our societies are constructed, what their basic characteristics are and how these are inter-related. Among the epistemological/methodological issues are the following:

1. Where the advocates of different paradigms see sociology located on the continuum between the arts/humanities and the sciences. As we shall see, Elias saw sociology as a 'human science' (*Menschenwissenschaft*) and himself as a 'human scientist' (*Menschenwissenschaftler*).

2. *If* they see sociology as a science, whether, for example, they see it as a science in a 'soft' sense, for example in a comparative-historical or participant observation sense, or in a 'hard', non-Comtean 'positivist' sense based on mathematics, statistics and equivalents to laboratory experimentation. Or, indeed, whether they subscribe to alternative models of 'science', as in the case of, for instance, critical realism and figurational sociology.

3. Whether they see the purpose of sociological knowledge as an 'end in itself' (that is, as something that is interesting and valuable for its own sake), as a tool for improving human performance, for example, in education, work, or sport; or as a means to identify and achieve desirable socio-political goals, for instance reducing class, 'race', and gender inequality, or violence and crime.

Among the ontological/factual issues are where the advocates of different paradigms stand in relation to such dualisms as 'materialism' *versus* 'idealism', 'agency' *versus* 'structure', 'social statics' *versus* 'social dynamics', and 'synchronic' studies *versus* 'diachronic' studies. The 'materialism' *versus* 'idealism' dualism centres primarily on the explanatory role of ideas in social processes relative to the role, for example, of 'economic forces'. The dualism of 'agency' *versus* 'structure' fundamentally concerns the degrees of choice that human individuals are able to exercise relative to the degrees to which their actions and beliefs are structurally determined or constrained. 'Social statics' *versus* 'social dynamics' – these concepts were first developed by Comte – and 'synchronic' *versus* 'diachronic' studies are both related to questions of processes over time and whether the advocates of different positions see sociology as concerned solely with the present, or whether they see it as primarily an historical or 'developmental' subject.

Approached in these terms, the abundance of sociological paradigms can be categorised as consisting of six basic types: functionalist paradigms; conflict paradigms; action paradigms; feminist paradigms; post-paradigms; and attempted syntheses such as: the structuration theory of Anthony Giddens, the reflexive sociology of Pierre Bourdieu, the neofunctionalism of Jeffrey Alexander, Jürgen Habermas's theory of communicative rationality, and the figurational sociology of Elias – the subject matter of this book. Mention of these syntheses suggests another source of basic differences between paradigms: the way that advocates of each of them deal with the relationship of sociology to philosophy. Thus, while, for example, Giddens, the primary architect of structuration theory, advocates a heavy dependency of sociology on philosophy,[8] Elias urged sociologists to maximise their autonomy in relation to other subjects, especially philosophy (Kilminster 1998; 2002; 2008).

Conflict, competition, and dissension of the kinds that have come to reign between the supporters of different sociological paradigms can, of course, be conducive to the advancement of knowledge. Such conflict was no doubt important to the early development of the discipline – bringing to light many of the shortcomings of once hallowed or axiomatic principles, orientations, concepts and ideas that would perhaps otherwise have remained unquestioned. However, the consequences of the disunity have arguably also been deleterious, especially since the 1980s and 90s. In those two decades in particular, paradigmatic variety and disunity in sociology gave way increasingly to paradigmatic fragmentation, with a series of problematic consequences.

Firstly, the proliferation of paradigmatic alternatives has greatly facilitated the decline of any kind of coherent 'core' to sociology. Indeed, in tandem with a poststructuralist 'decentring' of the human subject, the 'subject' of sociology itself has also lost its 'centre'. There is currently no clear agreement on the staple propositional knowledge required for even a basic mastery of the discipline. There is little consensus regarding what might constitute a standard sociological curriculum; no hierarchy of concepts or models to mark a commonly agreed upon learning trajectory for a newcomer to the subject. There is no set of 'paradigmatic texts' that are, by common consent, unequivocally agreed to form the basic 'building blocks' of sociology. Even the once relatively standard 'Marx, Weber, Durkheim' model of 'classical sociological theory 101' is no longer a universal one. Our point here is not so much a lamentation regarding the passing of a golden age in which 'we all knew what sociology was'. Indeed, such an age never existed, and there are in many cases good reasons for the 'decentring' of the discipline at this stage in its development. Rather, we wish to highlight the problem that arises because sociology, particularly relative to other social science disciplines such as psychology and economics, lacks a centralised intellectual consciousness. Partly in relation to this, there is little sense of a shared and consensual sociological enterprise, and with it, little basis for cross-paradigmatic collaboration; little intergenerational knowledge development; and few prospects for 'advances' in the discipline – let alone agreement upon what might constitute an 'advance', or even if such 'advances' are necessary or desirable. In suggesting this, we are not arguing that sociologists should emulate the models provided by psychology and economics in which, to oversimplify somewhat, logical positivism and empiricism are largely unquestioned as parts of a 'standard paradigm' for knowledge within these fields. It is nevertheless the case that, at the very least, the practitioners of these disciplines have a clearer sense of common endeavour, and have been, relative to sociology, more successful in developing institutional safeguards, professional standards, and the collaborative testing and revision of principles and models such that knowledge developed within these fields might be refined over time.[9]

Secondly, the paradigmatic disarray discussed above has also facilitated the growth of 'factions' within the discipline which, together with the emergence of established-outsider figurations surrounding the 'membership' of such groups, has compounded a tendency towards the development of misrepresentations, sometimes caricatures, of the work of others. Perhaps partly in relation to its immense paradigmatic complexity and fragmentation, a particular characteristic of the discipline of sociology seems to be the often rapid and somewhat wholesale dismissal by some members of the discipline of entire 'schools' or approaches without careful consideration and cross-paradigm dialogue. Sociology has become a subject so vast in scope and yet so heterogeneous in focus and specialisms that to have even a basic grounding in all branches and iterations of the discipline would constitute an entire life's work. An associated trend, perhaps understandably, is that of a tendency towards theoretical pluralism and eclecticism relative to paradigmatic synthesis and consolidation. With it has come an increasing separation of theory from research as a specialism in its own right, particularly one that is treated as an undertaking which is relatively 'context-independent'.

Thirdly, in relation to the latter point, such a divorce of theory from research has greatly augmented the possibilities for the import into sociology of theoretical models, orientations, and intellectual practices from other disciplines. Taken together with the inter-related processes of fragmentation and specialisation, such tendencies have weakened sociologists relative to specialists in other subjects, making it difficult collectively to resist the intrusion into the field of the representatives of higher status subjects such as philosophy. A key example is the enthusiastic embrace by some practitioners of the discipline of some of the more radical variants of postmodernist philosophy. Whilst, as we suggested earlier, the postmodernist intellectual movement may have initially been useful as a means of problematising (though perhaps not always constructively) some of sociology's foundations, in its wake, postmodernist theorising has left an enduring current of thought which involves notions that, in some cases, verge on solipsism and extreme epistemic relativism – the shortcomings of which have been convincingly demonstrated (see, for example, Sokal and Bricmont (1998)). It is, of course, crucial for sociologists to investigate what is knowable about the social world and, indeed, for natural scientists to investigate the universe as a whole. However, the lack of any coherent 'centre' to sociology – and we use the term quite 'self-consciously' – has prevented the formation of safeguards against, as Pierre Bourdieu puts it, people being able 'to utter all kinds of nonsense about the social world' (Bourdieu and Wacquant 1992: 53).

## Sociology and its discontents: Critical and political investments in knowledge

It is probably evident to most readers that the title of this Introductory chapter, 'Sociology and its Discontents', is modelled on a famous book by Freud, *Civilisation and its Discontents* (1930) – one of the texts that influenced Elias when writing his *magnum opus*, *Über den Prozess der Zivilisation* (1939), published in English as *The Civilising Process* (1978, 1982, 1994, 2000) and now reissued in a thoroughly revised edition in the Collected Works under the more accurate title *On The Process of Civilisation* (2012a). It is noteworthy that 'Civilisation and its Discontents', while now immediately recognisable as the title of one of Freud's key works, is rather a poor translation of the original German, *Das Unbehagen in der Kultur*. As Bruno Bettelheim (1985) observed, the term *Unbehagen* would have been better translated as 'discomfort' or 'malaise'. 'Discontents' has decidedly rational connotations, whereas Freud used *Unbehagen* precisely to designate a set of *feelings* (Bettelheim 1985: 98ff; Kilminster 2007: 168). A series of connotations in the original German are essentially lost in translation, notably Freud's central idea that 'discomforts' are integral to culture – that they are its inevitable and inescapable consequences. Moreover, as Elias discusses in the opening sections of *On the Process of Civilisation*, the term *Kultur* in the original German usage had a highly specific set of meanings, notably 'valued cultural accomplishments', and was in many ways antithetical to *Zivilisation*, which in German implies rather more superficial material and technical developments.[10]

Elias, too, faced problems with the translation of his work by others. However, notwithstanding such issues, there is much in this play on a mistranslated title that encapsulates a key aspect of our argument thus far: namely that within sociology there is currently considerable 'discontent', and for that matter, 'malaise' and 'discomfort'. And by further extension of the comparison with Freud's notion, such 'discontents' are inter-related with more general successive 'crises' that have come to characterise the 'human lot'. As we have argued, among a number of other defining problems currently faced by practitioners of the subject is the idea that there is at present little agreement on the very purpose or direction of sociology as an intellectual enterprise, let alone upon the meaning of key concepts and terminology. And yet, at the same time, within many sociological circles it has become something of an unspoken yet requisite credential to classify as 'critical' the approach to be adopted in almost any piece of academic writing, particularly one which deals centrally with the work of an important sociological writer. It is necessary to maintain 'critical distance', and at all costs to avoid the charge of 'uncritical' writing or analysis. It would seem that, whilst sociology as a discipline does not currently have a centralised intellectual consciousness, it does, nonetheless, have a relatively well-defined and widely disseminated, if on the whole unstated, set of scholarly mores and expectations for how serious practitioners of the discipline should conduct themselves intellectually, particularly in relation to what should *not* be said or done. Indeed, self-proclaimed 'critical sociologists' often implicitly, and in some cases explicitly, denounce as 'uncritical' others who choose not to announce themselves with this label. However, the term 'critical' – and its derivatives, 'criticism', 'critique' and 'critiquing' – are words that are themselves rarely defined, much less 'critically' scrutinised, and which are often taken for granted. It is worth exploring these in some detail since they raise important questions about the role of sociological knowledge in forming the basis, firstly for interventions in the social world, and secondly, for the relationships between political investments and sociological practice and the 'twin crises' discussed above, all of which represent important concerns for Elias's work. Moreover, they are central to our arguments in this book as a whole.

In his paper entitled Norbert Elias's Post-Philosophical Sociology: From "Critique" to Relative Detachment', Richard Kilminster (2011) has arguably gone further than most in teasing out the different layers of meaning of the terms 'criticism' and 'critical'. Kilminster starts with four everyday meanings, *viz*: one state about to change into another as in 'critical mass' in physics; decisive, crucial; estimating the qualities of literature, involving careful judgement, exact; and, currently most predominant, fault-finding, censorious, carping, passing judgement. It is this last set of meanings, or approximations to them, that come closest to the usage of the term by some contemporary sociologists who call themselves 'critical'. Critical sociologists in this vein write in opposition to a once-dominant Weberian orthodoxy in sociology, and in doing so are implicitly announcing their intention of passing 'critical' judgements on, for example, the capitalist mode of production, gender relations, colonial or neo-colonial[11] ethnic relations, etc. Thus, at the risk of some over-simplification, we might accordingly draw a distinction between normative judgements which stress how the world *should* be; empirical judgements which seek to stress how the world *actually is*; and critical judgements which stress, in particular, how the world *should not* be.

According to Kilminster, there have so far been three main technical uses of the term 'critical' in philosophy and sociology: the Kantian, where it means the demonstration of presuppositions through positing universal *a priori* logical concepts such as 'time', 'space', 'cause', 'morality' etc.; the Hegelian, where it refers to comparing particular phenomena with their ideal universal forms;[12] and the Marxian, in which 'practical-critical', that is, (in some cases) revolutionary, activity is said to involve re-fashioning the real world to make it become what it could ideally be. Most importantly, however, all three – and all their numerous variations – involve(d) utilising various forms of transcendental reasoning.

During the twentieth century, as the utopian ideals of the eighteenth and nineteenth century German philosophers (and their French and British counterparts) came increasingly to grief on the rocks of a complex, fluid, ever-changing and, in many respects, violent and unanticipated social reality, so philosophers and sociologists who continued to maintain the idea of themselves as 'critical' increasingly abandoned the conception of an historical *telos* ('end' or 'goal'). Examples of what was abandoned include the notion that history is marching inexorably towards socialism/communism, the disappearance of classes, the withering away of the state, and so forth. In their place, they opted for a deconstruction of 'grand theory' *per se* (as in the case of the poststructuralist movement in the wake of the systemic uprisings of the late 1960s). Alternatively, they erected equally transcendent, generally more abstract and metaphysical concepts and arguments such as Adorno's 'utopian moment of the object', or Habermas's 'ideal speech situation' as universal yardsticks with which to compare present-day society; and Bauman and Levinas's ideas of 'pre-social moral awareness' and that 'being for the other' is pre-social and thus universal.

It was largely this descent of some branches of philosophy into metaphysics that led Elias to claim that it is a subject which has outlived its usefulness (Kilminster 1998; 2007). In its place, as we shall see, he offered the theoretical-empirical idea of 'detours *via* detachment' followed by 'secondary involvement' as the only secure way of augmenting the stock of reliable knowledge, the existence of which is a vital precondition for human survival and comfort. This is not to suggest that Elias claimed his work to be 'neutral', 'value-free', or 'objective'. Rather, Elias advocated 'detours *via* detachment' as means of collaboratively and inter-generationally adding to a disciplinary stock of knowledge pertaining to the sphere of human figurations. What the metaphor of a 'detour' means is that, like other social scientists, sociologists have specific interests to defend emotionally involved positions but should strive to learn, at first, to distance themselves from and control them, and then return to them *via* a process of 'secondary involvement'. A useful example of what Elias meant in this connection comes from one of his earliest pieces of solo writing in the sociology of sport. In the extract that follows, his starting point was the Holocaust and its place in and significance for the 'civilising' of the West. He went on to discuss the issue of how best to instil civilising self-controls into children, and suggested that, in approaching the study of such concerns, sociologists should crucially seek, through the exercise of self-distanciation and self-control, to get beyond the level of 'popular', 'folk' beliefs and their own and other people's ideals and values, and to penetrate what occurs in socialisation processes and what the consequences of particular socialising practices actually are. Elias wrote:

> The Nazi episode served as a kind of warning; it was a reminder that the restraints against violence are not symptoms of the superiority of the *nature* of 'civilized nations', not eternal characteristics of their social or ethnic make-up, but aspects of a specific type of social development which has resulted in more differentiated and stable social control of the means of violence and in a corresponding conscience-formation. Evidently, this type of social development could be reversed... This does not necessarily imply that there are no grounds for evaluating the results of this development ... as 'better' than the corresponding manifestations of earlier developmental stages. Wider understanding of the nexus of facts provides indeed the only secure basis for value judgements of this type. Without it, we cannot know, for example, whether our manner of building up individual self-controls against physical violence is not associated with psychological malformations which themselves might appear highly barbaric to a more civilized age than ours (Elias and Dunning 1986: 143–44; 2008: 124–5)

In short, assuming that one does not get lost along the way, undertaking a detour *via* detachment can lay the foundations for a process of 'secondary involvement', for returning to a more 'involved' position in which – if the detour has been successful – armed with potentially *more* reliable, *more* 'reality-congruent' or *more* 'object-adequate' knowledge, subsequent generations of sociologists will have the potential to intervene in the social world in a manner that has more intended relative to unintended consequences than would have been possible hitherto. So, Elias and those who have taken up the mantel of his work, share with 'critical' sociologists, a desire to act, to 'make a difference' in the world (Giddens 1984), and in particular to change specific forms of social relations if they can be shown to embody constraints greater than are necessary, or which are inherently exploitative, dehumanising, or in other ways unsatisfactory. However, as will be seen in later sections of this book, particularly Chapters 4 and 5, the *ratio* between involvement and detachment (Elias 1987a; 2007a) – for it is arguably always a question of 'blends', 'balances', and 'alloys', and rarely if ever one of complete involvement or detachment – is in Elias's work envisaged in a diachronically structured manner with a considerable emphasis placed upon the importance of the 'detour' in order to avoid a collapse into either 'subjectivism' or 'idealism'. It is in some ways paradoxical that the very undertaking of writing papers and books on, or which utilise, sociology, including of course those of 'critical sociology', exemplifies a characteristic human 'detour behaviour': you cannot directly eat or drink what you think and write.

Where Elias parts company with the critical sociological tradition is that, while he felt with some degree of confidence that it is possible to make societies 'better', he considered 'utopias' – although they perform important functions for people – as in the end nothing more than dreams (Elias 1983b). Indeed, the original Greek derivatives of the term utopia, '*ou*', 'not' and *topos*, 'place', mean 'non-existing place', and not 'ideal place' (the latter set of connotations appears to date back to Thomas Moore's (1516) fictional epic, *Utopia*) (OED 2005). In fact, although he did not use that term, Elias in his later work distinguished 'dystopias' or 'fear-dream utopias' from 'utopias' of a solely positive kind. As he expressed it:

> In a number of fields, scientists have succeeded in raising the curtain of fantasies characteristic of the more spontaneous wishes and urges of humans which concealed from their eyes the real nexus of events. But the more realistic picture of the world revealed by scientists was often far from pleasant. Not only Darwin's theory of evolution, but many other scientific discoveries, too, replaced an emotionally far more satisfying fantasy picture with a more realistic but emotionally far less satisfying picture of the world in general and of humanity in particular. Copernicus' and Galileo's fight against the egocentric conception of the universe started the sequence of traumatic emotional disappointments that went hand in hand with many great scientific advances. To regard the earth and thus humanity as the centre of the universe was emotionally highly satisfying.

It flattered people's ego; it was at the same time for humans a meaningful arrangement of world affairs. To think of the earth as a petty satellite of the sun was disappointing as well as devoid of meaning.

Further advances in scientific cosmology have heightened again and again the sense of the grim and desolate meaninglessness of the physical universe. So far, human beings have entirely failed to draw conclusions from the fall of the illusions brought about by the blind social automatism of scientific advance, and from the more realistic picture of the universe on all its levels emerging from that advance. They have not yet come to terms with the fact that human beings themselves and, as far as we know, solely humans in the world, are the makers of meaning. Their fear-dream utopias reflect the slowly awakening disillusionment with the world as it is. So far they can only complain, as if someone owed them a better, more meaningful world. The traumatic shock, the mourning for lost illusions still blocks the realisation that no one can make this world better and more meaningful (other than) they, human beings, themselves. (Elias 2009c: 273)

Reading this passage in isolation might well lead one to conclude that Elias was bound to be deeply pessimistic. However, this was not the case. He was what one might call an 'optimistic realist' as emerges from the following extract from an essay he wrote which was published in 1991:

Cosmologists inform us that the sun is ... at the middle of its foreseeable lifespan ... and that they expect [it] to continue its role as a life-supporting star for several thousand millions of years. If humankind does not destroy itself, if it is not destroyed by a meteor or another cosmic collision – which are certainly ... real possibilities – the natural conditions of its existence will give humans the opportunity to tackle the problems of their life together on earth, or wherever, for a ... long time to come. A future of 4,000 million years should give humans the opportunity to muddle their way out of several blind alleys and to learn how to make their life together more pleasant more meaningful and worthwhile. (2011: 173)

As we have already stated, according to Elias a crucial precondition for contributing to and, above all, for gaining a degree of control over such a betterment of the human lot is the creation of a greater fund of reliable knowledge than has currently been attained, not only about the world at large in its physical, chemical, and biological aspects, but above all about ourselves and the societies we form. Where Elias was perhaps rather more pessimistic was in his assessment of the capacity for sociology, at least as the discipline has developed thus far, to rise to this challenge. In his view, and in ours, sociology was and is a subject in crisis, and one that without a fundamental shift of emphasis and direction, can never form the basis for the social 'fund' of knowledge required to address the recurrent human crises out of which the subject itself was born.

In the chapters that follow, we wish to show how Elias aimed to address such problems through the development of his own sociological orientation, and how he sought ultimately to provide ways of constructively dealing with aspects of the sociological and human crises. In Chapter 1, we shall explore how he came to develop his distinctive sociological approach, firstly by providing a brief biographical sketch of Elias's life and work, and secondly, through exploring the interweaving of biography and history in the formation of the central tenets of what he wrote. In Chapter 2, we examine some – but by no means all – of the key concepts of figurational sociology. Chapter 3 is devoted to a discussion of Elias's principal contribution to sociology, the theory of 'civilising processes'. This discussion focuses on describing the theory and its empirical base. It also involves reviewing some of the chief critiques of Elias's work, an undertaking to which we return later in the book. In Chapters 4 and 5, we engage with Elias's contributions to the sociology of knowledge and seek to distil the 'epistemological', 'ontological' and 'methodological' components of his distinctive sociological practice. In Chapter 6, we locate Elias's work within sociology more generally through a focus upon both the critical reception of his work by his contemporaries, and *via* an in-depth comparison with key figures in contemporary sociology, notably Anthony Giddens, Michel Foucault, and Pierre Bourdieu. Finally, in the Conclusion, we explore the implications of Elias's work for the future of sociology and consider the prospects for a possible 'relational turn' within the discipline.

# 1
# Working with Elias

Our task in this chapter is, firstly, to introduce readers to Elias as a person and, secondly, to develop a view of how and why he came to develop an approach to sociology which still continues to be regarded in certain quarters as outmoded, or at best as esoteric, and yet which in other circles has gained growing acclaim, and has come to be considered as one of the most innovative and important contributions to sociology of the twentieth century. In relation to this undertaking, this chapter is about working with Norbert Elias in a number of senses. It is about the fact that Eric Dunning studied and worked with Elias intensively and in person from 1956 to 1978 (the year Elias left England and returned to the continent), and somewhat less intensively from 1978 to 1990 – the year in which Elias died. Dunning's experience of working closely with Elias will be drawn upon as a source of biographical data, and as a means of providing a fuller sense of the interplay between 'Elias the person' and 'Elias the sociologist'. This chapter is also based upon Jason Hughes having been introduced to Elias's work by Dunning and the fact that the two of us have extensively 'worked with' Elias's ideas and approach in relation to a range of different topics.

In addition, this chapter is about some of the issues surrounding others 'working with Elias'. We think a book such as this is necessary in part because of the somewhat enigmatic position Elias's work currently occupies within the discipline. As we suggested earlier, since his death in 1990, Elias has come increasingly to be regarded as one of the leading sociological figures of the twentieth century, a 'classical' sociologist on a par with earlier figures such as Comte, Marx, Durkheim and (Max) Weber. And yet this growing recognition of Elias's importance has thus far not been matched by a corresponding rise in his influence on subsequent generations of scholars. While the numbers are growing, including outside of what might be called the traditional centres of figurational sociology in Leicester and Amsterdam, relatively few sociologists have come to 'pick up the baton' and participate in the 'relay race of knowledge' that Elias envisaged; his work still remains somewhat at the margins of the discipline. Our central aim here is thus partly to make sense of this enigma, but also to play our part in redressing it through developing one of the core arguments advanced throughout this book as a whole: namely that, despite the impression held by some that his work is a relic from a bygone age, Elias's contributions to the subject represent *a* basis – but by no means the only one – for a move beyond the fragmentation and crisis in which sociology currently finds itself engulfed, as we outlined in the Introduction to this book. To commence this line of argument we first turn to Elias the person, exploring in particular the interplay between his biography and the development of his distinctive sociological approach.

## Norbert Elias: A brief biography and some autobiographical insertions

Norbert Elias was born in June 1897 in Breslau, a city of some 500,000 inhabitants in the eastern part of the then recently unified German *Kaiserreich*, that is 'Imperial Germany'. Following Germany's defeat in the Second World War, Breslau was incorporated into Poland and given the name of Wrocław. Elias lived a long life and died in his home in Amsterdam in August 1990. In September 1999, a commemorative plaque was ceremonially unveiled on a wall of one of the houses in Wrocław where Elias had lived as a child.

Elias was of Jewish descent. His father, Hermann, was a prosperous textile merchant, and he and Elias's mother, Sophie, were sufficiently well off to be able to send the young Norbert to Breslau's distinguished humanistic *Johannesgymnasium*. In English, it was what we used to call a 'grammar school'. There, Elias received a German classical education, above all a grounding in Latin, Greek, French, mathematics, science and such classics of German literature as the works of Goethe, Schiller, Heine, Mörike and Eichendorff. This classical education was repeatedly put to good use by Elias in the course of his long and eventually distinguished career.[13] In 1987, he was to publish a volume of poems, two of them in English, under the title *Los der Menschen* ('The Human Lot') (Elias 1987b).

At the *Johannesgymnasium*, Elias became the member of a select group which met with a teacher to discuss the works of Kant. It was while at the *Johannesgymnasium* that he formed the ambition to pursue an academic career and learned that, as a Jew, he would encounter stiff hurdles in seeking to pursue his goal. The First World War broke out in August 1914 and, after graduating from the *Johannesgymnasium* in 1915, Elias enlisted in the Kaiser's army, joining the Signals Corps and seeing action on both the Eastern and the Western fronts. From that point in 1915 onwards, Elias's experiences provide some clues regarding why he developed a sociological interest in such problems as: (i) violence and civilisation; (ii) the relations between individuals and the societies they form, also referred to as the 'agency-structure dilemma'; (iii) the related problem of the relations between 'micro' and 'macro' phenomena; and (iv) the relations between 'the private' and 'the public' parts of social life. Kilminster (2007), Russell (1997) and, indeed, Elias himself (1994), have related this orientation to his Jewish origins and socialisation within the *relatively* non-oppressive Jewish culture. Elias's own vivid words are revealing in regard to how he formed his sociological perspective. In a series of interviews conducted by Arend-Jan Heerma van Voss and Bram van Stolk in Amsterdam in 1984, he replied to their probing about the First World War by saying concerning his recollections of the years before 1914 that he had felt very secure in that period largely as a result of the prosperity of his parents and their love for him, especially his mother's. He continued:

> in the world in which I lived ... I never heard the rumbling of the approaching thunderstorm. For me the world only changed with the war. I still cannot really quite understand how I coped with this situation; the change from the complete security of my family to the complete insecurity of the army. Suddenly my parents were no longer there. (Elias 1994: 14)

Regarding his years spent on the Western-front, Elias said:

> I still remember the dugout. We lived underground ... It wasn't just a trench, more like a mole's burrow. I still remember very vividly wooden steps going down, and then there were two narrow rooms deep down under the earth. When there was a near miss, lumps of earth came down the steps, the whole thing shook, and anyone outside was hit. I do not think that I was even in the most advanced trenches, because our task was to maintain the telegraph lines between the front trenches and headquarters. We were always sent out to mend the wires which were constantly being hit, and sometimes, during a barrage, one simply went into a shell crater and tried to sit it out ... I remember one comrade being wounded next to me, and we had to bring him back ... I have a vivid recollection of going to the front, of dead horses and a few dead bodies and that underground shelter ... Then there is some feeling of a big shock, but I cannot recollect. I cannot even remember how I got back. (Elias 1994: 26–27)

Like many young soldiers in the First and Second World Wars, whichever side they were on, Elias was not only traumatised by his war experiences but radicalised as well. He had been politicised as early as 1913 as has been shown by Hackeschmidt (1999). That was the year in which Elias joined the German radical Zionist youth organisation, the *Blau-Weiss Bund* (Blue-White League), a context in which he was to meet such subsequently prominent social/cultural science figures as Erich Fromm and Leo Strauss. Hackeschmidt suggests, in our view persuasively, that parts of Elias's theory such as aspects of 'his figurational model and his scholarly credo of "handing on the torch", can be traced back ... to his days in *Blau-Weiss*' (Hackeschmidt 1999: 73). Hermann Korte (1988: 63ff) has suggested that the Zionist radicalism of this phase in Elias's life is to be attributed largely to the effects on him of the war. In our view, however, to that has to be added the frequent radicalism of youth, especially of an 'outsider group' which is what the Jews in Germany at that time were. As Kilminster (2007: 26ff) shows, Elias himself later acknowledged the part which being a member of a 'stigmatised outsider group', especially of a radicalised younger generation who had come to doubt the wisdom of their parents, played in the shaping of his sociological thinking. Most important of all, however, is the fact that, by 1929 at the latest, and although he had earlier been associated with the secular part of *Blau-Weiss*, Elias was coming to abandon his youthful idealism for a more hard-headed realism. Before the 1914–18 war and in 1919 and 1920, he could dream of setting up a utopian society in Palestine but, by 1929, in an essay 'On the Sociology of German anti-Semitism', he had reached the conclusion that:

> in the present social state, there is no chance of a therapy, of a full-scale healing of the social body from the evil of anti-Semitism. The surge of anti-Semitism is the function of economic and social developments that cannot be altered by the small group of German Jews and scarcely influenced by them to any degree. The Jewish community in this regard is far more driven than driver. From such an understanding and in conjunction with other experiences, one can draw the conclusion that a social order in which a group of gifted, often spiritually and intellectually rich and creative people are consciously downgraded, devalued and so powerfully crippled is not worth preserving and must be fought against. It can also lead one to decide to go to Palestine, because the fight for a national home for Jews appears more promising than the fight for social equality for Jews in Germany. For those who are unwilling to draw such conclusions, there remains only resignation. A clear understanding of one's own position is preferable in any case to self-deception. That is, one thing always remains possible for German Jews as an answer to anti-Semitism: they can accustom themselves to the unobtrusive, determined and self-aware demeanour that is the only way of behaving appropriately in their position. (Authors' translation of German original; see Elias 2006a: 83 for alternative translation).

The German Jews, he had written in 1929, had had three options: to fight for a better social order in Germany; to fight for a Jewish state in Palestine; or, resigning themselves to their lot, to steer an unobtrusive path through a life increasingly scattered with minefields.

The years following the First World War were a period of great instability, tension and unrest in Germany. Kaiser Wilhelm II abdicated in the wake of the humiliating military defeat, and the Weimar Republic was formed. Large sections of the officer corps, many rank and file soldiers, and a large proportion of the old imperial upper and upper middle classes held the new republic, its parliamentary institutions, and its socialist/social democratic leaders in contempt. They called the republic a 'pig-sty'. There were attempts to overthrow it from the far Left and the far Right. From the Right, there was the so-called 'Kapp Putsch' of 1920 and the 'Hitler-Ludendorff Putsch' in Munich in 1923. And, under the influence of the 1917 Bolshevik Revolution in Russia, a 'Soviet Republic' (*Räterrepublik*) was formed in Munich in 1918 and, at the same time in Berlin, there was an uprising by the 'Spartakists' led by the 'Communists' Karl Liebknecht and Rosa Luxembourg. Both uprisings were put down by the 'official' army of the Weimar state and the *Freikorps*, fighting bands formed of demobilised officers and men from the disbanded army and navy. The *Freikorps* were politically to the right. They formed the backbone of an underground terrorist organisation, '*Konsul*', which killed large numbers of people, possibly 1,000, in the early years of Weimar (Elias 1996: 186). One of their victims, wrote Elias:

> was my schoolfellow, Bernhard Schottländer, a completely unathletic, highly intelligent person, who, with his thick spectacles, looked like a young scholar even as a first-former, and who tended to communism after reading Marx, and whose corpse, if I remember rightly, was found in Breslau's city moat, tied up with barbed wire. (Elias 1996: 186)

After the suppression of the *Freikorps*, the stability of the Weimar Republic was further undermined by the hyperinflation of 1922–23. In August 1922, it took over 1,000 marks to buy a US dollar. By October, that figure had risen to 3,000 and by December, 7,000 (Evans 2003: 104). Depreciation of the currency became increasingly compelling, taking on more and more the character, in Elias's terms, of a 'blind' or 'unplanned social process'. Richard Evans captured its unintended dynamics when he wrote:

> Anyone who wanted to buy a dollar in January 1923 had to pay over 17,000 marks for it; in April 24,000; in July 353,000. This was hyperinflation on a truly staggering scale, and the dollar rate in marks for the rest of the year is best expressed in numbers that soon became longer than anything found even in a telephone directory: 4,621,000 in August; 98,860,000 in September; 23,260,000,000 in October; 2,193,600,000,000 in November; 4,200,000,000,000 in December. (Evans 2003: 105)

Elias used to relate how he would go into a café for a cup of coffee in that period with the price listed at 5,000 marks and be asked to pay 8,000 or 10,000 marks when he had drunk it. More significantly, his parents' real income was substantially lowered by the galloping inflation and, not only were they unable for a while to support his studies financially, but *they* needed *his* support. He worked for two years as 'export manager' in a metal goods factory. It was, he said, an instructive experience. He learned a good deal about practical economics, liked his boss, and asked him one day: 'Tell me, Herr Meerländer ... why on earth do you do that? You are a rich man and yet you sit here eight hours a day ... Meerländer took his cigarette from his mouth, smiled and said: "You know, it's a hunt. A *hunt*. I *must* get this order and the others must not"...' (Elias 1994: 32). Such experiences outside the academy forced Elias to engage first hand with all that resided beyond the 'world of ideas'. To paraphrase how Elias himself expressed it: '... the onset of the great social crises' (the war, Germany's defeat, the severe post-war social tensions, the hyperinflation) 'drove me out of the ivory tower ...' (Elias 1994: 91).

Subsequently, Elias was to witness the bloody street and beer-hall battles between the Communists and the Nazis, and the rise of the latter to power in 1933. He described this process (1989; 1996) as 'a breakdown of civilisation' because the Weimar state proved incapable of maintaining monopoly control over the means of violence, and because, from that point on until 1945, as has been widely documented, the German state apparatus was abused in the pursuit of 'uncivilised' aims. One could even say that Germany in that period was ruled by criminals, though 'civilised barbarians' might be a more appropriate term (this is an issue to which we shall return in Chapter Three).

What Elias had to say about his activities, thoughts, and feelings as the Nazis rose to power is revealing. He was not politically active in a party political sense, but his physical and moral courage shine through in particular from three of the acts he used to recount to students and friends. The first occurred in 1932 as the street and beer-hall battles began to escalate. It was only then, Elias said, that he began to feel seriously alarmed. So he went alone to a trades union office in Frankfurt-am-Main in an attempt to persuade its pacifist and Social Democrat members to fight. He later wrote:

> I pointed out that the private armies were gradually becoming more important than parliamentary elections. I closed my little talk somewhat dramatically with the question: 'Gentlemen, what measures have you taken to defend your fine union building if you are attacked?' The answer was deep silence. (Elias 1994: 42)

That was because, Elias said, most Social Democrats and trades unionists at the time were pacifists and also believed that Germany was a constitutional state (a *Rechtsstaat*) governed by the rule of law. His father certainly believed it. When Norbert begged Hermann and Sophie to remain in England in 1938 – they had visited him to help with the publication of *Über den Prozess der Zivilisation* – the senior Elias replied to the effect that: 'What can they do to me, Norbert? I'm a German. Germany is a *Rechtsstaat* and I've done nothing wrong'.[14] His mother was later to die in a gas chamber in Auschwitz (possibly via Theresienstadt). Elias was understandably devastated by his parents' decision to return to Germany and utterly distraught over his mother's ultimate fate. He never forgave himself for his inability to help her. But sociologically, he later exclaimed, Germany during the 1930s helped to crystallise for him one of his key ideas, namely that 'law cannot function without the backing of physical force' (Elias 1994: 44).

The second act involved Elias going to hear Hitler speak in Frankfurt in late 1932 or early 1933. He (Elias) was accompanied by two tall, 'Aryan-looking' students and sported a feathered 'Tyrolean' hat in order to disguise his Jewish features. He went, he said, because, although he knew that there was little he could do to change things, he had an intense need to know and understand what was going on. Asked in an interview why, he replied:

> Because I think it is one of the most important tasks of human beings: if they want to arrange their lives better than they are now, they have to know how things are connected ... I mean that quite practically, since otherwise we act wrongly. The whole misfortune of people now is that they often let themselves be

guided by unrealistic ideas ... There was once great enthusiasm for communism. People sacrificed their lives for it – and look what has come of it. There was enthusiasm for liberalism. American presidents and economists still believe in it – and are they any more able to cure our economic ills? They act as if they knew the answers on the basis of ideals, but in reality they do not know how the economy or states function ... There should be more people like myself who are not afraid of what they discover ... That is the task of a scientist, in the social sciences as in the natural sciences... (Elias 1994: 47–8)

The interview from which this extract was taken was recorded in 1984 at a time when 'Reaganomics', 'Thatcherism', and the economic ideas of Milton Friedman were in the ascendant. Elias was firmly opposed to them as he was to any form of economics that was not allied with and integrated into a body of sociological theory and research, and in particular, that was ignorant of long-term social processes. His arguments, though he was by no means a lone voice in this respect, about the dangers of economic interventions based on inadequate, ideology-laden models and ideas appear to have been borne out in particular by an escalating global economic crisis in more recent times. As the *Guardian* columnist and London School of Economics lecturer, John Gray, has observed (2010), 'Ignorant of history, including that of economics itself, most economists not only failed to forecast the crash but, mesmerised by the spurious harmonies of their mathematical models, were blind to the mounting instability of the financial system and failed to grasp that an upheaval of the kind that is currently under way was even possible'. Gray penned these words as part of the scene-setting for his review of an iconoclastic (2010) text entitled *23 Things They Don't Tell You About Capitalism* written by Ha-Joon Chang, a leading economics thinker and currently Professor at Cambridge University. In the book, Chang set out to 'destroy the myths' (to use Elias's (2012b) term) of free-market economics that have long guided domestic and international economic policies. Chang squarely blames many of the present – he wrote this in 2010 – global economic problems on the flawed models advocated by professional economists. The 2008 economic crisis, he proposed, '... has revealed how the complexity of the world we have created, especially within the sphere of finance, has vastly outpaced our ability to understand and control it' (2010: 254). He writes:

Over the last three decades, economists played an important role in creating the conditions of the 2008 crisis (and dozens of smaller financial crises that came before it since the early 1980s, such as the 1982 Third World debt crisis, the 1995 Mexican peso crisis, the 1997 Asian crisis and the 1998 Russian crisis) by providing theoretical justifications for financial deregulation and the unrestrained pursuit of short-term profits. More broadly, they advanced theories that justified the policies that have led to slower growth, higher inequality, heightened job insecurity and more frequent financial crises that have dogged the world in the last three decades. On top of that, they pushed for policies that weakened the prospects for long-term development in developing countries. In the rich countries, these economists encouraged people to overestimate the power of new technologies, made people's lives more and more unstable, made them ignore the loss of national control over the economy, and rendered them complacent about deindustrialisation ... In other words, economics has been worse than irrelevant. Economics, as it has been practised in the last three decades has been positively harmful for most people. (Chang 2010: 247–248)

Chang's comments again bear out Elias's arguments regarding the importance for interventions in the social world (and Elias's model of 'the social world' by necessity includes 'economic' interventions and indeed the 'economic sphere' more generally) to be based firmly upon a reliable and expanding stock of reality-congruent knowledge, and of the corresponding dangers of acting on the basis of ideas that are more heavily 'value-congruent' – in this case the values of the 'free market' – than reality-congruent since the balance of intended to unintended consequences that follows from such interventions is likely to lean very decisively towards the unintended component of this ratio.[15]

The third act took place early in 1933, just after the Nazis came to power. It testifies to Elias's physical and moral courage but also to his concern for others. At this time, Elias was working under Karl Mannheim at Frankfurt University as 'University Assistant to the Sociological Seminar', a post which carried with it tutorial duties for undergraduate students, and a Doctoral supervision load (Elias 1961). As he related it in 1960 or 61 to Dunning who had asked him a question about 'critical theory' and the 'Frankfurt School', at a stage when Adorno, Horkheimer and many of their 'leftist' students were still in Germany, though a number were seeking to leave the country as was still possible at that time. Adorno had managed to purchase the necessary rail and boat tickets for the USA and a costly licence from the Nazi authorities to emigrate. Elias was in possession of keys to the 'Marxburg', the building which housed the Sociology Department (that is, Mannheim, Elias and Hans Gerth), when he heard that the Gestapo had learned about Adorno's left-wing involvements and were thinking of rescinding his emigration licence. He (Elias) accordingly went to the Institute, unlocked Adorno's room, picked up from his desk and bookshelves any material that the Gestapo might have regarded as incriminating and spent several hours tearing it up and flushing it down the toilet, fearing all the time that the Gestapo might burst in and catch him, a Jew, in what was, from their standpoint, a criminal act. The whole process lasted several hours. Some two or three days later, after Adorno had managed to escape, Elias was picked up at his flat by members of an SA (*Sturmabteilung*), that is, 'brownshirt' unit and driven across Frankfurt to the Institute in an open truck. He was quietly confident, he said, as it turned out rightly, that they would find nothing of importance.

It was around this time that Gret Freudenthal, one of the two women whose PhDs Elias was supervising in Frankfurt – the other was Ilse Seglow[16] – drove him on a fruitless journey to Switzerland to seek university employment.

He then visited his parents in Breslau and afterwards left Germany for France where he was again unable to find a post. He was, however, provided with support by the Steun-Fonds of Amsterdam which enabled him, as he put it, to enlarge his *Habilitationsschrift*, the post-doctoral thesis one has to write in Germany to become a university teacher and which he had completed in 1933. This involved, in Elias's words 'an extended study of nobility, royalty and courtly society in France' and formed the basis of *Über den Prozess der Zivilisation*.[17]

Elias left France and migrated to England in 1935, remaining there until 1978. At first, speaking little English, he obtained financial support from a committee set up in Woburn House, London, to help Jewish refugees. The stipend they gave him was small but allowed him to rent a bed-sitting room, to eat and to continue a book he had started in Paris. He worked in the Reading Room of the British Museum where, almost a hundred years before, another German-Jewish exile, Karl Marx, had written *Das Kapital*. At first, Elias said, his ideas about how to take his work further were rather vague but they crystallised when he came across the works on etiquette. Suddenly, he said,

> I ... found material which demonstrated that other standards of behaviour had been known, and how they had changed. So I began *The Civilizing Process*, fully conscious that it would be an argument against the psychological studies of attitudes and behaviour of that time ... For me it was quite clear that this well-trodden way was no more than an effort to fit humans into the methods of the natural sciences or biology, so that the whole human process of change was pushed aside. That was how it all began. (Elias cited in Mennell 1998: 18)

*On The Process of Civilisation* (*Über den Prozess der Zivilisation*) was published in Switzerland in 1939. In that same year Elias was appointed as a Senior Research Assistant at the London School of Economics (LSE) where he embarked on a study of the importance of the navy for understanding some of the key specificities of Britain's developmental path and the part the navy played in the development of the once powerful but now, in the context of the Second World War, declining British Empire. Elias's study of the British navy has recently been published by University College Dublin Press (see Elias 2007b).[18]

At the LSE, Elias was strongly supported by Morris Ginsberg, and also by his (Elias's) former Head of Department and PhD supervisor, Karl Mannheim, who now had a post at London University's Institute of Education. In a letter (written in English) to his parents in Germany and dated January 1941, he wrote:

> I am going on with my work as peacefully and quietly as ever, preparing a new book which I hope to write together with Ginsberg who is very kind to me and who, I believe, in his own hesitant way rather likes me. Uncle Karl [Mannheim], too, is here. He is not on the best of terms with Ginsberg and not very happy on the whole. But since I have dedicated to him the second volume of my last book on "the Civilising Process", he, too, is very kind to me.[19]

In his autobiography, the historian, Eric Hobsbawm, recalls regularly seeing Elias at the LSE in this period. Hobsbawm was then a student at Cambridge but divided his vacations between the LSE, where he used the library, and France. At the LSE's main building in Houghton Street, Aldwych, he informs us,

> student activists used to discuss politics ... usually observed by a silent lone central European rather older than ourselves, apparently one of those 'eternal students' who hang around inner-city campuses, but who was in fact the totally unknown and unconsidered Norbert Elias, just about to publish his great work on *The Process of Civilization* in Switzerland. Academic Britain in the 1930s was extraordinarily blind to the brilliance of the central European Jewish and anti-fascist refugee intellectuals unless they operated in conventionally recognized fields such as classics and physics. The LSE was probably the only place where they would be given house-room. Even after the war, Elias's academic career in this country was marginal... (Hobsbawm, 2003: 121)

Hobsbawm might have mentioned philosophy as another 'conventionally recognised field' in Britain where 'refugee intellectuals' were accepted. He could not have known, however, that the climate in British sociology was to change during and after the war partly as a result of the writings of the philosopher, Karl Popper, himself a refugee intellectual but one who *was* employed at the LSE. This 'climate change' was to work in the short-term to the academic disadvantage of Elias.

When the Second World War broke out in 1939, the LSE was evacuated to Cambridge and, shortly afterwards, Elias was interned as an 'enemy alien', first in a camp at Huyton near Liverpool, and then in one on the Isle of Man. Characteristically, Elias and one or two others formed their own 'university' in the camp. It was typical of Elias that, on the first page of the exercise book in which he wrote his lecture notes, he scribbled 'the lack of books as an advantage'. Clearly, Elias held his own ideas to be better than those in any book! It was there, too, that the subsequently famous American anthropologist, Eric Wolf, then an interned Austrian teenager, had his first encounter with the social sciences through lectures given by Elias on 'The Network of Social Relationships' and 'Monopolies of Power' (Wolf 1977). It was also whilst on the Isle of Man that Elias wrote and produced (in 1940) '*Die Ballade vom armen Jakob*' (*The Ballad of Poor Jacob*), which was put to music by the prominent composer and fellow internee Hans Gál (Korte 1996: 38). The opera tells the tale of Jakob, a Jew, and his ill-fated plight as an outsider.

After the war, Elias was employed by the British secret service in their attempts to 'de-Nazify' German prisoners of war. It was not until 1954, though, that he obtained his first full-time university appointment at the then University College Leicester. Its status then was as a satellite of the University of London. He was probably not fully aware at first, however, of the fact that the climate of British sociology had been changing substantially, especially during the course of the war.

Until the Second World War, the 'evolutionary' tradition in British sociology started by Hobhouse and Spencer was kept alive at the London School of Economics by Morris Ginsberg.[20] (As we shall see later, Elias rejected the appellation 'evolutionary' in favour of the terms 'developmental' or 'process sociology'.) It was a tradition that was compatible with the sociological perspective of Elias as can be seen from an essay, 'Recent Trends in Sociology', which Ginsberg published in 1933. He wrote:

> On the historical and evolutionary side of sociology recent work has brought out certain important distinctions. Alfred Weber and (Robert) MacIver stress the distinction between culture and civilisation and argue that the order of growth appears to be radically different in the two spheres ... With regard to the process of civilisation ... an important distinction is drawn by Thurnwald between ... processes that are cumulative and irreversible, for instance, technical discovery, and those that of necessity alternate between a number of limited possibilities, for instance, the forms of marriage, or systems of kinship. (Ginsberg 1956 [1933]: 120–121)

At Heidelberg during the 1920s, Alfred Weber had been Elias's *Habilitation* supervisor. Under him, Elias was researching the part played by Florence in the transition from pre-scientific to scientific forms of thinking. It is interesting to note that the culture/civilisation distinction that he presumably learned from Alfred Weber and Robert MacIver is the first topic examined by Elias in *On the Process of Civilisation* and that Ginsberg, citing Thurnwald (1932), used the term 'process of civilisation'. Elias had encountered Thurnwald at the 1928 Zürich Conference when he was a discussant of a paper by him (see Elias 2006a [1929]).

A measure of the change that took place in British sociology, especially after the Second World War – and, until the late 1950s/early 1960s, British sociology was virtually restricted to the LSE – is provided by an autobiographical note which A. H. ('Chelly') Halsey included in the Preface to his *A History of Sociology in Britain* (2004). He wrote:

> Popper's attack on historicism was deeply impressive to me. The Hobhouse tradition of seeking laws of social development, though never explicitly mentioned by Popper, was thereby rendered suspect and we were prejudiced against it and converted to Popper's version of 'positivism' as well as, admittedly reluctantly, to piecemeal social engineering. Our activism also led us to quantitative surveys. Popper was not apparently a philosopher but a physicist interested in the methods of the social sciences. It was his conversion of philosophy into methodological problems which attracted us – all very abstract but most persuasive... I was also a Victorian child, led by the promise of science to a new political and social order and inspired by idealistic novels and other arts to the creation, at last, of a new utopia. I have never subsequently lost these early orientations. (2004: vii)

Such orientations became dominant in British sociology in and after the 1950s. Dunning vividly remembers attending a British Sociological Association

Conference with Elias in Sheffield in 1962 or 1963. The topic was 'development', and when Elias expressed his views from the floor, he was heckled with the cry of 'Hobhouse! Hobhouse!' from a prominent female graduate of the LSE. With the exception of Hobsbawm, who happened to be attending, no one seemed to recognise that, with his new synthesis, Elias had arguably moved beyond Hobhouse and Ginsberg. Later on, Elias also provided a compelling critique of Popper's *The Poverty of Historicism* and *The Logic of Scientific Discovery* (see Chapter 5).

Without ever disappearing completely, the opposition to Elias as the proponent of a supposedly old-fashioned and occident-biased 'progress' theory began to be diluted in the 1960s and 70s as 'historical sociology' and the study of 'social development' in the sense of sociological research into the so-called 'Third World' began to achieve greater legitimacy. Elias used to stress in this connection, however, that terms like 'developed societies' and 'developing countries' are misleading because *all* human societies are in a state of flux. It is only the rates and directions of change that vary. He also attacked as uninformed the assumption that we already know all there is to know about the so-called 'developed' West and how 'it' came to be 'developed'. Accordingly, he called for a programme of comparative and historical research into Western as well as 'Second' and 'Third World' countries.

It was not only Elias's life-experiences but his formal education that influenced his thinking. At the University of Breslau between 1918 and 1923, he read philosophy and medicine, the latter in part because his parents wanted him to become a doctor. He studied medicine until he had completed the pre-clinical part of the degree but, at that point, gave it up to concentrate on obtaining his doctorate in philosophy. Not surprisingly, his unusual and in some ways even anomalous joint training in medicine and philosophy was another profound influence on the development of Elias's patterns of thinking. As he himself expressed it, one aspect of the resultant dilemma with which he found himself confronted, was 'the discrepancy between the philosophical, idealist image of [people] and the anatomical, physiological one', which, he commented, 'unsettled me for many years' (1984: 84). An example was provided in the dissecting room. In the 1950s and 1960s in his tutorials at Leicester, Elias used to relate how, as a result of his experiences in dissecting corpses, he began to puzzle over the popular-*cum*-philosophical dichotomy between 'the body' and 'the mind', wondering how these crude categories, which imply that 'the mind' is somehow separate from 'the body', fitted in with the structure and functioning of the complex organ which he observed and which, although it is still far from being fully understood, is now known to be the primary seat of consciousness, that is of 'feeling' and 'thought'. It was in the dissecting room, too, Elias told us, where he first observed and realised the significance of the complex, mobile musculature of the human face, leading him to reflect on the importance of smiling, laughing, and crying in human communication and social bonding. He speculated in particular in this connection that the emergence of this facial musculature and of the cognitive-emotional communicativeness of humans must have taken place interdependently in the course of long-term processes of biological evolution and social development.[21] In the course of such processes, *Homo sapiens* emerged as a social, language-forming, language-learning and language-using species which depends on expandable funds of knowledge which are symbolically, that is, mainly linguistically and mathematically, expressed and stored. Elias was, of course, aware of the fact that knowledge can contract and be lost as well as expand. An example of knowledge-loss is that experienced by most people in the urban-industrial-nation-states of today of the detailed knowledge of plants, animals, and animal behaviour which helped groups of hunter-gatherers to survive. Another example, as Foer (2011) explores, is how the human capacity to remember relatively large stores of information has declined in tandem with the ascendancy of the written word, particularly post Gutenberg's development of the printing press in 1440, and more recently with the development of new information technologies. An example that Foer provides is that of research that has demonstrated how over the course of the past decade the average quantity of telephone numbers that a person might be able to recall from memory alone has decreased tenfold. Such changes, he proposes, have emerged in tandem with the increasing availability and use of smartphone technologies.

Elias obtained his philosophy doctorate in Breslau in 1924 for a thesis entitled *Idee und Individuum: ein Beitrag zur Philosophie der Geschichte* (*Idea and Individual: a Contribution to the Philosophy of History*). In it, he explored the part played in history by individuals and ideas (Elias 1924). However, he quarrelled with his supervisor, Richard Hönigswald, over the issue of the Kantian *a priori*: the idea that certain categories of thought such as time, space, causality, and basic morality are inborn in people rather than socially formed and learned in particular socio-historical contexts. This played a part in leading him to decide to switch to sociology and go to Heidelberg to write his *Habilitationsschrift*. As we have seen, he registered to 'habilitate' under the 'cultural sociologist' (*Kultursoziologe*) Alfred Weber – younger brother of the more famous Max who had died in 1920 – at the *Institut für Sozial und Staatswissenschaften*. The choice of Elias's topic was principally related to the sociology of science, with a specific focus upon the relations between science and art in the Italian Renaissance. (His proposal is translated and republished in the Appendix to the first volume of the *Collected Works* published by UCD Press. See *Early Writings* (2006a).)

It was in Heidelberg that Elias met Karl Mannheim, one of the founding figures in what came to be known as 'the sociology of knowledge' (*Wissenssoziologie*). Strong traces of both Alfred Weber's cultural sociology and Karl Mannheim's sociology of knowledge can be found in the synthesis that Elias was to develop, particularly traces of Mannheim's sociology of knowledge. However, Elias was able skilfully to avoid both the descriptive particularism of Weber and the structure/consciousness dualism discussed at length by Mannheim. Other influences on Elias included: the sociologist Georg Simmel; the field theorist, Kurt Lewin; the *Gestalt* theorist, Wolfgang Köhler; the behavioural psychologist, J.B. Watson; and the physiologist W.B. Cannon. Above all, however, Elias's work can be seen as a synthesis principally of Marx, (Max) Weber and Freud, with Comtean and Durkheimian elements added later, perhaps in part as a result of the influence on him at Leicester of Ilya Neustadt.

In 1929, Mannheim accepted the Chair of Sociology at the University of Frankfurt, taking Elias with him as his Assistant. It is a mark of the power of German professors, then as now, that Mannheim called Elias to his room one day and said: 'Elias, I'm halving your stipend. The other half, I'm giving to Hans Gerth'. Gerth was later to achieve a degree of fame as collaborator with C. Wright Mills. Mannheim also took over from Alfred Weber as supervisor of Elias's *Habilitationsschrift*, promising to 'habilitate' him earlier. Elias abandoned the role of Florence in the development of scientific thinking as his topic and chose instead to write on 'the court society' of France. Elias 'habilitated' early in 1933, just after the Nazis came to power. His thesis was referred to in his work by Mannheim, but Elias mislaid his own copies and it was not published until 1969 when it appeared with the title, *Die höfische Gesellschaft (The Court Society)* (see Elias 2006b). Among other ways, it was remarkable – some might say remarkably prescient given what was about to happen in Germany in the 1930s and 1940s – in showing how a single individual, in this case Louis XIV, can come to exercise monopoly control over the levers of power in a large and complex state.

The advent of the Nazi dictatorship introduced another discontinuity into Elias's life. It forced him into exile, first of all to France where he spent two years in Paris and became informally attached to the *Ecole Normale Supérieure* through his association with the likes of Célestin Bouglé and Alexander Koyré (see Elias 1961). While in France, Elias published his first two sociological papers – one on 'changes in the character and function of art and architecture during a process of industrialisation' (Elias 1961: 1) entitled 'Kitschstil und Kitschzeitalter' (Kitsch-style and the age of Kitsch) (1935a) and another on the expulsion of protestants from France ('Vertreibung der Hugenotten aus Frankreich') (1935b), both published in English translation in *Early Writings* (2006a: 85–96 and 97–104 respectively). Elias subsequently moved to England (in 1935), and received British citizenship in 1952. It was not until 1954 that, at the age of 57, he obtained his first *full-time* university teaching post. It was at (what later became) the University of Leicester where, together with Ilya Neustadt, he succeeded – despite a prevailing climate in Anglophone sociology which was, as we described it earlier, strongly antipathetic to his views – in building up what was to prove to be, for some ten or fifteen years, one of the most rapidly expanding and influential sociology departments in Europe.

## Elias at Leicester

When Elias started to teach at Leicester in 1954, it was a University College and awarded London degrees. It was given a Royal Charter and the right to confer its own degrees in 1958. The then Head of Department, Ilya Neustadt, proved highly influential in securing Elias a teaching post at Leicester, and was for a considerable time to prove a powerful ally to Elias. It is together with Neustadt that Elias developed an innovative Introduction to Sociology course for the first intake of students reading for Leicester degrees, that is, the intake for the 1957–1958 academic year. The course arguably came to form one of the main bases for the success of the Leicester Sociology Department in the 1960s. It is worth reflecting at some length on this course, and more generally on the Leicester period of Elias's life, as this serves here to highlight his somewhat enigmatic place amongst, and rather sparse influence upon, in particular, some of the more prominent sociologists in Britain who emerged during this period. In Western countries generally, the 1960s were a decade of sociological expansion but, at Leicester, the rate of expansion exceeded that of anywhere else in Britain. Indeed, the Leicester Department came for a while to outstrip even the London School of Economics as the principal institution where British university teachers of sociology were trained or spent their formative years. A list of some of the personnel involved as staff and students will give an idea of the Department's success. They include (in alphabetical order): Martin Albrow, Sheila Allen, David Ashton, Clive Ashworth, Mike Attalides, Joe and Olive Banks, Anthony Barnett, Richard Brown, Chris Bryant, Percy Cohen, Chris Dandeker, John Eldridge, David Field, James Fulcher, Mike Gane, Anthony Giddens, Miriam Glucksman, John H Goldthorpe, Paul Hirst, Sydney Holloway, Keith Hopkins, Earl Hopper, Jennifer Hurstfield, Geoff Ingham, Nick Jewson, Terry Johnson, Mike Kelly, Richard Kilminster, Derek Layder, Mary McIntosh, Gavin Mackenzie, Rob Mears, Nicos Mouzelis, Pat Murphy, Chris Rojek, Graeme Salaman, John Scott, Ken Sheard, Dominic Strinati, Laurie Taylor, Ken Thompson, Ivan Waddington, Dave Walsh, Rod Watson, Ian Varcoe, Bryan Wilson and Sami Zubaida. Nearly all of them subsequently became at least moderately well known, though, with several notable exceptions, few acknowledged and most were probably unaware of the greater or lesser direct or indirect influence on them of Elias.

Elias's influence was a consequence of the fact that the Departmental agenda was largely set by whether members of the Department were for or against his ideas. Of those within the Department when he was there, Ilya Neustadt, Eric

Dunning and Richard Kilminster were perhaps the staunchest proponents of Elias's position apart from Elias himself. In Dunning's case, this was partly a consequence of the fact that he is sufficiently proficient in German to have been able to read *Über den Prozess der Zivilisation* in the original. That extended his insights into what Elias was attempting, especially into the fact that he was not proposing a throwback to the 'evolutionary', 'inevitability of progress', and teleological ideas of the eighteenth and nineteenth centuries as many claimed. However, only a few Leicester sociologists emerged in that context as what one might call 'fully-fledged Eliasians' or 'figurationalists', and principal among those who did were the Leicester sociologists of sport.[22] Somewhat indirectly, the University's Centre for Labour Market Studies is another of Elias's legacies. It grew, under the leadership of David Ashton, out of Elias's failed Departmental research project on 'The Young Worker' (see Goodwin and O'Connor 2006). It is worth noting that some of those who were involved with Leicester sociology during the period of Elias's prominence in the department later acknowledged, at least in private correspondence, how profoundly influenced by Elias they had been. A case in point is Richard Brown who in a letter to Elias himself in 1977 wrote that:

> Joop [Goudsblom] has commented on the absence of traces of your teaching or references to your writings in the case of publications by me and a number of others previously in Leicester, and in my case at any rate the comment is justified, at least with regard to references. It may well reflect something of the present state of industrial sociology, where I continue to do most work. It would not be so true of teaching, where I continue to be involved very considerably with problems of industrialisation and development and well aware of the lead you gave me in that respect. I also find that I draw on your teaching most of all perhaps when discussing (as in first year courses) formulations of individual-society 'relations', where most writing, it seems to me, is still very inadequate, posing some sort of dichotomy between 'individual' and 'society' and producing all sorts of false problems as a result. There is still a lot of work to be done! (Brown 1977)

The First Year Course devised by Elias proved to be popular with students and was central in leading them, in their droves and to the chagrin especially of the economists,[23] to abandon the other social sciences and flock to sociology. However, it was not so popular with teachers in the expanding Leicester Department, especially those who had come under the influence of the then-dominant, 'anti-historicist' current within then-contemporary sociology. In particular, it was to differing degrees unpopular with Anthony Giddens, John Goldthorpe, and Percy Cohen. Whilst it was likely that Giddens was principally critical of Elias's course – and of his approach to sociology more generally – on account of its explicitly anti-philosophical character,[24] Cohen and Goldthorpe,[25] in their different ways both devotees of Popper's arguments in *The Poverty of Historicism* (1957), were critical of its historical, process-orientation, or what Elias used in those days to call the 'developmental perspective' which underpinned it. This was a period in which advocates of the then-dominant sociological orthodoxy used to argue that the concept of development is of no scientific use because it is irremediably shot through with moral connotations. That is, it was held that 'development' is an inherently value-laden, 'Eurocentric', even 'racist', term which implies the intrinsic superiority of the West and the intrinsic inferiority of 'the rest'. In short, it was held to be equivalent to the in some ways wrongly discredited concept of 'progress'. In fact, contrary to a common misinterpretation of his theory of civilising processes which sees it as a form of 'Western triumphalism' which ethnocentrically celebrates the Western way of life, Elias developed the theory in the first place in the hope of contributing to an understanding of how what people think of as 'civilisation' is only a thin veneer, and which, through its own immanent dynamics, effectively 'produces' as an outcome its own discontents. Indeed, refuting the ideological fallacy of Western triumphalism was precisely Elias's starting point (Kilminster 2007).

It is apparent that both Elias and Neustadt were aware of the rapidly changing sociological 'fads and fashions' of the times, but in spite of these, both insisted on a developmental approach to teaching the subject. Prior to Elias's arrival, the developmental character of the course was largely confined to a relatively crude 'chronological' orientation. However, the historical scope of the existing programme no doubt was attractive to Elias. In personal correspondence from 20 October 1952, Neustadt, seeking here to encourage Elias to come to Leicester, described the then-existing programme and signalled some of the directions in which he hoped Elias might develop it:

> You can begin with Aristotle if you like!!! The best summary is Armand Cuvillier: Manuel de Sociologie, 2 vols. 1950. Vol. 1. First 2 chapters which gives you a bird's eye view from Aristotle to the present day. One can, for example, begin with discussing the various sources of sociology: political science, philosophy of history, history, influence of social reform movements and social investigations in the 19th C. (Booth, etc.), the influence of biology (tehory [sic] of evolution, Darwin, Spencer, the Eugenics movement, studies of heredity and environment, twins, etc. biological analogies). But then the main body is: Comte, Spencer, (the anthropologists if you like: Tylor, Morgan, etc.); Marx; Max Weber; some other German sociologists; Pareto; Hobhouse, Durkheim, Lévy-Bruhl, Westermark; comparative method; American tendencies... You are <u>perfectly free</u> to arrange the material as you think best; you are not expected to cover all those people – one usually selects... How you present it is your business entirely: for ex.: ... Weber: ideal type, capitalism, religion. Hobhouse: social development; Marx: materialist interpretation of history; Pareto: residues and derivations, elites. Ginsberg used also to deal with some problems: such as race and civilization, culture and civilisation (concepts), crime, war. Now that has gone out of fashion, and one deals, for ex., with various classifications of groups; or social surveys... But the main body remains an exposition and discussion of a number of representative

sociologists. There is in fact very little about 'methods'... Using Barnes, Cuvillier and even Sorokin (bad for students, but useful when in a hurry for us) you can devise 2–3 introductory lectures giving a bird's eye survey of names, works and dates and approaches: biological, psychological, sociological, etc. Then go on to Comte, etc. Or, for that matter, plunge straight into Durkheim. It does not matter a bit. Donald's criterium [sic], for example, is merely a chronological one! (Neustadt 1952)[26]

It is noteworthy to observe the key intellectual figures who are mentioned here by Neustadt. Marx, Weber and Durkheim are all included, but so are Comte, Spencer, Pareto and Hobhouse. Neustadt also alludes to the growing dominance of 'American tendencies' (implied here, for example, is the increasing influence of Parsonian functionalism), which include an emphasis on the classification of groups and the collection and analysis of survey data. In the development of the Leicester First Year Course – and here we are referring specifically to the course as given in 1960–61[27] when Dunning was a Tutorial Assistant, attended it and took course-related seminars – Elias indeed maintained a chronological orientation, bucking the then increasingly dominant trend to become present-centred, but came to develop this orientation in a number of key respects. Elias made a decisive move away from the existing 'great men', 'history of ideas', approach that appears to have been employed in the then-existing programme, and instead developed a series of lectures that would document the *longue durée* of human history, and, in tandem, the ascendancy of the social conditions in which sociology emerged as a distinct discipline. He retained a 'bird's eye' view, but extended this more generally to human history and global development. For example, he used the United Nations Yearbooks as a principal source of data on social development. On the basis of the figures contained in the Yearbooks on such issues as population, health and economic growth, he suggested – and it is noteworthy that he made this suggestion as early as 1957 – that the societies of the world could be divided into three basic types, what he called 'Type A', 'Type B', and 'Type C' societies. 'Type A' societies were structurally 'simpler' or 'underdeveloped' societies and had high birth rates, high death rates, small but relatively stable populations, agrarian and sometimes hunting and gathering economies, low levels of urbanisation, low levels of division of labour, weak or non-existent states and low levels of bureaucratisation. 'Type B', or 'industrialising' societies, had high birth rates, falling death rates, expanding populations, growing levels of industrialisation and urbanisation, increasingly complex divisions of labour and social structures, increasingly powerful states and growing levels of bureaucratisation. 'Type C' or 'industrial' societies had low birth rates, low death rates, large but relatively stable and occasionally declining populations, urban-industrial economies, large, complex and powerful states, and high levels of bureaucratisation. The most powerful Type C societies had developed overseas colonial empires and were also generally dominant in the world. However, Elias stressed in his course that, in conjunction with processes of global democratisation, such dominance was at that time coming increasingly under attack in the form of anti-colonial/de-colonisation movements.

Elias next looked critically at explanations of the changes involved in the development of and the transitions between these social types. First he examined the explanations proposed by the theorists of 'economic growth' – neither theories of modernisation nor the term 'modernisation' itself had yet become as misleadingly hegemonic as they are today. The works of William Arthur Lewis (1954) and Walt Whitman Rostow (1960) served as Elias's principal examples. He counterposed their largely reductionist, economistic arguments with nineteenth and early twentieth century sociological theories of development, for example, those of Comte, Marx, Durkheim, Weber and Hobhouse. In that context, Elias looked critically at, among other things, what he called, following Bertrand Russell (1948), the 'billiard ball' concept of social causation, arguing in its stead for a concept of 'causal nexuses', that is, of complexes of interacting and interdependent 'causes' and 'effects' in which 'effects' become 'causes' and *vice versa*. Finally, Elias undertook what he called, following Neustadt's cue (see again the earlier-cited correspondence) 'A Bird's-Eye View of the Social Development of Mankind' (*sic*). This started with a look at the origins and early biological evolution of *Homo sapiens*, went on to examine the earliest 'Stone Ages', and finished with a discussion of the 'Neolithic' (agricultural) 'New Stone Age', 'Metallurgical' (Bronze Age; Iron Age), 'Urban' (Egypt, Mesopotamia, Mexico, Peru), 'Scientific' and 'Industrial Revolutions'. Much of what Elias said in his 'Bird's-Eye View' was based on his reading of the work of the archaeologist V. Gordon Childe (1928, 1936). Interestingly, the Canadian historian W.H. McNeill and his son have, in the last decade, published a book entitled *The Human Web: a Bird's-Eye View of World History* (2003). It is a book redolent of ideas that could have come from Elias, and may possibly have been influenced by McNeill's exposure to 'figurational' work and thinking in the late 1980s and 1990s.

It does not, we think, require too great a stretch of the imagination to enable one to realise that Elias was anticipating *inter alia* in his First Year course what American sociologist Irving Horowitz (1966) later came to call the 'three worlds of development'. In short, we are suggesting that, as early as 1957, Elias anticipated the now standard distinctions between 'First World', 'Second World' and 'Third World' countries.

As we have said, Elias's course was popular with students. They were encouraged to explore and discuss a variety of issues such as the adequacy of his typology with its lumping together, for example, of varieties of in some ways very different African, Asian, South and Central American societies under the 'Type A' label. However, the course was decried by some members of the Leicester academic staff as hopelessly out-dated. What they meant, we can plausibly surmise, was something to the effect that:

(i) Elias's course dealt with issues such as social change and development which were either not covered or did not figure centrally in the then fashionable American introductory textbooks. Nor was it readily susceptible to Parsonian interpretations or researchable using statistical methods and present-centred survey techniques. These at that time University of Leicester critics of Elias, principal among them John Goldthorpe and Percy Cohen, evidently equated recency of publication with sociological value. In their view, the writings of Parsons (Cohen) and the methods of scholars such as Lazarsfeld (Goldthorpe) were what *modern, up-to-date, truly scientific* sociology should *really* be about;

(ii) these sociologists who were at Leicester at that time were similarly opposed to Elias's stress in his First Year course on the developmental and comparative theories of Comte, Marx, Durkheim and Weber. By the 1950s, the developmental/historical work of these and other 'classical' sociologists (such as Hobhouse) had been to a large extent confined to the dustbin by the advocates of the-then dominant functionalist and empiricist approaches to the subject (which were, of course, destined themselves to be similarly side-lined in the late 1960s). Elias, however, counselled against such arguments, claiming that many of the so-called 'classical' theories contained redeemable elements and accordingly urged sociologists 'not to throw the baby out with the bathwater'. More particularly, he advised them to jettison only those aspects of earlier theories that had been definitively refuted in terms of testable scientific criteria as opposed, as has recurrently happened in the social sciences, to fashion-shifts based on grounds of a more ideological, value-judgemental kind. Similarly, Elias integrated the concept of function into his synthesis on the basis that a move from a concept of action to a concept of function constitutes a shift in the direction of greater reality-congruence and hence scientificity. That is because, if properly interpreted, the concept of function is indicative of the existence of nexuses in the observable social world.

## Elias, Ghana, and British anthropology

During his time at Leicester (1954–1962), Elias rose to the rank of Reader before retiring from his post in 1962. Immediately upon his retirement, and before his return to Europe in 1964, Elias spent two years as Professor of Sociology at the University of Lagon, Ghana.[28] Whilst at Lagon, he became engaged in a considerable amount of fieldwork, and partly in relation to this, he began to amass a collection of African art. His collection had become sufficiently extensive by 1970 to warrant an exhibition at the City Art Gallery in Leicester.

According to the prominent anthropologist, Jack Goody, speaking at a conference in Metz (France) in 2002, Elias's fellow teachers at Lagon in 1962 – Goody was one of them – were up in arms against the way in which he (Elias) ran the Sociology Department there. While it was likely that Elias would not have made a good administrative head, it is possible that his Lagon colleagues may well have been opposed to him not only on that count but at least in some measure also on grounds that were similar to those on which he had been criticised at Leicester over the previous four or five years. That is, it may well have been the case that Elias's Lagon colleagues perceived him to have been 'old-fashioned' for trying to introduce an approach to sociology which, at that time, was considered to be outmoded. The opposition to Elias in that context also came from his (Elias's) attempt to remove anthropology from Lagon's sociological curriculum. In all likelihood, such a move was related to some of Elias's reservations concerning the British anthropology of this period.[29]

Nor did Elias seek to deny the contributions to knowledge that the best British anthropologists such as Radcliffe-Brown (1952) and Evans-Pritchard (1940) had made. He did, though, point to the fact that the origins of the discipline in Britain lay, in large part, in the perceived need of the rulers of the British Empire for information on the people they ruled. Elias was also critical of the tendency of many anthropologists to write, after only one or two years' fieldwork, as if they were describing *the* social structure of the Nuer, the Tiv, the Ashanti, or whoever, and not just giving *their own*, necessarily partial view of this structure. Nor, according to Elias in his lectures, tutorials, and private discussions, did such anthropologists typically try to account for how this structure had emerged in the first place, how it had developed over time, or how it had been affected by European colonisation.

In short, according to Elias there was a tendency, perhaps especially in the 1950s and 60s, for British anthropologists to treat 'tribal' societies as if they were self-contained, bounded 'systems' that existed independently of space and time, and, more particularly, independently of any wider and dynamic social and environmental context. There was also, he suggested, a tendency to accept – and perhaps even to believe – that what anthropologist X had written about tribal society Y had a high degree of congruence with the reality of that society. Furthermore, Elias proposed, tribal social structures tended to be seen as unchanging constants, so that there was no need for other anthropologists to return after a period of time to see whether anything had changed, or simply to test/check what their predecessors had written. In this connection, Elias used to make much of how, when Oscar Lewis (1951) returned to test what Robert Redfield (1947) had written on the folk culture of Yucatan, a Tepoztlán village in Mexico, he (Lewis) found a society that was considerably different. More particularly, Lewis found Tepoztlán to be conflict-riven, whereas Redfield had claimed it to have been largely harmonious (Elias and Dunning 2008).

Elias also used to argue that a good deal of twentieth century anthropology was characterised by a pervasive current of cultural relativism, in turn driven by a sometimes crude, romantic egalitarianism (see Dunning 1977). This contributed, he said, to a failure on the part of many anthropologists to appreciate, for example, that a people with and willing to use nuclear weapons is *ipso facto* more militarily powerful in an empirically demonstrable sense than, say, a people with only spears and bows and arrows. However, drawing distinctions of this sort had become, Elias suggested, eschewed by anthropologists as part of a more general attempt to avoid ethnocentrism, and their wish to disavow a colonial legacy in which a sharp distinction had repeatedly been drawn between those who are 'primitive' and those who are 'civilised' (see, for example, Anton Blok's (1982) critique of Elias's work along these lines; see also Stephen Mennell's more general discussion of anthropological critiques of Elias's work (1998: 228–241)). As we argued earlier in this chapter, Elias was more than just aware of this danger when drawing comparisons between societies at different stages of 'development'. Indeed, it was one of Elias's chief contributions in *On the Process of Civilisation* not only to explore how such distinctions as that between 'civilised' and 'primitive' people were employed by particular groups in the West as means of distinguishing their ways of life from those of their perceived social inferiors – and in so doing, mobilising the latter as justifications for colonial bloodshed – but also to examine the sociogenetic conditions under which such notions emerged in the first place. In fact, Elias saw it as his central undertaking to advance a *technical* concept of development that, quite consciously, avoids judgments such as 'backward' or 'uncivilised' through facilitating a primary engagement with differences in the 'actual patterns of interdependence binding people together' (Mennell 1992: 237).

## Elias's return to continental Europe

From 1964 to 1978, Elias maintained firm connections with Leicester. He continued to teach regularly on the MA (Sociology) degree, retaining an office in the University. During that period, he and Dunning also taught jointly at the University of Warwick for five years. Although he kept a flat in London for a while (in the White House next to Regent's Park), Leicester remained his principal place of residence until 1978, when he returned permanently to continental Europe, initially to Germany (1978–1984) after being awarded an honorary Doctorate by the University of Bielefeld in 1977. Thereafter, Elias came to set up home in Amsterdam where he had previously been a visiting lecturer in the early 1970s.

From the late 1960s and early 1970s, Elias's sociological reputation began to grow in continental Europe, especially in the Netherlands, Germany, and France. In addition to Bielefeld, Elias was invited to a number of other German universities, sometimes as a visiting scholar – these included Aachen, Bochum, and Konstanz. In 1977, Elias was made the first recipient of the Theodor Adorno Prize conferred at Frankfurt, where he was also awarded the title of Professor Emeritus at the city's principal university. During this period, Elias's star also began to rise outside the academy. For example, he became known to lay audiences when he came to feature in a series of interviews and documentaries by the press and television media, both within the Netherlands and Germany. His ninetieth birthday (1987) was marked by two conferences in his name, and an associated special issue of the journal *Theory, Culture and Society*. A year later, he was presented with the European Amalfi prize for *The Society of Individuals* (Elias 2010 (1987)) (at that time only available in the original German as *Die Gesellschaft der Individuen*) as the best book published within the continent during 1987. By the age of 92, Elias was almost completely blind and suffered recurrent strokes. He died at his home in Amsterdam on 1 August 1990. Virtually his last words to Dunning, who was visiting him the previous Christmas, were: 'Eric my dear, I'm dying'. They were spoken calmly, without visible emotion and in what appeared to be a rather detached and matter-of-fact way.

Summing up, the following aspects of Elias's life can be said to help in explaining characteristic features of his sociology:

(i) His experience, above all, of the First World War, the rise of the Nazis and the murder of his mother in a gas chamber, all sensitised Elias to the part played by violence and war in human life. Such experiences also intensified his awareness of '*de*civilising' as well as 'civilising processes' and provided him with first-hand experiences of the sorts of horrors that could be committed in the name of civilisation.

(ii) The repeated interruption of his career by wider events – the First World War, the German hyperinflation of 1923, the Nazi takeover ten years later, exile to France and then to Britain, internment as an 'enemy alien' – all helped to sensitise Elias to the interdependence and interplay of the 'individual' and the 'social'; 'the private' and 'the public'; 'the micro' and 'the macro'; 'agency' as well as 'structure'. As we suggested earlier following Kilminster (2007) and Russell (1997), Elias's experiences as a Jew played a part in this connection, too.[30]

(iii) Elias's simultaneous study of medicine – perhaps especially his observation in the dissecting room of the structure and functioning of the human brain – and philosophy, helped to problematise for him such aspects of philosophy as the mind-body dichotomy, contributing to his switching to sociology in the first place and to his making important and original contributions to what have come to be known as 'the sociology of emotions' and 'the sociology of the body'. That Elias was a pioneer of the sociology of sport is perhaps best understood primarily in that context, too.

It is worthwhile noting in this connection that many German social scientists in the 1920s and 1930s would, of course, have had similar experiences to Elias but took different scientific paths. However, none of them experienced the totality of what Elias went through and none had the same combination of academic training, determination, Jewish origins, familial background, and intellectual ability. Furthermore, some of Elias's conceptual innovations were developments only likely to have been made in Weimar Germany because they were elaborations on the earlier contributions made by scholars such as Max and Alfred Weber, Georg Lukacs, and Karl Mannheim. Besides, as is the case when considering the work of any key scholar, while the genesis of an individual's ideas cannot adequately be explained without an understanding of the biographical, intellectual, and more general historical conditions under which these took form, the development of such ideas is never in any simple sense *reducible* to such conditions.

## Recognition and dissemination

As suggested above, it was not until Elias was relatively advanced in years, principally when he was in his eighties, that his work came to gain anything like the widespread recognition for which he had hoped. At the time of its original publication in Switzerland in 1939, Elias's key study *Über den Prozess der Zivilisation* was little known and largely ignored by sociologists of the period. As Bryan Wilson (1977: 15–16) has suggested, the eve of the Second World War was perhaps not the most auspicious time for the publication of a two volume work on 'civilisation', and at that, by a German Jew. However, the republication of the text in the original German in 1969 did bring more widespread attention to Elias's work. It reached an even wider audience in the 1970s and 1980s as Anglophone scholars were finally able to read English translations of *Über den Prozess der Zivilisation*, notably the publication by Blackwell in 1978 of an English translation of Volume I sub-titled *The History of Manners*, which was followed in 1982 by Volume II sub-titled *State Formation and Civilization*. Also during this period, a number of Elias's other principal studies, some of which were partially or wholly written before the original publication of *Über den Prozess der Zivilisation*, began also to be published in English. These included (in their English translations) *The Court Society* (1969); *What is Sociology?* (1978); *The Loneliness of the Dying* (1984); *Involvement and Detachment* (1987); *The Society of Individuals* (1991); and, together with Eric Dunning, *Quest for Excitement* (1986; 2008), which was first written in English. It was not until 1994, though, that *The Civilizing Process* was published in English as a single volume, to be followed in 2000 by a revised edition, again by Blackwell, in which some of the issues relating to the translation from the original German were further addressed. At the time of writing, a major series entitled *Elias Collected Works*, published by University College Dublin Press, is nearing completion. A newly revised and partially re-translated version of *The Civilizing Process* has (May 2012) been published with the title *On the Process of Civilisation*. The new title, from the outset, helps to avoid the impression that Elias was attempting to theorise a singular, monolithic and universal process of social development. The title also constitutes, as we have suggested earlier, a far more accurate English translation of the original German title, *Über den Prozess der Zivilisation*.

To date, Elias's writings have been translated into some twenty-nine languages, mainly German (110 items as of June 2005) and English (72 items, also as of June 2005). Verbal testimony to Elias's current sociological stature is provided by a growing number of scholars. At a conference in Amsterdam in 1990 to mark Elias's death, the German Max Weber scholar, Dirk Käsler, described Elias as a 'sociologist for Europe in the twentieth century and a sociologist for the world in the twenty-first'. In a poll carried out in 1998 by the International Sociological Association, Elias's *On The Process of Civilisation* was ranked as the seventh most important sociological work of the twentieth century, coming ahead of books by Parsons, Merton, Habermas and many other famous figures. In 1998, Robert van Krieken wrote as follows on Elias's growing reputation. What he said is worth quoting in full:

> Since translation of his work into English began to accelerate in the 1980s, a growing number of books and articles on topics including health, sexuality, crime, shame, national and ethnic identity, femininity, and globalisation, in a variety of disciplines, made positive reference to Elias as an authority on the history of emotions, identity, violence, the body and state formation. Lewis Coser referred to him as 'one of the most significant sociological thinkers of our day', and Zygmunt Bauman described him as 'indeed a great sociologist'. 'Long before American scholars had discovered the idea of historical sociology', wrote Christopher Lasch, 'Elias understood the possibilities of this new genre and worked them out with an imaginative boldness that still surpasses later studies in this vein'. Anthony Giddens describes his work as 'an extraordinary achievement, anticipating issues which came to be explored in social theory only at a much later date'. Elias's teaching, writing and ideas are gradually exercising an increasingly pervasive influence on an ever-widening circle of sociologists as well as a broader lay public, in an expanding number of countries and languages, and he is now starting to take his place in the sociology textbooks and dictionaries. (van Krieken 1988: 2–3)

Two caveats are necessary to what van Krieken wrote. The first is that Elias's growing popularity is partly a consequence of the emergence and growth of 'the sociology of emotions', 'the sociology of the body', and 'the sociology of consumption' as sociological specialisms, developments of which Elias would probably have at least partly disapproved because these specialisms are not always located in the context of a wider body of theory. In this respect, echoing some of the ideas of Comte, Elias was opposed to the fragmentation that results from the contemporary trend towards overspecialisation. He also regarded 'the body' and 'the emotions' as central to *all* fields and branches of sociological endeavour and stressed the need (i) for analysis always to be accompanied by synthesis; and (ii) for *all* sociological specialisms to be related to a central corpus of knowledge.

Our second caveat relates to the fact that Elias's growing popularity is patchy and not literally world-wide. For example, his work first caught on and continues to be highly regarded in the Netherlands, France, Germany, Italy, Portugal and Spain. It is also highly regarded by some research groups in South America, especially Brazil, Colombia, and Argentina. In the United States and Britain, however, in fact throughout most of the English-speaking world, Elias's work remains somewhat marginal, little known outside specific paradigmatic enclaves, and somewhat divorced from the mainstream. An important exception to this more general rule is in relation to the sociological study of sport and, to a rather lesser extent, leisure, where Elias's work has long been centrally discussed by scholars in these fields. Relatively recently, for instance, the Canadian Michael Atkinson published his highly insightful *Tatooed: The Sociogenesis of Body Art*, in 2003; Joseph Maguire published his perceptive *Reflections on Process Sociology and Sport: 'Walking the Line'*, in 2011; and Dominic Malcolm published his imaginative *Sport and Sociology*, in 2012. All three were manifestly important sociological contributions – the latter two to the study of sport which, as we saw earlier in this book, had been pioneered among others by Elias and Dunning in the 1960s, 70s and 80s. All three of these books are fundamentally based upon, and have sought to advance, Elias's concepts and theories. Thus, they differ in a variety of ways from the work of other sociology of sport pioneers such as Günther Lüschen, John Loy, Peter Donnelly and Klaus Heinemann.

There are signs, nonetheless, that this situation regarding the reception of Elias's work – particularly with regard to its confinement to specific geographical and sociological 'enclaves' – may be set to change. Perhaps most significantly, it is in relation to the empirical applications and assessments of Elias's ideas on civilising processes that the most important developments have occurred over the last two decades. A noteworthy case in point is that of work by a number of key crime historians. For example, Eric Johnson and Eric Monkkonen's edited collection entitled *The Civilization of Crime* (1996, University of Illinois Press) contains contributions from European and North American scholars who have come to consider the work of Elias on the back of a reassessment of long-term trends in crime. As the authors of this volume explained:

> One of the most notable effects of recent work on the history of crime as demonstrated in this volume has been to force historians to reassess (or to assess for the first time) the work of the sociologist Norbert Elias. Without a doubt, his

work has gained the greatest respect of any single theoretician. Elias's significance has come to be recognized in part because his descriptions of the "civilizing process" match so well what crime historians have been finding. That he wrote his major works touching on violence in the late 1930s with little historical research to confirm his ideas makes his theoretical formulations all the more impressive ... [F]or historians of crime, the slowly growing conviction that crime has decreased, not increased, over the centuries; that the countryside used to be dangerous, not safe; that, as Barbara Hanawalt put it, "fur-collar crime" was a major threat – all of this changed the status of Elias from curiosity to prescient thinker. (1996: 4–5)

That this text was published in the US, and by two major North American scholars in the field, is particularly noteworthy. However, more importantly, to the extent that Johnson and Monkkonen are correct, it would appear that these scholars' motivation to engage with Elias has grown out of an increasing dissatisfaction with long established models of crime and society, rather than, say, the need to settle or resolve paradigmatic disputes. Indeed, until recently, Elias's thesis ran counter to most if not all other sociological models that had been dominant within the US, particularly those associated with Tönnies, Durkheim, Park and Burgess, and many related others, all of which held that crime had increased in tandem with processes of urbanisation, class alignment, industrialisation, and the more general demise of 'community' associated with the ascendancy of 'mass society' (1996: 5).

More recently, prominent North American social scientists such as Richard Sennett (currently in post at both the London School of Economics and the New York University)[31] and, to a much greater extent, Steven Pinker, the latter a Canadian who teaches at Harvard, have also come to recognise the significance of Elias's work. Pinker, a renowned and highly influential Canadian psychologist, like Johnson and Monkkonen, and the various contributors to their edited volume, came to engage with Elias's work not out of paradigmatic alignment, the pursuit of intellectual fashion, nor, indeed, because Elias's 'star was on the rise' in the US, but because his (Pinker's) empirical assessment of long-term trends in violence effectively made necessary a theoretical model that could better account for the processes he was observing. In his highly original book entitled *The Better Angels of our Nature: the Decline of Violence in History and its Causes* (Allen Lane, 2011), Pinker describes Elias as '... the most important thinker you have never heard of' (2011: 59). The book contains a seventy-page chapter devoted solely to Elias's work, and draws centrally on his theory of civilising processes. While we might cavil at some points of detail concerning his exposition of Elias, Pinker shows an admirable command of Elias's core ideas.[32] His work constitutes a major engagement with, assessment and extension of, Elias's theory of civilising processes. Above all, Pinker has arguably surpassed Elias with the very substantial body of statistical data that he introduces. Statistical methods were not highly developed in sociology during most of the years in which Elias lived and wrote, and he (Elias) spent far more time analysing literary texts, paintings and drawings. In addition, Pinker has effectively developed further specific aspects of Elias's thesis. For example, he has explored in some detail what we might call 'the civilisation of God'. Pinker documents through a panoply of examples how in the Judaeo-Christian tradition, there is a shift away from the understanding and depiction of God as a vengeful, impulsive, volatile, spontaneous and bloodthirsty deity – in, for instance, the Hebrew bible (the Old Testament) – and towards the depiction of an increasingly even-handed, temperate, pacifying, divine providence (in the New Testament and the Talmud).

We have shown in earlier sections of this chapter how Elias's own biographical circumstances, intertwined with a specific set of historical conditions – particularly the rise of the Nazis in Weimar Germany and the Second World War – had a significant role to play in his status as a relatively marginal figure, both within his own lifetime, and with respect to his enduring influence on other scholars. However, in addition to a consideration of such circumstances, there is a range of other factors to consider. These notably include some of the characteristics of Elias's work itself, which we think help to explain why it has not yet come to gain the recognition that it arguably deserves.

In an e-mail written to Chris Rojek in 2005 (which both of them have permitted us to cite), one of the few American sociologists to have engaged seriously with Elias's contributions, Alan Sica of Penn State University, commented incisively, albeit somewhat tongue-in-cheek, on this issue. He wrote:

> The reason Americans don't take to Elias is that he writes about European historical and cultural change and American sociologists don't feel comfortable with that sort of thing, except for Goldstone and that small lot; and because he is theoretically very adventurous and synthetic, and they don't go for that; and because he trashed Parsons, who many of them liked back in the day; and because he could be mistaken for a closet Freudian, which they don't like; and because he brings up really obnoxious qualities of humankind, which they particularly don't like; and because he wrote a helluva lot of stuff, which takes a long time to read, and they don't have time; and because 'figuration' is a word that has distinctly effete connotations in this country, and sounds like art history…

In our opinion, notwithstanding some notable exceptions not least those discussed earlier in this section, these observations apply to Britain as much as the USA. Put simply, Elias's work has never quite 'fitted' within the sociological mainstream in either the UK or North America. And as we have seen in this chapter, dominant intellectual trends seem on the whole to have disadvantaged Elias at pivotal moments in the development of his academic career. At a time when sociologists were turning their attention to 'macro' level social structures, particularly to the spheres of work, industry, and the 'economic forces' of production, Elias's work – with its focus on, say, the minutiae of table manners in the French Court – seemed out of place, indeed, rather 'effete' to use Sica's term, perhaps even antagonistic. Similarly, his later work, for example, on Mozart, or, together with Eric Dunning, on sport and leisure, was considered by some to be rather trivial at the time of its first publication. The question in such a context hardly needed to be spelled out: surely such topics were not worthy of serious sociological attention? And, while these topics subsequently came to be recognised as important fields of sociological analysis in their own right, Elias's approach was often considered (with, as we have seen, some notable exceptions) to be *one from the past* more than *one for the future*. Indeed, his work has almost always run counter to intellectual fashions. This tendency has extended even to the language and terminology he employed. Particularly in his first published work in English, Elias unapologetically used terms and formulations – with reference to, for example, 'civilisation'; 'development'; 'directions of change'; 'functions'; 'laws'; 'the nexus of facts'; 'scientific understanding'; 'factual knowledge'; and 'reality' – which variously offend the sensibilities of, or sound alarm bells for, many present-day sociologists. While Elias arguably employed such terms in ways that avoided their pitfalls (and with these, some of the main reasons why they had initially been called into question), this simple tendency alone has not helped his case.

More generally, Elias's developmental approach to sociology, and in particular, his insistence on the notion of sociology as a 'science', has led many (albeit mistakenly) to label him, variously, as an 'evolutionist', and more recently, as a 'naive empiricist', a child of the Enlightenment who, for example, is '... happily innocent of modern social studies of science' (Pels 1991: 181). While we shall return to such issues in Chapters Five and Six, and the Conclusion of this book, the points raised above are important in a key respect: whether or not such charges are 'real', they are, to paraphrase W.I. and Dorothy Thomas (1929), 'real in their consequences' to the extent that they have underpinned some rather hasty dismissals of Elias's work.

Such difficulties for subsequent generations of sociologists, quite literally, to 'come to terms' with Elias's work are perhaps compounded by the fact that, as we discussed in the Introduction, his sociology does not readily lend itself to short-term political causes. We have seen in this chapter that Elias's dogged determination to avoid ideological incursions into knowledge is related in important respects to aspects of his biography. Elias shunned straightforward and direct political investments in knowledge, and argued instead that these should be pursued by means of a *detour via* detachment. Elias's emphasis on 'detachment', in turn, has led some, albeit wrongly, to suggest that he appears to be making claims for a 'disinterested' or 'neutral science'. Furthermore, Elias envisaged the 'user group' for sociological knowledge ultimately to be *humanity as a whole*, not *specific* groups or interests.

In these and other senses, Elias's work does not provide easy 'answers'. The core premise that effective social interventions can only be made on the basis of the growth of a stock of knowledge that will take generations to establish may seem to some to be something of a 'cop-out'. Essentially, the notion appears to provide a good rationale for political avoidance along the lines that 'we can avoid becoming "politically" involved now, so long as we do our bit in the long run by playing our part in the knowledge relay race'. Typically, the social, economic and political problems of the day, irrespective of their long-term sociogenesis, are experienced rather more urgently. The temptation to 'retreat to the present' is all the greater for sociologists who are faced with institutional competition from other fields and disciplines – such as psychology and economics – the members of which feel more able to posit and peddle 'answers' and 'oven-ready solutions'. Of course, such a portrayal of Elias as a scholar who consigned political action to the future, is a misrepresentation, not simply of his approach, but of his life's work. As we have seen in this chapter, such work included in his youth, Zionist activism as part of the Blau-Weiss League, his later group-analytic work, and indeed the development of a path-breaking synthesis enshrined in his sociological approach that he hoped would help enable sociologists to become *Mythenjäger* – 'hunters' or 'destroyers' of myths (2012b: 46) – including the mythological and fantasy-laden political ideologies of the day. In a very immediate and direct political sense, Elias encouraged sociologists to challenge ideologies such as those which, to take the example discussed earlier in this chapter, underpin in important ways the enormous social and economic volatility which, in recent years in particular, has destroyed countless livelihoods and lives.

Dunne (2009) has suggested that Elias's position in this respect is inherently contradictory. On the one hand, Dunne argues, Elias views human history as following a largely 'blind' course, and yet on the other, he (Elias) envisages a future phase in which sociologists might be able to exert 'control' over human figurations. Furthermore, Dunne proposes that the issue of control in Elias's work is similarly ambivalent: Elias effectively observes the emergent human capacity for self-control through his empirical-theoretical work as an 'actual', and yet also posits such controls in a prescriptive manner – as something sociologists of the future *ought* to be able to develop. While, as we shall discuss in Chapter Six, we agree that there are a good many questions concerning what might be called the 'political status' of figurational sociology that require further working through, we disagree with Dunne's formulation of such problems. Firstly, Elias's model of human figurations is expressly intended to avoid both determinism on the one hand, and voluntarism, on the other – a point that Dunne recognises, but nonetheless neglects to accommodate. Put simply, Elias's approach avoids a view of human history as either 'the net outcome of human rationality and conscious planning', or of human history as a mere flow of unstructured and directionless 'chaos'. For Elias, human history arises from the 'web' of interdependencies – the nexus of planned and unplanned outcomes of interlacing human decisions, actions, and intentions, both rational and irrational, which shapes, more than it is shaped by, the choices of specific individuals (Mennell 1983: 6). As such, the course of large-scale human figurations has a degree of independence from *any particular* individual, but *not individuals as such*. Indeed, as Elias shows, for example, in *The Court Society* and *The Germans* – respectively in connection with Louis XIV and Adolf Hitler – under specific figurational conditions, single individuals have historically been able to monopolise state controls in order to secure a high degree of influence over large-scale human figurations, albeit with many consequences that these individuals had ultimately not anticipated. Elias demonstrates with his examples of 'the games models' (see Elias (2012b)) that the degree to which any particular figuration follows a 'blind' course is also related to the power ratios of the people who comprise it. In the case of those figurations which involve relatively high degrees of asymmetry in dominant power relations, the capacity for those in positions of relative advantage to exercise rational and conscious 'control' is considerably greater than within figurations characterised by more symmetrical power ratios. Thus, secondly, the question of 'control', or perhaps better, the degree to which particular groups of individuals, perhaps single individuals, might be able to 'steer' or otherwise influence the overall direction of change of specific human figurations is not simply a question of *either* 'control' *or* 'no control'. It is a question of *degrees* of influence, in turn related to power balances, and also a question pertaining to the ratio of intended relative to unintended consequences arising from conscious interventions in the sphere of human figurations. Elias's central thesis in this respect is that the more fantasy-laden the basis for such interventions, the more likely such interventions are to have a higher degree of unintended relative to intended consequences. Dunne is also, in our view, incorrect to conflate 'self-control' with 'control over human figurations'. Indeed, Elias's central argument is that while the human capacity for self-control that emerges in tandem with civilising processes is a necessary condition for a breakaway from the double-bind 'trap' that he posits, such 'controls' are not in themselves 'sufficient' to do so. Indeed, a further effort at 'distancing' is required, *both* in terms of psychic 'detachment', and in terms of 'scientific civilising processes' through which specific intellectual groups might come to gain a degree of autonomy from 'heteronomous evaluations'. Finally, Dunne is manifestly wrong to suggest that figurational sociologists are conspicuously silent on issues of policy, resigning such commentary to later generations, or perhaps altogether shirking such responsibilities. To take just the authors of this book as examples of 'working with Elias', Dunning *et al.*'s (1998) work on football hooliganism was highly critical of the-then Thatcher government's emotionally-charged and populist strategy of 'penning' rival supporters in football grounds since, they argued, such strategies served simply to escalate tensions between and among supporters, and to displace the violence such that it took place outside of the grounds instead of within them. Similarly, Hughes's (2003) work on smoking concluded with a series of observations and recommendations for health policy based upon his figurational analysis of long-term trends in tobacco use. Elias's model of sociology as a vocation, and more specifically, his depiction of sociologists as 'destroyers of myths' is itself of considerable 'political' import (see, for example, Mennell's (1983) explicitly 'political' pamphlet based upon figurational principles). It points towards forms of intervention in the social world that are applicable to sociologists at the current phase of the development of their discipline. At this early stage, current levels of knowledge are perhaps only sufficient for sociologists to draw upon in calling into question, for example, fundamental assumptions made within policy discourse. Indeed, as we mention elsewhere in this book, there is much in Elias's critique of *homo clausus* that, critically speaking, strikes at the core of neo-liberalist ideology and other forms of political and philosophical individualism. While destroying such ideological 'myths', in itself, is a form of 'political action' if we are to so label it, it stands towards one end of a gradual continuum towards more elaborate forms of political involvement, with, for example, explicit policy advice, the development of alternative, research-based models of government and governance, and so forth, towards the other end. If Elias is right, sociologists might, to the extent to which they are able to secure more reliable knowledge of the social world, be able to move gradually along the scale towards greater political involvement not, as Dunne depicts it, at a future stage when 'the day finally arrives' (such a notion is far too static), but by degrees, and by no means *via* a simple, unilinear 'march' towards progress within the human sciences as a whole. Indeed, though the 'anticipatory motif' (Kilminster 2004: 34) of Elias's work is expressly intended to help facilitate such a transition, it by no means guarantees this. Another axis upon which the degree of sociologists' capacity for effective research-based political involvement might vary relates to the degree of complexity involved. We might conceive, for example, of a further continuum with, for example, relatively simple (but still immensely complex) figurations, such as those between a parent and child, towards one end, and gradually more structurally complex figurations towards the other – for example, the figurational dynamics of entire families, schools, organisations, institutions, communities, neighbourhoods, regions, states, supranational entities, and ultimately, humanity as a whole. Accordingly, we could envisage the capacity for sociologists to proffer, for example, research-based models for the rearing of children, group analysis, organisational change, and so forth to be closer to the current reaches of sociological knowledge than, say, effective strategies for the aversion of escalating inter-state military conflicts. Elias's position on 'secondary involvement' is anything but an easy one to practice as a vocation. It demands considerable self-distancing, and, by extension, at the level of sociology as a discipline, the development of a series of more general institutional shifts (this is a theme to which we shall return in the conclusion).

Finally, following on from our arguments above, there is a more fundamental issue that ought to be considered when seeking to understand the somewhat patchy reception of Elias's work. Put simply, figurational sociology is not easy to practise. Developing an understanding of, in particular, long-term social processes often involves painstaking analysis of time-series data. To emulate Elias directly, one needs to have a solid command of classical and modern history, among other humanities, but, at the same time, there is a need to develop analyses which are quite different from those of historians, and which, accordingly, do not obey the rules of 'historical method', particularly with regard to the chronicling of events – a tendency which often causes figurational sociological work to fall foul of the methodological standards set by members of the 'historical establishment'. Moreover, the key concepts of figurational sociology are, at once, both beguilingly simple and immensely complex. In addition, their comprehension demands a considerable degree of cognitive investment and re-orientation. In particular, a full and proper orientation towards *processes* and a move away from *homo clausus* thinking, each demands a substantial degree of perceptual realignment and self-distancing. Such demands are all the greater given that there are no single or simple terminological/conceptual equivalents to Elias's core theoretical precepts. Nor can such concepts easily be 'disentangled', or indeed, meaningfully separated from, the theoretical-empirical work in which they take form. An exegesis of Elias's work, therefore, always faces the danger of artificially divorcing the 'empirical' and 'rational' components of his approach, or perhaps better, of separating Elias's theoretical insights from his empirical insights, and in so doing undermining a core aspect of his sociological practice which centred on the integration of 'research-theorising'. Yet at the same time, the enterprise of exposition itself demands, for the purposes of coherence, a degree of distillation and separation of core ideas from the corpus of the work from which such ideas are drawn.

It is with these two, albeit apparently contradictory, endeavours in mind that we shall start in the next chapter to examine some of Elias's major contributions to sociology.

# 2
# Some Basic Concepts of Figurational Sociology

Elias never considered his position to be 'unique'. He did, however, consider it to be distinctive. Indeed, he fought against a series of dominant intellectual currents to champion what was sometimes seen to be an outmoded approach by his contemporaries. It was one of Elias's hopes that, in the course of time, the central tenets of his work would come to be accepted simply as core parts of sociology. He was anticipating in this connection – and sought to contribute to – an end to the 'paradigm wars' that we have described in earlier sections, or at least a transformation of them in a more constructive direction.

The main distinctive features of figurational sociology are its emphasis on processes and relations. However, it is *radically* processual and *radically* relational in character; that is, it is processual and relational at its *roots* or *core*. The stress of Elias's sociology is centrally upon the explanatory importance of time. It correspondingly emphasises the importance of long-term as opposed to short-term processes, although Elias did not neglect the latter.

When he was President of the American Sociological Association in the 1960s, the late George Homans devoted a Presidential Address to the theme of 'bringing the people back in' (Homans 1961). He was advocating a sociology that would be less statistical/mathematical than what was then becoming dominant in the United States, a sociology in which it is never forgotten that it is *people* who act, occupy statuses, perform roles and form social structures. Like Homans, Elias, too, sought to lay the foundations for a 'scientific' sociology that did not simply involve the emulation of the more successful natural sciences but which was attuned, on the one hand, to those properties of the subject that it shares with other sciences; and on the other, to the balance of similarities and differences between humans, their societies and the rest of the known or empirically experienced world. It is an approach in which far greater stress is placed on what human beings are and how *they came to be* as they are than has conventionally been the case with sociology at least since the end of the Second World War. Dunning vividly remembers how, as a student, he was expected by Elias to have some understanding of human anatomy and physiology, and of biological evolution as well as human history and social development. Further to this, in his sociology, Elias eschewed the use of the more popular mechanical and organic analogies for the purpose of sociological concept-formation and stressed, instead, models taken from social life itself, for example, dances, games and the personal pronouns.

At the core of Elias's work is a stress on the observable fact that, like the universe at large, each human individual is a process: that is, we are born, mature and die – a set of facts which sound banal until it is remembered that the sociology of birth, death, and dying are marginal specialisms in our subject. Elias wrote of *Humana Conditio*, 'the human condition' (Elias 1985), in this connection. Our difficulties in coming to grips with the processual character of everything, he said, are compounded by our fears and hesitations regarding our mortality. Sociologists, he argued, need to develop a vocabulary which avoids the tendency to reduce processes to steady states (*Zustandsreduktion*). Such a tendency is characteristic of Western languages. As he expressed it:

> Our languages are constructed in such a way that we can often only express constant movement or constant change in ways which imply that it has the character of an isolated object at rest, and then, almost as an afterthought, adding a verb which expresses the fact that the thing with this character is now changing. For example, standing by a river we see the perpetual flowing of the water. But to grasp it conceptually, and to communicate it to others, we do not think and say, 'look at the perpetual flowing of the water'; we say, 'look how fast the river is flowing'. We say, 'The wind is blowing', as if the wind were actually a thing at rest which, at a given point in time, begins to move and blow. We speak as if the wind were separate from its blowing, as if a wind could exist which did not blow. ... This reduction of processes to static conditions, we shall call 'process-reduction' for short ... (Elias 2012b: 106–107).

It was in order to capture this idea of process that Elias insisted that the conventional sociological vocabulary which involves talking, for example, of 'social structure *and* social change', a formulation which implies that non-changing social structures could exist, should be abandoned and, even though they often sound ugly in English, replaced by process terms such as 'socialisation', 'civilisation', 'industrialisation', 'urbanisation', 'democratisation', 'courtisation', and 'sportisation'.

According to Elias, humans are also bound to others by fluid ties of interdependence which are a biosocial and not simply a social or learned fact of life. That is, we have a partly inborn, partly socially instilled tendency to seek the company of others, for example for sexual purposes, but also as an enjoyable 'end-in-itself'. Sociability is also important for human survival. The babyhood and infancy of humans last a relatively long time, and babies and infants cannot survive on their own. They have to bond with others and others with them. As Winnicott, the psychoanalyst famously put it: 'There is no such thing as a baby, there is a baby and someone' (Winnicott 1965). Humans also have a mobile facial musculature, a biological fact which is a precondition for smiling, another crucial inborn feature at the emotional level of human bonding.[33] It plays an important part in the bonding of parents and their newborn babies. Laughter is another uniquely human feature which can play an important bonding role. Although most people tend to take it for granted, there is an occupational group in modern societies – comedians – who specialise in making other people laugh, and there is now a substantial body of sociological research on this profession and on comedy itself (see, for example, the work of Lockyer and Pickering (2006); and Kuipers (2006)). And, of course, just as, among adolescents and adults, smiling can be used to deceive people, so laughter can be used to ridicule other individuals and groups. Both are sometimes used in 'legal' and 'illegal' murders. Examples include public executions of the kind that used to be common in European and other countries.

## Human figurations

Another way of expressing the radical interdependence of humans would be to say that we form dynamic 'figurations' with one another. Elias developed the concept of 'figuration' as an alternative to, but by no means the equivalent of, terms such as structure, society, and system. The notion is centrally related to a *homines aperti* view of humans – that human beings can only be properly understood as pluralities, and not as isolated individual 'actors' who variously 'interact' with other 'individuals', 'groups', 'organisations', or 'social institutions'. Elias argued that *homo clausus* formulations – which stem from an understanding of humans as 'closed off' 'essences of uniqueness' that 'stand in relation to' 'society' – can be understood as not simply in themselves conceptually problematic, but as reflective of a particular moulding of human psychic structures that emerges in tandem with particular social processes, notably those to which he referred as 'civilising processes'. Elias's aim in coining the term figuration, and in his work more generally, was to counter what has become to people in societies such as ours a socially intuitive reification: that we are individuals closed off from one another and from other 'social formations'. Moreover, Elias's term at its core is intended as a counter to the notion that 'social agencies', 'institutions', and 'society' are entities that exist somehow separately from the people who comprise them. That is, the concept of figurations is predicated upon an understanding of the fundamental interdependence of human beings, first in their biology, and then through their socially developed reciprocal needs (Elias 2012a: 525). Such human interdependencies comprise the nexuses of figurations: shifting networks of people with fluctuating, asymmetrical power balances. Sociologically, the concept directs attention towards shifting patterns, regularities, directions of change, tendencies and counter-tendencies, in webs of human relationships that are always changing over time. To think of the concept in relation to a more conventional sociological lexicon, the term invokes 'the individual', 'agency', 'society', 'social change', 'power', and 'structure' simultaneously, but purposely without being reducible to any of these components. Again, effectively built-in to the concept of figurations is the core idea that notions such as 'the individual' as an isolated abstraction, or 'agency' as some-*thing* that is 'held' or 'exercised' by 'the individual' or 'the state' are in themselves misleading terms which, to varying degrees, involve forms of conceptual reductionism and reification.

A guiding analogy for the concept of figurations is that of dance. Viewing dancers on a dance-floor as a mobile figuration of interdependent people is useful because it refers to 'real-life' social processes, and not abstract (and highly problematic) comparisons with, for instance, biological organisms or synthetic mechanisms. However, equally, in invoking dance as an analogy, Elias also wanted us, by extension, to envisage families, cities, nation states, and even feudal, capitalist, and communist societies, all as figurations, but with differing degrees of length and complexity. We can think of recognisable patterns emerging from such shifting figurations, just as we might, for example, be able to discern the 'tango', or the 'waltz', or simply 'dance in general' as distinct, say, from 'walking'. However, Elias argues, it is important not to conceive of 'dance' as a structure or 'thing' which is somehow 'outside' of 'the individual' (2012a: 525). While different people can dance the same dance figuration, there is no dance as such without dancers. Dance figurations, like any social figuration, are to a degree independent of the *specific* individuals forming them at any particular time, *but are not independent of individuals as such*. Neither, Elias proposed, are dances, or by extension figurations, mere abstracted mental constructions produced from the observation of individuals considered in isolation from one another. While figurations can persist even after the individuals who comprised them at one time died and became replaced, they only exist through the on-going participation of constituent members.

The analogy of dance, and indeed the concept of 'figurations', may appear simple at first sight, perhaps common-sensical, but the insights they yield are of great conceptual significance. In this concept – which, we shall show, must be understood in relation to the others he offers – Elias provides a means of *circumventing*, not so much resolving, the 'agency-structure dilemma'. The dilemma centres on the difficulties attendant upon developing formulations of the relationship between individuals and the societies they form which avoid the trap of 'reductionism' to 'individuals' and 'agency' on the one hand, and the 'reification' of 'society' and 'structure', on the other, whilst simultaneously doing justice to both 'the individual' and 'the social' sides of the equation. Sociologists have been embroiled in the agency-structure/individual-society conundrum since the inception of their subject when it separated from philosophy in the eighteenth and nineteenth centuries. Another name for the conundrum/dilemma is the 'nominalism' *versus* 'realism' controversy (Popper 1957). Emile Durkheim (1895) who saw sociology as the study of 'social facts' was a sociological realist who in some formulations came close to reifying social phenomena by playing down, perhaps even failing to see, that they are simultaneously individual. Max Weber who saw sociology as the study of 'social action' was a sociological nominalist because he denied the reality to which sociological constructs such as 'state' and 'society' correspond and refer (Gerth and Mills 1970). For Weber, they are ultimately nothing more than names.

It is important to recognise that Elias only came to develop his concepts, theories and methods gradually over time. They did not flow automatically or quickly from his pen. In his 1921 essay, 'On Seeing in Nature', for example, in which he discussed the balance of similarities and differences between 'the arts' and 'the sciences', he used the term 'laws' to express the discoveries unearthed by practitioners of the latter. Somewhat later, in his plan for his later abandoned *Habilitationsschrift* (post-doctoral thesis) which was to have been supervised by Alfred Weber (*Collected Works* (2006a), Vol. 1: 111–122) and likewise in his 1929 essay on 'The Sociology of German Anti-Semitism' (2006a: 78–80), he made explanatory use of the metaphor of 'constellations' to express the idea of structure but later abandoned it on account of its astronomical connotations. It was only when working in the 1960s on a joint article with Eric Dunning, 'Dynamics of Sport Groups with Special Reference to Football' (Elias and Dunning 1966), that Elias came to prefer the concept of 'configurations' because of its combination of structural and processual connotations.[34]

It soon became clear, however, that Elias had a considerably more complex set of concepts forming in his mind. He used the concept of 'law-like regularities' as explanatory of the relatively simple, recurring properties of the phenomenal universe such as light and gravity with which physicists and chemists have been centrally concerned. However, he did not think of them as necessarily universal and eternal as philosophers such as Popper seem to have done. Moreover, he spoke of the configurational dynamics of emergent organic structures such as DNA where the helix has to be double in order to result in genetic inheritance. 'Figurational dynamics' was the term he reserved for the highly complex and dynamic structures and processes that human societies involve, and that are the objects/subjects of sociological research. Elias expressed this latter point as follows:

> It is important ... to distinguish clearly the integration and organisation of sub-units in formations such as a cell or an organism from the integration and organisation of human beings in society. For this reason I have introduced the concept of the figuration of human beings, to designate the unique mode of organisation and integration of human individuals in societies. In this way, a clear distinction can be drawn between the configuration of large models in a cell and the manifold figurations of human beings that we call groups or societies. But what is paramount for me here are the differences in the things themselves. For these, conceptual symbols which are as reality-congruent as possible must be found. (Elias 2009c: 199, n12)

Earlier, Elias had sought to represent diagrammatically what he called 'some of the stages of integration' in the following way.

Figure 2.1 shows in diagrammatic form how Elias sought to develop a conceptual vocabulary which was attuned to the considerably higher levels of

SOME BASIC CONCEPTS OF FIGURATIONAL SOCIOLOGY 55

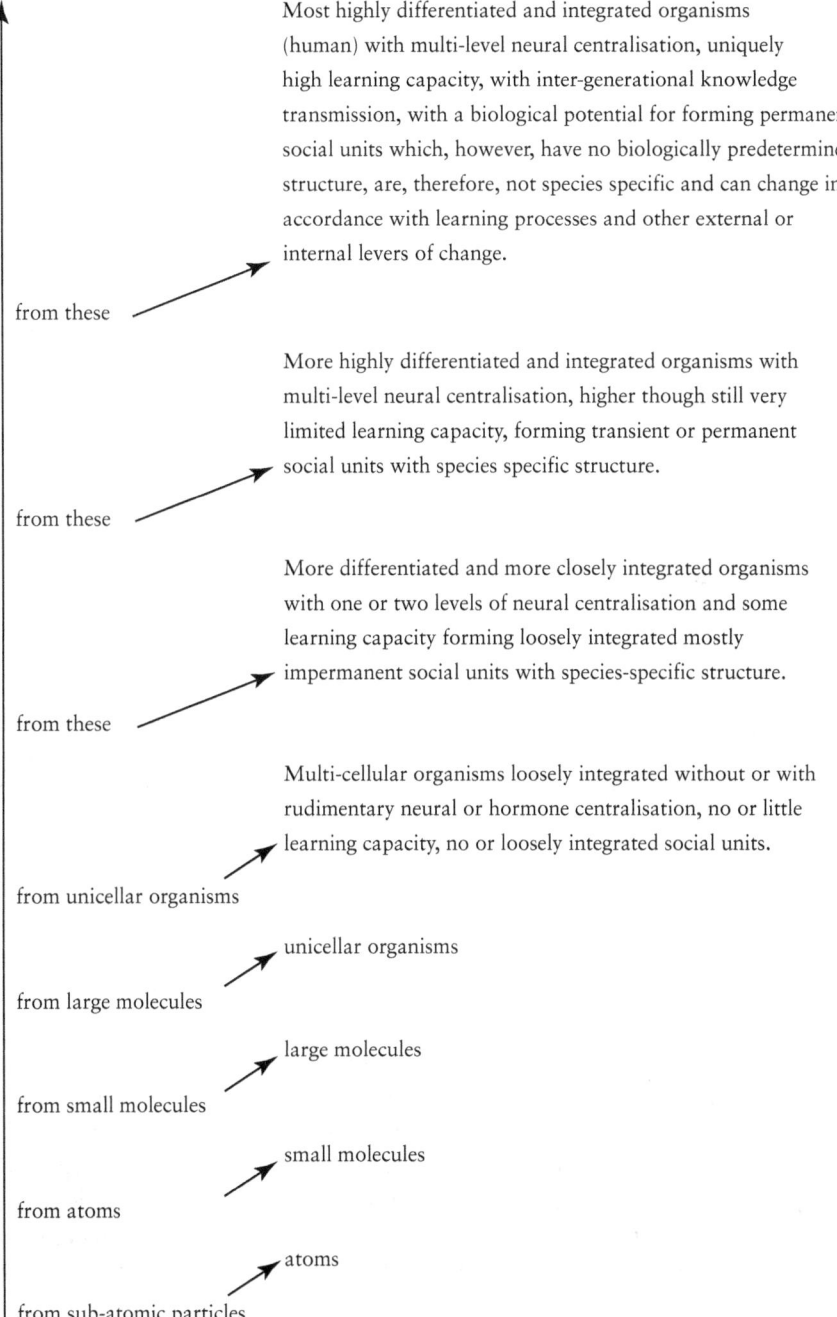

Figure 2.1 Some of the stages of integration as they can be presented today

complexity pertaining to human societies: in his terms – the levels of integration involved within the sphere of human figurations. We have already touched upon some of the important ways in which Elias's concept of figurations, in turn, also needs to be understood in tandem with the concepts of interdependence, *homines aperti* and *homo clausus*. It is thus pertinent now to explore these concepts in more depth for it is precisely this de-centring and re-orientation of the human self-image that is fundamental to Elias's sociological approach, and which marks his distinctive break from a pervasive current of post-Renaissance/Enlightenment thinking. To commence this undertaking, it is necessary once again first to return to the inter-related dilemma of structure versus agency.

## *Homo clausus* and *homines aperti*: Between the Scylla and Charybdis

In an interview with a journalist from *Woman's Own* magazine in 1987, former British Prime Minister, Margaret Thatcher, (in)famously said: 'There is no such thing as society... there are individual men and women and there are families'. The phrase later became celebrated as something of a neo-liberal mantra. Of course, the statement is entirely and inherently nonsensical. To use the term 'families' is already to posit the existence of an entity which is supra-individual. That is, implicit in what Mrs Thatcher said is the idea that a society consists of families and is, hence, more than the sum of its individual members. Her mentor in this mistaken way of thinking seems to have been the late Sir Keith Joseph – one of the home secretaries during her reign – and he, in his turn, seems to have got his understanding from reading the philosophers Hayek (1944) and Popper (1957), both of them advocates of varieties of sociological nominalism. Among other things, what this example shows is that the agency-structure/individual-society conundrum is not just a dry-as-dust academic issue but one with political implications.

In contrast to sociological nominalism, many, if not most of whose advocates come from the political right, the advocates of sociological realism tend, though again not always, to come from the political left. That is because, while people on the right are liable to advocate varieties of relatively unregulated entrepreneurship, rugged individualism, and unfettered markets, people on the left are more likely to champion government responsibility, state-intervention, and control, expressed through ideas such as 'no man is an island' and 'we are all responsible for one another'. An exception in this regard is provided by German National Socialism ('Nazism') with its extreme, *völkisch* racism, its idea of society ('the nation', 'the people' (*das Volk*)) as an entity which is somehow 'superorganic', and its stress on the subordination of individuals to 'the state'.

Much more typical of sociological realism is the 'structural Marxism' of Louis Althusser, a variant of Marxism from which 'the human being as a creative person is almost entirely absent ...' (Layder 1994: 41). People are seen from this standpoint as mere 'carriers' (*Träger*) of beliefs and structures which serve to support the *status quo* and bolster the power of the ruling class. It is a position which contrasts markedly with Marx's own, as can be seen from his famous statement that: 'Men make their own history, but they do not make it just as they please; they do not make it under circumstances chosen by themselves, but under circumstances directly found, given and transmitted from the past' (Marx in Marx and Engels 1942, vol. 2: 315). As we shall show, the balance between voluntarism and determinism expressed in this passage is close to Elias's position.

According to Elias, it is one of the chief tasks of sociologists to steer the sociological ship between the 'Scylla' of reification and determinism on the one hand, and the 'Charybdis' of individualistic reductionism and voluntarism on the other. What this means is that he urged them to use a combination of theory-based reasoning and empirical observation in which neither is allowed to become dominant. The idea is to build-up a picture of humans and their social worlds which is as congruent as possible with how individuals and their societies 'really' are. In short, based on his own researches, Elias was recommending a conceptualisation in which societies are neither conceived as wholly determining 'things' (reification), nor reduced to unstructured congeries of freely-choosing individuals (reductionism, individualism, voluntarism). Elias expressed his view of the 'individual–society' problem thus:

> Our conventional tools for thinking and speaking are to a considerable degree constructed as if everything external to the single person were an object, moreover an object usually in a state of rest. Concepts like 'family' or 'school' plainly refer to networks of people. But the conventional way in which we form our ... concepts makes it appear as if the groupings formed by humans were pieces of matter – objects of the same kind as rocks, trees or houses. This reifying character of the conventional means of speaking and thinking about groups of interdependent people – groups to which one perhaps belongs oneself – appears not least in the concept of society and the way in which one thinks about it. One says that 'society' is the 'object' which sociologists research. But this reifying mode of expression contributes not a little to the difficulties encountered in understanding what sociology is all about. (Elias 1970: 9–10. Authors' translation from the German)

Conventional modes of thinking and speaking, especially in the relatively 'civilised' urban-industrial societies of the modern era, says Elias, encourage the impression that 'society' is made up of 'structures' that are external to individuals, and that individuals are at one and the same time surrounded by 'society' yet separated from 'it' by an invisible wall. This common-sense model which dominates people's experience of their relationship to 'society' today is, according to Elias, 'naïvely egocentric'. Such a model is illustrated in Figure 2.2.

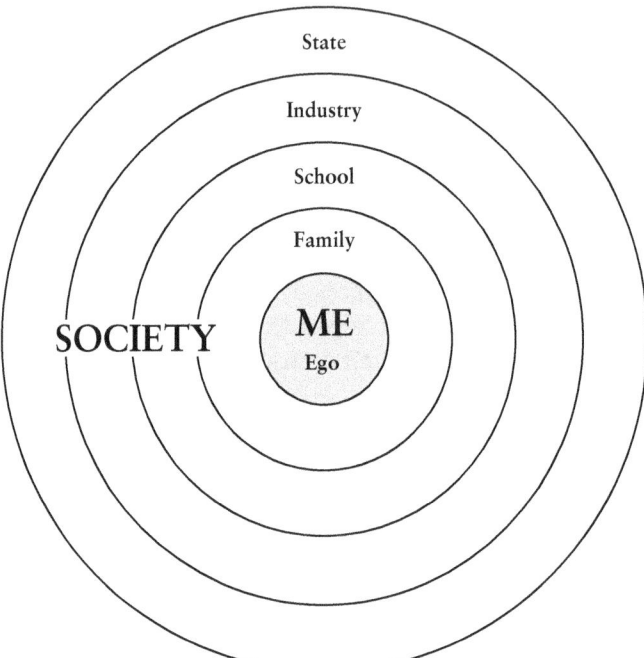

Figure 2.2 Basic pattern of the egocentric view of society

Figure 2.2 depicts what Elias called the *homo clausus* image of humans and their societies. In it, people experience themselves as isolated individuals ('egos') or 'I's who are walled off from others, separated from them as if by an invisible barrier, while at the same time experiencing the institutions that they form such as families, schools, economies, and states and which are nothing more than differently organised groups of individuals, as 'objects' or 'compelling forces' that are more, as it is sometimes metaphysically put, than 'the sum of their individual parts'. A more appropriate image, said Elias, is provided by Figure 2.3. This depicts a figuration of *homines aperti*, 'open people' who, 'through their basic dispositions and inclinations, are directed towards and linked with each other in the most diverse ways' (Elias 1978: 14–15). According to Elias 'people make up webs of interdependence or figurations of many kinds ... They are characterised by power balances of many sorts ...' (2012b: 10).

The first thing worthy of note in this connection is that Elias's understanding of the concept of interdependence is not the same as Durkheim's in *The Division of Labour* (1964). The French classical sociologist distinguished between 'bonds of similitude' based on likeness and 'bonds of interdependence' based on the division of labour. But, for Elias, 'bonds of similitude' involve forms of interdependence, too, for example, the bonds between husbands and wives, parents and children, and many more. That is, interdependence is far from being simply an 'economic' phenomenon. Dunning vividly remembers

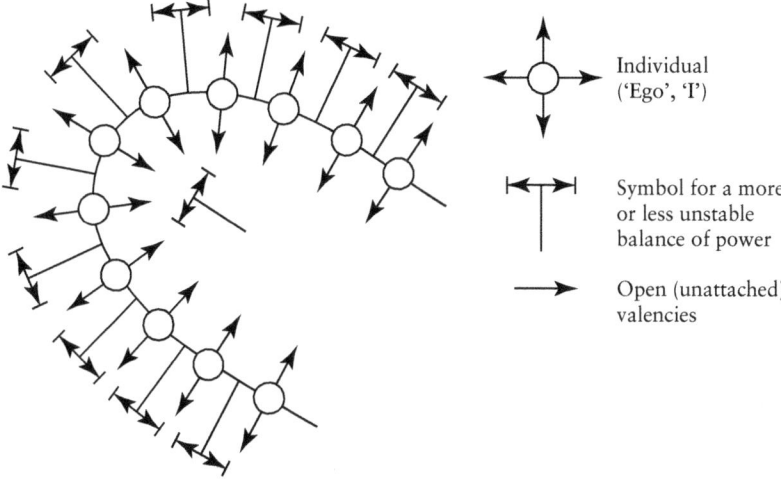

Figure 2.3 A figuration of interdependent individuals

driving Elias from Leicester to London along the M1 motorway in the 1960s and asking: 'Norbert, this is a form of interdependence in your understanding of the term, isn't it? All of us drivers are dependent on the others observing the rules of the road and not losing self-control. It's surely a kind of life and death interdependence'. Elias replied: 'Yes it is, Eric my dear. In fact, in *The Civilising Process*, you will remember, I contrast a medieval road where the main danger was from wild animals or deliberate attack from other humans and a modern road where the principal danger is that of other people losing their self-control' (see Elias 2012a: 406–7).

American sociologist Thomas J. Scheff has written on this issue as follows:

> In *What is Sociology?* (1978; 2012b) and *Involvement and Detachment* (1987a; 2007a), Elias implicitly uses interdependence to contrast it with two different types of relationship: 'independence', or a relationship characterized by detachment and 'dependence', a relationship so over-involved as to be suffocating to one or both parties. This more specific use of interdependence is also implied in his discussion of the 'I-we' balance in the preface to *Involvement and Detachment* (1987a; 2007a). In this passage a balanced I-we relationship would seem to correspond to interdependence. A relationship that did not involve a balance between the 'I' and the 'we' would not be interdependent; if one or both parties maintained an 'I-self', the relationship would be one of independence; if one or both parties maintained a 'we-self', the relationship would be one of dependence … [Elias] is not always consistent in his usage of the term 'interdependence', however. Although I have not found the reference, I have been told that Elias has written that war between two nations can involve interdependence (personal communication from Jon Fletcher)… (Scheff in Salumets 2001: 103)

Scheff is a prominent advocate of Elias's work, and one of the few American scholars to have engaged with his ideas in a sustained manner. However, his exposition of Elias above serves to highlight some of the principal sources of his misunderstanding of Elias's concept of interdependence. It is first important to note that, *pace* Scheff, Elias thought and wrote in terms of continua and balances or scales, not separate and discrete types of relationships. For Elias, as we saw earlier, humans are always and everywhere involved from birth to death in bonds of interdependence. Even though the bonds may vary, involvement in them – even of supposedly marginal exceptions such as hermits – is a constant. In fact, the isolation of hermits is illusory. Even they forage for food in neighbouring human settlements and are sometimes supported by them. They also tend to be affectively bonded to the people with whom they were once close. Seen in these terms, 'independence' and 'dependence' are not discrete types of relationships but positions towards polar ends of a continuum or scale. Furthermore, in Elias's usage, the term 'balance' has been shorn of all harmonistic value-conceptions. Scheff's misconstrual of the latter is perhaps given clearest expression in what he writes about interdependence and war (see, once again, the quotation above in which he refers to the work of Jonathan Fletcher). The passage Fletcher was referring to is in *What Is Sociology?* where Elias wrote:

> Fierce antagonists ... perform a function for each other, because the interdependence of human beings due to their hostility is no less a functional relationship than that due to their position as friends, allies, and specialists bonded to each other through the division of labour. Their function for each other is in the last resort based on the compulsion they exert over each other by reason of their interdependence. (Elias 2012b: 72)

Part of the source of Scheff's and others' misunderstanding of Elias on this issue appears, once again, to relate to Elias's terminology. The term 'function' has, particularly in relation to its use within major strands of American functionalism, long had 'consensus' connotations. However, as can be clearly observed in the passage above, Elias's usage of the term expressly avoided any such connotations, and indeed, was used in this instance to refer specifically to conflict-driven relationships. Indeed, such uses of the concept form part of Elias's attempt to rescue it in a way which was common to Weimar Germany sociologists such as Mannheim (we shall return to this theme shortly). Furthermore, Scheff's exposition also betrays another principal source of misunderstanding of the concept of 'interdependence', namely, the idea that the concept refers solely or mainly to the 'division of labour'. This, as we have said, is a common misconception.

There is a tendency in complex 'modern' societies, the 'urban-industrial-nation-states' which came to dominate the world in the eighteenth, nineteenth, and twentieth centuries, to think of 'the economy' as the central determining 'factor' in social life. Although it finds its clearest expression in some of the key variants of Marxism, such a tendency is by no means solely restricted to Marxist thinking. This is not the place for a full-scale investigation into why 'economistic' thinking has become prominent – a process which also finds clear expression in the taken-for-granted assumption that 'economics' is the leading, most necessary social science. It must be enough in the present context simply to suggest that what one might call the 'economisation of thinking' is probably connected, at least in part, with what Elias called 'functional democratisation', a process generated, as we shall see in Chapter 3, by the growing 'pressures from below' which ruling groups experience as societies develop beyond a given level of structural complexity. Such pressures are reinforced by the egalitarian ideologies which develop in these contexts and which involve the emergence and articulation of ideas such as 'the people', 'the commonwealth' and 'the economy'; the last term derived from *oikos*, the Greek for 'household'. In the dynastic states which preceded the nation states of modern Europe, 'the economy' was, in effect, coterminous with the household of the monarch. 'The economy', however, is best conceptualised, not as some separate 'part' of social life but, in complex 'modern' societies as people working – a term which covers manufacturing, trading, organising, administering, teaching, maintaining, cleaning and entertaining, and so forth – in order to earn money. This is reinforced, according to Elias, by the growing 'monetarisation' of social relations and the fact that the industrial, commercial, and governing bourgeoisie are 'the first working ruling class' in history. Earlier rulers had been warriors, priests, landowners, courtiers or members of a leisured elite.

It is the hegemony of 'economic reductionism' or 'economistic thinking' that lies at the heart of confusing the concept of division of labour with that of bonds of interdependence. The latter concept, as we have said, applies to the compulsions which make enemies in a war interdependent, as well as people driving on a motorway. It also applies to the compulsions operative on parents and children, masters and slaves, employers and employed, doctors and patients, rulers and ruled. Elias drew attention, in addition, to the impersonal bonds which form in conjunction with the emergence of larger social units and in which people become emotionally bound together through the medium of such symbols as coats of arms, flags and national anthems. 'What', he asked, 'are the common features of the various figurations which at different stages of development have bound individuals to them by this type of predominating emotional bond?' (Elias 2012b: 133). Earlier, he had posed the question: '… why do emotional bonds to state-societies – which nowadays are nation-states – take priority over bonds to other figurations?' (2012b: 133). In other words, why are people expected to sacrifice their lives at the behest of the rulers of their nation-states? Why, in so many cases, do they do so willingly? Why do they die defending their flags? Why have some people, for example, Josef and Magda Goebbels in Germany in 1945, sacrificed themselves and their children for the abstract ideal of their beleaguered and defeated *Volk* and its equally beleaguered and defeated *Führer*? Why did people in the past sacrifice themselves for their tribe or their religion, and why are some members of militant religious groups today willing to sacrifice themselves for their beliefs? Elias began to answer these questions as follows:

> First of all, these units all seem to have exercised comparatively strict control over the use of physical violence in relationships between their members. At the same time, they have allowed, and often encouraged, their members to use physical violence against non-members. To date, sociology has lacked any clear conception of the common features of this type of solidaristic grouping at different levels of social development. Its function is obvious: it knits people together for common purposes – the common defence of their lives, the survival of their group in the face of attacks by other groups and, for a variety of reasons, attacks in common on other groups. Thus the primary function of such an alliance is either physically to wipe out other people or to protect its own members from being physically wiped out. Since the potential of such units for attack is inseparable from their potential for defence, they may be called 'attack-and-defence units' or 'survival units'. At the present stage of social development, they take the form of nation-states. In the future they may be amalgamations of several former nation states. In the past they were represented by city-states or the inhabitants of a stronghold. Size and structure vary: the function remains the same. At every stage of development, wherever people have been bound and integrated into units for attack and defence, this bond has been stressed above all others. This survival function, involving the use of physical force against others, creates interdependence of a particular kind. It plays a part in the figurations people form, perhaps no greater but also no more negligible than 'occupational' bonds. Although it cannot be reduced to 'economic' functions, neither is it separable from them. (Elias 2012b: 133–4)

According to Elias, the division of humanity into 'survival units' (see Kaspersen and Gabriel (2008)) will probably last until we have become effectively integrated into one such unit: humankind as a whole. It is entirely possible, of course, that such a stage will never be reached or that, after being once formed, such a unit could disintegrate. It is also worth noting, once again, that whilst in general agreeing with and, indeed, taking part in the attacks on functionalism in the 1960s and 1970s, Elias insisted on retaining a concept of functions rather than altogether abandoning it. In his case, unlike that of Parsons, it was a non-harmonistic concept, closely tied up with Elias's concept of power and equally attuned to harmony and disharmony, order and disorder, integration and disintegration, unity and conflict. In short, for Elias, 'function' was a technical and empirically attuned concept that did not contain an axiomatic presupposition of any particular type of figurational dynamic, whether harmonious or otherwise. The same can be said for Elias's concept of 'social order'. According to Elias:

> The distinction between 'order' and 'disorder', so significant for the people involved, is sociologically speaking without significance. *Among men, as in nature, no absolute chaos is possible* ... [T]he word 'order' is not being used [here] in the sense in which it is used when people speak of 'law and order' or, in

adjectival form, of an 'orderly' as opposed to a 'disorderly' person. One is talking about an order in the same sense that one talks of a natural order, in which decay and destruction as structured processes have their place alongside growth and synthesis, death and disintegration alongside birth and integration. For the people involved, these manifestations seem, with good cause, to be contradictory and irreconcilable. As objects of *study*, they are indivisible and of equal importance. (Elias 2012b: 70–71)

According to Elias, furthermore, power is a central aspect of all forms of 'social order', a 'social universal', independently, firstly, of whether it is recognised as such by the people involved, and secondly, of whether these people experience it as 'good' or 'bad'. Thus, once again, Elias's concept of power is fundamentally inter-related with his other key conceptual innovations, in particular, as we have shown, with the concepts of interdependence and figurations. It is also closely related to, and finds clear expression within, Elias's theorisation of 'established-outsider' figurations. It is to this topic we shall now turn as part of our more general exposition of Elias's conceptualisation of power.

## Established-outsider figurations and Elias's theory of power

In a study that he carried out in the late 1950s and early 1960s with John Scotson entitled *The Established and the Outsiders* (1994 (1965)), Elias centrally examined a figuration formed by two working class groups in 'Winston Parva', his pseudonym for a suburb of Leicester, a medium-sized city in the English East Midlands. One of these groups, 'the established', was clearly dominant. The other, 'the outsiders', was clearly subordinate. According to Elias and Scotson, these groups were identical in terms of the conventional indices of social stratification – wealth, income, occupations, education, status/prestige – differing only in the fact that members of the 'established' group and their families had lived in the community for several generations, whilst the 'outsiders' and their families were relative newcomers. Yet a whole constellation of symptoms usually associated with class exploitation and social oppression was detectable in the relations between them. This led Elias and Scotson to ask: 'What ... induced the people who formed the first of the two groups to set themselves up ... as higher and better ...? What resources of power enabled them to assert their superiority and to cast a slur on the others as (people) of a lesser breed?' (Elias and Scotson 2008: 3–4). Elias found in 'Winston Parva' conflict-ridden figurational dynamics of the sort that would normally be encountered between groups that differed along national, ethnic, or class lines. What was particularly interesting about the case of this suburb, however, was that the 'full armoury of group superiority and group contempt' (Elias and Scotson 1994: xvii) was mobilised not in relation to obvious physical, cultural, or linguistic differences, but solely with regard to differences between residents in terms of how long they had lived within the neighbourhood, how 'established' they were within the community. Simply the length of association, Elias and Scotson wrote, was, in and of itself, sufficient to generate 'the degree of group cohesion, the collective identification, the commonality of norms, which are apt to induce the gratifying euphoria that goes with the consciousness of belonging to a group of higher value and with the complementary contempt for other groups' (Elias and Scotson 2008: 4). For Elias, Winston Parva presented an empirical crucible in which to develop a series of more general observations about power. It is evident in the passage that follows that Elias was, at least in part, developing these observations in response to long dominant conventional Marxist and Weberian formulations of power. He wrote:

> [O]ne could see here the limitations of any theory which explains power differentials only in terms of a monopolistic possession of non-human objects such as weapons or means of production and disregards the figurational aspects of power differentials due purely to differences in the degree of organisation of the human beings concerned ... [T]he latter, especially differences in the degree of internal cohesion and communal control, can play a decisive part in the greater power ratio of one group in relation to that of another ... [In the small community of Winston Parva], the power-superiority of the old-established group was to a large extent of this type. It was based on the high degree of cohesion of families who had known each other for two or three generations, in contrast to the newcomers who were strangers in relation not only to the old residents but also to each other. It was thanks to their greater potential for cohesion and its activation by social control that the old residents were able to reserve offices in their local organisations ... for people of their own kind and firmly to exclude from them people who lived in the other part [the 'outsiders'] and who, as a group, lacked cohesion ... Exclusion and stigmatisation of the outsiders by the established group, thus were two powerful weapons used by the latter to maintain their identity, to assert their superiority, keeping the others firmly in their place. (Elias and Scotson 2008: 4)

The power of the 'established' group in Winston Parva thus depended, according to Elias, on the fact that the 'oldness', that is, the length of time of their association, had enabled them to develop greater cohesion relative to the 'outsiders', many of whom started as strangers to each other, and this, in turn, enabled them to monopolise official positions in local associations. Such greater cohesion of 'established' relative to 'outsider' groups, Elias suggested, is a common, 'purely figurational' aspect of dominance-subordination relations, that is, of figurations in which some are dominant and others subordinate. The criticism implied here of the Marxian and similar approaches was later taken up by Elias explicitly. He recognised the sociological value of what he called Marx's 'great discovery', namely the idea that ownership and control of the means of production constitute the key determinants of class relations, but was critical of what he regarded as the tendency in some sociological circles – it was probably at its strongest in the 1960s and 1970s – 'to see in it the end of the road of discovery about human societies'. 'One might rather', he added, 'regard it as one manifestation of a beginning' (Elias and Scotson 2008: 18). In other words, Elias considered Marx to have developed an important and significant insight in uncovering a fundamental inter-relationship between the asymmetrical distribution of the means of production and a correspondingly uneven distribution of the means of satisfying human material needs (Elias and Scotson 2008: 18). However, Elias considered this to be only partially correct since Marx presented the struggle over 'economic' goals as the 'root source' of conflict between dominant and subordinate groups such that, 'to this day the pursuit of "economic" goals, elastic and ambiguous as this use of the term "economic" is, appears to many people as the "real", the basic goal of human groups by comparison with which others appear to be less "real", whatever that may mean' (Elias and Scotson 2008: 18).

Elias would not have sought to deny that Marx's theory of class formation deals with the generation of a particular form of social cohesion, namely that involved in the transformation of disunited 'classes in themselves' (*Klassen an sich*) into united 'classes for themselves' (*Klassen für sich*) (Bendix 1953: 30). What he would have denied is that such processes are to be universally understood solely intra-societally and in relation to modes of production. 'Economic' forms are socially structured and socially structuring but, Elias contended, they are not alone in that respect: other aspects of figurations which, especially in an age of increasing and increasingly rapid globalisation, have to be understood *inter*-societally and not simply *intra*-societally such as state-formation which is influenced, among other things, by war, the length and density of interdependency chains which have long since been spreading beyond national borders, and the relative cohesion of and balance of power between groups, all of which are equally structured and structuring and no less 'real'. Under specific circumstances, these other aspects enjoy degrees of autonomy in relation to and even dominance over modes of production. That is, in this as in other aspects of his work, Elias rejected the notion of universal 'law-like' relations between supposedly constituent social 'parts' such as 'the economy', 'the state' and 'civil society' (Elias 2009: 66–84). Consistent with this, he suggested that the degree to which 'economic' conflicts are paramount in a society is partly a function of the balance of power between its constituent groups. He wrote:

> The supremacy of the economic aspects of established-outsider relationships is most pronounced where the balance of power between the contenders is most uneven ... The less that is the case, the more recognisable become other, non-economic aspects of the tensions and conflicts. Where outsider groups have to live at a subsistence level, the size of their earnings outweighs all their other requirements in importance. The higher they rise above the subsistence level, the more does even their income ... serve as a means of satisfying human requirements other than that of stilling their most elementary animalistic or 'material' needs and the more keenly are groups in that situation liable to feel the ... inferiority of power and status from

which they suffer. And it is in that situation that the struggle between established and outsiders gradually ceases to be, on the part of the latter, simply a struggle for stilling their hunger, for the means of physical survival, and becomes a struggle for satisfying other human requirements as well. (Elias and Scotson 2008: 17–18)

According to Elias, in other words, *the phase of development* of the shifting balance of power between established and outsider groups plays a key part in shaping the aims and demands of the outsiders and in the responses of the established to them. This insight has more fundamental implications for Elias's discussion of power *per se*.

According to Max Weber, the 'classical' sociologist who devoted most time to articulating what is meant sociologically by the concept of 'power', 'we understand by "power" the chance of a man or a number of men to realise their own will in a communal action even against the resistance of others' (Weber 1946: 180). Elsewhere, he offered the following variation: 'power means any chance within a social relationship to realise one's own will, even in the face of resistance, regardless of the basis on which this chance rests' (Weber 1972: 28; our translation from the original German). It was this idea of the *relational* character of power that was seized upon by Elias. Thus he wrote of 'power-balances' or 'power-ratios' and suggested that:

> From the day of its birth, a baby has power over its parents, not just the parents over the baby. At least the baby has power over them as long as they attach … value to it. If not, it loses its power … Equally bi-polar is the balance between a slave and his [sic] master. The master has power over his slave, but the slave also has power over his master, in proportion to his function for his master – his master's dependence on him. In relationships between parents and infants, masters and slaves, power chances are distributed very unevenly. But whether the … differentials are large or small, balances of power are always present wherever there is functional interdependence between people … Power is not an amulet possessed by one person and not by another; it is a structural characteristic of a relationship – of *all* human relationships. (Elias 2012b: 69–70)

Elias went on to tie the concept of power more explicitly to that of interdependence. A solution to the problems of power more adequate than those on offer in sociology so far, he suggested:

> depends on power being understood unequivocally as a structural characteristic of a relationship … We depend on others; others depend on us. In so far as we are more dependent on others than they are on us, more reliant on others than they are on us, they have power over us, whether we have become dependent on them by their use of naked force, or by our need to be loved, our need for money, healing, status, a career or simply for excitement. (Elias 2012b: 88. Our translation from the German)

It is noteworthy that Elias wrote this in the late 1960s for publication in a German book which appeared in 1970, for the seemingly straightforward diagnosis that he offers is arguably sociologically profound. What Elias was suggesting is twofold: (i) that power is 'polymorphous', that is, many-sided and inherent in all human relationships; and (ii) that the key to understanding power lies in the interdependency of people. The examples Elias gives in the passages we have quoted all refer to 'bi-polar' or 'two-person' relationships but he was clear that power balances in the wider society and in the relationships between societies are always multipolar; that is, they involve large, complex and dynamic figurations of interdependent individuals and groups.

Elias's theory of what he called 'functional democratisation' is inherent in his concept of power as deriving mainly from interdependence. He contended that the social transformation usually referred to by terms denoting specific aspects such as 'industrialisation', 'economic growth', 'urbanisation', 'bureaucratisation' and many others, in fact involves a transformation of the total social structure (Elias 2012: 59ff). And, he suggested, one of the most significant aspects of such a total social transformation consists in the emergence of larger, more differentiated, and denser 'chains of interdependence' (Elias 2012a; 2012b). Concomitantly with this, according to Elias, there occurs a change in the direction of generally decreasing power differentials within and among groups, more specifically an equalising change to some degree in the balance of power between rulers and ruled, social classes, men and women, parents and children, and the generations more generally (Elias 2012b: 63ff). At the most general level, Elias maintained, such a process of 'functional democratisation' occurs when increasing specialisation takes place. That is the case because the performers of specialised roles gain from their specialisations chances of exerting varying degrees of reciprocal influence and control, for example, by withdrawing their services or, in the case of the purchasers of these services, refusing to pay for them. The power chances of specialised groups are further enhanced if they manage to organise since they then become able by collective action to disrupt the wider chains of interdependence on which a modern society depends. It is in ways such as these, according to Elias, that increasing division of labour and the emergence of larger chains of interdependence lead over time to greater, more even forms of reciprocal dependency and, hence, to patterns of multi-polar influence and control within and among groups. It is important, however, to stress that we have said here '*more even* forms of reciprocal dependency', not '*even*' forms. The comparative is significant. Elias's hypothesis is about processes of equalisation which can be demonstrated empirically to have occurred but is not intended to deny the vast inequalities which remain in Western societies and the world at large, and which have increased in certain respects in recent years.

It is noteworthy that our discussion above of Elias on power commenced in relation to an exposition of some of his other key ideas, and continued *via* an empirical analysis of established–outsider relationships, before moving on to a consideration of some of the long-term social processes involved in 'functional democratisation'. We stress this because it serves once more to demonstrate, firstly, the theoretical–empirical character of Elias's approach, secondly, the fundamental 'interdependence' of Elias's key concepts, and thirdly, the primacy of process in his sociological models. In the next part of this chapter, we shall explore more centrally the underpinning diachronic orientation of Elias's approach, with a specific discussion of his work on time, and a more general examination of some of his observations regarding the relations between history and sociology.

## Time and history in the work of Elias

Of all the major sociologists of the twentieth century, especially its second half, Elias was the one who argued most consistently in favour of an 'historical approach'. (The reasons why we have put 'historical' in inverted commas will become clearer as our exposition of Elias unfolds.) In order fully to grasp what he wrote on the subject of the sociology-history interface and the need for a process-orientated view to be dominant in both subjects, it is necessary to have an understanding of at least the basic elements of what he wrote on the subject of time. The principal contribution that Elias had to offer in this regard is best illustrated by comparing what he wrote with the views on this subject of Anthony Giddens. According to Giddens in *The Constitution of Society*:

> As the finitude of *Dasein* and as 'the infinity of the emergence of being from nothingness,' time is perhaps the most enigmatic feature of human experience. Not for nothing [*sic*] was that philosopher who has attempted to grapple in the most fundamental way with the problem, Heidegger, compelled to use terminology of the most daunting obscurity. But time, or the constitution of experience in time-space, is also a banal and evident feature of ... day-to-day life. It is in some part the lack of 'fit' between our unproblematic coping with the continuity of conduct across time-space, and its ineffable character when confronted philosophically, that is the very essence of the puzzling nature of time. (Giddens 1984: 34–5)

*Dasein* is the German for 'being' or 'existence' and, following his interpretation of Heidegger, Giddens is suggesting here that 'time' is unproblematic as a 'common sense', routine feature of daily life but massively problematic when viewed philosophically because, in the latter context, we are unable to escape 'ultimate' issues of a kind that we humans can only 'resolve' inadequately through the use of patently metaphysical ideas such as 'absolute beginnings', 'ultimate origins', 'uncaused' 'first' and 'final causes', and 'being emerging from nothingness'. Elias never pretended he had got anywhere near to solving the 'mysteries' of existence. As he expressed it in a poem in *Luciad*, the Leicester student magazine in 1962, 'There are no mysteries/only a lot I don't know'. He also claimed in conversations to have gone further than philosophers such as Heidegger and philosophically-minded sociologists such as Giddens regarding the understanding of time. More particularly, from Elias's standpoint both sides of the equation as formulated by Giddens are problematic. That is, while 'time' may be a 'banal and evident feature of human day-to-day life' in the modern world where we have inherited a workable calendar and efficient devices such as clocks and watches for measuring what we call 'time', this has not always been the case. According to Elias: 'One forgets that for thousands of years the calendars people used ran into trouble again and again; they had to be reformed and improved until one ... reached the near perfection the European calendar has attained since the last calendar reform' (Elias 2007b: 156–7). Indeed, so far from being 'banal and evident' is this taken-for-granted feature of human life that there have been times when people were opposed to calendar reforms because they believed they would shorten their lives!

The other side of what Giddens wrote is problematic because he does not appear to have considered the possibility that the 'daunting obscurity' of Heidegger's terminology may have been connected, not so much with the properties of 'time' as with the fact that Heidegger approached the problem in a purely rational and quasi-theological manner. More particularly, while the problems associated with 'time' remain *complex* if approached in a more theoretico-empirical manner, they are not necessarily 'daunting' and 'obscure'. At the most basic level, they are relatively straightforward. That is, 'time' is a concept which, in Elias's sociological terms, refers to a symbolic 'means of orientation' through which humans coordinate their lives – 'I'll meet you in the pub at 6.15'; 'the plane leaves Heathrow Airport at 18.30'; – and communicate their understanding of natural and sociohistorical processes of various kinds – 'light travels at 186,000 miles per second'; 'the Nazi dictatorship came to an end in 1945'. The reality of 'time' is as a social, collectively produced symbol in a world where only natural processes and events, including processes and events at the human-social level, occur; where, we might say, only events and processes of various kinds are 'real'. That, at least, was Elias's view. He expressed it thus:

> Linguistic habits ... constantly reinforce the myth of time as something which in some sense exists and as such can be determined or measured even if it cannot be perceived by the senses. On this peculiar mode of existence of time one can philosophise tirelessly, as has indeed been done over the centuries. One can entertain oneself and others with speculation on the secret of time as a master of mystery, although there is no mystery. It was Einstein who finally set the seal on the discovery that time was a form of relationship and not, as Newton believed, an objective flow, a part of creation like rivers and mountains which, although invisible, was like them independent of the people who do the timing. But even Einstein did not probe deeply enough. He too did not entirely escape the pressure of word-fetishism and in his own way gave sustenance to the myth of reified time, for example, by maintaining that under certain circumstances time could contract or expand. (Elias 2007b: 36–37)

So, processes and events, not symbols, are the only substantives, and 'time' is a humanly constructed symbol, not a process like a flowing river or an event like a flood. Furthermore, 'every change in "space" is a change in "time"; [and] every change in "time" [is] a change in "space"' (Elias 2007b: 82).

Part of the reason why is that the earth is constantly moving round the sun and the sun is part of a galaxy, 'the Milky Way', that, with the exception of local galaxies such as Andromeda which are moving towards us, is moving away at speed from the billions of other galaxies which constitute the currently known universe. We propose not to elaborate on the concepts of 'space' and 'time' any further here, except to add that, just as people today are the inheritors of more reality-congruent time symbols and more accurate time meters such as atomic clocks and the quartz watches that we in the more 'advanced' societies carry round on our wrists, so, too, are we the inheritors of a fund of more reality-congruent knowledge about 'space', especially the 'local space', namely the earth and the solar system, which we inhabit. That is, we have not only more effective calendars and chronometers – time-measuring devices – but also more detailed and reliable maps and devices such as compasses, radar, satellites and global positioning systems ('sat navs') for accurately measuring relative positions in 'space-time'. Our technologically buttressed abilities in these regards are crucial to the operation of the networks of global and local interdependence which characterise the present-day world.

The principal relevance for sociology of these issues is that the subject ought to be centrally concerned with the study of social events and processes in space and time. This means that the conventional view according to which sociology and history are separate subjects, one concerned with 'the present', the other with 'the past', is arbitrary and wrong. All studies are necessarily studies of 'the past'. A moment's reflection will show how this is so. Human societies exist in space-time, and time, as the old personifying adage has it, 'never stands still'. To express it non-metaphysically, human individuals, their societies, the earth, our solar system, the Milky Way and the universe are processes, constantly moving, constantly changing. This means that what we call the 'present' is a constantly shifting reference point in the ceaseless flow of physical, biological, social and individual processes and events. What was 'the present' on all these levels when we started writing this chapter had already become part of the past when we completed it. In a word, 'the present' is an ambiguous concept with multiple levels of meaning and it has to be read as having an historical connotation. It follows that, if it were to be accepted that sociology is the study of 'the present', some more or less arbitrary judgement about the relatively recent past would have to be made. One would have to decide whether the term 'past' refers to, say, the 1990s, the 2000s, or the 2010s, to the years since the 1960s, or to those since the end of the Second World War. However, whatever decision was made, any such studies would necessarily involve attempts to come to terms with aspects of 'the past'. In short, it would inevitably lead one to become involved in a kind of 'historical' study. Elias commented upon this fundamental relationship between sociology and history in some detail as we shall now discuss.

## History and sociology

One of Elias's lengthiest statements on the relationship between history and sociology is contained in the Introduction to his book, *The Court Society* (Elias 2006b (1969)). He began with a critical examination of the popular belief, expounded most systematically by the philosopher Karl Popper in his book, *The Poverty of Historicism* (1957), that history and historical sociology cannot possibly be 'scientific' because of the uniqueness and unrepeatability of historical events. It was Popper's contention that a 'science' is only possible with recurring events and phenomena because only then can you test and formulate testable 'laws'. Elias took issue with this popular view, suggesting that uniqueness and unrepeatability are not inherent in history as an 'object', that is, inherent in its 'nature' independently of the values and interests of people like Popper who make claims of this kind. On the contrary, such claims reflect the values of people in highly differentiated urban-industrial societies in which individual uniqueness is prized. Elias's case against Popper and others who propound similar views was complex. He began to unravel the complexity by suggesting that:

> unrepeatable and unique phenomena are by no means confined to the sequences of events that historians take as the object of their studies. Such phenomena exist everywhere. Not only is each human being, each human feeling, each action and each experience of a person unique, but each bat and bacillus. Every extinct animal species is unique. The saurians [that is, the dinosaurs] will not return. In the same sense, *Homo sapiens*, the human species as a whole, is unique. And the same can be said of each speck of dust, of our sun, the Milky Way and of every other formation: they come, they go and when they have gone they do not return. (Elias 2006b: 10)

These observations, said Elias, suggest that there are 'different degrees of uniqueness and unrepeatability, and what is unique and unrepeatable on one level can be seen on another as repetition, a return of the never-changing'. Take, for example, the often claimed uniqueness of individual human beings – one of the reasons advanced for the impossibility of a 'scientific' history or a 'scientific' sociology. According to Elias, it provides a good example of a phenomenon that involves uniqueness on one level and repeatability on another. That is so, Elias said, because 'individual human beings are themselves repetitions of an unchanging form, and what differs between people now appears as a variation of the ever-recurring basic pattern' (Elias 2006b: 10).

This observation allows Elias to question how 'object adequate' or 'reality congruent' – in more popular terms, how 'accurate' – is the argument that history consists of a unique sequence of unrepeatable events. Is it, he asked, a product of unprejudiced critical analysis or the result of an ideological manipulation in which the practitioners of history in highly differentiated and individualised societies project their specific social conditioning and short-lived values onto their 'object of study, the historical process itself'? This question, said Elias, cannot be answered in simple 'yes/no', terms; nor can it be reduced to a simple formula. Elias stressed the need to define clearly both the differences and the relationships between 'biological evolution', 'social development' and 'history'. The failure to do this up to now, said Elias, has acted as a blockage to knowledge.

Elias also contended that the biological constitution of social insects such as ants and bees is both relatively fixed and determines their social organisation. The evolution of *Homo sapiens* has led our species, too, to have a relatively fixed biological constitution. However, it is one which makes individual members of the species dependent on experience and learning. Humans *have to* learn in order to be able to function and it is this which makes it possible for human societies to have a history and to develop, that is to undergo changes of structure or form. According to Elias, however, while the biological evolution of *Homo sapiens* cannot be reversed – though the species could, of course, become extinct and, when our sun 'dies', probably will unless we have managed by then to transfer to a new habitable planet in a new sun system – their social development is reversible. As Elias put it:

> Change in human figurations is ... closely bound up with the possibility of transmitting experiences gathered in one generation to subsequent generations as acquired social knowledge. This continuous social accumulation of knowledge plays a part in the changing of human society. But the continuity of the collection and transmission of knowledge can be broken. The increase in knowledge does not bring about a genetic change in the human race. Socially accumulated experiences can be lost. (2006b: 13)

The terms 'biological evolution', 'social development' and 'history' denote layered yet separate sequences embracing the whole of humankind and they occur at different rates. In the long process of biological evolution, the species *Homo sapiens* emerged for the first time as a distinct species some 50,000 years ago. Its social development, though fast by comparison with the rate at which significant biological evolution generally takes place, was, at first, comparatively slow, speeding up following the agricultural and urban 'revolutions' and becoming even quicker following the 'scientific revolution' of the seventeenth century and the 'industrial revolution' of the eighteenth. Nevertheless, though fast by comparison with biological evolution, social developments are often so slow by comparison with an individual life-time that people do not recognise them as occurring at all. In Elias's words:

> Measured by the length and rate of change of an individual human life, social developments often take place so slowly that they seem to stand still. It is possible that the ... figurations formed by people change so little for a number of generations that they are regarded by those involved as immutable ... Thus, for a long period in the development of European society, people are embraced over and over ... by the figuration 'knight-page-priest-bondsman'. Today, and

for a number of generations past in the developed industrial societies, people are repeatedly found in relationships such as 'worker-employee-manager' or 'higher-middle-lower official'. The functional interdependence of these and all other divisions in a particular society entails ... a certain exclusivity. Knight and bondsman would scarcely fit into an industrial configuration. (2006b: 13)

Each human individual, said Elias, though a variation on the relatively unchanging pattern of the species as a whole, is 'unique' and 'unrepeatable' and, in the course of his/her life-time undergoes rapid change. Nevertheless, these unique, unrepeatable and rapidly changing individuals form relatively persisting figurations with one another which are 'just as real as the individual people forming them'. This is rarely recognised by the institutionalised establishment of historians, argued Elias, and it perpetuates both the inherent individualism of their approach and their feelings of superiority relative to newcomers such as sociologists. This leads to a terrible waste of human effort in the sense that each generation feels an urge to rewrite history in the sense of historians continually revisiting the same topics and events, bringing with them new values, new axes to grind, new sensibilities and new biases but little sense of the need for incremental knowledge.

## Elias as a radical sociologist

We commenced this chapter by arguing that Elias's sociological approach was *radically* processual and *radically* relational. However, that Elias's sociological insights might be considered 'radical' requires some qualification. As a means of concluding and distilling some of the key arguments of this chapter, we shall thus elaborate in more detail what we mean in this respect.

Johan Goudsblom of the University of Amsterdam has likened Elias to Charles Darwin (1977), the principal progenitor of the theory of biological evolution *via* 'natural selection'. An additional parallel – with Copernicus, the sixteenth century Polish astronomer – may also be pertinent. This is because Elias arguably succeeded not just in recognising that members of the species *Homo sapiens* are a kind of animals which evolved biologically to bond closely with each other, to be dependent on languages and the intergenerational transmission of acquired funds of knowledge, but also, as we have endeavoured to show in this chapter, in developing a conceptual repertoire attuned to this fundamental insight. Kilminster (2007: 154–5) elaborates on an idea of Freud's in this connection by referring to Elias's work as having delivered the fourth, sociological 'blow to human narcissism'; the first three having been delivered, respectively, by Copernicus, Darwin, and Freud. In his seminal essay, 'Resistances to Psychoanalysis' (Freud 1925: 273), Freud had pointed to: Copernicus as having delivered the first, that is, the *cosmological* blow to human self-love by discovering that the earth revolves around the sun rather than *vice versa*; Darwin as having delivered the second, that is, the *biological* blow, by discovering such basic facts about humans as that they had evolved out of earlier species of hominids; and the third, psychological blow that was delivered by Freud himself with regard to his highly influential and important thesis regarding the human repression of libidinal impulses.

In a manner that parallels Copernicus with respect to our solar system and astronomy, Elias pointed the way towards a sociology in which a resolution by means of theory-guided empirical research and research-based theorising could take the place of merely thinking about such age-old philosophical/sociological issues as the agency-structure dilemma (nominalism *versus* realism), the nature/society dichotomy, the nature *versus* nurture problem, body-mind dualism, materialism *versus* idealism, and many more. Elias's conceptual reorientation – aspects of which we have begun to explore in this chapter – has arguably laid the foundations for a 'post-philosophical' (Kilminster 2007) model for approaching such problems.

As was typical of Elias, he viewed his own contribution to sociology in terms of evolutionary scale processes of human development. In his text *The Symbol Theory*, Elias wrote of humans as having become equipped *via* evolution to undergo a process of 'symbol emancipation', that is, a potentially liberating increase in power and control made possible by language and knowledge-stocks in four main areas: (i) over their wider environment; (ii) relative to other animals, of humans developing from a 'hunt*ed*' into a 'hunt*ing*' species (Goudsblom 1994); (iii) over themselves as individuals; and (iv) over themselves as groups. A related notion is what Elias (1978: 156–7) called 'the triad of basic controls', that is, the control of self, society, and nature. Symbol emancipation, Elias suggested, must have involved simultaneous and interacting processes of biological evolution and social development, each mutually dependent on and not reducible to the other. Such processes are still far from being fully understood and the difficulty of understanding them is inhibited by a tendency to distinguish, as we have seen, between, for example, 'nature' and 'society', as if 'societies' could exist somewhere other than in 'nature'. The institutionally reinforced distinction between the 'social sciences' and the 'natural sciences' contributes further to the inhibition. In Elias's words:

> Most of [the social sciences], history and sociology among them, are concerned with aspects of human life which are uniquely human, which in other words are, or are due to, evolutionary innovations. They distinguish humanity from other species. As a rule, however, these human sciences ... do not ask how these uniquely human properties are connected with those which humans share with other species, such as birth and death ... [N]o attempts are made ... to discover the hinge connecting nature with ... 'non-nature'. Thus sociologists may see the body as a topic of interest. But the prevailing routines ... make it easy to treat the body as a topic of sociological research set apart from other topics, perhaps as the subject-matter of a specialism. There does not seem any need to explore the links connecting aspects of humans conceived as body, with other aspects

perhaps conceived as disembodied. On a larger scale, too, human sciences of this type tacitly work with the image of a split world. The division of sciences into natural sciences and others not concerned with nature reveals itself as a symbolic manifestation of an ontological belief – of the belief in a factually existing division of the world ... The question as to which unique biological characteristics of human beings make history possible has hardly been a talking point among historians. Nor have the distinguishing characteristics and the relationship of biological evolution and social development been a frequent point of discussion among sociologists. The term evolution is at present used indiscriminately with reference to both. How culture, rationality, knowledge, conscience and other similar aspects of human beings fit into the well-established theory of an evolutionary descent of humans is anybody's guess... (Elias 2009b: 141–58)

Just as Copernicus rejected the old geocentric or earth-centred picture of our local solar system and replaced it with a heliocentric or sun-centred view, so, to continue with Freud's model, Elias can be seen as having established crucial preconditions for the establishment of sociology as a human science (*Menschenwissenschaft*) by correcting the *homo clausus* or 'closed person' view of humans and replacing it with an orientation towards *homines aperti*, pluralities of 'open people'. Each of these reorientations involved a process of decentring: in the case of Copernicus, a decentring from humanity's primary anthropocentrism, that is their view of *Homo sapiens* and the earth as the centre of everything. In the case of Elias, a decentring from the Enlightenment/Judaeo-Christian view of humans as 'rational' beings created by an anthropomorphic conception, 'God', who stands 'above' and in some ways 'outside nature'. Further to this, humans are seen according to this view as apart from and above other animals, and as separated and alone in relation to each other.

In the next chapter, we shall develop this argument further through an exploration of how Elias attempted to add to a reorientation of sociology through what he regarded as his most important contribution to the subject, his theory of 'civilising processes'.

# 3
# Elias's 'Central Theory'

Elias regarded his theory of 'civilising processes' as a 'central theory'. As far as we are aware, he never wrote this down, but we know from his teaching and conversation that he developed the concept of a 'central theory' in partial agreement with C. Wright Mills's (1959) critical stance towards what Mills called 'grand theories' – theories which involve 'a level of thinking so general that [their] practitioners cannot logically get down to observation… [nor] from the higher generalities to problems in their historical and structural contexts. This absence of a firm sense of genuine problems, in turn, makes for the unreality so noticeable in their pages' (Mills 1959: 42).

The work of Parsons (1951) is probably the best example of a 'grand theorist' in this sense. Elias shared Mills's opposition to the generality, abstractness and non-empirical character of most of the writings of such scholars. He also shared Mills's stress on sociology as an historical subject concerned with structures. Hence the theory of civilising processes, as we shall see, involves the tracing of connections between the minutiae of developing social standards and social habituses on the one hand, and levels of state-formation, interdependency chains, functional democratisation and degrees of pacification under state control on the other.

In his Introduction to the 1968 edition of *Über den Prozess der Zivilisation*, Elias compared his own work with the 'grand theory' of Parsons in the following terms:

> What in this book is shown with the aid of extensive documentation to be a process, Parsons, by the static nature of his concepts, reduces retrospectively … to states. Instead of a relatively complex process whereby the affective life of people is gradually moved towards an increased and more even control of affects – but certainly not towards a state of total affective neutrality – Parsons presents a simple opposition between two states, affectivity and affective neutrality, which are supposed to be present to different degrees in different types of society, as being like different quantities of chemical substances. By reducing to two different states what was shown empirically in *On The Process of Civilisation* to be a process and interpreted theoretically as such, Parsons deprives himself of the possibility of discovering how the distinguishing peculiarities of different societies to which he refers are actually to be explained. So far as is apparent, he does not even raise the question of explanation. The different states denoted by the antitheses of the 'pattern variables' are, it seems, simply given. The subtly articulated structural change towards increased and more even affect-control that may be observed in reality disappears in this kind of theorising. Social phenomena in reality can only be observed as developing and having developed… (Elias 2012a: 497–8)

So, according to Elias, Parsons's work involved 'process-' or 'state-reduction' (*Zustandsreduktion*). Sociological explanations, Elias contended, have to be data-based and historical-developmental in character. Robert Merton (1957) shared some of Mills's and Elias's opposition to 'grand theories' and advocated instead what he called 'theories of the middle range'. Since a 'middle range theory' sounds as though it might be similar to a 'central theory', it is essential to clarify what Merton and Elias meant by their very different concepts. According to Merton,

> it would seem reasonable to suppose that sociology will advance in the degree that its major concern is with developing theories of the middle range and will be frustrated if attention centres on theory in the large. I believe that our major task *today* is to develop special theories applicable to limited ranges of data – theories, for example, of class dynamics, of conflicting group pressures, of the flow of power and the exercise of interpersonal influence – rather than to seek at once the 'integrated' conceptual structure adequate to derive all these and other theories ... I am suggesting that the road to effective conceptual schemes in sociology will be more effectively built through work on special theories, and that it will remain a largely unfulfilled plan, if one seeks to build it directly at this time. (Merton 1957: 9)

Elias would almost certainly have applauded the processual flavour of Merton's analogy between theory-building and road-building. However, despite the apparent similarity suggested by the words 'middle' and 'central', Elias was strongly opposed to the *ad hoc* character of Merton's concept. That was on account of his belief that Merton's strategy, whilst of undoubted potential value in addressing the need for a sociology based on a 'two-way traffic' between research and theory, would contribute to little or nothing being done to address the fragmentation which is rooted in the multi-paradigmatic character of the subject.

Hence Elias stressed the need for *central* theories, that is for theories based on meticulous, detailed and sensitive empirical observation couched at a level of synthesis sufficiently high to be applicable to a range of topics yet sufficiently down to earth to be clearly related to and relevant regarding the real-life experiences of humans. That Elias achieved a degree of success in this connection is suggested by the fact that the theory of civilising processes has been used to contribute to the advancement of knowledge with regard to such seemingly disparate subjects as – and we mention them in no particular order – time and timing, sport and leisure, the consumption of food and tobacco, war and violence, death and dying, scientific establishments, music in court and bourgeois societies, and many other aspects of human life. Let us look more deeply into Elias's central theory.

## Western 'civilising processes' and some of their major variations

Elias's theory of civilising processes involves an attempt to shed light, among other things, on the rise to global dominance of the West in the eighteenth, nineteenth, and twentieth centuries. It is concerned with exploring and explaining the undisputed, though far from permanent, fact of Western dominance and not with glorifying it (as some critics of Elias have suggested). Elias saw it in process terms. It was, at the time of writing (the 1930s), he suggested, the latest phase in a series of relatively discontinuous 'integration struggles' which have tended over long periods of historical time[35] and with numerous 'spurts and counterspurts' (Elias 2012a: 481) to become increasingly global in scope. In his later writings, Elias increasingly stressed as possibilities, not only further global unification and pacification under global state control, but also that humanity might destroy itself through nuclear war or global warming or at least propel itself back to a new 'Dark Ages'. It was one of his hopes that sociology might be of help to people in achieving the first of these possibilities and avoiding the second and the third. Let us explore the theory of 'civilising' processes in greater detail.

## Elias's central problem

Elias's first words in his Preface to *On The Process of Civilisation* were:

> Central to this study are modes of behaviour considered typical of people who are 'civilised' in a Western way. The problem they pose is simple enough. Western people have not always behaved in the manner we are accustomed to regard as typical or as the hallmark of 'civilised' people. If members of present-day Western society were to find themselves suddenly transported into a past epoch of their own society, such as the medieval-feudal period, they would find there much that they deem 'uncivilised' in other societies today. Their reaction would scarcely differ from that produced in them at present by the behaviour of people in feudal societies outside the Western world. They would, depending on their situation and inclinations, be either attracted by the wilder, more unrestrained and adventurous life of the upper classes in this society, or repulsed by the 'barbaric' customs, the squalor and coarseness that they encountered there. (Elias 2012a: 3)

Among the implications of this passage are the fact that Elias recognised that there are ways of 'being civilised' other than the Western one, and that, in the West at the time when he was writing, there was not a single, totally unified social habitus or behavioural canon. Thus Elias wrote that a 'civilised' person of his day would either have been in varying degrees attracted to or in varying degrees repulsed by the life of the medieval upper classes. Also, at pertinent points in his text, Elias placed inverted commas around terms such as 'civilised' and 'uncivilised' to signal his distance from their normative connotations (the emergence of which, indeed, was part of his central problem). His point was that most people in Western societies today have come to *regard themselves* as 'civilised', but that they would hesitate to apply this adjective to many people in 'tribal' societies or 'Third World' countries. However, it is also the case, according to Elias, that most people in the contemporary

West would not regard their own forerunners, for example, people in the 'medieval-feudal' period of Western history, as 'civilised'. They might like the relatively high degree of freedom of that period, particularly of the upper classes. They might dislike its coarseness and squalor, for example, the smell of horse dung and human excrement in the streets. Almost certainly, however, they would judge it in much the same manner as they would judge a 'Third World' country of today, that is as 'backward', 'crude', and 'uncivilised'. In a word, Western societies can be said to have undergone a 'civilising process', a series of transformations in the course of which their social structures and the social habituses of their people have become what they are today. This gives rise, said Elias, to a number of questions, in particular 'How did this change, this "civilising" of the West, actually happen? Of what did it consist? And what were its "causes" or "motive forces"? It is to the solution of these main questions that this study attempts to contribute' (Elias 2012a: 3). Thus, Elias was *attempting to contribute* to the understanding of how and why this 'civilising' of the West occurred. That is, he did not put *On The Process of Civilisation* forward as a final, definitive answer, some kind of 'grand theory', 'metanarrative' or 'totalising answer'. As Elias expressed it somewhat later in the text: 'This study ... poses and develops a ... wide-ranging problem; it does not pretend to solve it. It marks out a field of observation that has hitherto received relatively little attention, and undertakes the first steps towards an explanation. Others must follow' (Elias 2012a: 7).[36]

Elias also made it clear at the outset that he was motivated in his study by practical as well as scholarly concerns. It has been suggested by Stephen Mennell (1998: 26) that Elias never became involved in party politics. It is true that, even after gaining British citizenship, he admitted to never having been a member of a political party, nor to have voted in elections. People who stress this negatively, however, seem unaware of Elias's practical involvement, not only in teaching and the development of sociology but also, while he was on the permanent staff at Leicester, in university politics (partly in the role of advisor to Ilya Neustadt) and, after his retirement, in student politics as well. During the student revolt across the West in 1968, for example, he insisted that Dunning accompany him on visits to the students – the leaders were mainly sociology undergraduates – who were occupying Leicester's library and administration building. He was interested in their reasons for what they were doing and in the experiments in 'new forms of living' in which members of the younger generation saw themselves as engaged in the 1960s. He also took pains to keep abreast with developments in world politics. In the Leicester Senior Common Room, for example, he was a regular reader of *Time Magazine* and the *International Herald Tribune*. He also listened regularly to the World Service of BBC radio. During the 1940s and early 1950s, he was also practically involved in the development of group psychoanalysis in Britain. What he sought principally to do in that connection, much like Fromm and other members of 'the Frankfurt School' who attempted something not dissimilar from a mainly Marxist standpoint, was to contribute to the development of more sociologically informed forms of politics and psychotherapy than had existed hitherto. In fact, one could say that, *via* his use of aspects of the work of such scholars as Mannheim, Simmel and the two Webers, Elias succeeded better than Fromm *et al.* in producing a synthesis of the works of Marx and Freud. That had been something akin to the search for the 'philosophers' stone' or the 'Holy Grail' among social scientists in the first half of the twentieth century. A flavour of the sort of thing that Elias had in mind is captured in the following passage:

> [T]he issues raised by [this] book have their origin less in scholarly tradition ... than in the experiences in whose shadow we live, experiences of the crisis and transformation of Western civilisation as it has existed hitherto, and the simple need to understand what this 'civilisation' really amounts to. But I have not been guided in this study by the idea that our civilised mode of behaviour is the most advanced of all humanly possible modes of behaviour, nor by the opinion that 'civilisation' is the worst form of life and one that is doomed. All that can be seen today is that, with gradual civilisation, a number of specific civilisational perils arise. But it cannot be said that we already understand why we actually torment ourselves in such ways. We feel ... we have got ourselves, through civilisation, into certain entanglements unknown to less civilised peoples; but we also know that these less civilised peoples are ... often plagued with difficulties and fears from which we no longer suffer, or at least not to the same degree. Perhaps all this can be seen somewhat more clearly if it is understood how such civilising processes actually take place. At any rate, that was one of the wishes with which I set to work on this book. It may be that, through clearer understanding, we shall one day succeed in making accessible to more conscious control these processes which today take place in and around us not very differently from natural events, and which we confront as medieval people confronted the forces of nature. (Elias 2012a: 8)

Elias divided his study into four main parts. He called them:

1. 'On the Sociogenesis of the Concepts of "Civilisation" and "Culture"';
2. 'Civilisation as a Specific Transformation of Human Behaviour';
3. 'Feudalisation and State-Formation';
4. 'Synopsis: Towards a Theory of Civilising Processes'.

*Über den Prozess der Zivilisation* (1939; 1968) was originally published simultaneously in two volumes. So, as we mentioned in Chapter 1, was the first English translation. However, in the latter case they were given titles different from Elias's own. Volume 1 was called *The Civilising Process: the History of Manners* (1978) and Volume 2, *State-Formation and Civilisation* in the United Kingdom and *Power and Civility* in the USA. Both English translations of Volume 2 appeared in 1982. Elias objected strongly to 'the History of

Manners' and 'Power and Civility' as, respectively, sub-title and title, but his objections were overruled by Urizen, the first publishers. He objected to 'the History of Manners' because it was less accurate and hence more misleading as a characterisation of the contents of the first volume than Elias's own 'Changes in the Behaviour of the Secular Upper Classes in the West', a sub-title which makes explicit the fact that he was, above all, deliberately excluding from systematic consideration in the study of the part played in European 'civilising' processes by religious elites. *Power and Civility* is similarly misleading because it contains no reference to processes of state-formation and gives pride of place to 'civility', a concept which, as we shall show, Elias demonstrates to have been the second in the tripartite series, 'courtesy', 'civility', 'civilisation' by means of which successive Western ruling classes expressed their self-image. In the nineteenth century, as the West as a whole became a kind of 'global ruling class', 'civilisation' came to be a 'national' term which expressed the self-consciousness of 'incorporated' groups in Western countries more generally. In the late nineteenth and early twentieth centuries, that meant in the first instance principally France and England and, later, increasingly the one-time colonial offshoot of the latter, the USA.[37]

## The sociogenesis of the concepts of 'civilisation' and 'culture'

By the term, 'sociogenesis', Elias meant 'social generation' or 'social production'. He would not have accepted terms like 'social construction' in this connection which were popularised in the 1960s by authors such as Berger and Luckmann (1966) and which remain quite widely used today. That is because Elias saw such terms as overly voluntaristic and rationalistic, whilst he was concerned with establishing as precisely as possible the *balance* between choice and determinism or compulsion in the origins and development of concepts, social practices, and social structures. Elias wrote not only of sociogenesis but of 'psychogenesis' as well. By this he meant the part played in social processes by 'psychodynamics' – that is, processes at the level of the psyche, personality or habitus that have lasting social ramifications.

Following the structure of *On the Process of Civilisation*, it makes sense to commence our exposition by exploring what Elias had to say about the sociogenesis of the concepts of 'civilisation' and 'culture'. What he wrote is, in effect, an essay in the sociology of knowledge, and grasping it is crucial for understanding the adequacy and value of the theory of 'civilising' processes as a contribution to sociological understanding. Elias arguably anticipated in this connection many of the arguments later put forward by writers such as Edward Said (1978) on this score. He cannot thus be fairly accused of 'eurocentric' bias.

The concept of 'civilisation', said Elias, can be used to refer to a wide variety of facts: to a society's level of technology; to the habitus and manners of its people; to their religious ideas and customs; to their levels of bodily cleanliness and hygiene; to the way they play their sports; to the level of their scientific understanding; to the patterns of their class, gender and 'race' relations; to the ways in which they prepare their food; and many other things. In fact, there is practically nothing in the social lives of humans which cannot be described as more or less 'civilised' or more or less 'uncivilised'. This makes the concept of 'civilisation' difficult to define. However, it is not so difficult, according to Elias, to determine the general *function* of the term. What it has come to do, he wrote, is to express the self-consciousness of the West, especially of its dominant groups. It is, that is, a concept which is fundamentally bound up with power differentials and inter-group feelings and perceptions. As Elias put it, the concept:

> sums up everything in which Western society of the last two or three centuries believes itself superior to earlier societies or 'more primitive' contemporary ones. By this term, Western society seeks to describe what constitutes its special character and what it is proud of: the level of *its* technology, the nature of *its* manners, the development of *its* scientific knowledge or view of the world, and much more. (Elias 2012a: 15)

It is perhaps worth noting in passing that the Elias of the 1960s onwards would have sought to avoid the reification in this passage by referring to the beliefs of the *members* of Western *societies*. However, that minor correction is less important for present purposes than the fact that Elias went on to suggest that there are differences in the meaning which the concept of 'civilisation' has for the members of different Western nations, above all for the French and English on the one hand, and the Germans on the other. Even at this relatively early stage in his career, Elias was thinking in terms of what other German scholars have called the *Sonderweg*, Germany's partly separate or 'special path'. More particularly, while, for the French and English, 'civilisation' and its derivatives are terms that denote values of the highest rank, for the Germans, while 'civilisation' *can* be used as a praise-word, it is *usually* used only to denote second rate values. In German, it can also be used in a derogatory sense to mean 'superficiality' and a 'lack of solidity and depth'. As Elias put it: 'The word through which Germans interpret themselves, which more than any other expresses their pride in their own achievement and their own being, is *Kultur*, that is, "culture"' (Elias 2012a: 15).

A number of complex issues are raised by this discussion. For present purposes we shall dwell upon only one. Elias suggests that, while the concept of 'civilisation' is a universalistic term stressing common human characteristics that are either *in fact* or which *can potentially* be more or less widely shared, *Kultur* is, by contrast, a particularistic term which stresses difference. What Elias wrote on this is worth citing at length.

> To a certain extent, the concept of civilisation plays down the national differences between peoples; it emphasises what is common to all human beings or – in the

view of its bearers – should be. It expresses the self-assurance of peoples whose national boundaries and ... identity have for centuries been so fully established that they have ceased to be the subject of ... discussion, peoples who have long expanded outside their borders and colonised beyond them.

In contrast, the German concept of *Kultur* places ... stress on national differences and the particular identity of groups; primarily by virtue of this, it has acquired in such fields as ethnological and anthropological research a significance far beyond the German linguistic area and the situation in which the concept originated. But that situation is the situation of a people which, by Western standards, arrived at political unification ... only very late, and from whose boundaries, for centuries and even down to the present, territories have again and again crumbled away or threatened to ... Whereas the concept of civilisation has the function of giving expression to the continuously expansionist tendency of colonising groups, the concept of *Kultur* mirrors the self-consciousness of a nation which had constantly to ... constitute its boundaries anew, in a political as well as a spiritual sense, and again and again had to ask itself: 'What really is our identity?' The orientation of the German concept of culture, with its tendency towards demarcation and the emphasis on the detailing of differences between groups, corresponds to this historical process. The questions: 'What is really French? What is really English?' have long since ceased to be a matter of much discussion for the French and English. But for centuries the question, 'What is really German?' has not been laid to rest. One answer to this question – one among many – lies in a particular aspect of the concept of *Kultur*. (Elias 2012a: 17)

Elias wrote this in the 1930s, at a time when the British Empire appeared, at least on the surface, to be by and large intact. Now that the British Empire and its 'Commonwealth' have virtually ceased to exist and the United Kingdom has become a multi-ethnic, 'multi-cultural' society which is part of the European Community, the question of what it 'really means to be English' has arisen once again alongside what it means to be 'British', 'Scots', 'Welsh', 'Northern Irish', 'Hindu-', 'Sikh-' or 'Moslem-English', or an English/British person of African, Afro-Caribbean or Hong Kong Chinese descent. Much the same holds good for the French. However, according to Elias writing in the 1930s, the concept of 'civilisation' in French and English had by then come to be a high-praise term that expresses the national self-consciousness of colonising peoples who had enjoyed secure national boundaries and a corresponding sense of national identity for centuries. Together with this, went a tendency to want to 'civilise barbarians' in fact as well as in ideological justification of their colonial exploitation of them.

By contrast, the German concept of *Kultur*, the Germans' equivalent high-praise term, is a concept that mirrors the self-consciousness of a nation that has lacked secure boundaries, a secure national identity and that has not been able to engage in such continuous and successful colonial expansion as the French and the English. Finally, *Zivilisation* can be a praise-term of second rank in German usage as well as a term with a negative meaning.

How can this overall linguistic development be accounted for? Mathematical concepts, said Elias, can be separated from the groups that use them. You can explain triangles or rectangles without reference to socio-spatial, socio-historical and socio-cultural circumstances. They are the same in Ireland, England, Australia and Kurdistan. They are the same today as they were in the ninth, twelfth, sixteenth, and twentieth centuries. However, *social* concepts such as 'civilisation' and 'culture' cannot be understood independently of the groups that invented and use them. Nor can they be understood independently of the histories of these groups. They are terms which bear the stamp of whole peoples, or perhaps only of certain of their constituent classes. Early on, these were usually ruling classes but, later, to the extent that democratisation occurred, wider groups became drawn in.

A given-term may have been invented by a traceable individual. It may have been '*man*-made' as opposed to '*men*-made', (or '*person*-made' as opposed to '*people*-made'), that is, an 'individual' as opposed to a 'collective invention'.[38] However, the fact that a given term becomes established indicates, according to Elias, that it meets 'collective' and not merely 'individual needs'. How does Elias explain the emergence of the antithesis between *Kultur* and *Zivilisation* in German usage? And how and why did this antithesis take root?

According to Elias, the interaction among a combination of three part-processes helps to answer this question. More particularly, he suggests:

(i) German society did not undergo a process of national unification until a comparatively late stage, much later than the French and English;

(ii) the courtly ruling classes in Germany were more socially exclusive than their French and English counterparts and did not possess sufficient confidence to integrate bourgeois groupings into their social circles to the same degree as the more secure and self-confident French and English;

and

(iii) the ruling classes in Germany in the eighteenth and early nineteenth centuries spoke French rather than German and modelled their behaviour to a large extent on that of their counterparts in France. In fact, they used the French terms 'civilisation' and 'civilisé' to describe their own behaviour and to contrast it with that of their own compatriots lower down the social scale, members of the bourgeoisie included. As Elias suggests, the philosopher Leibniz, the only German in this period who won wide acclaim in European courtly circles, 'wrote and spoke French or Latin, seldom German' (2012a: 22). And Frederick the Great, the King of Prussia, published a book in 1780 which he entitled *De la littérature allemande* (*Of German Literature*) in which he said of German: 'I find a half-barbarous language, which breaks down into as many different dialects as Germany has provinces …' (2012a: 22).

Elias sought to explain this emergent antithesis thus:

> At the top almost everywhere in Germany were individuals or groups who spoke French and decided policy. On the other side, there was a German-speaking intelligentsia, who by and large had no influence on political developments. From their ranks, essentially, came the people on whose account Germany has been called the land of poets and thinkers. And from them concepts such as *Bildung* ('cultivation') and *Kultur* received their specifically German imprint… (2012a: 26)

At the roots of the antithesis between *Kultur* and *Zivilisation*, wrote Elias, lay the 'relative indigence' of Germany as a whole which followed from the country's post-medieval fragmentation and the frequency with which it was involved in wars. 'This', he suggested,

> impelled the nobles to cut themselves off, using proof of ancestry as the most important instrument for preserving their privileged social existence. On the other hand, it blocked to the German middle class the main route by which in Western countries bourgeois elements rose, intermarried with, and were received by the aristocracy: through money. (2012a: 31)[39]

Elias acknowledged that, at times, the meaning of *Kultur* for the Germans came close to that of 'civilisation' for the French and English. For example, Meyer wrote in 1897 that: 'Civilisation is the stage through which a barbaric people must pass in order to attain higher *Kultur* in art, science and attitudes' (2012a: 559). The idea of *Zivilisation* as second rate nevertheless persisted. It was 'an expression of Germany's self-assertion against the Western Countries' (2012a: 559) and had its counterpart in the belief of people in the latter that they had fought the First World War against Germany in order to defend 'civilisation'. Elias could not have had more than an inkling of this at the time when he was writing but 1939, the year in which *Über den Prozess der Zivilisation* was published, was also the year in which a second 'crusade' against Germany in the name of 'civilisation' was about to begin. As we shall see, Germany in that period was in the throes of a 'breakdown of civilisation' and members of the victorious 'allies' felt more than fully justified in going to war against the German 'barbarians' for a second and, in the case of the French, third time.

## 'Civilisation' as a specific transformation of human behaviour

We suggested earlier that Elias saw 'civilisation' as the latest term in the threefold series, 'courtesy', 'civility', 'civilisation', through which, in the context of societies that were experiencing what we now know to have been accelerating social change, members of the secular ruling classes expressed their self-consciousness and sense of social superiority. However, Elias did not deal with the concepts in the order in which they emerged. He started rather with the middle term, 'civility', a term first used, if the currently available records are correct, by the humanist, Erasmus of Rotterdam, in a book entitled *De civilitate morum puerilium* (*Of civility in boys*) which was published in 1530. It went through more than 130 editions, thirteen as late as the eighteenth century. It was translated into all main European languages (2012a: 62), a fact which indicates that it met a widely felt need among the secular ruling classes as the Middle Ages drew to a close and 'modernity' came into the ascendancy.

Elias dealt with 'civility codes' first because Erasmus's book enables readers to 'look', as it were, 'both ways', at what was, in the sixteenth century, the past as well as the future. It was, quite literally, a transitional text. It recommended ways of behaving to boys that were rooted equally in feudal and modern traditions. In that sense, it was indicative of 'civilisation' as a process. Listen to Erasmus on 'body language', in the first instance on how people use their eyes. 'A wide-eyed look,' he said,

> is a sign of stupidity, staring a sign of inertia; the looks of those prone to anger are too sharp; too lively and eloquent those of the immodest; if your look shows a calm mind and a respectful amiability, that is best. Not by chance do the ancients say: the seat of the soul is in the eyes. (2012a: 64)

The sentiments expressed here are neither shocking nor surprising to people with the habitus or affective moulding of people who consider themselves 'civilised' today. Shortly afterwards, however, Erasmus went on to write: 'There should be no snot on the nostrils ... A peasant wipes his nose on his hat and coat, a sausage maker on his arm and elbow' (2012a: 64). Later on, he said: do not expose 'the parts to which Nature has attached modesty' unless you need to. Some people, he wrote, demand that boys should 'retain the wind by compressing the belly'. But you can become ill if you do that. 'Fools who value civility more than health repress natural sounds' (2012a: 66).

This brings out clearly the 'Janus-faced' character of this stage in the development of Western manners. On the one hand, Erasmus does not hesitate to use the word 'snot' which is embarrassing to us. On the other, he uses circumlocutions instead of referring directly to the genitalia or, to use words which are still largely taboo in 'polite company', 'belching' and 'farting'.[40] This leads Elias to suggest that:

> [I]n following back the concept of civilisation to its ancestor *civilité*, one suddenly finds oneself on the track of the civilising process itself, of the actual changes in behaviour that took place in the West. That it is embarrassing for us to speak or even hear of much that Erasmus discusses is one of the symptoms of this process of civilisation. The greater or lesser discomfort we feel towards people who discuss or mention their bodily functions more openly, who conceal and restrain these functions less than we do, is one of the dominant feelings expressed in the judgement 'barbaric' or 'uncivilised'. Such, then, is the nature of 'barbarism and its discontents' or, in more precise and less evaluative terms, the discomfort with the different structure of affects, the different standard of repugnance which is still

to be found today in many societies which we term 'uncivilised', the standard of repugnance which preceded our own and is its precondition. (Elias 2012a: 66–67).

This raises the question, said Elias, of how and why Western societies actually moved from one standard to another, how they became more 'civilised'. In seeking answers, he wrote, feelings of discomfort, embarrassment and superiority will inevitably be aroused in us. The generation of such feelings, argued Elias, anticipating one of the central and frequently misunderstood planks in his treatise on 'involvement and detachment' (1987a), is a valuable part of the exercise. It is necessary, however, to try to control these feelings, 'to attempt to suspend all the feelings of embarrassment and superiority, all the value judgements and criticisms associated with the concepts "civilisation" or "uncivilised"' (2012a: 67). They refer to a 'beginningless' and still ongoing process. Our descendants may well be embarrassed by aspects of our behaviour. They may well regard us as part of an extended 'feudal' or 'medieval' era or even, as Elias later put it, as 'late barbarians' (1991b). Let us look at some of the evidence which formed the backbone of what one might call the 'microsociological' basis of Elias's theory, what has misleadingly been called 'the history of manners'.

## 'Courtesy', 'civility' and 'civilisation' as stages in a process

'Courtesy', 'civility', and 'civilisation' are, as we have seen, a temporal series. That is, 'courtesy' emerged first, in the medieval/feudal period. 'Civility' emerged second, in the era that historians, depending on whether they want to emphasise religious or secular aspects, conventionally call 'the Reformation' and 'the Renaissance'. It was a time when 'knightly society and the unity of the Catholic church were disintegrating' (2012a: 61). 'Civilisation' followed. Like 'civility', it can be traced to a specific individual: the elder Mirabeau in the 1760s (2012a: 47). '(A)t the moment of its formation', said Elias, it was 'a clear reflection of reformist ideas', those of 'the Physiocrats', the precursors of modern economists, a court clique (not yet a political party in the English sense) who wanted monarchs to become 'enlightened' and to rule according to 'rational' principles rooted in an understanding of the demonstrable dynamics of 'civilisation' which they believed they had discovered (2012a: 52).

According to Elias, 'two ideas were fused in the concept of "civilisation"'. On the one hand, it formed a 'counter-concept' to an earlier stage of development, 'barbarism'. On the other, it was perceived as a process which had to be taken further. This latter aspect, said Elias, was an expression of the interests of the rising middle class. In this sense, the term reflected the 'specific social fortunes of the French bourgeoisie to exactly the same degree that the concept of *Kultur*' reflected that of its German counterpart (2012a: 57).

So, the concept of 'civilisation' started 'life' as a middle class weapon.[41] As the middle classes gained in power, however, it came to express the national self-image and serve as a means of justifying French (and English) aspirations to national expansion and colonisation. For example, when Napoleon set off for Egypt in 1798, he admonished his troops: 'Soldiers, you are undertaking a conquest with incalculable consequences for civilisation' (2012a: 57). From that point on, said Elias, the French, and the English whom they were fighting, came to consider their own processes of civilisation as complete. He continued:

> the consciousness of their own superiority, the consciousness of this 'civilisation' from now on serves at least those nations which have become colonial conquerors, and therefore a kind of upper class to large sections of the non-European world, as a justification of their rule, to the same degree that earlier the ancestors of the concept of civilisation ... had served the courtly-aristocratic upper class as a justification of theirs. (2012a: 57)

To refer to the terms 'courtesy', 'civility' and 'civilisation' as a temporal series, as expressing stages in a process, is not to imply that each time a new term emerged, the earlier one or ones fell into disuse. All three continue to be used (along with synonyms such as 'politeness') to the present day.[42]

But the 'civilising process', according to Elias, has not involved merely a linguistic change. Using a variety of literary and pictorial sources, but primarily manners books aimed at the secular upper classes, the knights, the courtiers, and the bourgeoisie, Elias demonstrates the long term-term occurrence of a trend towards the increasing elaboration and refinement of manners and etiquette. This process was full of short-term and medium-term discontinuities, 'civilising' and 'decivilising spurts', and periods which were experienced at the time as stasis but in which the immanent dynamics were leading in the long-term to change. This went hand-in-hand with an increase in the social pressure on people to exercise stricter, more continuous, more even, more moderate and more nuanced self-control over a growing number of aspects of their feelings and behaviour in more and more social situations. The comparatives here are significant and all five adjectives are needed. That is, the trend involved pressure towards stric*ter*, *more* continuous, *more* even, *more* moderate, and *more* nuanced self-control in a *greater* number of social situations. At the levels of personality and habitus, this resulted in a deeper internalisation of social norms and taboos, that is, the emergence of a conscience which operates automatically and at an 'unconscious' level, much like the Freudian superego.[43] Today, we blush automatically if we violate a deep taboo in public, for example, if a man on a bus is told his fly-buttons are undone or if he realises that his penis is visibly erect. Together with the emergence of such a conscience, there has occurred what Elias called a raising of the 'threshold of repugnance' (*Peinlichkeitsschwelle*) and an advance in the 'frontiers of modesty and shame'. This means that people today are liable to experience feelings of revulsion and to get embarrassed more easily in relation, for example, to bodily functions than was the case with people in the Middle Ages. The evidence also suggests that medieval people were more liable than ourselves to experience sudden and extreme mood-swings. A present-day psychiatrist might well label them as having suffered from 'manic-depression' or 'bi-polarity'.

As we saw, the standard of 'good behaviour' in the European Middle Ages was expressed through the concept of 'courtesy'. It represented more clearly than the later terms, 'civility' and 'civilisation', a definite social location. It meant: this is how people behave in the courts of kings and other great feudal lords. It did not, says Elias, represent a beginning or the bottom rung in the 'ladder of civilisation' (2012a: 57). Elias ignored the small national differences that there were in courtesy codes and their spread to somewhat broader strata and stressed, instead, their simplicity. There were, he suggested, 'as in all societies where the emotions are expressed more violently and directly, fewer psychological nuances and complexities in the general stock of ideas. There were friend and foe, desire and aversion, good and bad people' (2012a: 71).

Let us give a few examples of changing manners to illustrate the long-term trend and its sequential order. *On The Process of Civilisation* is an empirically rich sociology book. What follows is nothing more than a selection from the mass of data presented by Elias. Following his practice, our time-series starts with a few items of table manners. It is important to remember in this connection that the courtly ruling strata in the Middle Ages were warrior leaders who took part directly in battles themselves. More often than today, a whole animal, fish or bird, including its head, was carved at table. They took meat from a common bowl with their fingers. The knife was the main implement for transferring food to their mouths. Contrasting these medieval warrior leaders and their courtly subordinates with ourselves, Elias wrote:

> What was lacking in this *courtois* world, or at least had not developed to the same degree, was the invisible wall of affects which seems now to rise between one human body and another, repelling and separating. This wall is often perceptible today at the mere approach of something that has been in contact with the mouth or hands of someone else, and which manifests itself as embarrassment at the mere sight of many bodily functions of others, and often at their mere mention, or as a feeling of shame when one's own functions are exposed to the gaze of others, and by no means only then. (2012a: 77)

## Selected examples of 'the courtesy', 'civility' and 'civilisational' codes

### Thirteenth century

> A man who clears his throat when he eats and one who blows his nose in the table cloth are both ill-bred, I assure you.

> You should not poke your teeth with a knife, as some do; it is a bad habit.

> It is not decent to poke your fingers into your ears or eyes, or to pick your nose while eating. These three things are bad.

(All three extracts in Elias 2012a: 92–94; from Tannhäuser's *Hofzucht* (Courtly Manners))

Do not spit over or on the table. Do not spit into the bowl when washing your hands. (Elias 2012a: 151; from *Stans Puer ad Mensam*)[44]

## Fifteenth century

Do not put back on your plate what has been in your mouth.

Do not offer anyone a piece of food you have bitten into. (Elias 2012a: 94; from *S'ensuivent les contenances de la table* (*These are good table manners*))

Before you sit down, make sure your seat has not been fouled (ibid., Elias 2012a: 129)

Do not touch yourself under your clothes with your bare hands. (Elias 2012a: 129; from *Ein spruch der ze tische kêrt*)

It is unseemly to blow your nose into the table cloth. (ibid., Elias 2012a: 142)

## Sixteenth century

It is impolite to greet someone who is urinating or defecating ... A well-bred person should always avoid exposing without necessity the parts to which nature has attached modesty. (Elias 2012a: 129; *De civilitate morum puerilium*, 1530)

It does not befit a modest, honourable man to prepare to relieve nature in the presence of other people, nor to do up his clothes afterwards in their presence ... [I]t is not a refined habit, when coming upon something disgusting in the sheet, as sometimes happens, to turn at once to one's companion and point it out to him. It is far less proper to hold out the stinking thing for the other to smell... (Della Casa, *Galateo*, Geneva, 1609: 32; quoted in Elias (Elias 2012a: 130–131). Della Casa's text originally appeared in 1558)

One should not, like rustics who have not been to court or lived among refined and honourable people, relieve oneself without shame or reserve in front of ladies, or before the doors or windows of court chambers or other rooms. (Elias 2012a: 131; from the *Wernigerode Court Regulations*, 1570)

Let no one, whoever he may be, before, at or after meals, early or late, foul the staircases, corridors or closets with urine or other filth, but go to suitable, prescribed places for such relief. (Elias 2012a: 131; from the *Brunswick Court Regulations* of 1589)

## Seventeenth century

Let not thy privy members be

layd open to be view'd,

it is most shameful and abhord,

detestable and rude.

Retaine not urine nor the winde

which doth thy body vex

so it be done with secresie

let that not thee perplex.

(Elias 2012a: 131; from Richard Weste, *The Booke of Demeanor and the Allowance and Disallowance of Certaine Misdemeanors in Companie*, 1619)

The smell of the mire is horrible. Paris is a dreadful place. The streets smell so badly that you cannot go out. The extreme heat is causing large quantities of meat and fish to rot in them, and this, coupled to the multitude of people who piss in the street, produces a smell so detestable that it cannot be endured. (From the correspondence of the Duchess of Orleans, October 9, 1694; date also given as August 25, 1718. Quoted in Elias 2012a: 132)

[At table] to blow your nose openly into your handkerchief, without concealing yourself with your serviette, and to wipe away your sweat with it ... are filthy habits fit to make everyone's gorge rise ... You should avoid yawning, blowing your nose and spitting. If you are obliged to do so ... do it in your handkerchief, while turning your face away and shielding yourself with your left hand, and do not look into your handkerchief afterwards. (Elias 2012a: 144; from Courtin, *Nouveau Traité de Civilité*, 1672)

## Eighteenth century

At table you should use a serviette, a plate, a knife, a spoon and a fork ... It is improper to use the serviette to wipe your face; it is far more so to rub your teeth with it, and it would be one of the greatest offences against civility to use it to blow your nose... (Elias 2012a: 100; from La Salle, *Les Régles de la bienséance et de la civilité Chrétienne*, Rouen, 1729: 7)

It is a part of decency and modesty to cover all parts of the body except the head and hands. You should ... not ... touch with your bare hands any part of the body that is not normally uncovered ...

It is far more contrary to decency and propriety to touch or to see in another person, particularly of the other sex, that which Heaven forbids you to look at in yourself. When you need to pass water, you should always withdraw to some unfrequented place. And it is proper (even for children) to perform other natural functions where you cannot be seen.

It is very impolite to emit wind from your body when in company, either from above or from below, and it is shameful and indecent to do it in a way that can be heard by others.

It is never proper to speak of the parts of the body that should be hidden, nor of certain bodily necessities to which Nature has subjected us, nor even to mention them. (ibid., Elias 2012a: 132; from La Salle, 1729, *loc. cit*)

It is very impolite to keep poking your finger into your nostrils, and still more insupportable to put what you have pulled from your nose into your mouth ...

> It is vile to wipe your nose with your bare hand, or to blow it on your sleeve or your clothes ... You should always use your handkerchief... (Elias 2012a: 145–6; from La Salle, 1729, *loc. cit*)

> You should not abstain from spitting, and it is very ill-mannered to swallow what should be spat. This can nauseate others ... Nevertheless, you should not become accustomed to spitting too often ... When you are with well-born people ... it is polite to spit into your handkerchief while turning slightly aside. (Elias 2012a: 153)

### Nineteenth century

> Forks were undoubtedly a later invention than fingers, but as we are not cannibals, I am inclined to think they were a good one. (Elias 2012a: 103; from *The Habits of Good Society*, London, 1859)

> no epicure ever yet put a knife to an apple, and ... an orange should be peeled with a spoon. (Elias 2012a: 125; *The Habits of Good Society*, *ibid*)

> Spitting is at all times a disgusting habit ... besides being coarse and atrocious, it is very bad for your health. (Elias 2012a: 154; *The Habits of Good Society*, *ibid*)

## Elias's use of literary and other sources

Although they constituted his major source of systematic time-series data, Elias did not rely solely on manners books in his attempt to shed light on the Western 'process of civilisation'. He used literary and pictorial sources to great effect as well. Take, for example, what we now call 'sex' and 'gender relations', that is, respectively, the unlearned biological and the learned social aspects of the relations between males and females. The shame feelings surrounding sexual relations, says Elias, have become noticeably stronger in the course of the civilising process. This fact is 'manifested particularly clearly in talking about these relations to children' (Elias 2012a: 167). In his *Colloquies*, for example, a book intended, like *De civilitate morum puerilium*, for the instruction of young boys and dedicated to his six- or eight-year old godson, Erasmus depicts a young man wooing a girl, a woman complaining about her husband's bad behaviour, and a discussion between a young man and a prostitute. An influential nineteenth century German pedagogue called Von Raumer fulminated against this by saying: 'Erasmus here paints fleshly lust in the basest way' and proceeds to ask: 'How could such a book be introduced in countless schools? What had boys to do with these satyrs?' (Elias 2012a: 167). This example of what we in Britain today might call 'Victorian morality' provides an illustration of the social and psychological distance which had grown between adults and children. It is also marked by the growing length of childhood/adolescent dependency, childhood and adolescent socialisation and by such facts as that the clothing of adults and children used to be far less different in the Middle Ages and early modern period than is the case today. Although this has more recently changed somewhat as a consequence of the so-called 'permissive revolution' of the 1960s – a better term would be the 'era of informalisation' (see Wouters 1977; 1986; 2008) – sex, sexuality and childbirth were hidden from children and spoken of mainly through circumlocutions.

Also pointing in the direction of lower inhibitions and a different standard of shame regarding the body, sex and sexuality than our own are the wedding customs of the upper classes. In the courts of the early Middle Ages, for example, there was a procession into the bridal chamber led by the best man. The bride was undressed by her bridesmaids and the bridegroom had to mount her in the presence of witnesses, otherwise the marriage was invalid. 'Once in bed you are rightly wed' was the old saying. Later on, this custom changed in that the couple were allowed to lie on the bed fully clothed. Even in the French absolute courts of the seventeenth and eighteenth centuries, this custom persisted with the couple being taken to bed by the guests, undressed and given their nightclothes (Elias 2012a: 174).

Members of the court aristocracy often regarded the restriction of sexual relations to marriage as 'bourgeois' and, according to Elias, women in that context experienced a degree of liberation that was lost in the bourgeois society of the nineteenth century. What was involved was a changing balance between freedom and constraint. As Elias put it:

> [T]he bourgeoisie as a whole became freed from the pressures of the absolutist-estates social structure. Both bourgeois men and ... women were now relieved of the extended constraints to which they were subjected as second-rate people in the hierarchy of estates. But the interweaving of trade and money, the growth of which had given them the social power to liberate themselves, had increased. In this respect, the social constraints on individuals were stronger than before. The pattern of self-restraint imposed on the people of bourgeois society through their occupational work was in many respects different from the pattern imposed on the emotional life by the functions of court society. For many aspects of the 'emotional economy', bourgeois functions – above all, business life – demand and produce greater self-restraint than courtly functions. (Elias 2012a: 181)

Other things which point towards there having been a more relaxed outlook on sex and the body in the Middle Ages and early modern period were attitudes to prostitution, illegitimacy, and public nakedness. Take the case of prostitution. It was a low status occupation but more open than is the case today. A telling illustration is provided by the fact that, in 1434, the (Holy Roman) Emperor Sigismund 'publicly thanked the city magistrate of Berne for putting the brothel at the disposal of himself and his attendants for three days' (Elias 2012a: 173). In similar fashion, 'illegitimate' upper class men in the Middle Ages often allowed themselves to be called 'bastard', or called themselves by this label 'expressly and proudly' (Elias 2012a: 179). They did not seek to hide it. A somewhat more advanced stage of shame-feeling, however, says Elias, is revealed by the fact that, in the eighteenth century, the Marquise de Châtelet, Voltaire's mistress, could sit naked and unconcerned in her bath with her manservant there and scold him for not pouring in the hot water properly. Given his low status, she did not regard him as a man in any sexual sense (Elias 2012a: 138). In the absolute courts, whether or not a person became embarrassed was evidently in large part a matter of relativities of rank.

Changes in the standards regarding violence and aggression point in the same direction. In the 'civilised' nations of the West, says Elias, aggressiveness – he was referring primarily but not solely to the aggressiveness of males – has become bound, 'even in directly warlike actions, by the advanced state of the division of functions, and by the resulting greater dependence of individuals on each other and on the technical apparatus. It is confined and tamed by innumerable rules and prohibitions that have become self-constraints' (Elias 2012a: 187). During the Middle Ages, by contrast, even though that period was nowhere near constituting a zero-point of standards in this or any other regard, 'rapine, battle, hunting of people and animals', all formed part of the pleasures of life for the knightly ruling classes. 'The only threat, the only danger that could instil fear was that of being overpowered in battle by a stronger opponent' (Elias 2012a: 189).

Medieval knights lived for battle. They had been trained for it from an early age. They took pleasure in torturing and killing others. Indeed, social conditions to some extent pushed them in this direction. According to Elias:

> What, for example, ought to be done with prisoners? There was little money in this society. With regard to prisoners who could pay and who, moreover, were members of one's own class, one exercised some degree of restraint. But the others? To keep them meant to feed them. To return them meant to enhance the wealth and fighting power of the enemy. For subjects (that is, working, serving and fighting hands) were a part of the wealth of the ruling class of that time. So prisoners were killed or sent back so mutilated that they were unfitted for war service and work. The same applied to destroying fields, filling in wells and cutting down trees. In a predominantly agrarian society, in which immobile possessions represented the major part of property, this, too, served to weaken the enemy. (Elias 2012a: 189)

Given the relative instability of their lives, medieval knights were less emotionally stable, more prone to sudden mood shifts, than tends to be true of their counterparts today. They were liable suddenly to switch between extremes of joy and sadness, love and hate, anger with and pity for others. Starting around the fifteenth century, the open and unalloyed joy they took in battle began to be tempered by feelings for their war comrades, the code of chivalry (Elias 2012a: 207), and beliefs in the justice of a cause. Later still, in the eighteenth and nineteenth centuries, nationalistic ideologies and the belief that fighting and dying for one's nation was a supreme value increasingly took pride of place.

According to Elias, similar patterns prevailed among the nascent bourgeoisie. Feuding, belligerence, hatred, and joy in tormenting others were all more uninhibited among rising members of the 'Third Estate' than later became the case. Echoing Marx on this, Elias suggested that it was not only 'the weapon of money that carried the burgher upward. Robbery, fighting, pillage, family feuds – all this played a hardly less important role in the life of the town population than in that of the warrior class itself' (Elias 2012a: 192). Elias went on presciently to comment on the much touted role of religion in this connection as follows:

> Much of what appears contradictory to us – the intensity of their piety, the violence of their fear of hell, their guilt feelings, their penitence, the immense outbursts of joy and gaiety, the sudden flaring and the uncontrollable force of their hatred and belligerence – all these, like the rapid changes of mood, are in reality symptoms of one and the same structuring of the emotional life. The drives, the emotions were vented more freely, more directly, more openly than later. It is only to us, in whom everything is more subdued, moderate and calculated, and in whom social taboos are built much more deeply into the fabric of our drive economy as self-restraints, that the unveiled intensity of this piety, belligerence or cruelty appears to be contradictory. Religion, the belief in the punishing or rewarding omnipotence of God, never has in itself a 'civilising' or affect-subduing effect. On the contrary, religion is always exactly as 'civilised' as the society or class which upholds it. (Elias 2012a: 194–5)

Summing up, the overall direction of the microsocial and psychogenetic changes in habitus, norms and behaviour documented by Elias was towards:

(i) the 'privatisation' or 'pushing behind the scenes' of the performance of major bodily functions. They, and the associated body parts, came over time to be viewed as distasteful, and Elias wrote in this respect of the 'rising threshold of repugnance' and advances in the 'frontiers of modesty and shame'. People began in this connection to feel uncomfortable at the sight of blood and, correspondingly, animals which were to be eaten came to be killed in abattoirs and butchers' shops. The performance of toilet functions was confined to the bathroom and specially designated public buildings, and sex and sleeping were confined primarily to the bedroom. During the Middle Ages and early modern periods, executions had been public spectacles attended by large animated crowds but, as part of the same overall trend, they began during the nineteenth century to be carried out behind closed doors and, during the second half of the twentieth, were widely abolished. The United States forms an interesting exception in this latter regard.[45]

(ii) also as part of this overall complex of changes, the fork and the spoon came to be the main eating implements, the only ones allowed for transferring food from plate to mouth. Correlatively, the knife came to be increasingly surrounded with prohibitions out of proportion to its actual danger. This, explained Elias, was on account of the fact that knives are not only eating implements but also weapons and are thus symbols of aggressiveness and violence, forms of behaviour, which were coming increasingly to be subject to controls.

(iii) the courts of kings, queens, princes and dukes etc. were the principal model-making centres where the standards of good behaviour associated with the courtesy, civility, and civilisational codes developed, and from which they spread through processes of downwards diffusion. According to Elias: 'What slowly began to form at the end of the Middle Ages was not just one courtly society here and another there. It was a courtly aristocracy embracing Western Europe with its centre in Paris, its dependencies in all other courts, and offshoots in all other circles which claimed to belong to the great world of "Society", notably the upper stratum of the bourgeoisie and to some extent even broader layers of the middle class' (Elias 2012a: 218). This Europe-wide 'court-society' was characterised by what one might, using an apparently contradictory term, call 'conflictful integration'. That is to say, despite the political differences among them and the numerous wars they fought against each other, its members were unified by a common language, French, and a common code of behaviour derived from Paris. For a long time, the patterns of social distance and communication within this Europe-wide court society were closer than between them and members of their respective national lower classes. It is worth pointing out that one of the major differences between Elias's understanding of European social development and that of Marx consisted precisely of the fact that the former regarded this court society as a crucial transitional stage, whereas the latter, given the economistic tenor of his thinking, failed to see its significance, preferring to think in terms of a direct transition from feudalism to capitalism. Anthony Giddens is one of the few 'non-Eliasian' sociologists to agree with Elias on this score.[46]

(iv) manners books for upper class adults in the Middle Ages and early modern period included instructions on behavioural rules which adults in the West today take for granted because they have been firmly instilled in them as children. One of the implications of this is that the period of primary socialisation has been extended in the course of contemporary processes of civilisation. This means that the period of childhood dependency has been lengthened, too, and that the social and psychological distance between adults and children has grown correlatively.

Let us turn our attention now to the 'macrosocial' levels of Elias's theory, that is to say, what he had to say about state-formation, pacification under state-control, the lengthening of interdependency chains and related 'macro-social' processes. We do not pretend that what follows details the whole of his case.

## State-formation and the lengthening of interdependency chains: the 'macro-social' levels of 'civilising processes' in the West

According to Elias, 'The question why people's behaviour and emotions change is basically the same as the question why their forms of living change' (Elias 2012a: 199). More particularly, it was Elias's contention that the manners, personalities and habituses of the people of Western Europe changed in a 'civilising direction' in conjunction with the following macro-social changes: state-formation, in particular the formation of state monopolies of violence and taxation. According to Elias, these are the 'major means of ruling' in societies with a money economy. Correlatively came growing production, growing trade, and growing wealth. All of these, Elias conceptualised as a complex of interacting processes that involve(d) the lengthening and concentration of interdependency chains, that is, growing social differentiation or division of labour, and the growth of towns; together with demographic growth, that is, the growth of populations. Another way of putting all of this would be to say that, according to Elias, the 'civilising processes' of Western Europe occurred correlatively with the emergence of capitalist-urban-industrial-nation-states, and such social units were initially primarily formed through and for war. In short, 'civilising processes' were conflictful affairs which involved 'hegemonic struggles' *within* the emergent nation states and 'integrational struggles' *between* them.

It was another of Elias's contentions that what we call 'societies' are best conceptualised as 'survival units' or 'attack-and-defence units'. These are self-explanatory terms through which Elias sought to capture the simultaneously military and economic functions of human societies (Elias 2012b). These units have ranged historically from clans and tribal groupings, through city-states and feudal states, to absolutist states and modern nation-states. The phases of European history focused on principally by Elias in *On the Process of Civilisation* involved a shift from feudal states, through absolutist states, to nation-states. More importantly for present purposes, however, such 'survival units' are all multi-faceted with regard to violence. This means that, whilst they typically involve an attempt to limit and control *internal* violence, violence *against* 'outsiders' tends to be condoned and, especially in times of war, even regarded as legitimate and rewarded (Elias 2012b: 164–70). As we have seen, Elias also argued that power is a property of *all* social relations. This means that he held social relations to always involve an element of internal conflict and competition. Correlatively with this, and implicitly following Lewin (1952) and anticipating Bourdieu (1984) by nearly fifty years, Elias suggested, without explicitly using these terms, that human societies can also be fruitfully conceptualised as 'social fields' or 'fields of forces'.[47] It is interesting to note that Elias's *Habilitation* sponsor, Karl Mannheim, developed a concept of 'structure' as a dynamic configuration of antagonistic and conflicting forces.

According to Elias, the balance of competitive pressures in a society can range between extremes in which either 'centrifugal', that is, disruptive, dis-unifying, de-centralising tendencies, or 'centripetal', that is, integrating, unifying, centralising tendencies are dominant. In Part II of *On the Process of Civilisation*, he discussed centrifugal tendencies under the heading of 'feudalisation', a kind of 'decivilising process' that was dominant in Western Europe following the decline of the Western Roman Empire in the fifth century AD.[48] Centrifugal tendencies remained dominant until about the eleventh century (Elias 2012a: 263). From then until today, despite fluctuations, centripetal tendencies have been in the ascendant. Elias discussed this dominance of centripetal tendencies under the headings of the 'monopoly mechanism' and the 'royal mechanism', terms upon which he later cast doubt.[49] That is, relatively stable central rule by monarchs and later, parliaments, began to become the general norm. According to Elias, however, stable central rule did not emerge as part of a continuous, unilinear process. That is, discontinuities and differences of timing were involved. Let us elaborate.

It is first necessary to examine how Elias dealt with this early 'decivilising process' or 'breakdown of civilisation'. One of his central contentions was that recurrent tendencies towards 'feudalisation', that is towards local economic self-sufficiency and independent local rule (economic and political 'autarky') were inherent in the structure of the societies of early medieval Europe. Contrary to a Marxist view, he suggested, economic and political processes worked interdependently in this connection. Neither was dominant. Expressed differently, what was happening was as follows. After waves of tribal invasion from the East and North and the correlative breakdown of Roman control in the West – Elias did not see one as 'cause' and the other as 'effect' – money, trade and towns *virtually* disappeared from Western Europe. They did not disappear *entirely*, however, and in the longer term this helped to speed and spread the 'recovery' which began around the eleventh century.

Between the fifth and the eleventh century, centrifugal pressures were dominant. Centripetal pressures did 'enjoy' short periods of ascendancy, as was especially apparent during the reign of Charlemagne (768–814). He was the founder of the 'Carolingian' dynasty and the most successful ruler during the so-called 'Dark Ages' which followed the decline of the Western Roman Empire. At its height, Charlemagne's empire embraced large parts of what we now know as France, Belgium, the Netherlands, Germany, Austria, Italy and

Spain. It became 'the Holy Roman Empire' when Charlemagne was crowned by the Pope in Rome in AD 800.

When one takes into account the then available means of transport and communication, the Holy Roman Empire can only be described as huge. It owed its existence largely to Charlemagne's personal warrior charisma and success in war. Economic autarky, however, meant that he did not have tax revenues at his disposal at a level that would have permitted the employment of a civil service and a standing army, essential prerequisites for ruling a state of considerable size. As we have discussed, according to Elias, tax and violence monopolies are the major 'means of ruling' in societies with a money economy. Stable state-societies are also usually ruled from a single centre, for example, London, Paris, or Berlin. Charlemagne and his entourage, however, had to travel from one to another of his estates in order both to feed themselves and maintain control. He had a 'peripatetic' court.

Charlemagne also had to rely on relatives and friends to rule distant parts of his empire and newly conquered territories. However, these 'vassals', even though they had sworn 'oaths of fealty' to their liege lord, recurrently came to see imperial lands as their own. They also lacked Charlemagne's charisma. As a result, when the great king died the empire began immediately to fragment. In 843, in the context of a fierce struggle for the succession, the empire was split into three by the Treaty of Verdun. This failed to resolve matters, and, in 870, a further treaty – the Treaty of Meerssen – came to be viewed as necessary in what proved to be a vain attempt to shore up the crumbling empire. Increasingly insistent centrifugal pressures were once again in the ascendant.

In seeking to explain what happened in that context, Elias focused primarily on the 'Western Franks' who were destined to become what we now call 'the French'. He began by noting how, at the time, centrifugal pressures were weaker in the Eastern parts of Charlemagne's one-time empire with the result that the forerunners of what we now call 'the Germans' were considerably stronger in the early Middle Ages than the forerunners of the French and English. The Germans' strength was forged in the more or less constant battles they had to wage against invading tribes from the North and East. It was not until the Reformation and the beginnings of what is nowadays misleadingly called 'modernisation' that the German medieval empire (the second, smaller 'Holy Roman Empire' which had been consecrated by the pope in the tenth century) started to crumble. By that time, the initially weaker French and English were in the ascendant.

In that early period, too, because of their geographical location, the Western Franks faced no external threats comparable to those which kept their Germanic Eastern counterparts on their toes (apart, of course, from the threat of the Normans, which a lack of space prevents us from dealing with in this context). A consequence was that Western Frankish rulers had less chance of conquering new territories and were compelled to reward loyal vassals by giving them sections of their own (the central rulers') lands. In that way, the power of the rulers was weakened while that of their vassals grew stronger. Take the case of Louis IV (936–954), one of the last Carolingians and still nominally King of France. When he inherited the crown, he was called 'le roi de Monloon' because little was left to him of his family's once vast possessions other than the castle at Laon (Elias 2012a: 232). He was, in effect, just one feudal lord among others in a society with a cell-like structure of economically self-sufficient, mainly self-ruling units of roughly equal power.

The situation of Louis VI (1108–1137; known as 'Louis the Fat') makes an interesting comparison. It was in some ways similar to that of Louis IV but in others instructively different. After a protracted struggle, the Carolingian house had been succeeded by the 'Capetians', offspring of Hugh Capet (987–996), Duke of Francia (the 'Île de France'), themselves to be succeeded later by the Valois and the Bourbons. 'In the person of Louis VI', Elias tells us, 'the Capetian house struggled against the houses of Montmorency, Beaumont, Rochefort, Montlhéry, Ferté-Alais, Puiset and many others (Elias 2012a: 251). In such a context, the castle of the Montlhéry family proved to be of decisive significance because it commanded the main route between Paris and Orleans, the two most important parts of the Capetian domains. Louis VI felt compelled to mount a series of expeditions against the castle until he finally captured it towards the end of his reign. Montlhéry is only 24 kilometres (about 15 miles) from Paris! Louis needed three further expeditions to subdue the most powerful family in the Orleans district, and it took him fully twenty years to establish dominance over the houses of Rochefort, Ferté-Alais, and Puiset, and add their possessions to his own. In this way, Louis VI became not only the nominal king but also the *de facto* ruler of his territory. He could not have known it but he was taking the first steps towards the crystallisation of what was to become France. According to Elias, 'By concentrating on the small area of Francia, by creating ... hegemony in this restricted ... territory, Louis VI laid the foundations for the subsequent expansion of his house. He created a potential centre for the crystallisation of the greater area of France, even though we may certainly not assume that he had any prophetic vision of this future' (Elias 2012a: 293).

At the roots of the power of the absolute monarchs of Western Europe, lay their monopoly control over what Elias, building on what was originally a conceptual innovation of Max Weber's, described as the major 'means of ruling' in societies with a money economy and a level of structural complexity above that of clans and tribes. As we have seen, these were their monopolies of taxation and military force. Such 'means of ruling', Elias suggested, worked interdependently. The tax monopoly provided central rulers with the financial wherewithal to pay and equip powerful armies and this, in turn, enabled rulers over time to disarm nobles, that is, to prevent the latter from keeping armies of their own. It also enabled the rulers to embark on the general pacification of the population and to maintain social conditions conducive to more rational government, long-term planning, material production, and the flow of trade.

The violence monopolies of the central rulers simultaneously enabled them to maintain their monopolies of taxation and, as production, trade and wealth grew, so the tax revenues available to central rulers expanded. Further to this, the custom of (especially) males carrying arms in public was abandoned and guns began to be licensed by the state. Specialised 'police' forces also emerged and, in Britain, these moved about the street most of the time armed with only a whistle and a truncheon.

At least three consequences flowed from the tax and force monopolies:

(i) although this was not a simple, always one-way process but also involved regressions that were usually sparked in connection with internal revolts and/or international wars, more and more people began to be brought up under conditions of relative peace. That is, at an *intra*-societal or domestic level, though not *inter*-nationally, violence became a less frequent part of the lives of growing numbers. People came to be less fearful of violent physical attacks by others. Such processes of pacification came to be reflected in the emergence of a dominant collective habitus in which violence was increasingly regarded with abhorrence at the levels of law, custom, individual conscience and feeling and thus pushed increasingly 'behind the scenes'. As this process ran its course, rulers and socially dominant groups more generally changed in a 'civilising' direction, more particularly from warriors into courtiers, and later into politicians, bureaucrats, business people, and top level military personnel. Also involved, according to Elias, was a shift from private ownership of the means of ruling to more public forms. That is, from a situation in which the apparatus of government had been the personal property of a monarch, more public and eventually more democratic forms of ruling gradually emerged;

(ii) as pacification increasingly took root, the predictability of social activities increased correlatively. So did the frequency of forward-looking, rational planning. In its turn, this contributed to the emergence of more rational, less emotional ways of ruling and more rational, more effective ways of conducting material production and trade. At the same time, chains of interdependence, which were largely but by no means entirely economic – for example, patterns of friendship were involved as well – grew longer and denser. That is, as we saw earlier, more and more people came to live in heavily populated towns and cities;

(iii) in conjunction with this, the power of bourgeois groups gradually increased and that of the landed nobility correlatively decreased.

In fact, the bourgeoisie were destined in the longer term to emerge as *the* ruling class and there were signs by the twentieth century of rulers being recruited from the other industrial class, the working class or 'proletariat' as well. At first, however, the interrelated state-formation and 'civilising' processes favoured the great lords – the dukes, the earls, the counts and others with the largest possessions – and the central rulers, leading eventually to the victory of the central rulers who, unlike Charlemagne some seven or eight hundred years beforehand, had at their disposal tax revenues, administrative apparatuses and means of transport and communication which enabled them to expand their territories and pass them on to their successors relatively intact. That is, the Western nation-states we are so familiar with today were gradually emerging. They are currently showing signs of merging into a larger, supra-national unit, the European Community. This process has so far been largely peaceful and it is multicausal and multidirectional in character (at the time of writing, there are signs of increasing disintegration of the European Union). It is also centrally connected with globalisation.

Besides enabling central rulers to prevent other nobles from keeping private armies, the growing power of monarchs, as we have seen, enabled the latter to bring the chief nobles to their courts where they could be kept under strict surveillance. In such a setting, the talents, experience and connections of the nobles could also be exploited in the business of ruling. Elias called this process *'die Verhöflichung der Krieger'* – the 'courtisation of the warriors' – a term which signifies the gradual transformation in the setting of the royal courts of 'knights' into 'courtiers'. In the royal courts, members of the feudal aristocracy became less able to use impulsive violence to secure objectives, protect interests and express themselves than they had been hitherto. They were subjected to more effective control 'from above' and hence forced to engage in longer-term, more 'rational' plotting, dissembling, and intrigue. Their manners and behaviour also grew more polished and urbane, and the 'civility' and 'civilisation' codes gradually took over from the 'courtesy codes'. According to Elias, however, 'court rationality' continued for a long time to be different from 'bourgeois rationality', being more orientated towards status and honorific considerations than money.

As we saw earlier, according to Elias there gradually emerged during the sixteenth, seventeenth, and eighteenth centuries, a Europe-wide 'court society' in which the French court was the major 'model-making centre' and French manners were generally followed. Although members of this court society continued to engage in dynastic and increasingly 'national' struggles with each other, they tended to have more in common than they did with members of the middle and lower classes of their emerging nation-states.

Another mark of this overall process was the gradual transformation of the dwelling places of rulers from fortified castles into palaces and country houses. A parallel process was the gradual disappearance of city walls, both being further marks of domestic pacification. A crucial underlying part of this development all the time was the fact that, in the longer term, internal societal pacification favoured capital-owning, money-earning, bourgeois groups more than it did those aristocrats who remained dependent, in the first instance on the warlike skills and attributes of their medieval forebears and, in the second, on the more fixed, less easily transferable resource of land. This contributed further to the processes of democratisation which were already inherent in the lengthening and growing density of interdependency chains and which were leading to growing pressure on rulers 'from below'. More particularly, rulers began to grow increasingly dependent, first on their middle class 'subjects' and later, as national income grew and to some extent 'trickled down', on their lower class 'subjects' as well. They depended on them for the taxes they paid, for their votes and, in periods defined as times of 'national necessity', for the military services of both groups. As we said earlier, this led over time to a shift from private ownership of the means of ruling to more public forms and, correlatively, to the transformation of 'subjects' into 'citizens', a process which is in some ways less advanced in the United Kingdom than in most Western countries. Elias had much more to say on these subjects but, given limitations of space, we shall conclude this chapter with a discussion of his position on the thorny issue of whether social developments are 'unilinear' or 'multilinear'. As we shall try to show, Elias's views on this and related issues were more complex than those commonly attributed to him by some of his critics.

## Social processes: Unilinear or multilinear?

A view of Elias's theory of 'civilising processes' held in different ways by such critics as Armstrong (1998), Bauman (1979), Giddens (Giddens and Mackenzie 1982), Giulianotti (2005), Goody (2002), and Williams (1991) involves problematically projecting onto it an abstract, general character. Such critics have falsely read Elias as having dealt with a simple unilinear and irreversible change, supposedly for the better, from one social 'state', 'barbarism', to another, 'civilisation'. More or less explicitly, according to such critics, Elias saw this process as having taken place at the same time, the same rate, in the same way and with exactly the same 'causes' and consequences in all the countries of Western Europe. In short, these writers see Elias as having proposed a simple 'modernisation' or 'progress' theory, a theory which is Eurocentric, little more than a paean to the West and an expression of 'Western triumphalism'. As they see it, Elias's theory, to repeat one of the issues we touched on earlier, is, in effect, a 'throwback' to the supposedly falsified and discredited 'evolutionary' and 'progress' theories of the eighteenth and nineteenth centuries which emerged as justifications for Western imperialism and colonial expansion.

The title *Über den Prozess der Zivilisation* and perhaps its English translation as *The Civilising Process* – the new title, *On the Process of Civilisation*, is rather better – certainly give an impression of unilinearity. As we have shown already, however, Elias's study is solidly based on historical data and thus far from abstract. It is easy, moreover, to show that Elias embraced such notions as multilinearity and reversibility all along. For example, he entitled one of the sections in what was originally Volume 2 of *On the Process of Civilisation*, 'Excursus on Some Differences in the Paths of Development of Britain, France and Germany' (Elias 2012a: 294–301). He also dealt with these and similar developmental differences in footnotes and on several occasions in his main text. At the time he was writing, of course, England, France, and Germany were still major players on the world stage and Elias, having been born in Germany was then living in England, having just spent almost two years in France. Thus his grasp of the balance of similarities and differences of social structure and habitus between these three countries was formed *in vivo* and not just from books. Let us enquire briefly into what he wrote about the French, the English and the Germans – especially the latter two – before closing this chapter with a short discussion of some of the hypotheses that Elias developed in *On The Process of Civilisation* about non-Western 'civilisations'.

According to Elias, of all three countries, France was the one – under Louis XIV – where the strongest form of monarchical absolutism developed. It accordingly became the chief model-making centre in the whole of Europe as far as courtly manners were concerned. England, by contrast, experienced the shortest phase of court-absolutism of the three. It was also the first in which a rural population of more or less free peasants emerged and where, along with a class of landowning noblemen, there developed 'a class of landowners who were untitled, a class who were only "gentlemen"' (Elias and Dunning 1971: 129). Elias also discussed at some length the hoary old idea that many features of the English/British collective habitus or 'national character' are explainable by the fact that Britain is an island. This merits elaboration.

If the national habitus of the English/British were simply a consequence of the fact that they are island dwellers, said Elias, 'then all other island nations would have to show similar characteristics, and no people should be closer to the English in character and habitus than, for example, the Japanese' (Elias 2012a: 599). This was a timely comparison because, at the moment of writing, the Japanese were involved in their conquest of South Asia, a context in which the military values and traditions of their nation were being thrown into sharp relief. In England/Britain, however, according to Elias, the nobility were 'relatively pacified' early on, a coalition of aristocratic and bourgeois groups succeeded in limiting the monarch's control over the state monopoly of violence, and the military enjoyed lower prestige than their counterparts in Japan and on the continent. Elias elaborated on this as follows:

> How closely certain features of the British superego ... are bound up with the structure of the monopoly of physical force is shown ... by the social latitude given in Britain to the 'conscientious objector' ... We should probably not be wrong in assuming that non-conformist ... organisations have been able to remain as strong and vigorous as they have ... in England only because the official Church of England was not backed by a police and military apparatus to the same extent as were, for example, the national churches in the Protestant states of Germany. At any rate, the fact that in Britain the pressure of foreign military power on the individual was from an early stage much less heavy than that in any other major continental [European] country is extremely closely connected to the other fact, that the constraint which an individual was expected to exercise on himself, above all in everything connected with matters of state, became stronger and more all-round than in the great continental nations. In this way, as an element of social history, the island character and the whole nature of the country have, indeed, affected the formation of the national character in a whole variety of ways. (Elias 2012a: 599–600)

Elias's principal contention in his 'Excursus on Differences in the Paths of Development of England, France and Germany', however, was that the ease with which centralised states emerged in Western Europe and hence the timing of such state-formation processes depended largely on the physical size of the territories to which they laid claim, the size of their populations, and the extent of the geographical and sociocultural, especially linguistic, differences they contained. He wrote:

> The task implied in the struggle for dominance, that is, for both centralisation and rule, was ... different in England and France from that in the German-Roman empire. The latter ... was very different in size to the other two; geographical and social divergences within it were also ... greater. This gave the local, centrifugal forces ... greater strength, and made the task of attaining hegemony and thus centralisation incomparably more difficult. The ruling house would have needed a far greater territorial area and power than in France or England to master the centrifugal forces of the German-Roman empire and force it into a durable whole. There is good reason to suppose, that, given the level of division of labour and integration, and the military, transportational and administrative techniques of the time, the task of holding centrifugal tendencies in so vast an area permanently in check was probably insoluble. (Elias 2012a: 294)

Elias went on the show how the 'Holy Roman' or 'German Roman Empire' crumbled away for centuries at its borders, a process only partly compensated by expansion to the East. Ignoring irregularities, examination of the long-term trend, he suggested, gives an impression of 'the Empire's constant attrition ... accompanied by a slow shift of the direction of expansion, and a drift in the centre of gravity from west to east' (Elias 2012a: 299).

In 1800, at a time when Britain and France were already nation-states with relatively high degrees of unification, the Holy Roman Empire consisted of more than 400 autonomous or semi-autonomous units. Two of them, however, those of the Hohenzollern and Habsburg dynasties, that is, Prussia and Austria, were larger and stronger than the rest. The Holy Roman Empire was replaced by a Confederation early in the nineteenth century but proved unable to accommodate the tensions caused by the hegemonic rivalries of the Hohenzollerns and Habsburgs. This led to what Germans came to call the '*kleindeutsche Lösung*' (the small Germany solution), that is, the split between Germany and Austria. There was a further diminution after 1918 in consequence of the territorial losses suffered by Germany following their defeat in the First World War. In one of his last books, *The Germans*, Elias went on to show how a major consequence of Germany's defeat in the Second World War was a continuation of this trend: yet another split occurred, this time between the Federal and Democratic Republics.

Elias contended, then, that the large territory occupied by German-speakers and the size and sociocultural heterogeneity of their population led them to encounter greater difficulties regarding state-centralisation and unification than the British and French, the size of whose territories and populations was considerably smaller. This led to stronger centrifugal tendencies and a more discontinuous pattern of history and social development. One mark of this was the comparative recency of Berlin as a capital compared with London and Paris which had grown relatively continuously for something like a thousand years. Vienna and Prague sometimes served as capital of the Holy Roman Empire; and Berlin only became capital with the rise of Prussia. Another mark of discontinuity was the fragmented character of the German middle classes whose power-chances relative to the aristocracy were, as a result, less than those of their counterparts in Britain and France. According to Elias, the weakness of the German middle classes was reinforced by the fact that the old empire lacked a generally acknowledged capital which could have served as a focus for revolutionary action. As a result, they were relatively easy to defeat in the revolution of 1848.

The fragmentation of the Holy Roman Empire also meant that no 'court society' such as emerged in France, and no 'great society' such as grew up in Britain, centred on London, could arise and 'courtise' the German aristocracy. As a result, the latter retained a militaristic ethos for longer than the aristocracies of Britain and France. They also excluded the middle classes from their scattered courts, ensuring that middle class elites obtained little experience of participation in the business of ruling. This, Elias suggested was one of the roots of the originally humanistic ethos of the German middle classes whose orientation was towards philosophy, science, and the arts rather than politics and economics.

Throughout the twentieth century, the dominant outside image of the Germans portrayed them as a warlike people. From the sixteenth to the end of the nineteenth century, however, they tended to be viewed as non-militaristic and weak. Madame de Staël, for example, wrote of them in 1814 that: 'the nation is by nature literary and philosophical ... the realm of the seas belongs to the English; the realm of the earth to the French; the realm of the air to the Germans' (De Staël 1985: 28–9). She meant by 'realm of the air' philosophy, science and the arts, not domination of the skies by Zeppelins, Messerschmitts, 'flying bombs' (V1s) and V2 Rockets!

Germany experienced a massive power loss in the sixteenth century when, largely in conjunction with wars between Catholic and Protestant princes, the medieval empire began to break up. As a result, in the seventeenth century – remembered by the English and French mainly as a century of glorious achievements – Germany became the 'cockpit of Europe'. This was marked by the devastating 'Thirty Years War' in which it is estimated that Germany lost a third of its human population as well as some 90 per cent of its horses. Towards the end of the seventeenth century, Germany was invaded by Louis XIV, a process repeated by Napoleon at the beginning of the nineteenth century. In consequence, according to Elias, Germans became acutely conscious of their low status in the rank hierarchy of European states and many developed chronic doubts regarding their own and their nation's worth.

Germany did not become a unified nation-state until the second half of the nineteenth century. This process occurred through a series of wars under the leadership of the Prussian king and military caste. In its course, the balance between adherence to 'humanist' and 'anti-humanist' values among the dominant sections of the middle classes began to shift decisively in favour of the latter. According to Elias, Germany's victory in 1871 in the Franco-Prussian war played a decisive part in both this value-shift and Germany's national unification. The liberal *Bürgertum* in the eighteenth and early-nineteenth centuries had aspired to the achievement of national unification by peaceful means. The fact that, in the event, unification was achieved through war under the leadership of the warrior class made such an impression on a majority of middle class Germans that militaristic values increasingly permeated their ranks. As Elias pithily expressed it: 'the victory of the German armies over France was at the same time a victory of the German nobility over the German middle classes' (Elias 1996). In the eighteenth and early nineteenth centuries, German middle class culture had been exemplified by the work of people like Goethe, Kant, and Schiller; after 1871, it was the work of authors such as Friedrich Nietzsche and Ernst Jünger who glorified violence and military values, which came to express and reinforce the dominant view.

Elias described Germany's more unified Second *Reich* – the First had been the Holy Roman Empire and the Third was the *Reich* of Adolf Hitler – as a *satisfaktionsfähige Gesellschaft*, a term which cannot be meaningfully translated directly into English but refers to a society orientated around a harsh and unbending code of honour in which the demanding and giving of 'satisfaction' in duels occupied pride of place. According to Elias, Germany's unification thus involved a 'brutalisation' of the leading sections of the middle classes. One manifestation of this was the fact that, whereas in France and England, the incidence of duelling declined during the nineteenth century, in Germany it increased. The student fraternities in the universities played an important role in this process of brutalisation. Just like the public schools and Oxford and Cambridge Universities in England, the German universities were institutions where a partial unification between the aristocracy and the middle classes occurred. Membership of a fraternity became a precondition for being regarded as *satisfaktionsfähig* – worthy of being challenged to a duel – and thus for being admitted to the local 'good societies' throughout the Second *Reich*. In this context, according to Elias, the middle classes were even more 'brutalised' than their aristocratic rulers because the latter were subject to greater restraint through the honorific ethos of their warrior code. It was Elias's contention that this ethos of *satisfaktionsfähigkeit* was one of the preconditions for the rise of Nazism. As he expressed it:

> I have treated the expansion of military models into parts of the German middle class ... because I believe that National Socialism and the decivilising spurt which it embodied cannot be completely understood without reference to this context ... Above all ... the unbridled resort to acts of violence as the only realistic and decisive vehicle of politics, which was at the centre of Hitler's doctrine and the strategy used already in his rise to power, can be explained only against this background. (Elias 1996: 15)

It was another of Elias's contentions that, whilst the rise to power of the Nazis was by no means inevitable, such a development was more likely to have occurred in Germany than in France or Britain. It is thus also worth briefly examining some of the things that Elias wrote about social developments *outside* Europe.

## The theory of 'civilising processes: A 'eurocentric' theory?

As we saw earlier, one of the most frequent criticisms of Elias's theory holds it to be 'Eurocentric', a celebration of the global power and 'progress' of the West rather than a social scientific contribution to its understanding. It certainly is a 'Eurocentric' theory in the sense of being *focused on* Europe and trying to contribute to the understanding of how and why France and Britain became powerful enough to develop global empires, in the process equating themselves with 'civilisation', whilst Germany was a 'late developer' and, latterly, 'prime mover' in the attempted bureaucratic-industrial genocide of Jews which has come to be known as 'the Holocaust'.

However, whilst Elias's theory is mainly *centred on* Europe, it is not *'eurocentric'* in the sense of being an exemplification of European or Western 'triumphalism'. On the contrary, it is an observation-based theory concerned, not so much with making value-judgements of this sort, but with advancing a sociological understanding of the processes with which it is concerned. In order to make this crystal clear, Elias cited from a 1935 article on 'social evolution', published in the *Encyclopaedia of the Social Sciences* and written by Alexander Goldenweiser, an American anthropologist who argued: 'If there is a social evolution, whatever it may be, it is no longer accepted as a process to be contemplated but as a task to be achieved by deliberate and concerted human effort' (New York, 1935, Vol 5: 656 ff; cited in Elias 2012a: 592–3). This reflected the empiricist trend in Western sociology we referred to earlier and stung Elias into responding that his 'study of the civilising process differs from these pragmatic efforts in that, suspending all wishes and demands concerning what ought to be, it tries to establish what was and is, and to explain in which way, and why, it became as it was and is. It seemed more appropriate to make the therapy depend on the diagnosis rather than the diagnosis on the therapy' (Elias 2012a: 593). In thus using language which reveals his medical training and psychoanalytic interests, it was not Elias's intention to claim that his theory was fully-fledged or complete, a theory which explains all there is to know about state-formation and 'civilisation' and which can be used for therapeutic purposes whether at the individual or the societal level, but rather, that he had laid down foundations on which he hoped others would be able to build in at least four ways:

(i) by testing, deepening and elaborating upon his theory by means of further studies of Britain, France and Germany;

(ii) by studying 'civilising' and state-formation processes in other Western countries, non-European (for example, Australia, Canada and the USA) as well as European;

(iii) by studying processes of this kind in oriental, other Asian, South American and other non-occidental settings; and

(iv) by adding to the stock of knowledge through studies of special subjects such as food, fire, art, leisure and sport.

As a means of bringing this chapter to a conclusion, we shall now briefly examine the third of these ways in which Elias hoped that others would build on the foundations he had laid down.

A glance at the index of *On The Process of Civilisation* shows that Elias saw himself as having provided in that book just the first of what he hoped would become a comprehensive series of equally theoretical and empirical comparative-developmental studies which would eventually encompass the 'history' of humanity in its entirety. He referred in particular in this connection at differing lengths and in a preliminary way to China, Ethiopia (Abyssinia), the Incas, and Japan. Ethiopia and Japan were, of course, hot topics in the late 1930s on account of the Italian invasion of the former and the latter's invasion of South-East Asia. What Elias wrote about China and Japan, and, more generally, about the need for comparative-developmental studies, is of greatest interest for present purposes.

Elias starts by commenting on how astonishing it was that, given the means of transport and communication available to them, the Chinese and Inca empires should have remained comparatively stable for relatively long periods. He claimed in this connection that precise and detailed sociogenetic or 'structural-historical analyses' of the interplay of centrifugal and centralising tendencies and interests in such contexts would be necessary to explain the relative cohesion of such vast agglomerations. He went on to develop the following hypothesis regarding the Chinese:

> The Chinese form of centralisation, compared to that developed in Europe, was certainly very peculiar. Here the warrior class was eradicated relatively early and very radically by a strong central authority. This eradication – however it happened – is connected with two main peculiarities of the Chinese social structure: the passing of the control of land into the hands of the peasants (which we encounter in the early Western period only in a very few places, for example, Sweden) and the manning of the governmental apparatus by a bureaucracy always recruited in part from the peasants themselves and at any rate wholly pacified. Mediated by this hierarchy, courtly forms of civilisation penetrated deeply into the lower classes ... [T]hey took root, transformed in many ways, in the code of behaviour of the village ... [W]hat has ... been called the 'unwarlike' character of the Chinese people ... resulted from the fact that the class from which the people drew many of their models through constant contact, was for centuries no longer a warrior class, a nobility, but a peaceful and scholarly officialdom. It is primarily their situation and function that is expressed in the fact that, in the traditional Chinese scale of values – unlike the Japanese – military activity and prowess held no very high place. Different as the Chinese way to centralisation was, in its details, from that in the West, therefore, the foundation of the cohesion of larger dominions was in both cases the elimination of freely competing warriors or landowners. (Elias 2012a: 589.)

It is not within the realms of our competence to say whether or not these suggestions by Elias regarding the Chinese pattern of development held good at the time of writing or whether or not they are now out-dated, having long since been superseded by advancing knowledge. Our point is rather to show that Elias was an imaginative scholar who wrote primarily about European societies because of the readily available data. Hence he cannot reasonably be charged with having been ethnocentric, the proponent of a theory about the inherent 'superiority' of the West. Others of his arguments in *On The Process of Civilisation* point in a similar direction. For example, he contended (Elias 2012a: 601) that we do not yet have a good understanding of why the degree of what he called 'social pressure', that is, the pressure imposed on one another by interdependent people, varies from society to society, 'cultural area' to 'cultural area', and from time-period to time-period. For example, he suggested that the level of social pressure and hence of social tensions was higher within the figuration of European states than among the states of Central and South America, but concluded that we do not yet have adequate conceptual tools for exploring issues of this kind. However, what is certain in this connection, said Elias, is that such problems are best approached in processual and comparative, dynamic and relational terms. Moreover, social pressures and tensions are generated, not simply 'endogenously', that is, within particular societies, but also by the positions of societies within inter-societal figurations. In the next chapter, we shall explore the significance of some of the insights that Elias developed in relation to his specific empirical work on civilising processes for his more general approach to sociology, particularly his approach to the sociology of knowledge.

# 4

# The Development of Knowledge and the Sciences as Social Processes

In this chapter, we shall explore the implications of Elias's central engagement with social processes for the understanding of issues related to knowledge and the development of the sciences. As we shall see, his approach to such issues involved a consistent attempt to develop sociology as a discipline distinct from philosophy. In a direct and conscious sense, Elias sought to translate problems relating to knowledge and the sciences that continue to this day to be typically posed in largely 'philosophical' terms into more 'sociological' formulations. Of course, the distinction we have drawn between sociology and philosophy is by no means shared by, nor even immediately recognisable to, a broader sociological audience. But, in many ways this was precisely Elias's point: he sought to establish a sociological approach which, *pace* the arguments of Winch (1958) among others, would stem from a break both from the discipline of philosophy and what we might loosely call 'philosophical modes of theorising'. As we shall endeavour to illustrate in this chapter, Elias had a remarkably lucid vision of what a properly sociological approach in contradistinction to a philosophical one should entail.

While there is some disagreement regarding Elias's depiction of philosophy and, indeed, regarding the alleged degree of his residual dependence on philosophical thinkers (see, for example, Maso's (1995) discussion of Elias and Cassirer, and the response of Kilminster and Wouters (1995) and Goudsblom (1995)), Elias's views on knowledge and the sciences involved a fundamental rejection of the classical oppositions and related modes of theorising which have long dominated debates over 'epistemology', 'ontology' and 'methodology'. To this end, Elias made much of his intellectual debts to Comte and Marx.

## The primacy of process

Comte and Marx, Elias argued, attempted in their own ways to escape the 'fables of classical European philosophy' (Elias 1997: 355; Elias 2009b: 9), in particular, the notion of 'eternal reason' and the idea of 'consciousness' or the human 'spirit' as the timeless, unchanging, 'motor' of social change. These principles were also used in classical philosophy as starting points for all questions concerning 'knowledge' and 'science'. For Comte, the philosophical edifice of 'eternal reason', the idea of an unchanging mind shared by all people and all classes in all historical periods, was fundamentally flawed. In rejecting it, Comte made what Elias called 'a sociological breakthrough'. More particularly, he developed the hypothesis that human thinking, in tandem with a complex of more general social structural changes, has passed, and is continuing to do so, through a series of empirically verifiable stages. Elias recognised, of course, that Comte's 'law of the three stages' – marked by the sequential ascendancy of theology (itself subdivided between fetishism, polytheism and monotheism), metaphysics and science – cannot strictly speaking be called a 'law' and involved an overly simple view of knowledge, especially as it has developed since Comte's death. Elias nevertheless saw the model as providing a useful indication of an empirically demonstrable overall 'direction' of change and that it was in that way helpful in securing a break from the predominantly static forms of thinking of classical European philosophy (we shall later discuss the concept of directionality in greater detail). In this way, says Elias, Comte was able to redefine the relationship between 'a reasoning subject of knowledge' and the 'objects of knowledge' as itself a social process and, accordingly, as a properly sociological concern that could be empirically investigated through an examination of how the development of different types of knowledge involves a partly necessary sequence of developmental stages (Elias 1997: 355; Elias 2009b: 9)).

By contrast to Comte, Marx based his reorientation of human intellectual activity on a break from the philosophy of Hegel who, in turn, had been dependent on an inherited notion of 'spirit', the idea of mental activities as a domain wholly autonomous in relation to the structure and development of societies, and yet at once the hegemonic impetus behind all other aspects of social change. As we touched upon in Chapter 2, Marx's crucial departure from this philosophical legacy, said Elias, was to substitute for 'spirit', the relations involved in the material production and distribution of goods for the satisfaction of elementary human needs (Elias 1997: 356; Elias 2009b: 10). In so doing, Elias argued, Marx's work constituted a decisive shift from philosophy to sociology. More specifically, Marx's work involved a departure from the reduction of 'humanity' to 'mental activities', and a shift away from the notion of a single, isolated, and 'rational' human mind, towards a consideration of people in the plural, of human societies, including a focus on human relationships, people's biological constitution, and their need to find sustenance for their elementary needs.

Marx recognised the lack of a clear-cut correspondence between the depiction of the social world in the books of learned scholars such as Hegel, and the objects to which such accounts refer. For Marx, this lack of agreement between posited 'knowledge of the world' and 'the world to which such knowledge pertains' does not derive so much from a philosophically postulated gulf between 'subject' and 'object', or from the structure of a pre-given human consciousness, as it does from the fact that the interests, values, ideals and commitments of groups – to which those who reflect upon such matters variously subscribe – distort or obscure their perceptions of the world (Elias 1973: 376; Elias 2009a: 11). Elias suggested that this crucial insight of Marx's was 'eminently promising' since such 'blockages' and 'distortions' can be studied empirically and systematically in relation to the development of societies. Indeed, Elias noted, this insight provided the foundations for many subsequent sociological theories of knowledge (1973: 376; Elias 2009a: 12). Another, now largely overlooked, aspect of Marx's insight is the idea that such interests, ideas and values, tied as they are in important ways to broader social relations, develop over time. In this way, Marx can be said to have laid the foundations for a processual theory of the growth and development of knowledge.

In thus railing against this one-sided image of humans, Elias suggests, Marx 'overshot the mark' somewhat. Fighting directly, as he was, against the philosophical idealism of Hegel, Marx paradoxically came to subscribe to a materialist mode of theorising that mirrored in certain ways that of his opponent (Elias 1973: 376; Elias 2009a: 12). Marx's posited relationship between 'being' (existence) and 'consciousness' implied an eternal, unchanging relationship between all forms and levels of consciousness and all manifestations of 'social reality' in all historical ages. In this context, consciousness was conceived as a kind of 'eternal froth', lacking a structure of its own. It was seen as little more than a 'superstructural' reflection of a structured socio-economic base – as though 'social reality', indeed the human 'means of production', could be produced without consciousness, and as if people could be involved in relations of production as owners and employees somehow devoid of consciousness (1973: 376; Elias 2009a: 12). In this sense, Marx can be said to have effectively replaced an autonomous philosophical 'spirit' with an equally autonomous 'economy' or 'mode and relations of production'. Thus, according to Elias, Marx's substitution of a 'material' for an 'ideal' 'prime mover' was ultimately rooted in and indicative of the fact that his break from the philosophical legacy was incomplete.[50]

Regarding his use of concepts such as 'the economic' and 'the material', Elias proposed that Marx came to treat the social satisfaction of elementary human needs as the basis of all other human functions, and to posit in this connection, to use his (Marx's) own Hegel-derived terms, a 'dialectic of historical movement' (Elias 1997: 356; Elias 2009b: 10). In this way, Marx's 'dialectical exuberance' gave way to a kind of 'chicken-and-egg' problem. In Elias's deceptively simple words, it can be expressed thus: 'people are in no position to satisfy their elementary physical needs without thinking and without the knowledge to orientate themselves in their world, and that they are incapable of orientating themselves in this manner without satisfying their elementary needs' (Elias 1997: 356; Elias 2009b: 10–11).

Elias sought to move beyond this apparent paradox by avoiding Marx's tendency to accord primacy to 'the economy' and to relegate all other areas of human functioning to a secondary 'superstructure'. Elias's contention was that 'consciousness', 'knowledge', 'ideas' (or whatever we choose to call them) and 'society' or 'social reality' are terms which refer, not to separate objects which exist independently, but rather to different, inter-related aspects of a complex whole. The historical tendency, particularly in Western thought, towards conceiving of, for example, 'consciousness' and 'society' as ontologically distinct and 'separate' was, for Elias, itself of considerable sociological interest and, again, something worthy of empirical investigation (see our discussion of *homo clausus* and *homines aperti* thinking in Chapter 2). For Elias, it makes little sense to conceive of humans without consciousness or, conversely, to conceive of consciousness without 'society' – as something existing outside a plurality of living people – an idea which is ultimately implied by the argument that 'material conditions' or 'relations of production' (the 'cause') are generative of 'consciousness' (the 'effect') (Elias 1973: 375; Elias 2009a: 12).

Elias's position was, in a relational sense, more 'radical' than even that of Marx. For Elias, 'consciousness', 'knowledge', and 'ideas' are a component of everything social. And like all things social – indeed, everything in the known universe – these terms imply phenomena that are dynamic. That is, for Elias: '"consciousness" is an inherent *dimension* of *any* society. ... [I]t is present in the feeding of a child by its mother, the ploughing of his field by a farmer, in the spinning of cotton by workers of a nineteenth century mill' (1973: 376; Elias 2009a: 11). Further to this, Elias's emphasis on the processual character of 'consciousness', 'knowledge' and 'ideas' had 'epistemological' as well as 'ontological' significance. If 'consciousness' or 'ideas' and 'society' are seen as essentially static entities, albeit entities which 'move' or 'change' from time to time, our questions concerning knowledge must inevitably centre on issues of primacy. Thinking in essentially static terms, we are compelled to seek to identify the 'active' or 'prime mover', as well as the 'moved', 'acted upon' or passive 'recipient' of 'change'. Put simply, adherents to an 'epistemology' which stems from a static orientation are compelled to ask questions which are themselves flawed in certain respects. To illustrate this point, it is worth returning to Elias's example of the 'chicken-and-egg' problem, a subject that featured recurrently in his teaching. How might this dilemma be reframed using process concepts?

The problem of 'which came first, the chicken or the egg?' seems impossible to resolve. A chicken obviously has to exist to lay an egg but, equally, a chicken has to grow out of an egg. So how can the problem be resolved? From a process perspective at the present level of knowledge, the short 'answer' is: 'the Big Bang' – at least if one subscribes to this widely accepted theory of how the universe 'began' and, indeed, to the very notion of any such 'absolute beginning'. That is because the problem of the chicken and the egg is only impossible to resolve if one accepts the manner of its posing: the chicken and the egg are offered as equivalent and exclusive opposites. One has to choose between one and the other. Such a formulation begs for an 'answer' rather than an investigation. Moreover, the problem is posed statically; it is blind to the processual character of that to which it refers. In other words, it is not a helpful question because it leads one to make a selection between only two choices and these are treated as 'eternals'. In short, the intractability of the dilemma is to a large extent a product of how the question has been framed.

Adopting the sort of process orientation advocated by Elias, one would attempt to 'resolve' the chicken and the egg question, not through 'armchair theorising' but *via* a different and more reliable knowledge-producing vehicle: 'research-theorising' – that is, theorising in tandem with empirical observation in which neither the theoretical nor the empirical component is allowed to become dominant over the other. Using such an approach, it would be necessary to gain an understanding of the evolutionary emergence of chickens and their characteristic reproductive cycles over time. If we were really interested in what came 'first' – accepting, for present purposes, that this is a pertinent question – we would need ultimately to consider the origins of the universe, hence our earlier reference to 'the Big Bang', because, given our present level of understanding, everything, all life on earth, and everything else in the cosmos is, in the 'final' analysis, connected to that. From there, we would seek to trace the origins of the earth, then move on to considering the development of life, perhaps studying how the earliest, single-cell life-forms emerged from 'the primordial soup'. We might then explore how these evolved into more complex organisms such as animals, including saurians (dinosaurs) and, then, how these in turn gave way to other life-forms. We might go along with those who claim that birds evolved from dinosaurs which also reproduced using eggs, and eventually we could study the species that we have now come to recognise as 'chickens'. The question of 'which came first?' would thus be reframed to become a research-based investigation through which we would seek to discover which was the earliest life-form to reproduce using eggs. But even this is too static a question, too static a starting-point for research. We would need, for example, to investigate the development of membrane-like coatings surrounding the young of some species which eventually evolved into egg-like 'shells', and so forth. In short, to resolve this question more adequately than through the inevitably flawed selection between two static choices, we would need to refocus our enquiry to accommodate the relational and developmental dynamics of the 'real' universe as scientists have so far come to understand it.

## On the concepts of 'process' and 'development'

The chicken and egg example is intended here as allegorical. We have introduced it in order to highlight the importance of reframing in processual terms questions about knowledge and social dynamics. One of the respects in which the allegory is limited is in the lack of a correspondence between the kinds of processes involved in the development of life on earth, specifically 'organic' or 'biological evolution', and those involved when we speak of the 'development' of societies. It is, accordingly, important to consider exactly what Elias meant, firstly, when he used terms such as 'process', 'development', and 'direction', and, secondly, by his broader conceptual vocabulary that was centrally attuned to facilitating diachronic analysis and the study of social dynamics at various levels.

Two main sets of issues arise in this context. They are interconnected but we have separated them for purposes of clarification. The first set is more 'substantive'. It relates to the specificities of Elias's thesis concerning the developmental 'directions' of 'civilising processes' in France, England, and Germany, the three most powerful West European nations when Elias wrote his book. Particularly since its publication in English, Elias's *magnum opus* has attracted criticism on the grounds that his thesis is shot through with teleological, or more specifically, 'progress' overtones. Perhaps the exemplar of this is Cambridge anthropologist Sir Edmund Leach's statement concerning *On the Process of Civilisation*: that, at the very time it was being written, 'Hitler was refuting the argument on the grandest scale' (Leach 1986).

We have discussed such readings of Elias's work, and the issues to which they pertain, in some detail in earlier sections of this book (particularly in Chapter 3). It is important to add that these criticisms betray a pervasive caution among sociologists and anthropologists of the late nineteenth and twentieth centuries over the very concept of 'development' and, indeed, many cognate terms, a tendency that Wittfogel (1957) described as 'developmental agnosticism', though 'developmental atheism' might have been a better term. Herein lies the second set of fundamentally inter-related concerns we alluded to above. Put simply, as theoretical 'objects' for Elias's theorising and research, what is the status of terms such as 'process' and 'development'? And by similar extension, to what extent, if at all, does Elias's use of process descriptor terms such as 'direction' and 'curve' imply unilinear development and historical continuity? As we have seen already, and as we will discuss in greater detail in Chapter 6, such questions have been central to critiques of Elias by authors from within the disciplinary domain of anthropology in particular (see, for example, Blok (1982), and Goody (2002) discussed in this volume; see also Mennell's (1998: 227–250) rebuttal of such critiques). They are arguably all the more important in the wake of post-modernist accounts of what their authors deem to be the 'grand narratives' of classical sociology. Indeed, what we understand to be the widespread post-modernist emphasis on 'discontinuities', 'ruptures' and historical 'disintegration' would at the very least appear to raise important questions regarding concepts such as 'development' and related terms.

Critics have often viewed Elias's commitment to a developmental perspective as having been related in large part to his positioning at a particular socio-geographical and historical conjuncture, namely as a European scholar who wrote his most important work in the first half of the twentieth century before the attack on 'social evolutionism' of figures such as Talcott Parsons (1937) and Franz Boas had had time fully to sink home. It was at a time when Elias could still be envisaged as 'standing on the shoulders' of optimistic Enlightenment thinkers who placed their faith in the progressive triumph of Western rationality. However, particularly in view of the massively troubled era, especially in his native Germany, in which he began to develop his key ideas, Elias was able in important ways to remain remarkably detached from the prevailing social climate. Far from being naïve or ignorant of the tendency of particular groups in Western European societies, including some of their leading public intellectuals, to take it for granted that *their* societies, *their* values, *their* ways of life were the most advanced, and those of others by comparison 'primitive', for Elias, the growing ascendancy of such ideas was in and of itself a problem of sociological interest. As we showed in Chapters 2 and 3 of this book, the opening sections of *On The Process of Civilisation* are devoted to exploring how the very word 'civilisation' came to emerge as a notion employed as a means of legitimising the dominance of the then-ruling groups in France, later coming to spread throughout Europe and the wider world and to perform a similar legitimising function for European rule over supposedly 'barbarian subjects'. Indeed, *pace* Leach, rather than constituting an empirical refutation of Elias's arguments, the development of what was then the nascent Third Reich and Hitler's rise to power were among the points of departure of Elias's work, namely the 'experiences in whose shadow we all live' to which he referred in the Preface to *On The Process of Civilisation*. The difficulties that Elias experienced in getting his book published in the first place were also intimately bound up with the Nazis' rise to power.

For Elias, the emergence in the twentieth century of a powerful trend in the social sciences and related subjects towards viewing terms like 'development' and 'process' with suspicion, if not outright condemnation, poses a problem of sociological interest and importance. It is not all that difficult to understand, he used to argue, why such terms have come to attract a taboo-like status. You do not need to be a professional historian specialising in the twentieth century to know of the horrendous atrocities that were legitimised in that century by notions of 'development' and 'progress' in a normative sense and which more or less explicitly implied judgements of 'superiority' and 'inferiority' whether in terms of 'race' or belief systems of a political or religious character. If anything, in so far as it is possible to make such a generalisation with meaning, the dominant mood in Western societies since the latter part of the twentieth century has been characterised by growing doubts over whether the direction of social change taken, in particular in the more 'advanced', more affluent societies of the West, can be said to involve any 'progress' in the sense of increasing human happiness and well-being. As Mennell cogently expressed it, '[it] is also partly because any mode of speaking and thinking which appears to rank the peoples of the world as "higher" and "lower", as more or less advanced, is seen as casting doubt upon the fundamentally equal worth and rights of all human beings. This is a very civilised way of viewing humans' (1998: 27).

According to Elias, furthermore, such judgements are paradoxical. On the one hand, he suggests, the twentieth century was a period of significant technical advance in which an exponential expansion of knowledge took place, together with a correlative trend towards planned reform of the 'social order'. At the same time, however, the twentieth century was a period marked by deepening doubts about the value of such 'progress'. Any advantages secured in conjunction with the latter were accepted but its simultaneous dangers were increasingly feared. Elias commented on the apparent paradox thus:

> The increasing stream of innovations makes the affected people insecure; the growing tempo of change strengthens their desire for enclaves of peace and for symbols of changelessness. Above all, however, people search for deliverance from the unremitting conflicts of human groups – whether they delude themselves that everything could be peaceful and harmonious if only the others, the disturbers of the peace, the agitators, did not rebelliously threaten the good life, or whether they see the means of salvation in an overthrow of existing power relations and the establishment of another order in which they hope for greater peace, harmony and freedom from conflict'. (1997: 358; Elias 2009b: 13).

In fact, when viewed in the longer term, the idea of humanity advancing towards a 'better' future – an idea which arguably reached its zenith in Europe between the mid-eighteenth and the mid-nineteenth centuries – is in many respects quite novel (Elias 1997: 357). For centuries, Elias argued, people saw social development mainly as a 'decline': 'Paradise lay in the past. The Golden Age was followed by the Silver Age and the Iron Age [and] by many wars. At best, people dreamed of a journey back to the lost paradise, of the return of the better part, of the renaissance of antiquity'. (Elias 1997: 357; Elias 2009b: 11). The enthusiastically held belief in 'progress' which had been dominant in the eighteenth and early nineteenth centuries – more specifically the faith in a continuous improvement in the human condition that was to be brought about through advances in knowledge and its application *via* technology – was followed in the twentieth century, particularly in the more advanced industrial nations, by 'a kind of dialectical pendulum swing by a no less exaggerated judgement that this belief in progress was the expression of a naïve optimism' (Elias 1997: 357; Elias 2009b: 12). However, again paradoxically and albeit on the most laudable grounds, such wholesale condemnation of the belief in progress impeded access to a whole range of sociological problems not only concerning the 'age of optimism' itself but also regarding the more sceptical period that followed it. For Elias, more fundamental questions concerning the social conditions within which a 'progress movement' had gained the ascendancy in the first place; the shift and reconfiguration of power relations that was expressed in ideas such as 'progress', and, indeed, the circumstances under which the 'chorus of opposing voices' later came to gain wider acceptance, including in academic communities, necessitated an engagement with 'process' and 'development', concepts that had been rejected earlier as part of a more general reaction against notions of social 'progress'.

Within academic circles, the disavowal of notions of social 'progress' was bound up with a widespread but by no means total renunciation of social 'evolutionism', particularly in the fields of anthropology and sociology. This rejection arguably undergirded a shift towards variants of historical and cultural relativism. As Mennell (1998) has observed, a long dominant American school of anthropology whose principal progenitor was Franz Boas had been founded on a critique of theories of social evolution of precisely the type that underpinned such variants of 'scientific racism' as 'eugenics' – ideas which had grown up in the eighteenth and nineteenth centuries and which widely influenced social policy and practice in the USA and Europe, but which are nowadays best remembered as having been mobilised by the German Nazis as a justification for genocide. The Boasian argument for cultural relativism, based on a meticulous and detailed analysis of cultural traits and their (lack of) association with 'racial' differences, thus served as a necessary corrective to Social Darwinist models of social 'evolution' which sought to explain socio-cultural differences between 'primitive' and 'modern' societies in terms of supposed differences in biological, especially biologically inherited mental, endowment (Mennell 1992: 235). What we have called here 'the Boasian' approach, later came to be influential upon the British and French structuralist, including structural-functionalist, schools of anthropology and among social scientists more generally.

While Elias by and large agreed with this rejection of Social Darwinism and, indeed, shared many of Boas's views, he nonetheless sought to retain a notion of 'development' that is neither 'evolutionary', unilinear, nor imbued with ideas of 'progress' in a normative and value-judgemental sense. Elias's view was that, when considered at a 'technical' level, the differences between the biological and social levels of integration demand, respectively, different kinds of process concepts. For example, human societies develop through socio-cultural not biological differentiation and change. As a result, unlike biological evolution, social development is reversible: 'de-development', 'de-differentiation', and 'de-civilisation' are just as possible as 'development', 'differentiation' and 'civilisation' (we are using this last term in its process sense). Moreover, again by contrast with biological evolution, social 'stages' do not follow one another with the same degree or kind of necessity. While it may be possible to establish retrospectively that a set of earlier changes made a later set of changes possible – formed a precondition for them, in other words – there is no 'logic' or 'pattern' to social development in the sense of a series of stages necessarily following one another according to a fixed sequence.

Nor – and we are again in agreement here with Stephen Mennell (1992: 235) – is there any exact equivalent in social development to biological speciation.

There are two distinct aspects to this issue. The first is typological. Thus, as early sociologists such as Durkheim – who used the terms 'species' and 'speciation' in this connection – tried to show, it is possible to classify societies in terms of such properties as their degrees of structural complexity, population sizes, and densities, and so forth (Durkheim *Rules*). The second aspect is biological and crucially involves the fact that humans are biologically a single species, able to communicate knowledge to one another *via* oral and written symbols, thus allowing the direct exchange of knowledge and the indirect exchange of social characteristics between groups at different developmental levels. The point is that, for Elias, the challenge is to work out a concept of development that avoids problems such as process- (or state-) reduction, essentialism, and teleology on the one hand, and epistemic relativism or a view of history as consisting only of constant and unstructured transformation on the other.

The concept of 'development' that Elias sought to construct was one by means of which he tried to approximate at different levels of abstraction the diachronic structure of changes in human societies. Where Elias refers, for example, to the overall 'direction' or 'curve' of a 'civilising process', he is at pains to stress that such terms denote a *balance* between 'trends and counter-trends', 'spurts and counter-spurts', 'shifts and counter-shifts', aggregates of changes that, conceptually speaking, are rendered as regression sequences plotted against time-series data. To talk of an overall 'direction' is thus not to imply a simple arrow-like trajectory. Similarly, to posit a 'curve' – and here again we might think of an undulating graph representing a sequence of rising and falling data – in order to capture and to describe the character of certain long-term social processes is an example of Elias forming a conceptual vocabulary through which he sought to avoid depicting 'development(s)' as sequences that are universally simple, linear and incremental while, at the same time, avoiding a collapse into historical relativism. Indeed, Elias's meticulous commitment to mapping in detail the 'diachronic structures' involved in, say, the long-term development of table manners in Western Europe, has sometimes led to the charge that he was primarily an empirical historical analyst and only secondarily a sociological 'theorist' (van Krieken 1998: 43). And yet, conversely, his use of shorthand summary process descriptors – such as his characterisation of European civilising processes as involving 'diminishing contrasts and increasing varieties' – is sometimes treated as though he was denying the vastly complex sequence of often apparently and sometimes 'really' contradictory changes that Elias painstakingly documented in his study of those self-same processes.

As van Krieken observes, an orientation towards a directional rather than a teleological approach to development can also be found in the work of writers such as Ginsberg (1934) and Ogburn (1922), both of whom Elias cited in *On The Process of Civilisation* (van Krieken 1998: 29). However, van Krieken also suggests that, while Elias's concept of social development avoids teleology and is multi-linear, and while Elias successfully distanced himself from progress theories, there remains a degree of ambiguity regarding whether or not he saw 'civilising processes' as involving changes that amount to an overall 'progress' in certain aspects of human life. On the one hand, van Krieken proposes, Elias often casts the relatively higher levels of human control over non-human nature that tend to accompany 'civilising processes' in a positive light. On the other, as we have seen, Elias suggested that 'civilising processes' could at any time be accompanied by or contribute, independently of the intentions of a majority of the people involved, to decivilising processes. He was also acutely aware of the 'dark side' of civilisation, not least following his experiences in the two World Wars, and perhaps especially on account of the murder of his mother in one of the Nazi gas chambers (van Krieken 1998: 70–71). Van Krieken adds that the chief danger of employing a concept of directionality is that it can be read, albeit incorrectly when viewed against the background of the totality of Elias's work, as a conflation of trends and counter-trends into a single overall 'arrow' of change. This helps in part to explain why Elias's work has sometimes been wrongly charged with 'unilinear evolutionism' (1998: 68). We agree by and large with van Krieken's observations on this subject, but with one main qualification.

As we saw in previous chapters, Elias refused simply to dismiss 'civilisation' as 'the worst form of life and one that is doomed' (Elias 2012a: 8). He was also reluctant to embrace wholesale the growing tide of pessimism about humans and the development of their societies. However, this was part of a more general effort to avoid 'evaluating' in a simple normative sense the phenomena he was studying. He recognised that the 'civilising processes' experienced in the West up to his time of writing had contributed at one level to 'specific civilisational difficulties' by means of which 'we torment ourselves', yet, at another, compared with our medieval ancestors, to a diminished level of 'difficulties and fears' (Elias 2012a: 8). Elias was referring in this latter connection to the higher degrees of control over non-human nature facilitated primarily by the development of the sciences. He recognised clearly that this latter development is an ambivalent, Janus-faced process, with, for example, the growing ability to understand and control atomic fission and atomic fusion entailing both an ability to create bombs with the power to destroy human-kind and to make available abundant cheap energy for constructive and peaceful purposes, whilst again, even in the latter case, involving new kinds of problem – such as those attendant upon the disposal of radioactive waste with its long life spans. However, rather than 'blaming science' for its negative consequences, Elias sought to contribute to the development of 'better', more 'scientific' means of orientation to the social world than have been available up to now. In turn, Elias also understood such means of orientation as being a vital resource for humanity as a whole to draw upon in their attempts to avoid the escalation of destructive inter-state and 'inter-faith' conflicts, together with the more general 'shadows' and 'discontents' that 'civilising processes' and other social developments have tended so far in human history to entail. We understand van Krieken's charge that Elias's attitudes towards the greater human capacity for control of the natural world 'could easily be put in the category of "progress"' (1998: 70) by others. However, this is a judgement that Elias would not himself have made. It was more Elias's endeavour to study people's attitudes towards the 'positive' and 'negative' aspects of science, its triumphs and its failures, whilst avoiding making value-judgements of an overly simple, non-empirically based kind.

This last point raises a number of related concerns. Firstly, what did Elias understand a more scientific 'means of orientation' to the social world to involve? Secondly, to what extent did he subscribe to an ideal of 'science' that could be 'value-neutral' or 'value-free'? Thirdly, in positing the natural sciences as models for the social sciences to emulate – whilst taking due note, following Comte, of the need to take account of the specificity of 'the social', for example, its complex and labile character – in what sense was Elias advocating a variant of 'positivism' and/or 'empiricism'? These are questions, albeit pursued in a different order below, that are worth discussing in detail.

## Knowledge and the sciences

Before commencing a discussion of what Elias understood when referring to a 'more scientific' sociology, it is necessary to consider what he had to say about the concept of 'science' itself. It is also necessary to examine some of his key ideas about the history and philosophy of science. The first thing worthy of note in this connection is the fact that, for Elias, it is highly problematic to talk of 'science' as though the term refers to something monolithic. Indeed, he suggested, a sociological theory of science needs to take centrally into account the diversification of 'the sciences' which has taken place since the late eighteenth/early nineteenth century (1972: 117; Elias 2009a: 67). Elias was critical of a prevailing tendency in philosophical and philosophically-influenced sociological discussions of science to treat the fund of knowledge of a science at any given time as constituting a coherent and self-contained system that is understandable without reference to the processes by which it 'came to be'. More particularly, he was critical of the tendency to divorce systems of knowledge from 'their' development. He was critical, furthermore, of accounts of sciences in which their histories are introduced as a kind of 'backdrop', where such a 'history' serves merely as a brief 'introduction' which recounts a medley of ideas, seemingly without order or structure. For Elias, once again, what we call 'science' has to be understood developmentally, that is as involving structured and directional change. In fact, in this sense it is better from a process-orientated perspective to posit 'science' as *consisting of* 'structured and directional change', rather than as a system of knowledge that somehow happens to be *contextualised* by such developments. Furthermore, Elias suggested, any philosophical, historical or, for that matter, sociological approach to understanding the sciences needs some kind of theory of the 'development'/'growth' and 'loss'/'decay' of scientific knowledge. Indeed, it is not always recognised in this connection that, as we suggested earlier, he wrote of 'knowledge-loss' as well as 'knowledge-gain' (1987a).

It is, of course, impossible meaningfully to generalise in any simple sense about either philosophical accounts of science or historical ones. In fact, Elias found a measure of agreement between his own views and those of developmentally-minded philosophers of science such as Imre Lakatos and theoretically-minded historians of science such as Thomas Kuhn (Elias 1972).[51] In a paper devoted to their contributions, Elias wrote:

> [I]f Kuhn argues – and I would agree with him – that a theory of the history of science has to prove itself and may have to be changed in the light of relevant empirical evidence, Lakatos appears to argue – and again, that is how I see it myself – that the evidence may have to be changed, that it, may have to be selected, connected and interpreted differently in accordance with a different theory of the history or the 'progress' of science. (1972: 121; 2009a: 89–90)

The debate between Kuhn and Lakatos arose in conjunction with a more general problem regarding the development of knowledge, a subject to which Elias devoted considerable attention particularly in his later years. Put simply, it appears to be the case that, for scientific knowledge to advance, general theoretical models need to be revised, refined and sometimes completely transformed in order to make them consistent with new empirical evidence. Sometimes they need to be abandoned altogether. Conversely, it is inevitably the case that empirical evidence will be selected and interpreted in the light of existing theories. How, then, to use Kant's classical formulation, *is science possible*? Or perhaps better, how can the occurrence of 'advances' in scientific knowledge be established? Part of Elias's approach to this problem involves once again reframing it in more processual terms. If we are concerned with exploring the issue of how knowledge 'grows', 'expands', 'advances', 'progresses' or 'regresses', he suggested, it is crucial to realise that it is not so much a question of selecting between (or, indeed, of reconciling) two static logical extremes – such as are suggested, for example, by the terms 'deductivism' and 'inductivism' – as it is of asking questions about the structure of a specific kind of order, more specifically about the connections involved in the sequential order of knowledge development. According to Elias, however, the kind of connectedness involved in such sequences is different from that with which, say, classical physics, the physics of Newton, was concerned. It is an order in which each datum that comprises it '… presupposes an antecedent datum as its necessary (though not necessarily its sufficient) condition and may in turn become a necessary (though not necessarily sufficient) condition for a further stage within that process of growth or development' (Elias 1972: 121; Elias 2009a:90). Thus, for Elias, the endeavour of establishing the criteria of 'progress' or 'regression' in the development of this type of order, of determining the character of the connections in a diachronic succession, is of crucial importance (1972: 121; Elias 2009a:90).

The goal of the sociological theory of any particular science is thus, for Elias, that of shedding light on the 'nexus of the sequential order' involved in the discoveries its practitioners make. Classical historians of science, he suggested, have tended on the whole to neglect any such undertaking. Their focus, instead, has characteristically been upon 'the history of ideas', pursuing questions such as 'who said this first?', 'who stole whose ideas?', 'how did this particular individual achieve that breakthrough?', 'what was his/her reasoning?', 'what individual idiosyncrasies were involved in this discovery?', etc. While such questions have their place, Elias suggested, their importance has been elevated to such an exaggerated extent that the history of science has tended to involve more the history of 'great men', 'scientific pioneers' and 'great inventors', than it has the study of the diachronic structures involved in the sequential development of knowledge within particular sciences. Historical accounts of this individualistic sort tend to rely upon references to relevant documents as the basis for certainty regarding the authenticity of a particular scientist's ideas. But the selection and connection of such, albeit textually authenticated, individualised fragments of the development of knowledge within a scientific field are characteristically left to the imagination of the historian (Elias 1972: 12; Elias 2009a:90). To use Lakatos's term, the 'rational reconstruction' of the order of succession of the particular fragments that comprise an historian of science's narrative of the history of science is somewhat arbitrarily conceived.

Kuhn (1962), of course, made important contributions in breaking from a tradition of historical writing about the sciences which has no 'theory of growth' or 'development'. He did so through examining what he called 'the structure of scientific revolutions'. Expressed simply, what he did was to advance an analysis of the 'internal' and 'external' history of science by recourse to a series of empirical cases. More particularly, he posited a distinction between 'normal science' and 'revolutionary science'. 'Normal science' was held to involve relative stasis and a tendency to rationalise as anomalous or to reject altogether evidence perceived as presenting an 'internal challenge' to the currently dominant paradigm. 'Revolutionary science', by contrast, was held to involve dramatic change and revision of knowledge, challenges to the 'rules and standards of scientific practice', 'paradigm ruptures', 'revolutions', and 'discontinuities'. In putting these ideas forward, Kuhn was, in effect, challenging the 'logical positivist' or 'logical empiricist' tradition in philosophy which posits an overly simple 'development by accumulation' model (Friedman 2003: 19). It is a tradition according to which the growth of scientific knowledge is understood to involve nothing more than the progressive uncovering of 'facts' through systematic observation.

Like Kuhn, Elias was acutely aware that the 'development-by-accumulation' model falls short on account of its neglect of extra-scientific issues. For example, whether or not a scientific hypothesis is regarded as worth testing, or whether or not a given finding is regarded as valid, is often related to the phase in the development of the social group and/or society in which the hypotheses/findings were generated. Similarly, it may have been related to the relations between such groups and societies and their rivals. In a nutshell, extra-scientific contingencies and developments frequently, perhaps even invariably, have an important part to play in the development of a science (Elias 1972: 130; Elias 2009a:96). However, Elias also felt that Kuhn placed rather too much stress on 'ruptures' and 'discontinuities' in his model of 'scientific revolutions', and over-separated 'normal science' from 'revolutionary science'. He suspected that Kuhn's preoccupation with discontinuity and 'spectacular advances' may have betrayed a residue of 'great man', 'history of ideas' thinking in his (Kuhn's) theorising. Put simply, according to Elias we are more likely to find ruptures, breaks and revolutions if our focus is fixed firmly upon the 'great innovators' and the question of distinguishing those thinkers 'who said it first' (the progenitors of scientific revolutions) from those 'who merely continued or elaborated an existing innovation' (the proponents of normal science). If instead, Elias contended, our central engagement is with the development of specific scientific problems and concepts, it is likely that we will find a picture of the balance and blend of historical continuity and discontinuity different from that portrayed by Kuhn.

Kuhn can be understood in this regard as standing in the 'epistemological break' tradition exemplified by Gaston Bachelard according to which:

> irrespective of what one might assume, in the life of a science, problems do not arise by themselves. It is precisely this that marks out a problem as being of the true scientific spirit: all knowledge is in response to a question. If there were no question, there would be no scientific knowledge. Nothing proceeds from itself. Nothing is given. All is constructed. (Bachelard 2002: 117)

As part of the 'pendulum swing' away from the traditional continuist, incremental model of science, the stress in this intellectual lineage is characteristically upon how knowledge does not march onwards somehow independently of 'the knowers' who produce it – 'Nothing proceeds from itself. Nothing is given'. Instead, knowledge is said to be 'constructed', that is, inextricably tied to the values, interests, efforts, abilities and lives of the individuals who generate innovations and, ultimately, paradigm revolutions.

This stress on epistemological rupture can be seen as complementary to the 'great man' model of scientific development. Elias depicted the latter by invoking the metaphor of swimmers who jump into the stream of knowledge at particular times and places, and who are dependent, within the constraints of time and place, on their individual strengths, abilities, decisions, and deeds for being able, within limits, to swim further or faster than others. The history of science, he tells us, is full of 'outstanding swimmers' who are understood to have 'solved' the key scientific problems of their day through their outstanding ingenuity. Like Bachelard before him, even Kuhn understood the theory of relativity to be totally unconnected with the developments in theoretical physics which preceded it (Elias 1972: 133; Elias 2009a:93, n. 13), almost as if the great figure of Einstein effectively cast all others into the shadow. Those whom Kuhn groups together under the banner of 'normal science', who do not quite manage to gain recognition as great innovators and who appear only to continue and perhaps to elaborate a little on an existing paradigm are, as such, denigrated and metaphorically 'thrown to the wolves'. And yet, Elias suggests, such proponents of 'normal science who make less spectacular advances, even though these might be 'overthrown' in the course of dramatic paradigm revolutions, nonetheless form a lineage or line of succession without which no problem could be posed. Indeed, as Bachelard recognised, 'if there were no question, there would be no scientific knowledge'.

It follows that the process that he metaphorically depicted as a 'stream' into which individual scientists 'take the plunge' is better conceived, from Elias's perspective, as an 'intergenerational grouping of knowledge-carriers and knowledge-producers' (Elias 1972: 124; Elias 2009a: 93). The structural conditions experienced by, the resources available to, and the control and direction of any such grouping may be such that, during some phases in its development, its representatives will face problems which none of them, no matter how great their individual abilities, can solve. During other phases, by contrast, the conditions might favour innovation. The 'great men' model of scientific development, in particular the questions of 'who said it first?' and 'who merely continued it?', appear to a degree to have been reproduced in Kuhn's demarcation between 'revolutionary' science and 'normal science'. But on their own, Elias contended, such questions are inadequate as a basis on which to determine and explain 'advances', 'slow-downs' or 'regressions' in the development of scientific knowledge. The 'discontinuity thesis', of which Kuhn can be understood as a proponent, involves the assumption of a relatively stable patterning (inevitably leading to rupture) of the developmental relationship that exists between 'the problems that a scientist seeks to solve with the help of his theoretical innovation and the antecedent developments in his or her neighbouring scientific fields' (1972: 133; Elias 2009a:93, n. 13). In a much more straightforward manner, the 'incremental growth' theory of knowledge development reaches the same kind of assumption, albeit of 'continuity' instead of 'discontinuity'.

For Elias, both assumptions are problematic. It is always necessary, he contended, to investigate the balance between continuity and discontinuity or rupture in knowledge growth. A key related concept is that of 'relative autonomy', used with a dynamic, developmental or processual connotation. For example, it would be wrong, according to Elias, to understand the relationship between innovations and antecedent developments in scientific knowledge as involving simple, direct 'cause-and-effect' diachronic sequences such as the following: *datum or theory 'A' led to 'B' which in turn led to 'C' (as in a simple continuist model)*; or *datum or theory 'C' broke from 'B' which, in turn marked a discontinuation of 'A' (as in a simple discontinuist model)*. Instead, invoking the concept of relative autonomy, the sequential structure might be better expressed as: *datum or theory 'A' was a necessary, but not sufficient, condition for 'B', which, in turn, was a necessary but not sufficient condition for 'C', and so forth*.

The concept of relative autonomy also plays a crucial part in Elias's argument in another sense. It is one which testifies to a degree of agreement between Elias and Lakatos. More particularly, both authors agree that scientific knowledge can come to have a degree of independence, not from individuals *per se* but from *any particular* individual. That is, knowledge can be 'handed on' between knowers and generations of knowers. It is, in Elias's terms, under certain figurational conditions, *communicable*. In this sense, returning to Elias's metaphor, the 'stream of knowledge' can be said to have a degree of independence from the intergenerational groupings of knowers and the individual 'carriers' and 'producers' of knowledge who comprise these groupings. Accordingly, knowledge can be understood as having a (diachronic) 'structure of its own' or, to use Elias's formulation, 'a sequential order to its expansion or decay' (Elias 1972: 124). However, once again the autonomy of knowledge from the groups who produce and exchange it is always relative, never absolute and complete.

The idea of knowledge having relative autonomy in this way avoids the dangers of both epistemic relativism and logical positivism (empiricism). For Elias, it also invites a theoretical-empirical investigation into how the relative autonomy of knowledge varies both historically and between the sciences. How is it, for example, that knowledge in the physical or so-called 'natural' sciences has gained a relatively high degree of autonomy, while that in the social sciences, perhaps particularly in sociology, is relatively low? What problems stem from the relatively high degree of autonomy in some sciences and scientific fields relative to that of others? It is to these and related issues that we shall address ourselves in the remainder of this chapter and in the chapter which follows.

## On sociology as a 'science'

Our last discussion points towards a need to resurrect the question of the degree to which sociology is, or indeed ever can be, 'scientific'. Since the 1960s, in the UK at least, undergraduate students of the discipline have characteristically been trained from their first year onwards to treat with abject suspicion, if not wholesale rejection, the idea that sociology can be a science. This is, perhaps, for what appears to be a good reason. It is abundantly clear that sociology deals with a subject-matter which is in important ways different from that of the 'natural sciences'. Attempts to model sociology on the 'natural sciences' in a 'positivistic' fashion have well documented limitations. Indeed, as we have discussed in earlier sections of this book, even Comte himself, the coiner of the terms 'positivism' and 'sociology', argued against sociologists emulating the models and techniques of the natural sciences too closely, and would have lamented above all the so-called 'positivist' preoccupation with measurement and quantitative methods. Comte's vision of sociology as a science involved, not so much a question of using other sciences as models from which to derive methods and procedures – these he saw as having fundamentally to depend upon the levels of complexity, rates of change, and degrees of human involvement in phenomena at the different emergent levels of reality, and which give rise to the need for different sciences – but rather to promote sociology as the *'queen'* of sciences, a discipline that would play an integrating role for all fields and branches of knowledge. But 'positivism', at least as the term has come subsequently to be understood, by no means represents the only possibility for sociologists to proceed more 'scientifically'. From Elias's perspective, sociology can become *more* 'scientific' in the sense of there emerging a trans-generational community of producers, carriers, and users of sociological knowledge who collectively concern themselves with developing and refining the means of orientation towards human societies. In other words, according to Elias, it is possible for sociology to be 'scientific' in the sense of its proponents concerning themselves, whatever methods they may use, with developing a systematically ordered fund of demonstrable knowledge about the social world.

The legacy of debates stemming from what Rojek and Turner (2000) call the 'decorative turn' in sociology over the last twenty years appears to boil down to a pervasive faith in more or less sophisticated variants of epistemic relativism and a stress upon the importance of recognising the social contingency of knowledge. Against this backdrop, to insist on using the term 'development' or to speak of 'advances' in sociological knowledge is to invite the charge of naïve empiricism and immediately to be seen as aligning oneself with the 'steady incremental' model of knowledge accumulation. Worst of all, it is to be seen as subscribing to a unilinear, evolutionary, 'progress' theory of knowledge development. Again, as discussed earlier in this chapter, it is not difficult to understand the currently prevailing sensitivity towards the notion of an 'advance' in knowledge. Such a term appears to be invoking an Enlightenment assurance that science moves inevitably towards progressively 'superior', intrinsically 'better' forms of knowledge, and that scientific practice involves the discovery of 'truths' which are considered to be progressive approximations to 'reality' and devoid of moral investment or purpose.

Sociologists of science have long since highlighted an inherent paradox in the ideas of Enlightenment social thinkers, remnants of which can be seen in the work of subsequent generations. The paradox is that Enlightenment thinking is invariably shot through with an unspoken moral project which centres on notions of Western superiority and an endemic blind faith in 'progress' which is little different from the religious, metaphysical, and philosophical convictions bound up in the beliefs that science is understood to supplant. But recognition of the social contingency of scientific knowledge, the uncovering of 'hidden' moral visions underpinning Enlightenment thinking and, indeed, the thinking of scientists today, is not, for Elias, an 'end-point' to debates about knowledge and the possibilities for sociology as a science. Rather, it marks a beginning, a point of departure. In rejecting Enlightenment notions of social 'evolution' and 'progress', there has been a tendency, according to Elias, to use one of his favourite metaphors, to 'throw out the developmental baby with the evolutionary bathwater'. A consequence of this almost total rejection of at least this aspect of Enlightenment thinking, Elias argued, has been the effective blockage of access to a means of conceiving problems concerning the sociology of knowledge, and, indeed, key questions concerning the 'human sciences' generally, in a processual and developmental manner. In particular, it has effectively tabooed use of the conceptual tools by means of which sociologists might be able to escape the impasse of conceiving of knowledge as either socially contingent or value-free.

Part of the means by which sociologists might succeed in moving beyond this impasse, Elias suggested, is by reframing the more general problem to which it relates. In the language of epistemology, the dilemma pertains centrally to the split between 'empiricism' and 'rationalism' and related divides such as those between 'objectivity' and 'subjectivity', and 'deductivism' and 'inductivism'. It is typically posed as a kind of conceptual riddle which is ultimately insoluble. According to Elias, however, the problem is better conceived, not as a choice between static, 'logical' alternatives, but as a question which pertains to 'embodied' pluralities of humans 'in the round', and to investigations into *the figurational conditions under which knowledge develops*. A key task in addressing the 'philosophical riddle' alluded to above is that of reconciling the insight that empirical evidence and 'social facts' are not somehow 'given' *a priori* to a researcher – that researchers select evidence more or less consciously and deliberately on the basis of existing theories, understandings, and values (both professional and extra-professional) – with the understanding that scientific knowledge develops through revising existing theories in the light of new evidence, new 'facts'. To this end, Elias introduced as conceptual alternatives the terms 'involvement' and 'detachment'. In addition, he adopted formulations which always involve 'degrees', 'blends' and 'alloys' between the former and the latter and which refer to '... changing equilibria between sets of mental activities which, in human relations with other humans, with objects and with self ... have the function to involve and to detach' (1956: 227; Elias 2007a:69).

We shall discuss the concepts of involvement and detachment further in the next chapter. For the moment, it must be enough to say that, in positing an alternative to the standard dichotomy between 'subjectivity' and 'objectivity', Elias was reaching for a formulation that would facilitate a consideration of the conditions under which *greater* 'value-incursion', or expressed more precisely, the 'autonomous' values of a scientific discipline such as a commitment to understanding the world *as it is* and *as it has developed*, have greater influence than the heteronomous values of the societies to which the scientists involved belong and which instead privilege the world *as we want it to be*, or, indeed, *don't want it to be*. Such terms are designed to bring questions concerning what one might call 'the developmental exigencies' of knowledge to the fore in place of static and idealised conceptions of the relationship between knower and knowledge. Here, Elias was again arguing against a Kantian model of 'objectivity' centred on the idea(l) of a cognitive effort at self-distancing by an isolated, supposedly rational being. In place of this, Elias wanted to contribute to the development of a psychoanalytical and sociological conception of *detachment* based on a recognition of both the configurations of psychic structures that facilitate an optimal balance between involvement and detachment, and the relationship of these structures to the social arrangements – the figurational conditions – that make potentially more constructive balances of involvement and detachment possible. In short, Elias wanted to explore, not just the social contingency of knowledge but also the *different ways* in which knowledge is tied dynamically to different and differentially emergent human psyches and figurations.

According to Elias, it is a main task of sociologists to develop knowledge which will hopefully be of greater potential than, say, many of the ideology-driven beliefs which have tended to govern politics and everyday social life so far. He had a whole repertoire of formulations with which to describe such knowledge. More particularly, he spoke of: adding to the 'social fund of more reality-congruent knowledge'; the development of theories with greater 'object-adequacy'; advances in 'the means of orientation' towards human figurations; knowledge with 'greater cognitive value'; and so forth. He also spoke of knowledge-gathering and developing as a psycho-social process in which, for example, highly involved individuals might add to what they know experientially about, say, smoking or playing football, by undertaking a 'detour *via* detachment' – a concept we have touched upon in earlier sections of this book. In this, they 'distanciate' themselves from their objects of study in an attempt to construct as accurate a picture of these as possible. And then, deploying the potentially more 'reality-congruent' or 'object-adequate' understandings thus obtained in a process of 'secondary involvement', they seek, to continue with the examples employed above, to help people to stop smoking, to improve their understanding of sport dynamics, and so forth. As such, Elias posited a kind of diachronic structure as inherent to the 'detour', one involving a *blend* of, first, the insights derived from having an experiential 'involvement' in that which is studied; then, following on, greater 'detachment' whereby such insights are complemented by viewing the same topic, as it were, from a 'distance'; and finally, 'secondary involvement' where the combined insights of involved and especially detached knowledge might facilitate social interventions which have more intended relative to unintended consequences than has typically been the case than those based solely on highly involved knowledge.

## 'Reality congruence'

Critics of Elias have suggested that, while his position regarding knowledge may involve a different terminology, it does not so much resolve classical epistemological dilemmas as side-step them. For example, Derek Layder (1990) has argued that adopting concepts such as 'involvement', 'detachment' and 'reality-congruence' as alternatives to 'subjectivity', 'objectivity' and 'truth' fails to remove the key problem of how to distinguish between knowledge-claims. As Layder put it: 'To talk of something as being "more true'" or "more false" no more resolves the problem of what constitutes the moment at which something becomes true rather than false, that is, how someone classifies something as false rather than true and *vice versa*' (Layder 1990: 44). Leaving aside for the moment his reduction of Elias's concepts to the static binaries of 'true' and 'false', Layder's formulation of the issue is in many ways reminiscent of Popper's in *The Logic of Scientific Discovery* (1959). It is a formulation in which a person conceived as standing apart from the stream of knowledge is envisaged as arbitrating between the falsity and truth of knowledge-claims according to an 'external' and *a priori* 'logic'. Indeed, Layder's dependence on Popperian thinking is explicit: in developing his critique of Elias's position, he invokes Popper's distinction between 'naïve' and 'sophisticated empiricism'. Like other sophisticated empiricists, Layder proposes, Elias distances himself from a 'naïve empiricist' position by recognising that observations of the world are not made in a vacuum but are, in fact, theory-laden. However, he (Layder) suggests that, again like other sophisticated empiricists, Elias provides no criteria of validity with which to distinguish scientific from non-scientific statements (1990: 44).

It would be misleading for us to suggest that, in his work on knowledge and the sciences, Elias somehow forgot to discuss the issue of criteria of validity or, perhaps better, the 'standards' by which to determine 'advances' in knowledge according to their degrees of reality-congruence. It is rather the case that he rejected this mode of formulating the problem precisely because it is premised upon a rather unrealistic, somewhat static and imaginary cognitive process, not a developmental and fully 'social' one. The idea of an authority figure measuring 'truth' claims against timeless and universal standards of 'validity' is, it seems to us, an enduring myth that is by no means confined to imagery in the work of writers such as Layder and Popper. It can be seen, for example, in the pervasive tendency in Western sociology to assess the worth of a piece of research against standards of methodological procedure or rigour – a tendency towards the fetishisation of methodology as the principal means by which to gauge the adequacy of any particular claimed contribution to knowledge. But the idea that the degree of correspondence between 'knowledge of the world' and the 'world itself' might thus be somehow 'settled' or 'determined' in an absolute and final sense, and at that, through a process of cognitive arbitration is, at best, rather unrealistic. Indeed, the very depiction of the process by which knowledge develops as involving a solitary individual selecting between logical oppositions such as 'true' or 'false', 'valid' or 'invalid', is, according to Elias, highly problematic regarding concrete social processes. Terms like 'true' and 'false' may well have considerable utility in the resolution of problems that pertain, say, to the prescribed order of a logical system such as many of those relating to a predominantly deductive science like mathematics. However, these terms have considerably less adequacy for the problem of determining advances in means of orientation towards the social world – an undertaking central to Elias's model of sociology. As Elias wrote in critique of Popper:

> [T]he term 'scientific discovery' used in the title of his book is slightly misleading. Scientific discoveries on the theoretical level are not really Popper's concern. He is concerned with the logical consistency and coherence of the series of statements which follow from the theoretical postulates or axioms. These themselves are apparently arbitrarily chosen by the individual scientist. How and why, according to Popper, is not a question into which a theory of science needs to go. Yet, in fact, the relationship between the theories and experiments of different scientists, the way in which they influence, learn and struggle with each other, in short, the relationship between the hypotheses and theories of a particular scientist and both the preceding development of his [sic] field and the current scientific situation in it, is of supreme importance for the understanding of the former. Quite arbitrarily, Popper's thinking and argument stop at the point where the individual forms an hypothesis. (Elias 2009c: 165–66)

Elias's critique of Popper, and by extension, of the more general and pervasive mode of posing the problem of developments in scientific knowledge that underpins Popper's formulation, thus amounts to considerably more than a question of terminological differences. Rather than shirking or 'side-stepping' the problems posed by Popper and Layder, Elias poses instead alternative modes of conceptualising them. As can be seen from the above quotation where Popper characteristically framed such issues more in terms of ideal situations of how a science *ought* to proceed, Elias (and in this sense what he wrote was positioned firmly within the 'sociology of knowledge' tradition) was concerned with the problem of how inter-generational pluralities of scientists *actually* proceed and, more specifically, with questions relating to the psychic and social conditions under which advances and regressions of knowledge occur.[52] This is an important point. While Elias's formulation might well have 'epistemological' implications and is likely to be seen as such by philosophers and sociologists with philosophical leanings, much of his sociological reorientation is lost in the translation of his concepts into their perceived philosophical equivalents. In Layder's formulation, Elias's concepts are rendered as banal neologisms which translate to 'degrees of truth' as if he (Elias) were referring to 'degrees of pregnancy'. While, to continue with the comparison, it might well make sense to think of 'pregnancy' as a process involving varying degrees, it, and by comparison, the concept of 'truth', steer our thinking towards 'states' and 'essences' and away from arguably more realistic ways of conceiving developments in social scientific knowledge – ultimately, a female is *either* pregnant *or* she is not. 'Truth' is similarly an 'either-or' concept which serves to steer thinking inevitably towards 'finalities', 'states' and 'essences' and away from arguably more realistic ways of conceiving developments in knowledge.

Elias's usage of the term 'reality congruence' implies a 'process', not a state. It is a 'flow' term not an 'essence' term, one which refers to varying degrees of approximation, of agreement, between the dynamism of scientific knowledge and the dynamism of the social reality of which that knowledge forms part. We realise, of course – as did Elias – that use of the terms 'reality' and 'congruence' in this connection is liable under present conditions to arouse suspicion. But Elias did not think of 'reality' as something fixed, monolithic and ultimately 'fully knowable'. He did not see it as a 'thing out there', but rather as a dynamic totality which includes humans and their expanding (and sometimes contracting) knowledge as an integral part. It follows that, in Elias's view, knowledge can never be 'absolute', never 'finished' or 'final' as is implied by a static concept like 'truth'. It is worth observing that, as an alternative, a term such as 'value-congruence', and indeed, the sociological investigation into how scientific knowledge is, to varying degrees, consistent with extra-scientific values is, in the current sociological climate, considerably less controversial. It is perhaps useful, then, to qualify Elias's usage of the term 'reality-congruence'. In using it, he was also inevitably implying a consideration of 'value-congruence': the key question is which values (note, not simply 'whose' values – as in a 'history of ideas' model of science)? Put simply, Elias's stance on knowledge suggests that a consideration of 'value-congruence' without a consideration of 'reality congruence', as in a solely relativist position, is as problematic as a consideration of 'reality congruence' without 'value congruence' as in a naïve empiricist stance.

When considered developmentally, we might thus understand an 'advance' in a given field or specialism as involving a phase in its overall development in which the knowledge produced is more consistent with the 'autonomous' values of its scientific community – such as, once again, understanding 'the social world as it is' – relative to the 'heteronomous' values of a wider society – such as those which tend towards portraying 'the social world as we want it to be or don't want it to be'. Of course, not all sciences conform to this somewhat idealised contrast between 'autonomous' and 'heteronomous' evaluations. At the current stage of its development, sociology is a case in point.

It was Elias's firm conviction that, for sociological knowledge to 'advance' in any sense, one of the central pre-requisites is the gradual establishment of an inter-generational, international community of scholars committed to a set of values which centre on the enterprise of developing a more reliable fund of knowledge about humans and the societies we form than has been achievable thus far. The problem of reality congruence pertains, in this respect, to the extent to which such a community will be able to establish higher degrees of certainty over time. More particularly, it is a question of whether any particular models, 'claims' concerning the structure, 'direction', or even enduring characteristics of social processes, have lasting utility, 'fit', demonstrability within the course of subsequent research-theorisation. Such a process is by no means inevitable, and, particularly at the current stage of the development of sociology as a discipline, is unlikely to be characterised by a steady, incremental, linear development towards an expanding and more reliable fund of knowledge. We shall add to and elaborate on this discussion in Chapter 5.

# 5

# Problems of Method and Values in the Development of Sociological Knowledge

Thus far we have described Elias's work as constituting a radically processual, relational and synthesis-orientated approach to sociology. We have argued that this engagement with relationships, processes and syntheses extends equally to Elias's treatment of problems relating to method and the role of values in the development of sociological knowledge. In this chapter, we shall consider – to use terms which he fundamentally rejected – Elias's 'epistemological', 'ontological', and 'methodological' position, and explore his reframing of the sociological lexicon as part of an attempt to facilitate a reorientation of problems that have historically been the chief concerns of the philosophy of the social sciences and that he saw as belonging to the sociology of knowledge.

## Involvement and detachment and the problem of 'values'

As we argued in the previous chapter, it was one of Elias's key contentions that sociological research and theory, the conjoined, indivisible and equally necessary basic components of the subject, are hindered rather than helped by thinking in terms of such simple dichotomies as 'value-bias' and 'value-neutrality', or their equivalents such as 'subjectivity' and 'objectivity', 'irrationality' and 'rationality'. It is better, he maintained, more in tune with and appropriate for understanding the complex and dynamic, that is, processual and relational character of humans and the societies they form, to think in terms of fluid and complex balances in which emotional as well as rational aspects of human behaviour and life together are taken into account. Elias subscribed neither to a view of scientific knowledge as completely 'value-free', nor to the notion that the social contingency of knowledge renders all accounts of the social world equally 'valid' as in the case of a crude epistemic relativism. The key for Elias was to consider, and in small part contribute towards, conditions under which an inter-generational community of social scientists might develop more adequate understandings of the world, and, indeed, develop a more secure *basis* for their value-judgements (Elias and Dunning 1986: 144; Elias 2008: 125) than they have managed so far. That is, Elias's aim was to provide a basis for constructing more autonomous sociological values that are 'sounder' than those currently available. For Elias, they would be 'sounder' to the degree that they would facilitate the foundation of a collective orientation towards developing more reliable knowledge in relation to the sphere of human figurations. Ultimately, such values would be sounder to the degree that they would possess the potential to make life more meaningful and enjoyable than it has tended to be up to now for large numbers of people, as well as helping humanity as a whole to adjust successfully to such threats as nuclear war and 'global warming'.

It is useful to compare Elias's position on these issues, firstly, with that of the original members of the 'Frankfurt School' – 'critical theorists' such as Adorno and Horkheimer – with whom, as we have seen, Elias was personally acquainted, and, secondly, with some of the key arguments put forward more recently by proponents of a 'cultural studies' approach and adherents to some of the principal variants of poststructuralist theorising.

The position of critical theorists on questions of involvement and detachment was cogently summed up by Robert Bocock in 1983. He wrote:

> Epistemologically critical theory stresses the importance of sociology and social theory being critical of scientism in the realm of methodology. Scientism means here the uncritical attempt to copy the methods of the natural sciences in doing social science. Critical theory tried to retain links between social philosophy and ethics, rather than severing them in order to make sociology seem more like a natural science – something which it is in principle impossible to do anyway as far as this epistemological position is concerned. The social world is *appraised* in the very language used to describe, analyse, explain and understand it. Neutral scientific sounding language does not avoid such an appraisal: it merely suggests that there is nothing in that which it is analysing to get worked up about either politically or morally. Critical theory developed its epistemology under the shadow of the Nazi regime, and it has always held that liberal, well-intentioned 'value-neutrality' in the social sciences aided the rise of Nazism by appearing to students and others to be unable to offer any political values worth caring for, thus providing a gap which fascism filled. (Bocock 2002: 22)

As we noted earlier, Elias was one of Karl Mannheim's assistants – we would perhaps say in English 'teaching assistants' – in the Sociology Department at the University of Frankfurt from 1929 to 1932, a time which coincided with the early days of Max Horkheimer and Theodor Adorno's privately funded Institute for Social Research, the institutional setting of 'the Frankfurt School'. In fact, the University rented rooms for the Sociology Department in the Institute. The building, which they jointly occupied, came to be known by students and teachers at the University as 'the Marxburg' on account of the communist affiliations of many of the Institute's staff. As we saw earlier, Elias related to Dunning and others in the early 1960s more than once how, at considerable personal risk, he (Elias) had been instrumental in helping Adorno to escape the Nazis.

We have mentioned this incident again in order to make it crystal clear that Elias, too, and not only the 'Frankfurt School', developed aspects of his 'epistemology' – as his distance from philosophical modes of thinking increased, he came to prefer to refer to it simply as a 'theory of knowledge' – under the shadow of the Nazis. Yet despite his contacts with members of the Frankfurt School, familiarity with their writings, and exposure to many of the self-same dangers, Elias came to different conclusions regarding issues of involvement, detachment, methods and 'methodology'. He shared Adorno and his colleagues' opposition to 'scientism' – the inappropriate attempt to use natural science methods in social science research. But, as we suggested earlier, he did not share their largely uncritical embrace of an unreformed 'Kantian' or 'neo-Kantian' philosophy and the idea that there can be *a* 'methodology', that is, literally a science of method that is equally applicable to the physical, chemical, biological, psychological and social realms. What he insisted on, instead, was that sociology can, indeed must, be made *more* scientific than it is at present but that, for that to happen, its practitioners will have to develop methods, concepts and theories appropriate to the complex and dynamic character of its subject matter and the fact that it is comprised of thinking, feeling humans, each endowed with a capacity to act and, except in marginal circumstances, make choices. For Elias's preferences to become a reality, however, it is not just a question of creating methods, concepts and theories, but of institutionalising autonomous evaluations strongly enough to prevent the intrusion of heteronomous evaluations. This is not easy for at least two reasons: firstly because social processes continually generate involved thinking; and secondly because the institutional boundaries surrounding sociology have remained porous up to now.

Except in his 'Adorno Prize' speech in 1977 (Elias 2009b: 82–92), Elias never criticised the work of the 'Frankfurt School' at length. He did, however, part company with them over what he regarded as their non-dynamic/non-developmental, that is, non-processual view of language and values. He did not seek to deny that the language employed by the practitioners of some forms of social science, for example, those which Mills (1959) dismissed with the label 'abstract empiricism', while making claims to be 'neutral' and merely 'descriptive', can nevertheless mask a concealed, perhaps even unconscious 'appraisal' of the social world. Elias contended, however, that 'appraisal' – making 'value-judgements' – is not a simple 'either-or' matter, a dichotomy, but yet again a question of nuances and degrees of 'scientificity' or, to put the same thing the other way around, a question of *types* and *degrees* of subject-orientation or *types* and *degrees* of 'value-bias'. In short, Elias felt it to be a much more complex and fluid issue than is usually assumed. More particularly, there are different *kinds* of 'values', or 'evaluations' in Elias's terminology.

Ideologies, or 'belief systems' to give them a more neutral-sounding name, differ in their degrees of reality-congruence, too. For example, the secular ideologies of the modern world – 'conservatism', 'socialism', 'liberalism', 'humanism', 'agnosticism', 'atheism', etc. – are all relatively more congruent with observable 'reality' than were the 'magical-mythical', 'other-worldly', mainly religious belief systems of former times (Elias 2012b). That is because the secular ideologies of today contain more empirically ascertainable elements than do (or did) magical-mythical beliefs because the latter are fundamentally concerned with human constructs such as 'God' or 'the gods' which are not empirically observable in anything other than their human manifestations. Secular ideologies, by contrast, contain a greater number of empirically testable components. To say this is not to suggest that religions of various kinds are entirely lacking in reality-congruence. If that were the case, they would probably have low survival-value for their adherents. However, it is known, as archaeologists such as V. Gordon Childe (1928: 36), on whom Elias partly depended, have shown, that the priests in Ancient Egypt, although they believed the Nile was a deity, observed it closely and became able to predict the time of its annual flood. They used this knowledge to control the subject population of peasant-farmers because the latter who depended on the flooding for growing their crops, believed the priesthood were able through their prayers and invocations to persuade the 'river god' to flood and this became a major source of priestly power. Similarly, an important part of Comte's 'law of the three stages' held that the fetishism-polytheism-monotheism sequence occurred as a consequence of advancing knowledge and that the belief in a single, all-powerful 'God' was an early stage in the realisation that there are universal and observable 'natural laws' such as Newton's 'inverse square law', popularly known as the 'law of gravity' (Comte in S. Andreski (*ed.*) (1974)). It is important, finally, in this connection, to point out that, although modern science fundamentally developed in the first instance in post-Reformation, post-Renaissance Europe, important contributions had been made in the Middle East, the Arab world, and China at a time when Europe was mired in the 'Dark Ages'. Indeed, the much celebrated fourteenth century Islamic scholar, Ibn Khaldun, was a polymath who is credited, variously, with being a forerunner if not a progenitor of many 'modern' social science disciplines, among them sociology and economics (see, for example, Gates (1967); Alatas (2006); Khaldun (1958)).

According to Elias (Elias 2007a: 32), 'the capacity for detachment is a human universal'. We *all* possess it in some degree or another. It is a constitutive feature of the species *Homo sapiens*. Take, for example, such ostensibly simple activities as the earliest, stone-age humans making tools or weapons. We have chosen this example because it is easier to understand than would be the case if we started by referring to the present-day West where this universal capacity has to some extent become masked by a complex division of labour, a high level of material affluence, and a high degree of routinisation, mechanisation and automation. As Elias put it, in order to undertake such tasks as making tools or weapons, the earliest humans had to learn 'to detach themselves to some extent from their immediate internal or external situation'. They had to learn to be able not to act immediately in response to hunger pangs, sexual urges, fears of wild animals, threats from other humans and dangers in the physical environment. In other words, making artefacts such as tools and weapons is not a direct means of sating hunger or dealing with an environmental threat. It involves 'the capacity for distancing oneself from the situation of the moment, for remembering a past and ... anticipating a possible future situation where the work of one's hands ... might be of use' (Elias 2007a: 32). These operations, said Elias, 'are essentials of the variety of self-regulation described as detachment' (Elias 2007a: 32). In other words, a greater or lesser capacity for detaching oneself cognitively (rationally) and affectively (emotionally) from a given situation or bodily state is a property of all human beings, part of the condition of being human. It is *not* just a property of scientists in their research.

This universal human capacity for detachment is dependent in part on the biological constitution of the species, above all on the directing, coordinating, problem-solving functions performed by the cerebral cortex and the fact that this organ is generally dominant over the lower parts of the brain.[53] It is also dependent on the related fact that the cortex, which at the start of life is virtually a *tabula rasa*, a 'blank slate', crucially depends on learning from experience, especially from what Elias called humanity's 'social funds of knowledge' (Elias 2007a) which are stored, not only in the brains of individuals but extra-corporeally in libraries and, increasingly nowadays, digital information retrieval systems. However, according to Elias, detachment is necessarily always blended with involvement. He expressed this form of psychic interdependence thus:

> One cannot say of a person's outlook in any absolute sense that it is detached or involved (or if one prefers, 'irrational', 'objective' or 'subjective'). Only small babies, and among adults perhaps only insane people, become involved in what they experience with complete abandon to their feelings here and now; and again only the insane can remain completely unmoved by what goes on around them. (Elias 2007a: 68)

We think that Elias would have agreed that the only 'completely detached' human beings are dead ones. In *all* human societies, adult behaviour normally lies between the two extremes and shifts to and fro between one and the other during the day, from day to day, season to season, and at different stages in the life-course. As Mennell (1998: 160) observes, Elias's 'emphasis on this point is in clear contrast to Parsons's notion that the distinction between *affectivity* and *affective-neutrality* ... is a clear-cut, dichotomous, mutually exclusive choice between opposites'. In other words, for Elias yet again, it is a question of continua, of overlapping and shifting balances or degrees.

Crucial in this regard is the degree to which a society's fund of knowledge is understood primarily in 'magical-mythical' terms or in terms that are more 'scientific'. The concept of 'magical-mythical' thinking refers to thinking in terms of anthropocentric, that is, human-centred, and anthropomorphically conceived 'demons', 'spirits', deities' or 'gods' which are believed to have a super-powerful, essentially human form, or at least the capacity to take one on. The concept of 'scientific' thinking refers to thinking that can be shown empirically and theoretically to be *more* congruent with 'reality' than its magical-mythical antecedents. An example would be the shift from thinking of the sun as a 'god' as opposed to a gaseous body that generates heat and light. Another would be the shift towards thinking of our solar system in 'heliocentric', that is, sun-centred, as opposed to 'geocentric' or earth-centred terms, together with the realisation that our solar system is but one small part of a galaxy, the 'Milky Way' which, in turn, is but one among billions of observable galaxies. A sociological example might be the shift from Hegelian thinking in terms of spirits and ideas, for example, the idea that 'democracy' is part of the contemporary *Zeitgeist* or 'spirit of the times', to Marxian materialistic thinking which directs researchers to deeper, more determining aspects of the social world. Indeed, it is arguable that a shift from Marxian thinking in law-like, monocausal terms to Elias's stress on the need for 'structure-and-process models' like the theory of 'civilising' processes serves as another sociological example.

It is worth stressing yet again that this is a question of balances and degrees. Even the funds of knowledge of the scientifically most 'advanced' societies that have existed so far – 'advanced' in the sense of having knowledge such as of the working of electricity or nuclear fission and fusion which permit these forces to be recurrently put to constructive or destructive human use – contain layers or residues of magical-mythical thinking. Similarly, many, even of the most famous scientists, have continued to adhere to religious ideas. Some two-thirds of Newton's published work, for example, dealt with theological issues and Einstein, when he first encountered quantum physics, is famously reputed to have said: 'God didn't play dice with the universe'! It is worth adding, however, that Einstein is also known as having said that 'The word God is for me nothing more than the expression and product of human weaknesses'. His key point, however, concerned the observable regularities in this connection which pointed to relativities rather than metaphysical laws.

Parallel to the idea that there remain traces of magical-mythical thinking in even the scientifically most 'advanced' societies is Elias's contention that the members of no human society, no matter how 'simple' in material terms and no matter how 'knowledge-poor' relative to the 'scientific-industrial' nation-states of the modern West, could ever have survived without a measure of reality-congruent knowledge about themselves and their immediate socio-geographical environments. Indeed, as we have seen, extreme forms of magical-mythical thinking have been gaining prominence in recent years, not only in Middle Eastern and Eastern contexts with the shift to Moslem extremism but in the West as well with the rise of forms of Christian fundamentalism and beliefs in 'creationism'. Coupled with this is the fact that the members of 'tribal' societies had or have funds of orally transmitted knowledge about, for example, local flora and fauna the counterparts of which have been lost by people in the West or which are perhaps stored in libraries and known only to a few specialists. However, notwithstanding provisos such as these, it remains the case that, throughout most of humanity's existence, magical-mythical thinking has predominated, and the level of reliable knowledge remained correspondingly low. That is, people were trapped in a 'vicious circle' or what Elias, following Bateson et al. (2000 (1956)), called a 'double-bind'. Although, as Comte recognised, the people thus caught were unable to prevent the slow, long-term development of understanding which contributed in important ways to the transition through the stages of the fetishism-polytheism-monotheism and the theology-metaphysics-positivism sequences, magical-mythical thinking was not, in general, conducive to amassing reality-congruent knowledge, and the lack of reality-congruent knowledge kept people's ability to exercise control low. As a result, the dangers to which they were subject and their corresponding fears remained high and their levels of fear kept them locked into magical-mythical thinking, for example, in praying to their 'God' or 'gods' asking for deliverance from individual and collectively experienced traumas such as plagues, pestilence, drought and attack by outside groups. This gave them emotional comfort, but failed to help them in a practical sense. (See Elias's 'The Fishermen in the Maelstrom' 2007a: 105–178.)

According to Elias, there have so far been two main breakthroughs from the double-bind trap experienced in this connection. The first occurred in the Ancient World and involved a limited flowering of science as expressed, for example, in the geometrical and other discoveries of the Greeks. Subsequently, as Elias colourfully and mischievously expressed it at a conference held at Balliol College, Oxford, in 1980, this flowering 'drowned in a sea of Christianity'. He was, of course, aware that much of the Greek legacy was preserved in monasteries. The second breakthrough began in Renaissance Europe and proved considerably more substantial and enduring. It is a process in which we are still caught up today, though in a similar manner, it, too, is under threat from the revival of the forms of extremism found in the Christian and Moslem worlds to which we referred earlier.

Implicit in our arguments so far in this chapter is the fact that Elias's position on questions of scientific method is bound up with a theory of the development of knowledge. This theory is based partly on the observation that, over the millennia, but with quickening pace since the Renaissance, people have succeeded in building-up larger funds of more reality-congruent knowledge. They have been able, as Elias put it, to construct 'small islands of certainty in the vast oceans of their ignorance' (Elias 2009c) and these, in turn, have enabled them to exercise a greater degree of environmental control. However, these developments have occurred faster with respect to physical, chemical and biological processes than regarding humans and the societies they form. In Elias's words once more:

> Over the millennia, human groups, with the help of the growing social fund of their knowledge, have been busily building into the undiscovered and uncontrollable universe a widening safety area for themselves – an area of known connections which they can more or less control. As a result, people are now able in certain areas to steer their way through the flow of blind and unmanageable processes better than their forebears – at least at the physical levels, if less so at the human levels, just as people aboard ships steer their way through the unmanageable waters of the ocean or, in spaceships, through the uncontrollable processes of the sun-system. In that way, by expanding their control within the uncontrollable flow of events, humans, in the more advanced societies, have managed to provide themselves with a larger protective shell designed, as far as possible, to keep out the dangers that emanate from the non-human levels of the overall process. They have not yet managed to develop an equally comprehensive and realistic fund of knowledge at the human or social levels. Hence, they are not yet able to bring under control the dangers that human beings constitute for each other and themselves. (Elias 2007a: 115–16)

Dutch sociologist Johan Goudsblom (2002) named this area where humans have established an ability to exercise relatively high degrees of control 'the anthroposphere', after the Greek word, 'anthropos', meaning in the general, non-gender-specific sense, 'man'. It is important to add a rider here about Elias's use of language, more particularly about his use of the adjectival phrase 'more or less control'. It is a verbal device he used frequently. It strikes many people as sloppy and imprecise. However, in Elias's usage it is rather an acknowledgement of the belief that, at the present stage of knowledge, it is impossible accurately to quantify many phenomena, in this case the degree of human control over some area of 'nature'. It is thus more precise than the scientistic or pseudo-scientific attempts of some sociologists to claim that they have available to themselves, forms of mathematics capable of being accurately applied to phenomena in the complex, fluid human social world (see Goldthorpe 2000).

One of the central hypotheses advanced by Elias in relation to this general area is that the growth of knowledge since the Renaissance has been, in part, a consequence of and in part contributory to a 'civilising spurt', a speeding-up in the 'civilising' process which began around that time. As we saw earlier, he had in mind in this respect such discoveries as Copernicus's demonstration that the earth revolves around the sun rather than *vice versa*. We could add Newton's discovery of the 'inverse-square law' and Harvey's discovery of the circulation of blood in this vein (if readers will excuse the pun). Putting it differently, Elias suggested that one of the preconditions for the growth of modern science has been an increase within specific but later widening groups, first of all inside but later on outside Europe as well, in the socially instilled capacity of their members to exercise self-distanciation and self-restraint. This is revealed, for example, in the shift from the Ptolemaic to the Copernican or Galilean view of the solar system. The Ptolemaic view was anthropocentric and geocentric, and appealed to human self-love in thus regarding humans and their earth as being at the centre of all things. It was also based on immediate appearances rather than scientific, observationally based fact because the sun does *appear*, like the moon which really does, to revolve round the earth. The Copernican, or Galilean, view, by contrast, is based on detailed and systematic in-depth observation – which was aided by the invention of the telescope in Galileo's case – and required its advocates to distance themselves from the comforting view that our planet stands at the centre of all things and was created for the benefit of its human inhabitants by their anthropomorphic construct, 'God'.

However, by consolidating the experience of the self as a *homo clausus*, Elias argues, the self-same process which facilitated the growth of the natural sciences acted as a blockage to the emergence of their social counterparts, contributing to the later, slower, lesser and more contested growth of the latter inside and outside academic circles. Added to this, in sociology in particular, have been the paradigm wars we discussed in our Introduction. At the same time, according to Elias (1956; 2007a), the growth of the natural sciences has contributed to an exacerbation of social problems such as war, for example, by increasing the destructiveness of weapons and the ranges over which they can be used. In the course of the twentieth century, weapons were developed with the capacity to destroy humanity and perhaps even life on earth in its entirety, all of which prompted Elias to advocate the need for more adequate understanding of the sociogenesis and psychogenesis of wars.

Elias was realistic but not entirely pessimistic in this regard. For example, he recognised that the social sciences, including sociology, *have* grown to *some* degree and saw himself as having made a small but hopefully significant contribution which, he hoped, would come to be recognised and built upon by future generations. More particularly, he saw himself as having contributed to the development of a post-classical, post-functionalist, scientific-humanist form of sociology which came to be called 'figurational' and later 'process sociology'.

Towards the end of his life in discussions with friends, Elias added 'global warming' and other present day 'ecological crises' to the problems he saw as having been at least partly caused by the application of findings from the natural sciences and which, in his view, increase the need for advances in the sociological, psychological, and related fields to deal with them. That is because they are partly based on such social roots as individualisation and status- and achievement-striving which are fuelling human dependency on cars, and other consumer goods, especially in the West. However, just as important, if not more so, it is because they will almost certainly require for their solution changes in human behaviour and social structure on a substantial if not massive scale. It is also easy to see that, if the social and environmental roots of global warming are not effectively tackled, resultant problems such as land and water shortage could easily contribute to the causing of wars. These in turn could contribute to the further uncontrollable consumption of oil, in that way representing a threat to the success of attempts to curb carbon emissions and hence global warming, and so forth in a compelling and possibly long-lasting and destructive double-bind trap. These wars might 'go' nuclear, and the combination of nuclear war and global warming could lead to destruction and impoverishment on a massive scale, if not to the wiping out of humanity in its entirety and perhaps even of life on earth.

It was not only the slow crystallisation of sociology and related subjects such as anthropology, politics and economics as fledgling sciences that led Elias to suggest that people, especially in the more 'advanced' societies, are gradually coming to adopt a more detached view of themselves. He contended, as we noted earlier, that the emergence of such a view is also to some degree inherent in the secular political ideologies of our age that had no real counterparts in the Middle Ages and emerged in conjunction with what has widely come to be called 'modernisation'. That is the case because these ideologies, notwithstanding the fact that there are religious political parties in some European countries, tend to be secular rather than religious in character and hence devoid to a greater or lesser degree of anthropomorphic concepts such as 'spirits', 'gods' and 'demons'. It is also inherent in the fact that the more secular ideologies of today contain at their roots beliefs such as the systemic idea of 'society' and ideas in terms of which it is believed that 'societies' can be made 'fairer', 'more affluent' or 'more efficient' through the implementation of policies by 'the state'. That said, however, present-day ideologies, whether of the left, centre or right, continue to contain 'voluntaristic' ideas such as that it is possible on the basis of currently available knowledge to 'engineer utopias', that is to mould societies according to fantasies, wishes and dreams.

According to Elias, however, voluntaristic thinking about human relations is in many ways akin to magical-mythical thinking. If you want something strongly enough, that is the gist of it, it will be possible to achieve it in the 'real' world. Beliefs of this kind, he suggests, may provide a degree of comfort, emotional warmth and satisfaction in what is for many people a cold, impersonal, rapidly changing, complex and puzzling social world, especially if the beliefs are shared with others and involve the group performance of apparently meaningful rituals. However, experience up to now suggests that, when translated into action, ideology-driven policies lead as often as not to a higher degree of unanticipated and undesirable consequences relative to those that are intended. It was for such reasons that Elias regarded it as vital for sociologists to strive for greater autonomy in relation to political, religious and other movements and ideologies. Even though they represent a development towards greater detachment in certain respects, present-day belief systems of a predominantly ideological kind continue to place items of blind and insufficiently examined faith at the forefront of the agenda. Examples are the idea that public ownership of the means of production will lead, *ipso facto*, to greater equality, that the maximisation of individual wealth is a certain route to happiness and fulfilment, or that unregulated markets generate the greatest wealth for all. At the risk of over-repetition, in Elias's view, by contrast, a greater current need is for a larger fund of more reality-congruent knowledge than is available today about ourselves and the societies we form, that is for knowledge that will increase our capacity to control social processes and events and to avoid the age-old problems associated with what Merton (1936) famously called 'the unintended consequences of intended social actions'.

Elias never ceased to talk and write about how rudimentary our sociological knowledge is at the current stage of the subject's development and that included his own contributions. He never pretended that he 'had all the answers': only that he had some ideas about how to 'set the ball rolling' in the direction of knowledge-growth. While Elias never explicitly said so, it would, we think, be consistent with his assessment of the present level of sociology's development to say that, if Marx's work constituted one symptom of a beginning, his own constitutes another. However, because he was able to build on the foundations laid by Marx – and others such as Comte, Weber, Mannheim, Simmel and Freud – Elias's work may be in some senses more advanced. It is a symptom of a beginning nevertheless. All sociologists are workers in a fledgling science. Elias never claimed that any of his theories were anything but starting points, incomplete and needing further theoretical-empirical work. They were, he was fond of arguing, small but hopeful breakthroughs in the process of people's growing knowledge about themselves. Indeed, at the present level of the development of sociology, a fully-fledged or 'final' theory of civilisation, manners, power, knowledge, state-formation, food, sport, leisure, smoking, football hooliganism or, indeed, anything else is a chimera. Elias wrote of scientific method thus:

> The aim of (scientific) inquiries is to find the inherent order of events ... independently not of any, but of any particular observer, and the importance, the relevance, the value of what one observes is assessed in accordance with the place and function it appears to have within this order itself. In the exploration of nature ... scientists have learned that any direct encroachment on their work by short-term interests ... is liable to jeopardise the usefulness which their work may have ... The problems which they formulate and, by means of their theories, try to solve, have in relation to personal or social problems of the day a high degree of autonomy; so have the sets of values which they use; their work is not 'value-free', but it is, in contrast to that of many social scientists, protected by firmly established professional standards and other institutional safeguards against the intrusion of heteronomous evaluations. (2007a: 72–3)

Elias's reference to 'heteronomous evaluations' was again indicative of his opposition to the argument that sociology should be the tool of a particular class, 'race', interest group or gender. He accepted in conversation that there had been a destructive, to some extent unconscious and unintended masculine bias in much work in the discipline's earlier phases, but argued that it would be wrong to replace this with any form of equally biased politics of representation. Nor did he accept the idea that a sociology which is not expressive, say, of the interests of the working class is, by virtue of that fact, expressive of the interests of their rulers. Rather, he urged sociologists to strive for autonomy and against heteronomy, that is against interference in determining their work agendas and findings by any outside, that is, non-sociological, group or its representatives whether these be governments, employers, trades unions, political parties or whatever. To this end, he advocated the development of standards, institutions and modes of proceeding similar to those of the 'natural' sciences but moulded to the specific properties of humans and the figurations that they form.

## 'Methodology', 'epistemology', 'ontology', and the problem of method

Beyond this broad stipulation – of the need for sociologists to attune their methods to the specific properties of human figurations – Elias did not dwell extensively on problems of 'methodology'. Nor, in this sense, did he focus on issues concerning his 'epistemology' and 'ontology' as such. Indeed, as we suggested earlier, Elias abandoned these terms as part of a more general attempt to develop a conceptual vocabulary less imbued with modes of thinking at odds with the sociological or 'post-philosophical' (Kilminster 2007) reorientation that he sought to advance. At the simplest level, problems of 'epistemology' characteristically relate to the kinds of *questions* asked; problems of 'methodology' typically pertain to *how* such questions are pursued; and problems of 'ontology' relate to the *character* of that to which such questions are addressed – of what can be said to 'exist', in our case in social 'reality'. Thus, while one would search in vain to find Elias's definitive statement of his 'methodological', 'ontological' or 'epistemological' position, he, nonetheless, addressed such concerns both in discussions of substantive topics – such as in his analyses of scientific establishments and of established–outsider relationships between community groups in particular locales. He dealt with such issues, that is to say, through the very medium of his work, his sociological 'practice', that is, his distinctive approach to *doing* sociology and the theoretical-empirical vehicle for his analyses that this implied.

The task of extracting from Elias's corpus of work a comprehensive exegesis of his 'methodological' and 'epistemological' positions is beyond the scope of our focus here. Nonetheless, we shall offer to this end a number of tentative observations. In order to elucidate Elias's position on these issues, it is necessary to return, once again, to the central components of his distinctive sociological approach. His key sociological foci are processes, relationships and syntheses. These components are, at once, the 'subjects' and the 'objects' of Elias's approach. As such, they inform – to consider questions of 'epistemology' and 'methodology' first – both the kinds of questions that he asked, and the manner in which he approached their 'solution'. As our earlier chicken and egg example of the impossibility of determining which comes first serves to demonstrate, some conceptual problems are intractable only as a consequence, firstly of how they have been formulated, and secondly, of their consideration in isolation from empirical study. Further to this, how such problems are presented, including the very terms employed and the conceptual axioms they embody is, in itself, a topic worthy of sociological investigation. For Elias, the dominant but by no means uniform tendency, particularly in Western philosophy since the Enlightenment, to formulate problems which centre on a singular, static, ideal, 'developed', adult, 'reflexive' 'subject' and the terms of 'its' 'engagement' with the 'objects' of 'its' knowledge is in itself not simply expressive of a particular strand of rationality, but of a particular historical juncture, a particular phase in a series of interconnected long-term social processes. In the same way, the current tendency within much sociology towards an embrace of epistemic relativism, conceptual eclecticism, the conceptual oscillation between the twin pillars of 'the autonomous social agent' and 'impersonal structures of subjugation', the increasing engagement of poststructuralist theorists with 'culture' and 'cultural artefacts', and the tendency to assume that history is structureless and characterised by patternlessness and social decline are all, in their own ways, indicative of more than the ascendancy of particular sociological paradigms.

If we were to distil Elias's epistemological position into a single question, putting aside for the moment all the difficulties attendant upon doing so, it would be this: *how did 'this' come to be?* Such a question immediately facilitates an engagement with processes. As Elias expressed it in *Involvement and Detachment*: 'By "Why questions" ... I mean genetic questions' (Elias 2007a: 182n). To take an example that has been considered in detail elsewhere by one of the authors of this book (Hughes 2003), the question 'Why do people smoke?' involves a formulation which in itself invites a process-blind 'answer'. It is as though there is *a* 'reason' for smoking, and at that, a reason shared by all smokers in all historical periods. Adopting a process-orientated approach necessitates a re-formulation of the question along the lines of 'how did this come to be'. A reformulation of the kind referred to above involves making the question itself an on-going substantive and not merely *a priori* concern. As a starting point, it might prompt one to ask several other questions such as: to what extent and how have understandings of tobacco use, including the questions of why people smoke and why they say they smoke, changed over time and in different cultures? To what extent and how have tobacco consumption and patterns of its use changed over time and in different cultures? To what extent and how might these understandings mediate experiences of tobacco use and of being a 'tobacco user'?, and so forth. At the level of an individual smoker, one might seek to pursue the question of the different ways in which a person 'becomes' a 'smoker'. But even this is in some ways process-reducing – very few smokers can define a specific 'moment' at which they made the transition from non-smoker to 'smoker', or after having stopped, from 'smoker' to 'ex-smoker' (while some claim they will always remain 'smokers' whether or not they continue habitually to place cigarettes, cigars, or pipes into their mouths) (Hughes 2003).

Howard Becker (1998) provides a similar example, not in exposition of Elias's approach, but in highlighting a processual 'trick of the trade' used in qualitative research. A researcher might, for example, be interested in how it came about that a man 'decided' to undergo a sex change operation. The question might be asked in the following way: 'What would lead a seemingly normal American man to have his penis and testicles amputated?' (Becker 1998: 26). But such a line of investigation would, Becker suggests, ignore the process of 'becoming': how, by degrees and successive approximations, and not by a simple and continuous trajectory of development, a man might move from being drawn towards some kind of homosexual activity, towards entering a social world in which homosexuality is viewed positively and as 'normal', to encounters with others who suggest possibilities he had not previously considered, to perhaps experimenting with female clothing and make-up, to mimicking the physical mannerisms of a woman, to wondering how it would feel to become like a woman in a more permanent physical sense, and so forth.[54] Viewed in such a processual manner, we are able to understand a 'decision' to have sex change surgery, not so much as the sudden radical 'choice' of a person gripped by spontaneous impulses, but as just one in a series of relatively small but connected decisions; a sequence of 'small steps' that must be understood as a processual whole. As Becker writes:

> At each of these points, our mythical young man finds himself doing some things he had at some earlier time never heard of and, having heard of them, had not imagined he might do. The steps he takes are never so very radical. Each one is simply another small step on a road from which he might at any minute turn to some other of the many roads available. Each small step is intellectually and emotionally understandable to people who themselves are nothing like this young man, *once the circumstances are made intelligible to them*... (Becker 1998: 27; emphasis in the original)

Beyond illustrating, once again, the importance of understanding social issues as processes, the examples of transvestism, sex change, and smoking also have significance for questions of methodology. The examples serve to highlight Elias's more general point regarding the need for sociologists to adopt methods matched to and appropriate for the relational and dynamic, that is, processual, character of their subject matter. Elias's personally favoured method was that of documentary analysis since this is particularly well suited to the more general historical-comparative approach he advocated. His work in *On The Process of Civilisation* is replete with examples of this method in use. Typically, as we saw in Chapter 3, Elias presents a number of textual examples in time series, each numbered as a sequence. He then reflects upon the changes from one example to the next – both what has been added as well as what has been removed, what has changed as well as what remains more or less basically the same, what was said and what was unsaid. Crucially, such examples are always conceived as diachronic *Gestalten* or patterns: that is, it is not so much the individual fragments of historical documents – their authority, authenticity, reliability, or representativeness – that concern Elias, as it is the connections between such data. To use the analogy of an old-fashioned motion picture film roll, which Elias sometimes used in his lectures and tutorials, his method involved focusing less on the individual 'stills' than on the 'movie' these generate when viewed as a sequence. While each frame in a motion picture might have particular characteristics – it might be shot from a particular angle, have particular lighting, contain an aberration caused by dust or some other intrusion – no individual frame can be properly understood in isolation from the film as a whole or its position in a sequential order.

In his other research, whilst he was by no means totally hostile to a limited use of quantitative methods (see, for example, his use of 'game models' in *What is Sociology?* (2012b) and road accident statistics in his essay, 'Technisation and Civilisation' (1995)), Elias most commonly used qualitative methods. In the 1960s, for example, he secured government funding from the UK Department of Scientific and Industrial Research (DSIR), the predecessor of the Social Science Research Council (SSRC), now the Economic and Social Research Council (ESRC), for a large-scale study of *The Adjustment of Young Workers to Work Situations and Adult Roles*. This aspect of his work is now little known, partly because the project was ill-fated, ending in a dramatic fall-out between Elias and some of the researchers employed to conduct the fieldwork (for a fuller account of the project and its demise, see Goodwin and O'Connor 2006). Part of the disagreement centred on the research methods and orientations adopted by the researchers. Some decades before what has been termed the 'reflexive turn' in sociology, Elias tried to encourage these researchers to adopt the method of depth-interviewing *in situ*, recording lengthy written transcripts of the conversations that took place, and, most interestingly, noting their own reflections on these conversations. These contained everything from comments on how the researchers felt the interviews had gone, through to their 'subjective' evaluations of (and moral judgements on) the participants' living conditions and personal appearances (see Goodwin and O'Connor 2002). Clearly, Elias felt that the patterns of researchers' involvement in a process of research is as important a consideration as the data gleaned from their more detached role as 'investigators' or 'observers'. The methods adopted in the 'Young Workers' study involved an attempt to explore the intersection between life phase and orientations to work, and more generally, between history and biography. In the original application, Elias summarised the project thus:

> The project is concerned with the problems which young male and female workers encounter during their adjustment to their work situation and their entry into the world of adults. When they go to work, or begin to train for work, young workers have to make a wider adjustment to a situation and to roles which are new to them, whose implications are often imperfectly understood by them and by the adults concerned, and for which they are in many cases not too well prepared. The project will differ from other studies investigating this wider adjustment which young workers have to make in their relationships with older workers and supervisors in the factory or workshop: to job problems and to their role as workers; and to their roles as money earners in home relations and in their leisure time. The factors to be examined will include differences between age groups, between sexes, in size of the organisation, in nature and status of job, and between young workers from working class and middle class home backgrounds. We intend to pay special attention to the overall characteristics of industrial societies responsible for the specific problems of adjustment for people in this age group.

To readers familiar with Elias's approach in works such as *On The Process of Civilisation* and *The Court Society*, it may be surprising to read his summary of what looks by today's standards like a fairly 'conventional' empirical study. However, it is clear that the key ingredients of Elias's characteristic mode of sociological analysis – the relationship between sociogenesis (here, the overall characteristics of industrial societies) and psychogenesis (here, the adjustment of young workers to work environments); the idea that the experience of work should be studied as a process of continual transition; indeed, the very notion that an important distinction should be drawn between younger and older workers – underpin the inception and design of the research and relate to the more general principles of process sociology.

The lack of a lengthy discussion of methodology in Elias's work, or to use a formulation with which he would have found more agreement, with problems of method, is no accident. Elias's position was that such problems should not be so much a matter to be finalised prior to undertaking research through the resolution of 'timeless methodological dilemmas', as they should be substantive, 'live' concerns germane to the particular problems and topics under investigation. Moreover, as discussed in the previous chapter, Elias objected to the notion that the 'worth' or 'value' of any piece of research can be established through determining the extent to which the researchers adhered to specific methodological standards and procedures. He did so partly because he saw this tendency as a hangover from ill-conceived attempts by sociologists to ape the practices of the natural sciences (and what he regarded as a caricatured and idealised model of the natural sciences at that), and partly because, as we have seen, the issue of establishing the occurrence of 'developments' or more specifically 'advances' in knowledge involves considerably more than questions of method. More particularly, it pertains to a consideration of the connections between theoretico–empirical research contributions as part of an ongoing knowledge process. Two cases which Elias used repeatedly to refer to were Fleming's serendipitous discovery of penicillin and Crick and Watson's discovery of the double-helix structure of DNA. Looking solely at the latter, the American, Linus Pauling, was the first to hit on the idea that a helix is involved in genetic inheritance but Crick and Watson (Watson 2001 (1968)) report how one of them saw in an X-ray crystallograph taken by Rosalind Franklin of King's College, London, that this basic genetic process is a question of two intertwined helixes. They did not tell her but, on their return to Cambridge, were able immediately to construct a model and write a paper for which they won a Nobel Prize. The history of science, Elias used to say, is littered with examples of such serendipity/accidentality and sharp practice. In a word, it is not the simon-pure affair often depicted in idealised accounts but a social process characterised by unplanned as well as planned components and involving a labile, shifting balance between cooperation, rivalry and outright conflict within and between groups. It needs, Elias said, to be studied as such.

To return again to the example of a motion picture film reel, questions of methodology demand that we should become preoccupied more with the particular fragment of data in hand, with individual frames and stills, and with their peculiar characteristics – 'Who said this?' 'Why was it said?' 'How "true" is it?' 'Can it be corroborated by what others have said?' 'How reliable is this?' 'How valid is this statement?' 'What lies "behind" this?'. Insofar as one can generalise, methodological questions – at least as these have tended to have been discussed in the field of sociology up to now, tend, on the whole, to be somewhat less concerned with the connections between frames, the *diachronic Gestalt*, and the procedures by which the film might be played back than they ought to be if seen in relational, dynamic, and synthetic terms.

## Sociology and historical analysis

Elias's emphasis on the need for sociologists to engage with social phenomena as longer-term processes, and in particular, his stress on the largely 'blind' course of social development, runs counter to the dominant present-day idea that humans can control the processes in which they are entangled. That is, Elias's characteristic focus on long-term processes is an approach that renders 'events' and 'intentions' secondary to the shifting course of social development. Such an approach is, in important ways, at odds with conventional 'historical analysis', particularly that which is allied to political ends and in which analysts seek to find the 'smoking gun' of intent behind the origins say, of a particular social problem or the subjugation and exploitation of a particular group. It is ostensibly far more politically useful, in a short-term sense, to posit unambiguous models of historical causality in order to show how specific social problems can be traced to the actions of particular groups or individuals, in order to assign – and, indeed, to cease such analysis after assigning – unequivocal 'historical blame'. Equally, however, Elias's emphasis on long-term 'blind' historical processes should by no means be taken as denying how, at particular historical junctures and under certain figurational conditions, specific individuals have been able for a while to 'steer' the course of social development in limited but nonetheless important ways. As suggested earlier, Napoleon in France in the late eighteenth/ early nineteenth centuries and Hitler in Germany in the 1930s and 1940s are obvious examples. In an article in the special edition of *Der Spiegel*, the German magazine, in 1989 (42–44), published to mark the 100 years since Hitler's birth, Elias wrote of the would-be destroyer of the Jews as a 'charismatic ruler' and went on to show how Hitler had substantial power until he declared war on the USA in 1942 and thereby sealed his own and Germany's fate (See Elias's discussion of the 'charismatic ruler', 2008: 164–9).

The idea that *all* sociological analysis is, by virtue of its subject matter, inevitably historical, or perhaps better, processual and developmental, is not without its critics. Derek Layder (1994), for example, warns against treating 'historical sociology' and 'social analysis' as though they were identical. He proposes that those who claim these enterprises are 'identical' are in danger of making the 'analytic mistake' of claiming that '[An] historical analysis of general social processes can give us an adequate framework for the development of research which has a contemporary focus and which relies heavily on observational data culled from situated interaction' (1994: 177–178). It would seem that Elias, from Layder's perspective at least, is in danger of making such a mistake in much of his empirical work which has a 'contemporary focus': the earlier cited example of the 'Young Workers' study is a case in point. Another is the research Elias conducted with John Scotson into the 'established-outsider' figurations of Winston Parva. Layder's key reservation concerning the idea that 'historical sociology' and 'social analysis' can be treated as equivalent enterprises appears to reside in his insistence upon a distinction between 'situated interaction' and 'general social processes'. He is, accordingly, critical of Elias's tendency, as he (Layder) sees it, to 'mask' important differences between, in Layder's words, 'general institutional changes' and 'situated encounters'. He writes:

> Elias's (1978) analysis of the development of a personality type emphasising internal (superego) control of behaviour from a previous type which lacked such controls – as a consequence of a civilising process general throughout western societies – is excellent as a general analysis of behavioural changes that occurred in tandem with various institutional changes... However, in the absence of a clearly delineated appreciation of the quite distinct properties of situated

encounters as compared with general institutional processes, there is always the possibility that such a general framework is seen to be sufficient in itself for the analysis of present-centred research drawing on situated data.

The danger is compounded in Elias's case by his insistence that there is no real distinction between the individual and society and that for all intents and purposes they should be viewed to be part of the same phenomenon. Such a view obscures an important distinction between the formation of general personality types and the development of specific personalities through unique biographical circumstances. Overall, Elias's position masks significant differences between, on the one hand, general institutional change and situated encounters, and on the other, between general personality types and unique individuals. In this respect, Elias's framework appears rather more comprehensive than it really is. (1994: 177–178)

Implicit in Layder's critique is a normative assumption regarding a supposedly clear-cut and unequivocal distinction between 'past' and 'present'. It is as if 'historical processes' somehow stand as ontologically separate from the 'here and now stuff of social life'. Indeed, the notion that a 'contemporary focus' is separate from an historical one reproduces the idea of a dichotomy between an eternal 'present' that is divorced from 'its' 'historical' context. But, as we have argued in previous sections of this book, even if we subscribe for the moment to such a clear-cut separation between past and present, and by extension, between historical sociology and social analysis, where should the line be drawn? How can the distinction be anything other than arbitrarily conceived? Put simply: at what 'point' does a 'contemporary' focus become an 'historical' one? At what 'moment' does the 'present' become the 'past' – after a period of years? Months? Days? Seconds? Nanoseconds? The issue is not merely a question of timing, or even simply of time perception or temporal semantics. Once again, Elias's apparently simple concept of 'process' has fundamental and wide-reaching implications. In stressing an understanding of social reality as fundamentally dynamic – as processual and developmental – Elias's endeavour involved him precisely in seeking to *avoid* the tendency to reduce social processes to static phenomena, albeit ones which are held to 'have' an 'historical context' or 'backdrop', or which 'move' at certain 'points', and which led him explicitly to challenge the crude, seemingly self-evident (to certain groups in certain historical periods) dichotomy between concepts such as 'past' and 'present'.

That Layder should find it axiomatic to divorce 'the past' from 'the present' or 'historical' from 'social' analysis relates to a topic to which Elias devoted considerable attention in his *Time: An Essay* (1991), which we discussed in Chapter 2. It is an issue to which it is worth returning. The tendency relates in part to a socially learned self-distanciation. The very ability to think in terms of 'past', 'present' and 'future', Elias argued, stems from an historically emergent capacity that humans have to engage in 'detour behaviour'. An example of such self-distanciation is where early humans learned to distance themselves from their immediate situation and to restrain spontaneous impulses in order to fashion tools which would help them better in serving their survival needs. The use of tools, in turn, required the capacity to picture, in the 'mind's eye' as it were, a 'future' in which ends are being met – a capacity dependent on the formation of mental abstractions relating to temporal categories including the notions of 'now' and 'the future'. But this human tendency to think of past, present, and future as separate, and indeed, the more general *homo clausus* tendency to think of 'society' (or general institutional changes) as something 'out there' and separate from the 'in here' as experienced through 'situated encounters' – both of which are based in a particular kind of self-distancing – is, Elias argued, inadequate as a means of orientation towards social processes. In Layder's case, it underpins a reproduced variant of the 'structure-agency' dilemma whereby 'general institutional changes' are viewed as separate, and as having 'a life of their own', existing beyond the level of human beings and the figurations that they form. It is almost as though 'general institutional changes' are not, at any level, constituted from 'situated encounters'.

Layder's insistence on sustaining such a dualism can also be seen in relation to central concepts in his work – 'interaction' and 'structure'. His use of the term 'encounters', for example, implies 'face-to-face' 'interactions' which, in turn, are seen to be 'situated' in social 'structures'. As we discussed elsewhere in this book, however, according to Elias what people may experience as face-to-face 'encounters' always involves more than just 'interaction'. Take, for example, the following very much oversimplified hypothetical example of a 'situated encounter' between a customer and a clerk ('teller' in the USA) in a bank. The customer is a married schoolteacher with a wife and three children, two of them of school age, and he wants to cash a cheque, among other things to pay his bus fare and provide his children's school dinner money. The bank clerk is an unmarried woman who lives with her parents, both of them retired, and who is engaged to be married to an airline pilot. It does not take much imagination to realise that each person in this encounter is variably interdependent, not only with the others and the people in the bank at the same time but also with countless family members, work colleagues in other branches of the bank, neighbours and, through the medium of money and the banking system, countless thousands of other people at the national and international levels as well. This is the sort of thing that is meant by saying that such interactions always involve chains of interdependence with others whom the people 'interacting' may never 'meet' or 'see' 'face-to-face'. Thus a person's 'plans', 'intentions' and 'actions' within any 'encounter' are always inter-related and interdependent with the 'plans', 'intentions' and 'actions' of others, and these interdependencies are parts of chains which stretch across time and space. For Elias, the intermeshing of human 'strivings' and 'impulses' forms a 'tissue', a 'web' which gives rise to an order that is 'more compelling and stronger than the will of the individual people composing it' (Elias 1994: 444) – once again, a 'figuration'. At one level, this order can be seen as involving 'general institutional change'; at another 'social structure', at another 'society'. Elias argues that it is because this 'order' at the most general level largely follows a 'blind' course that it is often conceptualised as having 'a life of its own' or as having an existence beyond the level of human beings. But, according to Elias, it is an order that, while not reducible to any particular individual, nor to the actions of any particular group, is not independent of individuals and groups as such. For Elias, the key 'analytic mistake' in this respect is precisely the reverse of what Layder takes it to be: it is to reproduce the idea of structures and agents as if they were ultimately separate and ontologically distinct – in Layder's case under the guise of a posited dualism between 'general institutional change' and 'situated encounters', the 'past' and the 'present', 'historical analysis' and 'social analysis', and ultimately, in his implicit understanding of the difference between the terms 'process' and 'interaction'.

It follows from this that Elias's approach is arguably not so much one which '… masks significant differences between … general personality types and unique individuals', as it is one that seeks to provide a means by which to explore the historically variant relationships between the lives of 'unique individuals' such as, for example, Louis XIV (Elias 2006b; 1969), Mozart (Elias 1993a), Velázquez (Elias 2007a; 1987a) or Hitler (Elias 1996) and 'general personality types'. And rather than ignoring the different properties of 'institutional change' and 'situated encounters', Elias explicitly aimed at developing a conceptual vocabulary that sensitises researchers to the different characteristics of, for example, processes of 'sociogenesis' and 'psychogenesis' whilst avoiding the tendency to treat such processes as ultimately separate. Beyond these points, however, it should be noted that it was one of Elias's key concerns to build an understanding of the processes by which 'the individual' – with all the connotations this term now evokes such as 'uniqueness', 'sovereignty', 'freedom', 'difference', 'knowledgeability', etc. – has come to be an overriding concern, even a guiding ideal, in political ideologies such as neo-liberalism, and in much recent theorising in sociology. Indeed, from Elias's perspective, research which stems from *homo clausus* theorising – in which humans are studied as 'essences of uniqueness contained within individual vessels' – is far more likely to find and reveal 'individuality' since, conversely, such thinking serves to obfuscate how ostensible 'uniqueness' may in fact be related in important ways to more general social processes.

Ultimately, it may well be that Elias and Layder are in greater agreement than the latter appears to recognise. In a later critique of Elias, Layder writes that:

> What is needed more than anything else is a clear distinction between general and specific claims as they relate to … different levels of analysis… For example, a concentration on the socially constructed nature of sexuality or self-identity, as they can be traced over long periods of development, must be distinguished from

a specific individual's identity and sexual development. Although all people must to some degree be affected by the social contexts in which they are raised... this does not and cannot mean that they are simply reflections of these circumstances. (Layder 2006: 145)

While he would have disagreed with how Layder has formulated the problem here, the intersection between what we might for shorthand purposes call 'historical' and 'biographical' processes, is, if anything, Elias's principal concern throughout the bulk of his work. The key point for Elias was to recognise that 'biographical' processes are inevitably 'historical ones' and, conversely, that 'historical' processes are 'biographical' ones – and in doing so not to reduce one to the other, but rather, to recognise their indissolubility at the same time as their analytic distinctness. For example, the specific details of the Dutch Renaissance humanist scholar, Desiderius Erasmus's, life, his particular biographical circumstances, his personal idiosyncrasies and proclivities, the perhaps unique aspects of his character, all have their place in understanding the man and his work (various aspects of which are at times discussed by Elias in *On The Process of Civilisation*). But of equal if not greater sociological importance is Erasmus's positioning at a particular historical juncture and how his writings as an individual, albeit with their own distinctive nuances and character, are related to more general, historically specific social mores, manners, customs, and codes of etiquette. Moreover, if Elias's analysis is accurate, they are indicative of broader processes of social development.

## 'Involved detachment'?

Building on an argument developed by Richard Kilminster (2004), the above discussion of *homo clausus* thinking can be seen to raise a further issue relating to Elias's ideas on involvement and detachment. In much of his writing on this subject, Elias provides examples – notably Edgar Allan Poe's 'The Fisherman in the Maelstrom' and, as we saw earlier, the astronomer Copernicus's pivotal role in the shift from a geocentric to a heliocentric cosmology – which highlight the importance of developing more detached knowledge with rather fewer illustrating the significance of its logical opposite, more involved knowledge. It is somewhat paradoxical that, on the one hand, Elias viewed the human capacity for detachment as central to the development of knowledge, and yet, on the other, his central thesis concerning civilising processes is that psychic detachment, and more specifically, self-distancing, emerge as part of civilising processes and underpin a socially-instilled disengaged self-experience which also informs *Homo clausus* thinking. For Elias, it requires a further effort at self-distancing to realise how such disengagement, specifically the feeling of a dividing line between 'me in here' and 'society out there', might inform our approaches to the social world, and yet, at the same time, it is only through a degree of disengagement and self-distancing that such insights are possible. This point serves to illustrate the highly complex character of the relationship between involvement and detachment as conceived by Elias.

It would be misleading to suggest that Elias discounted more involved knowledge altogether. His notion of a 'detour *via* detachment' bears out more generally his argument that '… while one need not know, in order to understand the structure of molecules, what it feels like to be one of its atoms, in order to understand the functioning of human groups one needs to know, as it were, from inside how human beings experience their own and other groups, and one cannot know without active participation and involvement' (Elias 1956: 237). For reasons such as these, Elias often encouraged postgraduate students to carry out research into areas in which they were directly interested and involved. Thus, in Frankfurt, as we saw in Chapter 3, Ilse Seglow, the actress, and Gisele Freund, the photographer, were encouraged by Elias to write their doctoral theses on, respectively, the acting profession and photography. In Leicester, university footballer Eric Dunning was encouraged to write his Masters thesis on the development of football, his favourite sport. At the same time, however, students were urged by Elias to strive as hard as possible when they were engaged in the research process to distance themselves from the objects of their research, to take a detour *via* detachment in order to maximise the degree of reality-congruence of their findings, that is to make these findings correspond as far as possible to the structure and qualities of the research objects themselves rather than to their own (the researchers') personal fantasies and feelings, or to personal and/or group interests and myths of various kinds. Then, armed with potentially more reality-congruent and in that sense more practically reliable knowledge, researchers were encouraged by Elias to apply, *via* what he called 'secondary involvement', their more reliable knowledge to the addressing of social and political problems of various kinds. In a similar way, the work of painters such as Masaccio, van Eyck and Velázquez also involved, Elias argued, a detour *via* detachment. Elias was able to show, for example, how the illusion of three-dimensional space *via* a more realistic sense of spatial perspective in the work of these painters was a capacity based on their greater detachment: an approach which made an appeal both to a viewer's self-same capacity for detachment, and then to stimulating their (the viewers') emotional involvement through visual clues and aesthetic arrangements (Kilminster 2004: 33).

Elias's position was that adding to knowledge *per se* should be paramount over short-term interests, values, and concerns both in research and in deciding the merits of particular authors and pieces of work. However, Elias was crystal clear about the fact that, in striving to achieve these aims, sociologists cannot and *should not* abandon their political interests and concerns. As he expressed it:

> The problem confronting [social scientists] is not simply to discard [their more individual, political] role in favour of … [a more detached, scientific one].

They cannot cease to take part in, and to be affected by, the social and political affairs of their group and their time. Their own participation and involvement, moreover, is itself one of the conditions for comprehending the problems they try to solve as scientists... The problems confronting those who study one or the other aspects of human groups is how to keep their two roles as participant and enquirer clearly and consistently apart, and, as a professional group to establish in their work the undisputed dominance of the latter. (2007a: 84)

Elias can be observed, here as elsewhere in his work, as envisaging sociology as an emerging science which, at the current stage of its development, has yet practically to resolve the dilemma generated by the tension between degrees of involvement and detachment as he conceived it. His argument was that part of the means by which this difficulty may be practically overcome involves reframing it by using more sociological concepts, and by considering at once both degrees of individual psychic distancing and the development of social conditions conducive to the greater detachment of academic communities from the pressures of heteronomous, that is, 'outsider' evaluations. However, as Rojek (1986) argued, while Elias provides useful examples of the detour *via* detachment, and while the concepts of involvement and detachment represent a useful re-orientation towards key problems concerning the development of sociological knowledge, these are not sufficient in themselves as a basis for guiding an individual sociological researcher towards what needs to be undertaken in order to follow the 'detour *via* detachment'. In short, Elias provides no 'clear' drill for sociological research other than the model embedded in his own sociological practice. That is, Elias's work has less explicitly to say on how, at the level of an individual social researcher, greater detachment can be achieved, greater self-distancing maintained, and such knowledge blended and alloyed with knowledge which is more involved. Moreover, if sociologists are resigned to the fact that, at its current stage of development, the subject is generally not one in which autonomous evaluations take precedence over heteronomous evaluations, and that in order for sociological knowledge to develop, there needs to be greater and more widespread acceptance and establishment of the former relative to the latter, how might an individual researcher – albeit one committed to 'autonomous evaluations' – proceed? To this end, Kilminster has offered a useful means of addressing the concern. He suggests that part of the answer resides in adopting the *anticipatory motif* of Elias's sociological practice (2004: 34). That is, researchers who are committed to 'autonomous evaluation':

> should apply in their practice of sociology the criteria of cognitive evaluation and the standards of detachment which *would* be widely taken for granted if the discipline, as a special science, had achieved a higher degree of self-perpetuating, institutional autonomy, and a corresponding authority, than at present. The consistent application of these criteria and the standard of detachment anticipates their future embodiment in a stronger institutionalisation of the discipline and,

hopefully, will help bring it about. Although there are no guarantees as to how far this process can go. (Kilminster 2004: 34; emphasis in the original)

Such an anticipatory motif, Kilminster suggests, is, as we discussed earlier, in important ways less problematic than certain other conceptions of 'ideal states' as regulatory models for research such as, for example, Habermas's or Apel's notion of 'ideal speech situations'; Adorno's 'utopian moment of the object'; or Bauman's notion of 'being-for-the-other' (Kilminster 1998: 50–54). The motif of 'greater detachment and secondary involvement' is thus best conceived as a kind of 'controlling imperative' which, unlike a philosophical eternal or transcendental argument from which to derive regulatory principles, has neither logical necessity nor a metaphysical status: it is instead an orientation towards the concrete social and psychic conditions which inhibit or facilitate, as Kilminster put it '… the achievement of *greater* self-perpetuating institutionalised standards of detachment, without assuming that a final state of pure detachment can be achieved' (2004: 34; emphasis in the original).

As Kilminster suggests, it would be profoundly at odds with the ideas of Elias to assume that sociology is, as Smith (1984) proposes, somehow being pulled towards a preconceived ideal state of complete detachment by some kind of eternal *telos* or *logic* of its own development. Indeed, this is unequivocally *not* what is meant by Elias's anticipatory motif. The idea of '*greater* detachment and secondary involvement' necessarily implies that sociology, like any other science, is never 'complete', never 'finished'. It is in a 'continuous process of becoming' (2004: 34). A key condition for it to become more established and self-perpetuating, argues Kilminster, is the '… *sustained transfer of controlled affect into 'autonomous evaluations'* through a process of institutionalisation' (2004: 35; emphasis in the original). In other words, the sociological passion that has come, in many ways, to be a defining characteristic of the discipline, particularly in the sense of being associated with specific political views, or with a general commitment to eradicating social injustice, should instead be channelled, *via* an intergenerational 'detour' (in the way that Elias intended this term) into the pursuit of sociological knowledge which has greater congruence with the *world as it actually is* – knowledge which might well demonstrate the one-sidedness, perhaps the false character of understandings of *the world as we might think or want it to be*.

Ultimately, Kilminster's arguments suggest a different kind of relationship between involvement and detachment than is usually assumed of Elias's work. It is one which allows for alloys and blends along the lines of 'passionate detachment' – for example, a fervent commitment to the *discipline* of sociology – and equally, 'dispassionate involvement' – for example, in seeking to build a more detached understanding of both the influence and insights deriving from one's own involvement in that which is studied. Such formulations serve, once again, to illustrate that, rather than expressing a 'dialectical' or bi-polar formulation, and rather than simple logical alternatives or a zero-sum relation, the concepts of involvement and detachment refer to different aspects and components of the development of knowledge, and may well point towards particular strategies and orientations towards sociological research – a few of which we have endeavoured to highlight in this chapter and throughout this book as a whole.

# 6

# Elias and 'The Habits of Good Sociology'

In the acceptance speech that he gave in Aachen, Germany, in 1977 when he was presented with the Festschrift, *Human Figurations: Essays for Norbert Elias* (Amsterdam, Stichting Amsterdams Sociologisch Tijdschrift), to mark his eightieth birthday, Elias started by recalling a nightmare which, he claimed, had regularly disturbed his sleep in the 1950s and 60s. It started to become less frequent in the 1970s, he said. It involved him repeatedly shouting into a telephone, 'Are you there? Can you hear me?' He never got an answer.

The dream is simple to analyse. Elias had been convinced from a young age that he had important things to say. However, as we have shown in previous chapters, a combination of external events such as the rise of the Nazis, his enforced migration to France and then Britain, the Second World War, and the death of his parents, especially his mother, had contributed to preventing him from getting all his ideas into publishable form. Added to this were such more personal circumstances as that he found himself forced in the late 1930s to start writing in a foreign language, English, and the self-confessed neurotic difficulty which he admitted to having in allowing manuscripts to be taken from him for publication. Both of these had contributed further to his not having been able to convey as many of his ideas to a wider sociological and educated lay public as he had wanted. Ilse Seglow, one of his PhD students in Frankfurt and later a successful group psychoanalyst in London, used persuasively to say that Norbert's writings were his 'children' and that he was a 'possessive father' who found it difficult to let his 'children go'. In a word, as Michael Schröter has suggested, Elias was ambivalent towards publishing. (See Schröter's editorial afterword to Elias's *Mozart: Portrait of a Genius*, 1993.) Using a term that Elias had experimented with in conversation, Stephen Mennell, who worked closely with Elias on the English translation of *Was ist Soziologie?*, described Elias's tendency in this regard as indicative of his 'counter-ego' (Mennell 2006). Indeed, Elias's fear that 'no-one was listening' was often set against his frustration with the presentation of his ideas by others. He initially opposed the publication of Mennell's, *Norbert Elias: Civilisation and the Human Self-Image* – a text that is now widely regarded as a seminal introduction to Elias's work. In fact, it was not until late in his life that Elias came to accept that there was scope for any kind of secondary introduction, and even then he only did so with some resignation (Mennell 2006).

## Elias: Established *and* outsider?

During the late 1960s and the 1970s, Elias's work began to attract substantial readerships, especially in the Netherlands, Germany, and France. In that period, as we saw in previous chapters, Elias gradually came to be recognised as a sociologist of world stature and, as his reputation grew, his recurring nightmare correlatively subsided. But this wider recognition of his work by no means constituted its acceptance – nor arguably its full comprehension – by Elias's contemporaries. Indeed, as we have discussed throughout this book, the question of determining Elias's enduring influence within sociology, and his broader intellectual legacy is not a straightforward one.

Elias's work continues to this day to have a somewhat ambivalent status. It is perhaps surprising, particularly given the central foci of his work, that it is not more widely known. For example, as Newton and Smith (2002) observed in relation to the field of organisational studies, while there has been a rapid expansion of interest in recent years in areas such as the study of: 'networks'; 'power, control and resistance'; 'culture, language and knowledge'; 'change'; 'identity, the self and emotionality'; etc., there has not been a corresponding rise in engagement with Elias's work which arguably offers a framework in which all these themes are woven into a unified perspective (Newton and Smith 2002: viii). In some cases, Elias's work is embraced but misconstrued in important ways; in others, as we have seen, it is dismissed as a naïve, crude, teleological progress theory. It has attracted a curious mix of passionate advocacy and vehement dismissal, in one or two cases at different times by the same authors (see Mennell's discussion of this tendency (1992: 227–250)). On the whole, Elias retains a somewhat marginal 'outsider' status in relation to 'mainstream' sociology. However, by a few authors, his approach is considered as constituting an 'orthodoxy'. In the early 1990s, Dutch sociologist, Dick Pels (1991: 178), went so far as to suggest that, in the Netherlands, 'figurational sociology' had '... risen into what is today one of the most distinctive, prestigious and successful academic establishments'. This was probably not an over-estimation of figurational sociology's reputation in the Netherlands at the time of Pels's writing, though it is perhaps less the case today.

Sociologists who have been directly influenced by Elias have, at various times, been described as a 'sect'. Alternatively, they are said to be an 'industry' who seek only to canonise the 'great man and his work'. According to Pels (1991), they are involved in an unspoken politics of theory that entails a kind of symbolic violence based around paradigm conquest. Those who have argued that Elias's work constitutes a sociological 'breakthrough' have also been charged with 'intellectual immodesty' (Pels 1991: 177) – a term that Elias would, no doubt, have found sociologically interesting, and perhaps also amusing, given his central engagement with the nexus between power, notions of 'modesty', and the development and transgression of codes of etiquette more generally.

This latter point is more than simply flippant. Pels may well be correct in depicting Elias as a scholar who would not have been satisfied with the establishment of a 'mere school' based upon his ideas (1991: 177). However, Elias's tendency in this respect amounted to considerably more than personal ambition, empire building, 'immodesty', and egoism. Indeed, it is evidently Elias's interest in and passion for the development of sociology as a subject with an expanding knowledge base, rather than a simple preoccupation with self-interest, that underpins his entire approach. Following his ideas concerning the development of knowledge, Elias understood the widespread tendency within sociology towards multi-paradigmatic conflict and the more general lack of agreement and consensus regarding the sociological enterprise itself, as themselves constituting problems to be addressed. To borrow Kuhn's (1962) terms, sociology has thus far been a mostly 'revolutionary' science, with little or no 'normal' science in its output. While, from Elias's perspective, paradigm specialisation, inter-school rivalry, and theoretical heterogeneity have at times been quite significantly productive and of considerable importance to the expansion of sociological knowledge, the self-same tendencies have also come, from his standpoint, to impede the development of the discipline.

As has been discussed throughout this book, Elias sought to establish a sociological re-orientation in which he envisaged his own work as representing little more than a theoretical-empirical point of departure – one which might at best sensitise growing numbers of subsequent researchers to conceive of sociological problems in a relational and processual manner. As such, his ambition was for other sociologists, not simply for himself, to embark upon a programme of research-theorising that would hopefully lead over time to the establishment of a set of agreed-upon standards, principles, methods, and analytical approaches, together with a body of relatively certain knowledge, that could be used to shift the balance of 'autonomous' and 'heteronomous' evaluations employed in the development of such knowledge decisively in favour of the former and away from the latter. Of course, the very notion of theoretical 'reconstruction', and Elias's 'project' (as some no doubt would construe it) of epistemic consensus-building, transgresses a dominant intellectual code within current sociology premised, as the latter is, upon the legacy of deconstruction, paradigmatic divergence, and eclecticism. In particular, Elias's undertaking falls foul of a prevailing sentiment that might best be described as 'relativistic egalitarianism'. It is a sentiment which encourages liberal theoretical pluralism over and above conceptual usefulness. It also involves the implicit stipulation that no single perspective or orientation should be elevated or 'privileged' over and above any other (see, again, Pels 1991).[55] Indeed, as we have sought to demonstrate in this book, the underpinnings and consequences of such an intellectual code – the prescribed 'habits of good sociology' as it is at present understood – themselves constitute a subject deserving closer scrutiny than they have so far received.

The question of how Elias's proposed 'sociological reorientation' might be realised, and, more specifically, the extent to which the premises of his work can be reconciled with those of other authors, past or present, remain pertinent concerns. In what follows, we shall explore some of the applications and appraisals of Elias's work in relation to a number of key studies. Whilst noting some of the misapprehensions and misrepresentations of Elias's work that have arisen in this connection, our ultimate goal is to explore the utility of his insights *outside* the 'figurational paradigm' through a comparison and dialogue with other key sociological thinkers, especially those who have been in some way influenced by him.

## Key issues and controversies

An examination of a recently published collection of essays, edited by Mary Fulbrook, provides a useful starting point for our consideration of the adoption and appraisal of Elias's work in sociology more generally. In a number of key respects, Fulbrook's book serves to exemplify the reception of Elias's work within what we might call the 'critical cultural studies' genre. The volume is entitled: *Un-Civilising Processes? Excess and Transgression in German Society and Culture: Perspectives Debating with Norbert Elias* (Fulbrook 2007). Almost without exception, its contributors argue against a crude caricature of Elias's work as some kind of twentieth century 'throwback' to the rudimentary eighteenth and nineteenth century theories of Western superiority and inevitable 'progress'. However, Elias is simultaneously presented here as an important and in many ways sophisticated social thinker who, in *On The Process of Civilisation*, has provided a 'path-breaking' and 'searching' study that has much to offer in relation to a series of substantive concerns. Lack of space means that it is only possible in this context to examine Fulbrook's Introduction to the book.

In her exposition of Elias's work, Fulbrook repeatedly uses the terms 'civilisation' and 'modernisation' as synonyms. As an aside, it is worth noting that Elias was highly critical of the concept of 'modernisation' when it crept into sociological usage in the 1960s. The point is more than merely pedantic. His major objection to the term is that it has a time-reference only and is lacking in any connotation of content or structure in the way that structure and process concepts such as 'industrialisation', 'urbanisation', 'bureaucratisation', 'democratisation' and 'civilisation' manifestly do. 'Modernisation' is also, Elias repeatedly pointed out in lectures and tutorials, a term which implicitly resurrects the old ideas of social development as unilinear, inevitable and irreversible progress as found especially in the work of Comte and, to a lesser extent, Marx, and their eighteenth century predecessors. By contrast, as we have seen in this book, in *On The Process of Civilisation*, Elias concentrated mainly, though by no means solely, on the differential developmental trajectories of the three countries in which he had lived up to the time of writing it – England, France and Germany. He was at pains to depict processes of development as invariably complex, multi-linear, multi-levelled and reversible. Briefly, what he attempted to show was that the emergent social units that in the course of time became England and France, were unified earlier than the emergent unit which became Germany. As we have discussed in earlier sections of this book, this was largely because the territories they occupied were smaller, their populations smaller and more homogeneous, and their languages and cultures more uniform. Such overall basic unity gave them initial advantages in European power struggles and in colonising the rest of the world, helping them to become successful imperialists, while the more disunited Germans lagged behind both domestically and in the scramble for territories overseas. However, despite such shared properties, France and England (or, more properly, Britain) differed from one another in numerous ways. France, for example, was more highly centralised and bureaucratised, while, as an island, Britain depended more on its navy than a land army for purposes of attack and defence. It was perhaps in part because he regarded every society's (and every person's) development as in some ways a unique variation on a common pattern that Elias deliberately refrained from referring to Germany's *Sonderweg* (special path), although Dunning and Mennell used this term in the Preface to their English translation of *The Germans* (1996). One of Elias's central points was that, in an overall European context where anti-Semitism was widespread and where France in the late nineteenth century displayed the highest incidence of anti-Jewish feeling – as manifested most infamously in the Dreyfus case – Germany's late unification contributed in a myriad of interacting ways to that country's becoming what retrospective analysis shows to have been the European country where a Nazi takeover and genocidal policy towards the Jews were most likely. Germany's in some ways singular developmental path, however, was largely a 'blind' or unplanned and unintended process. We have returned above to the original arguments of Elias's text to show some of the principal problems with what is probably the most frequent criticism, exemplified by Fulbrook, namely that his study of the 'breakdown of civilisation' in Weimar Germany is an example of what she calls 'long-term structural teleology' (2007: 10).

It is evident that Fulbrook's reading of Elias is, in large part, informed by the work of Dennis Smith. Whilst Smith's account of Elias in *The Rise of Historical Sociology* (1991) is on the whole accurate, parts of his *Norbert Elias and Modern Social Theory* (London, Sage: 2001) are problematic. Tellingly, however, it is precisely on parts of Smith's miscomprehensions that Fulbrook seizes. She writes (2007: 7) that:

> Smith suggests that lower classes had long had a history of 'disciplined practices' but that there is a lack [of] appropriate records on the basis of which to write this history. And in contrast to Elias, Smith sees the aristocracy as 'almost the last major group within medieval and early modern society to be confronted with the challenge of being tied down to a particular place and being forced to do what they were told by an overlord. They were latecomers to the modern game'. Once the aristocracy were forced into self-restraint, in Smith's view, it acquired a degree of prestige.

The implication of this seems to be that, *pace* Elias, it was the lower rather than the upper classes who were the first to become more 'civilised' because of the work disciplines to which they were subjected. By contrast, fighting, leading wars and ruling, the main activities of the upper classes, were undisciplined and unruly practices. There is, of course, something in the idea that written history tends to favour the literate classes because they have left the majority of records, but Smith neglects in this connection that it was members of the priesthood and not the warrior rulers who were the principal recorders in the European Middle Ages. More to the point, the term 'lower classes' is a general one which covers, among others, proletarians, peasants, serfs, slaves and craftsmen. It also covers people at varying levels of poverty/relative deprivation. Above all, Smith's argument fails to take into account the historically shifting balance between 'external constraint' (*Fremdzwang*) and 'self-restraint' (*Selbstzwang*) and the oscillating and irregular part played by violence, power struggles, competition for monetary and prestige rewards, and variable levels of pacification in the formation of habituses and emergent social patterns. Smith also seems to suppose, wrongly in our view, that Elias was offering some kind of 'total', 'fixed and final' theory of 'civilisation'. Such an idea ignores how *On The Process of Civilisation* was deliberately delimited in its focus to the upper classes of Western Europe, with only occasional forays into the lives and experiences of the middle and lower orders. Indeed, this is why Elias called Part I of his book 'Changes in the Behaviour of the Secular Upper Classes in the West', clearly implying that he expected others, or perhaps himself, to carry out comparable studies of elsewhere in Europe and non-Western societies, as well as studies of religious groups and European groups lower down the social scale. That said, Smith's observation in this regard raises some interesting empirical questions. For example, we might imagine a situation in which under a feudal system of servitude, a serf who is bound to an unruly master might at his (the master's) arbitrary will taunt, beat, and otherwise torment the serf and possibly members of his family, including raping them. Such a situation would place tremendous demands on the serf to exercise self-restraint, to not 'lose it' and strike back at his master, and to day-after-day supress feelings of resentment and imagined revenge. This, once more, highlights the need for further empirical-theoretical extensions and possible revisions to Elias's theory of civilising processes.

Similar ideas regarding Elias's work – particularly, as we have discussed, concerns about the allegedly normative or teleological connotations of the term 'civilisation' – have become enduring themes in critiques of his work, particularly by anthropological writers. Probably the most eminent of the anthropologists to have taken issue with Elias is – and here we shall further elaborate on a discussion that we commenced in Chapter 1 – Sir Jack Goody, Emeritus Professor of Social Anthropology at the University of Cambridge. Central to Goody's critique of Elias is how he met the latter in Ghana in the early 1960s and formed an impression of him as 'somewhat isolated from what went on around him'. He appeared, said Goody, 'the very opposite of an ethnographer'. Goody proceeded to write:

> I believe my impressions are fully supported by looking at his (Elias's) autobiographical account of his experiences in (Ghana) and of his encounter with what he referred to as *Naturvolk*. The term is significant since it refers to those who have yet to undergo 'the civilising process'. They are nearer to nature and to the expression of man's biological nature.

As we saw earlier, with his training in philosophy, medicine and sociology, Elias never pretended to be an ethnographer. More importantly, as we have been at pains to point out in this book, he *never* used the concept of 'civilisation' in anything like the way of which Goody is rightly critical. Nor did he use the term *Naturvolk*. His (Elias's) discussion of 'civilisation' as a technical term always centrally involved, as we have seen, the argument that there is 'no zero-point of civilisation' and no 'absolutely uncivilised' human individual or society', with the partial exception of a newborn baby. According to Elias, 'civilising processes' are, and always have been, a human universal, a consequence of the biological evolution of *Homo sapiens* as a social species dependent on the cognitive and emotional learning of such universal 'social facts' as languages and social funds of knowledge. It goes without saying, of course, that, just as the 'civilising' or 'socialising' processes of individuals vary from person to person, group to group, and society to society, so societal 'civilising processes' vary considerably over space and time.

It should be clear from this argument that Elias would not have referred to the people of Ghana as a '*Naturvolk*'. This, we suggest, is Goody's projection onto Elias's text of a notion with which the latter disagreed as profoundly as any modern anthropologist would. That this is the case can be seen from some of the answers Elias gave in an interview published in his *Reflections on a Life* (1994) about his time in Ghana:

> Q: And where did you find the primitive culture you were looking for?
>
> A: I would not use the word 'primitive', I do not like it – 'simpler' is the right word, in the sense of 'less differentiated'.

Q: Much of what you say about Africa makes us think of children.

A: In that case you misunderstand how different it is ... With regard to such an experience there are two attitudes, both of which I consider wrong. The first is – the usual colonialist attitude: that we are more rational, more advanced, and that they are simply more irrational, more childish. In a word, we are better. The second attitude, just as wrong, stresses how much better it is to give free rein to one's feelings and affects. It is indeed more colourful and easy to romanticise. My own attitude is, I think, distinct from both. I see quite clearly that our way of life is only possible because our physical safety is incomparably greater than theirs. If we lived in similar insecurity, we too would seek the help of invisible powers. (Elias 1994: 68–71)

Elias, then, aimed explicitly at avoiding the very notion of a totally 'uncivilised' *Naturvolk* that Goody attributed to him. Goody next proceeds to argue that, while at the University of Ghana, Elias tried to have anthropology removed from the syllabus on the grounds that 'Africa should not be left to the anthropologists who had failed to understand its particular strangeness'. He wanted to replace it with sociology, says Goody. Similarly, in the Sociology Department at Leicester which Elias helped to set up, there was, according to Goody, 'effectively no element of anthropology in its curriculum'. Furthermore,

> ... (Elias's) book on 'What is Society?' [*sic*] has virtually no reference to anthropologists, except to Levi-Strauss in relation to the Whorf hypothesis and to Evans-Pritchard's *Nuer*. If anthropologists in Britain neglected Elias, it was perhaps partly because he neglected them and showed little interest in the range of society with which they were mainly dealing and which his universalising hypotheses might have expected him to include. (Goody 2002: 402)

The title of Elias's book is, in fact, '*What is Sociology?*' not *What is Society?* as Goody suggests. It is accordingly perhaps rather unreasonable to expect Elias to have provided extensive discussion of, and reference to, anthropological work in such a text. Perhaps more importantly, it is simply inaccurate to suggest that the Leicester Department in the 1960s effectively had no element of anthropology in its curriculum. The second-year courses on Empirical Sociology contained a substantial anthropological component and two trained anthropologists, Tanya Baker (who left after one or two years), and Percy Cohen, were appointed to the staff. They were ably assisted by Peter Duncan, Tony Giddens, and Sami Zubaida, all taught by anthropologist Peter Worsley at Hull, and by Geoff Hurd and Terry Johnson, two Leicester graduates who followed Elias and Neustadt, the Head of the Leicester Department, to Ghana. Few British sociology departments in that period can have boasted comparable competence in teaching about the kinds of societies regarding which anthropologists used, not without justification, to claim a particular expertise. Related to this, while we do not doubt that Elias tried to get rid of anthropology at the University of Ghana, we do doubt that his grounds for doing so would have rested on a notion of the failure of anthropologists to understand Africa's 'particular strangeness'. It would have been far more consistent with his line of thinking to have argued against his anthropologist contemporaries because he perceived them as treating less differentiated societies as self-contained, static 'systems' and as ignoring their historical, colonial and wider world contexts.

We have seen in the previous chapters how, from Elias's perspective, a rejection of 'developmental' concepts such as 'civilising processes' by some anthropologists might be understood to relate, at least in part, to a more fundamental rejection of notions of 'social progress' and 'evolutionism' in the wake of both world wars, the rise of Nazism, the Holocaust, and the demise of the British and other European empires. Such ideas also found expression in sociology. For example, in the early writings of Parsons was the implicit idea that nation-states are enduring, harmonious systems (Parsons 1951) which do not need to be studied historically or developmentally because ideas of 'social evolution' have fallen foul of the 'evolution of ideas'. 'Who now reads Spencer?' wrote Parsons (1937: 3). His work is 'the victim of a jealous god, Evolution, in this case the evolution of scientific theory'. Such deeply entrenched ideas may well have played their part in the general unreceptiveness towards Elias's work shown by some key anthropologist and sociologist members of these generations. And yet, as we sought to argue earlier, Elias did indeed explore such issues head-on, and arguably presented a synthesis which satisfactorily addressed most of the principal objections of these scholars. It was a synthesis which also had a greater affinity and resonance with French *anthropologie* than it did with British and American anthropology. This is especially apparent in the work of writers such as Lévy-Bruhl, Mauss, van Gennep, and Bloch.

It is also pertinent in this connection to note that this hostility towards the term 'civilisation' – culminating in its status as a 'watchword' which arouses particular sensitivities – is not extended to anything like the same degree to the term 'culture'. That is to say that, while generally speaking there is widespread acceptance of a distinction between the normative, value-laden, term 'culture' on the one hand, and the technical use of 'culture' as an anthropological concept, on the other, the same cannot on the whole be said of 'civilisation'. As we have seen, Elias provides important insights into why this may be the case in his Introduction to *On The Process of Civilisation*. As we discussed in Chapter 3, what he centrally argued is that the anthropological concept of culture had its origins in the specifically German concept of *Kultur* which '... places special stress on national differences and the particular identity of groups' (Elias 2012a: 17). It is, he suggested, a term which reflected the concerns of a nation which had continuously to form and reform its political boundaries and associated 'we-images' and repeatedly ask the question 'what really is our identity?' (Elias 2012a: 17). It is precisely by virtue of its origins in this German linguistic usage, Elias proposed, that the concept of 'culture' found widespread currency and adoption in anthropological and ethnological circles.

To expand again on an issue that we examined in earlier sections of this book, the term 'civilisation', by contrast, embodies a different structure of meaning. In the first instance, it expresses the national consciousness of countries, notably England and France, which had attained a high degree of political integration significantly earlier than Germany. Accordingly, it gives expression to the 'expansionist tendency of colonising groups' (Elias 2012a: 17) – to nations which had found some degree of resolution to the question of 'who are we?' precisely through their power over and perceived contrast with the 'others' whom they colonised. It was Elias's preoccupation with the processes by which particular groups came to see themselves as 'civilised' relative to others whom they deemed 'uncivilised', rather than a tacit acceptance of the veracity of such notions, that underpins his technical usage of the term. Elias, in fact, devoted a good proportion of his life to researching the competing and contested meanings of 'civilisation', its denotative and connotative associations, and how these emerged out of much broader processes of inter- and intra-state conflict and broader patterns of social development. Perhaps more than any other scholar of his generation, he was not just aware of the normative meanings of the term, but understood how such connotations came into use, and of what they express and reveal about different human figurations. His heightened awareness of the term, his reflexive understanding of its meanings, including of their inherent contradictions, was no doubt underscored by his first-hand experience of the horrors committed in the name of the relative 'civilisation' of different so-called 'races'. And yet, in 'civilisation', Elias also found a term which had certain linguistic advantages over 'culture'. Where the term 'culture' is somewhat static, the term civilisation is processual, and, in addition to questions of difference, distinction, and identity, also lends itself to investigations of social development and, in particular, to the structure of such processes.

It is somewhat paradoxical, then, that the focal point of Elias's contribution to sociology is also the single greatest source of its rejection by some. Even as his work has become increasingly widely known, and there has correlatively emerged a somewhat broader recognition of a distinction between Elias's technical and normative usage of 'civilisation',[56] the term continues to present an enduring hurdle. Time and again, Elias's work is dismissed without serious engagement with his ideas, seemingly on the grounds of little more than a repeated misapprehension of what he meant by 'civilisation'. For example, a year after Johnson and Monkkonen (1997: 2) arrived at the conclusion that '… a large number of historians of crime have become more interested in Elias because his work better describes what they have found than does that of other social thinkers', Elias's thesis on long-term trends in violence was abruptly dismissed by Bonnie Smith as one which is '… utterly fanciful' (Smith 1998: 216). In Smith's case, the dismissal of Elias was again based upon a fundamental misunderstanding of his ideas relating to 'civilisation'. Smith cites the introduction to Jacques-Louis Ménétra's eighteenth-century *Journal of My Life* – in which rape is characterised as a 'normal' aspect of male sexuality – as evidence that disproves Elias's more general thesis. She says that Elias cannot 'see' such evidence because it lacks the 'credibility of official government sources' (216). Such 'non-official' sources and kinds of evidence, of course, were central to Elias's work. In particular, they were central to his arguments concerning how 'violence' became 'pushed behind the scenes' into 'private' life (rather than simply 'disappearing', as Smith wrongly interprets and portrays Elias's thesis).[57] Unfortunately, Smith makes no attempt to assess the degree of accuracy of Ménétra's portrayal. Nor does she present any analysis of whether a putative increase in male violence against women may in some ways be a *consequence* of processes of civilisation. Once again, the ideas are superficially dismissed, seemingly on the grounds of their perceived normative connotations. Thus, while Elias had excellent sociological reasons for highlighting 'civilisation' as a technical concept in his work, when conceived in terms of the promotion and 'marketing' of his ideas to other scholars, it has remained to date an important if in many ways superficial obstacle to their more widespread dissemination.

## Elias and contemporary sociology

The arguments we developed in the previous section are not intended to suggest that Elias's work has continued to be widely rejected within sociology. Indeed, the man and his ideas were and are known by some of the most influential and important sociologists of the last few decades. Among these, three key figures stand out: Anthony Giddens, Michel Foucault, and Pierre Bourdieu. All of them were familiar with Elias's work and, to varying degrees, came to appreciate some of his contributions. In the remainder of this chapter we shall consider each in turn.

### Giddens and Elias

If one were to enquire among present-day British sociologists which of their fellow countrymen they regard as having made the most important contributions to sociological theory since the Second World War, it is a fair bet that a substantial number would name Professor – now Lord – Anthony Giddens. Prior to teaching at Cambridge and the London School of Economics, Giddens spent eight years – 1961 to 1969 – at Leicester.[58] These were the years in which, as we have discussed in previous sections, the Leicester Department of Sociology was at the forefront of the expansion of the subject in Britain. Elias, together with fellow émigré scholar, Ilya Neustadt (the then Head of Department) held considerable sway over the intellectual agenda of the Leicester Department at the time. However, there remains some debate concerning who out of Neustadt and Elias was the more significant *intellectual* influence over Giddens. Chris Bryant and David Jary in their Introduction to a book of readings on Giddens's work, suggest somewhat unequivocally that it was Neustadt who was the more important of the two, with Elias serving as more of a 'scholarly model'. They write:

> With hindsight, the contribution of Elias to [the Leicester] concept of sociology is plain enough but it was not visible to students at the time and one of us, Chris Bryant, managed, not untypically, to leave Leicester in 1966, after three years as an undergraduate and a fourth as a postgraduate and tutorial assistant, without appreciating Elias's part in it and without knowing anything about Elias's figurational sociology. Giddens has told us that Neustadt was the greater intellectual influence ...; but he also says it was Elias who impressed him as a model of what a sociologist should be – the single-minded scholar willing to pursue a large-scale personal project, heedless of distractions, over ... many years ...
> There are certainly some, especially in Britain and the Netherlands, who argue that Giddens owes more to Elias than he acknowledges ... [But] we have no reason to question Giddens's claim that he never knew enough about Elias's (at the time, largely unpublished) work for it to have been a major influence, although in 1961–62 he did attend Elias's first-year lecture course ... which was organised around the theme of development, and he did read Volume I of *The Civilising Process* in unpublished translation and later in German ... But there is a ... more profound sense – the provision of a role model – in which the influence of Elias may have been decisive. (Bryant and Jary 1991: 4–5)

There was, of course, never a single 'Leicester concept' of sociology. Nor would we wish to deny the influence that Neustadt exerted on Giddens. However, we suggest that it was primarily editorial rather than sociological/ intellectual in character. That is, Neustadt was centrally involved in using his considerable editorial and linguistic talents – he was a fluent speaker of six languages – to instruct Giddens and people like Dunning in the skills of intellectual craftsmanship. Nor do we wish to deny Elias's influence on Giddens as a 'role model'. He (Elias) was certainly that in Frankfurt and for many of his students in Leicester and Amsterdam. It seems to us, however, that Bryant and Jary's arguments are overly individualistic and fail to see that Elias's influence on Giddens (and one or two others) is best understood as less a question of direct influence in lectures, seminars, tutorials etc. or through reading Elias's books – little by him was available in English until the 1970s and 80s – than of influence in a tightly-knit and dynamic department *via* exposure to a departmental culture in which Elias and his views of sociology were central foci of debate. Let us elaborate briefly on this.

In the early 1960s when Giddens taught at Leicester, the principal departmental opponent of what Elias then called 'developmental' sociology was Percy Cohen, later Professor of Sociology at the London School of Economics. The heated but always on the surface apparently friendly rivalry between these two contributed to a lively but polarised intellectual environment.

This was enhanced by its cosmopolitan character, a cosmopolitanism evidenced in the fact that Neustadt and Elias, the two central Europeans, attracted to the teaching staff scholars from the USA, Germany, Greece, Cyprus, Israel, Iraq, and South Africa, besides a minority of native Britons. At the time, as we noted earlier, Elias seemed to many of his departmental opponents to be championing a regressive return to an outmoded 'evolutionism' rather than arguing, among several other things, for a synthesis of the best elements of classical and modern theories. To his credit, Giddens was one of those who grasped Elias's synthesising aims. However, there are great differences between his sociological practice and that of Elias. Let us sum up what we take to be the principal similarities and differences between the sociological work of Giddens and Elias.

Giddens's work undoubtedly constitutes what Bernstein described as a 'remarkable achievement'. However, while Elias's greatest strength lay in his capacity as an original thinker and in the synthesis he began to forge between biology, psychology, history and hitherto antithetical approaches to sociology, and that his greatest weakness lay either in ignoring, or in the not fully substantiated comments that he sometimes made on the work of others, with Giddens the balance of strengths and weaknesses arguably lies the other way around. That is, if we are right, Giddens – and we are referring to what might be called the primarily theoretical phase of his career in the 1960s, 70s and 80s – developed most of his key ideas and insights on the back of interpreting, summarising, and critiquing the work of others. That said, however, there are a number of similarities between the sociological approaches of Giddens and Elias. Both share a commitment to an historical and comparative approach. Both acknowledge a dependency on Marx, yet are simultaneously critical of Marxian theory and seek to move beyond it. Probably the greatest similarity between Giddens and Elias in this regard is that both – to express it in terms of which Elias would have partly disapproved – see 'the state' as relatively autonomous from 'the economy' and stress that a process of pacification under the aegis of developing state-control was one of the preconditions for the development of modern capitalism. Although his language is less 'Eliasian', Giddens seems to us to have made precisely this point in what is in our view his most important book, *The Nation-State and Violence* (1985).

Giddens and Elias are both concerned to seek a better way to handle problems of 'structure and agency' than has proved possible in sociology up to now. Both, too, reject Parsons's claim to have made a decisive epistemological breakthrough; locate their respective contributions within the heritage of classical sociology; and seek to synthesise that with modern achievements. However, despite their common desire to build on classical foundations, it is in what they take to be most significant in the classical heritage that the differences between Giddens and Elias become most readily apparent. For example, while Giddens identifies Marx, Weber and Durkheim as having been the most significant 'founding fathers' and rejects Comte almost entirely, Elias, while acknowledging his debt to the 'holy trinity' and others such as Simmel, Mannheim, and Lévy-Bruhl, deliberately laid emphasis on the work of Comte as one of the most important influences on his emergent synthesis.[59] Along with the fact that he worked with Mannheim, this helps to explain, as we saw in Chapters 4 and 5, the centrality in Elias's work of what philosophers call 'epistemological' concerns. By contrast, Giddens dismissed Comte as a somewhat eccentric and outmoded nineteenth century figure who held a naïve faith in science and focused equally deliberately on what philosophers call 'ontological' issues, as if it were possible meaningfully to discuss 'ontological' issues entirely independently of 'epistemological' ones. Elias, in short – unlike Giddens – set great store by the need to develop an empirically researchable theory of knowledge. This, of course, as we saw again in Chapters 4 and 5, is one of the keys to a proper understanding of Elias's work.

It was Elias's concern with the sociology of knowledge, together with his experiences as a doctoral student of philosophy in Germany in the early 1920s, that led him to believe that the Western, Kantian, and neo-Kantian philosophical traditions are irremediably flawed and that sociologists should fight against philosophers' claims to be the arbiters of scientific method. To repeat an argument developed earlier in this book, Elias used to argue that 'methodology', i.e. a 'science of method' as opposed to particular methods *per se*, is a philosophers' invention. In a criticism of an early draft by Eric Dunning of the Preface to the first edition of their *Quest for Excitement* (1986) he wrote: 'Eric my dear, I do not have a *methodology*. It is an ideology foisted on us by philosophers who have outlived their usefulness. I may have a "method"; I'll have to think about it'. By contrast, Giddens argued that 'the social sciences are lost if they are not directly related to philosophical problems by those who practise them'. In saying that, he provided confirmation of Kilminster's (2007) telling argument that late twentieth-century sociologists were more deferential to the professional culture of the philosophical establishment than their precursors had been in the nineteenth and early twentieth centuries. In other words, in marked contrast to Elias, Giddens believes (or used to) that what Elias would have described as a 'flight into philosophy' is an essential precondition for the development of sociology. Perhaps this helps to explain why Giddens has, for the most part, eschewed empirical research while, throughout his life, Elias constantly immersed himself in and tried to make theoretical sense of the details of empirical data? Nowhere is this difference between Giddens and Elias more apparent than in their treatment of problems of 'agency and structure'. It is to these hoary old issues that we shall now return.

Giddens claims to have 'resolved' the 'agency-structure dilemma' – in more old-fashioned language, the conundrum posed by trying to synthesise 'nominalist' and 'realist' ways of conceiving the relationships between human individuals and the societies they form – by means of what he calls the 'theorem of the duality of structure'. In *The Constitution of Society* (1984), he summarised his basic argument thus:

> Structure, as recursively organised sets of rules and resources, is out of time and space, save in its instantiations and co-ordination as memory traces, and is marked by an absence of the subject. The social systems in which structure is recursively implicated, on the contrary, comprise the situated activities of human agents, reproduced across time and space. Analysing the structuration of social systems means studying the modes in which such systems, grounded in the knowledgeable activities of situated actors who draw upon rules and resources in the diversity of action contexts, are produced and reproduced in interaction. Crucial to the idea of structuration is the theorem of the duality of structure ... The constitution of agents and structures, are [sic] not two independently given sets of phenomena, a dualism, but represent a duality. According to the notion of the duality of structure, the structural properties of social systems are both medium and outcome of the practices they recursively organise. Structure is not 'external' to individuals: as memory traces, and as instantiated in social practices, it is in a certain sense more 'internal' than exterior to their activities in a Durkheimian sense. Structure is not to be equated with constraint but is always both constraining and enabling. (1984: 25)

Despite his complex language and the high level of abstraction at which he wrote, Giddens's stress on structures as enabling as well as constraining can, we think, be said to represent an advance relative to many earlier formulations. In our view nevertheless, it is doubtful – as critics have already pointed out – whether the 'theorem of the duality of structure' can be said in any meaningful sense to 'resolve' the 'agency-structure dilemma'. There are at least six reasons for suggesting this:

(i) Unless it is an unnecessarily complex way of suggesting that 'structures' do not exist as such, that is, independently of their particular manifestations, the idea of structure as 'out of time and space' is a literally metaphysical construct;

(ii) The idea that structure exists only in its 'instantiations' and as 'memory traces' seems to us to be little more than a complex way of saying that it exists only in the behaviour and memories of individuals. The impression that this is what Giddens meant is reinforced when he writes that: 'structure is not "external" to individuals ... (I)t is in a certain sense more "internal" than exterior to their activities in a Durkheimian sense' (1984: 25). This is a nominalist, highly subjective formulation. It fails to embrace what might be called the 'relational' dimensions of social structures, for example, those signified by concepts such as 'interdependency chains' or 'social networks'. Although nothing readily visible or tangible links the individual human beings who form structures of these kinds, they, in some ways like electricity which, although it is factually traceable, is also invisible most of the time, are as 'real' as the individual men and women who form them and not reducible to their individual components. More particularly, they involve material linkages *via* sight, sound and brain activity, together with such properties as the length, density and duration of interdependency chains and the degrees of openness/closure of social networks. As Elias and Elizabeth Bott (1957), among others, have shown, such properties play a part of some importance as determinants of the personality and behaviour of individuals. Giddens writes, we think scientistically rather than scientifically, about what he calls 'time-space distanciation' and 'time-space stretching' but does not seem to see that these concepts are arguably incompatible and inconsistent with his nominalist definition of structure;

(iii) While rules self-evidently play an important part in producing and reproducing the patterned character of social life, they are not exhaustive as determinants of social structure. For example, as Durkheim (1982) recognised when he wrote of growing 'material density' as a necessary though not sufficient condition for an increase in the division of labour and as Simmel (1964) recognised when he wrote of the 'significance of numbers in social life', variables such as group size and population density are important influences on social patterning at both the 'micro' and 'macro' levels of social integration. In fact, in tying his conception of structure so closely to rules, Giddens appears close to an idealist position and to be endorsing a variant of the 'Parsonian' or 'normative functionalist' concept of social structure. However, structure in the sense of 'order', 'pattern' or 'regularity' exists even in the absence of rules as Durkheim (1952) showed through his concept of 'anomie' and as Elias (2012b) showed through his discussions of the 'primal contest' and the scientific as opposed to the normative concept of 'order';

(iv) The idea that agents and structures are not 'independently given phenomena, a dualism, but represent a duality' seems to us to be little more than a play on words. As Callinicos (1985) has pointed out, it involves nothing more than the substitution of two letters – 'ty' – for two others – 'sm' – and, as such cannot be held to constitute a 'resolution' of the 'agency-structure dilemma'. Simple plays on words, even simple reasoning, cannot on their own tell us anything about the relationships between agents and structures because such a task cannot possibly be accomplished by philosophical reasoning, only by theory-informed scientific observation. That is, in order to contribute to an advance in the understanding of such issues – not a once-and-for-all 'resolution' of the kind Giddens has attempted – what is needed is the kind of detailed, painstaking observation-guided research, informed by and orientated towards the testing and elaboration of theories undertaken by Elias of how the structure of habituses, personalities, and individual behaviour are formed and changed over time in conjunction with changes in social organisation, and *vice versa*;

(v) By providing a subjectivist definition of structure, Giddens reduces structure to agency. In addition, he also arguably reproduces the agency-structure dilemma by introducing a dichotomic distinction between 'structure' and 'system';

(vi) Lastly, as Kilminster (1991, 1998, 2002) has argued, Giddens's concept of the 'human agent' is overly rationalistic and prevents him from developing an adequate theory of emotions, more particularly of the interdependence of and balance between cognitive and affective processes in human behaviour. That this may help to explain Giddens's neglect of 'pleasure-producing' activities as was suggested in 1991 by John Urry when he wrote that: 'Giddens's conception of human activity is too routinised, too boring, and it is difficult in his framework to conceptualise pleasure-producing activities such as travel, leisure, holiday-making, sightseeing, playing sport, visiting friends and so on' (1991: 168).

This hiatus in Giddens's work is all the more surprising when one takes into consideration that his 1961 MA thesis at the London School of Economics was a pioneering study in the sociology of sport. Although Urry did not refer to them in his stimulating (1991) text on tourism, it was precisely this range of activities that Elias and Dunning sought to grapple with in the 1960s when they wrote their essays on excitement and the 'sparetime spectrum', later published along with a number of other joint and solo essays as a book entitled *Quest for Excitement* (1986; revised edition, 2008). During the 1980s and 90s, it began to become widely recognised, centrally by authors such as Scheff and Retzinger (1991), that one of Elias's major contributions was to the sub-field which acquired the label 'the sociology of emotions'. Scheff's work in particular has focused centrally on Elias's contributions to the sociology of shame and shaming (see, for example, Scheff 2004). Elias would have welcomed this growing recognition but not, we think, unequivocally. His concern was with a synthesising sociology focused on the study of what he called 'human beings in the round' (Elias 1970) and we are sure too, that Elias would have sought to alert us to the dangers of this new – to use a phrase of Max Weber's – 'parcelling out of the soul' (Weber 1944 (1909): 127).

## Foucault and Elias

Another centrally important figure, both in presenting a potentially complementary perspective to that of Elias, and as a scholar who engaged with the latter's work, is Michel Foucault. It is a little known fact that, towards the end of his life, Foucault produced his own French translation of Elias's *The Loneliness of the Dying* (1985).⁶⁰ While Foucault clearly had an interest in Elias's work, and for that matter, Elias in Foucault's, the degree to which one may have influenced the other remains unclear. It is noteworthy that, in *The Order of Things* (1966), Foucault devoted the first chapter of his book to an analysis of the painter Diego Velázquez's masterpiece, *Las Meninas*. Perhaps not coincidentally, Elias discussed the same painting at length in the Introduction to *Involvement and Detachment* (2007a: 49–63). There are some shared elements in the two analyses which are, to a degree, illustrative of the more general common ground of the two authors. For example, both Foucault and Elias used Velázquez's painting to explore the representation of representations, the interplay between aesthetic perspectives and intellectual perspectives and between visual reflections and self-reflections, and the corresponding more widespread shift in cognitive structures that the picture serves to exemplify. Both also consider the particular kind of reflexive consciousness that is represented and enshrined in the painting.

For Foucault, *Las Meninas* signals a sharp contrast between the 'rationalities' of the modern and the classical ages. The painting, he explains, can be understood as standing at the juncture between the two epochs. Its aesthetic structures express a characteristic kind of reciprocal, internally contradictory, self-reflecting rationality – that of a person who stands in a relationship to 'their own' involvement in and reflection upon the world. In *Las Meninas,* this is played out through an array of visual cues, most centrally in the ambiguous relationships of rendered 'visibility' between the observers *of* and the depicted observers *within* the painting. For example, Foucault suggests that Velázquez has depicted himself in the composition, precisely figured in the process of 'depicting' and 'observing the observer'. His:

> dark torso and bright face are half-way between the visible and invisible... As though the painter could not at the same time be seen on the picture where he is represented and also see that upon which he is representing something. He rules at the threshold of those two incompatible visibilities... We are observing ourselves being observed by the painter, and made visible to his eyes by the same light that enables us to see him. And just as we are about to apprehend ourselves, transcribed by his hand as though in a mirror, we find that we can in fact apprehend nothing of that mirror but its lustreless back. The other side of a psyche. (Foucault 2002: 4, 7)

Elias's analysis of the painting is also centrally concerned with the distinctive kind of self-consciousness expressed by the inherent ambiguities of Velázquez's composition. For Elias, *Las Meninas* illustrates a shift towards a cognitive self-distancing characteristic of a nascent court society. It is also, he argued, a painting which, through its indeterminate open-endedness, places a particular set of demands upon the imaginations of those who observe it. In its own way, it expresses, on the one hand, the nexus of Velázquez's 'involvement' in the composition, for example, the inclusion of his own image in the scene; and on the other, it expresses his simultaneous 'detachment', more particularly, *via* Velázquez's use of perspective to create a realistic illusion of three-dimensional space. In a similar manner, a viewer of the painting is first drawn into the composition through its realism and subject matter, and then through the use of subtle aesthetic clues. In particular, the open-ended relationship between observer and observed in the composition is secondarily involved through a central focus upon such qualitative visual arrangements.

This pattern of a 'detour *via* detachment' followed by 'secondary involvement', Elias suggests, underpins Velázquez's exceptional capacity to capture the enigmatic facial expression that precisely characterised his own (Velázquez's) highly involved preoccupation with the act of painting. But how, Elias asks, was he able to do this? How did he know how he himself would appear when engrossed in his pictorial apprehension? This problem of acting simultaneously as the subject and object of one's own 'reflection', or perhaps better, of the inherent competition of demands for simultaneous involvement and detachment is, for Elias, a defining one. Indeed, he suggests, it came to preoccupy many subsequent painters, notably Picasso when he painted his own version of *Las Meninas* in 1957. Elias wrote:

> Picasso may have felt that Velázquez in his painting *Las Meninas* was, like himself, occupied with the problem of the painter's peculiarly divided self-consciousness, as someone who stood outside, who observed the world and formed pictures of it in his mind, and who, at the same time, was also very much part of this world – who was, in a word, detached and involved at the same time. (Elias 2007a: 63)

However, Elias argued, a particularly notable characteristic of Velázquez's self-representation is that the artist showed himself, not as an isolated individual, but as the member of a social group of which he actually formed part. Moreover, he depicted himself in a prominent, but, importantly, not *the most* prominent position within this group. This judgement led Elias to direct his analysis, rather more than Foucault had done, towards the social relationships expressed in the painting. In particular, Elias was led to the differences in social rank characteristic of the courtly figuration to which Velázquez belonged. According to Elias:

> To perceive and to represent oneself as such required a high capacity for seeing oneself from a distance as one might be perceived by others. I have already indicated that this self-representation by Velázquez as one amongst others was closely connected with the characteristics of a court society. For members of such a society, it was more difficult than it is for members of industrial societies to forget that individualisation has its limits, that every human being is almost continuously dependent on others. In contemporary industrial societies many people experience themselves as a little sun around which the universe revolves. It is much more difficult in these societies to find full understanding for the fact that individual identity is closely linked to a group identity. For members of a

court society it was far easier to recognise that an I-identity goes hand in hand with a we-identity ... As [Velázquez] presented himself in this group portrait his personal pride in what he had achieved as court painter and the king's personal servant was unmistakable, but so too was his awareness that he was not the centre of his world. (Elias 2007a: 63)

Once again, we can observe here a similarity between the analyses offered by Elias and Foucault. Like Elias, the post-structuralist Foucault was reacting against the idea of a Cartesian *cogito*, a Kantian 'autonomous agent' or, perhaps better, the image of a 'we-less I', both ways of thinking that have come to dominate Western thought since the Renaissance. Elias, however, couched his argument in terms of his more general critique of *homo clausus* thinking. Velázquez, he suggested, took a decisive step towards more accurately perceiving himself as others might, a step towards, to use Elias's terms, 'distancing himself from himself' (Elias 2007a: 57). Such a step, Elias suggested, also underpinned more general shifts in the human self-image and the development of scientific knowledge, notably the transition from the geocentric world-view towards the heliocentric model. A similar shift was involved, Elias argued, in the development of philosophical theories of knowledge that assume as their point of departure a fundamental subject-object relationship: 'This hypothesis, too, demands that people can distance themselves sufficiently from themselves to be able to perceive themselves as people acquiring knowledge about objects existing outside, and apart from, their own persons' (Elias 2007a: 57). But, he continued, such a step in itself is not sufficient. It:

> represents one to oneself as if one existed in isolation, as a *'wirloses Ich'* – an 'I without we'. It does not go beyond it; the subject-object hypothesis makes it appear that an individual person – oneself – can acquire adequate knowledge about objects alone and single-handed, without learning knowledge from other human beings. It requires yet another step of self-distancing to integrate into theories of knowledge the awareness that every individual step of enlarging the social fund of knowledge presupposes the acquisition, by the individual subject concerned, of a social fund of knowledge, including knowledge and language, from others. (Elias 2007a: 57–8)

For Foucault, the departure from Descartes and Kant leads in a similar, but ultimately distinct, direction. Again, one of his aims in the *Order of Things* was to problematise the Cartesian '*cogito*' and the Kantian ideal of the autonomous social agent by reconstructing the history of their 'constructions'. According to Foucault, the painting by Velázquez illustrates how both notions are the product of an inherently contradictory form of reflexivity emblematic of the modern age. Put simply, in the classical age the 'representer' was understood to be standing separately from the 'represented'. He or she was not viewed as 'part of the picture': classical reflexivity involved the understanding that people use language, painting, music and other symbols to present in a transparent manner a God-given order. Human knowledge, as such, was understood to be the relatively unmediated expression of God's creations. By contrast, Foucault argued, the modern age involves a new epistemological foundation or 'regime', one in which humans are themselves increasingly 'centre stage'. This regime is characterised by a rapidly increasing level of interest in our-'selves' as 'objects of our own reflection'. At the same time, it involves a heightened awareness of how language, culture, and our 'individual uniqueness' set limits to knowledge of the world. And herein lies the paradox of this form of reflection: on the one hand, there is in the modern era a growing capacity to understand that humans are 'part of the picture' – they are inextricably bound up with the conditions of knowledge and, as such, can never fully come to 'know themselves' or penetrate to the origins of thought itself. On the other hand, modern individuals have the insight '... that we can know the world in a way that transcends the limitations of our own positioning within the order of things' (Dreyfus and Rabinow 1982: 48). As such, Foucault sought to highlight the paradoxical character of 'the reflecting human subject' as itself a 'reflection', a 'modern' 'discursive formation' which involves at once the representer and the represented, the creator and the created. Such notions, he argued, are logically deficient. They are contradictory, and ultimately tautological. They involve a series of simultaneous 'doubles' or dichotomies which are inherently irreconcilable. Modern thought, Foucault wrote, is predicated upon:

> the simultaneous appearance of the Double, and that hiatus, minuscule and yet invincible, which resides in the 'and' of retreat *and* return, of thought *and* the unthought, of the empirical *and* the transcendental, of what belongs to the order of positivity *and* what belongs to the order of foundations. Identity separated from itself by a distance which, in one sense is interior to it, but, in another, constitutes it, and repetition which posits identity as a datum, but in the form of distance, are without doubt at the heart of that modern thought to which the discovery of time has so hastily been attributed. (Foucault 2002: 370)

The 'doubles' to which Foucault is referring in this passage are, respectively: the retreat/return of origin – the epistemological foundation of critical theory and hermeneutics; the thought/unthought double of phenomenology; and the empirical/transcendental double of positivism. In each case, Foucault argues, the logical premises of these positions encounter the same core dilemma: a 'hiatus' between, on the one hand, seeking to provide a basis for positive knowledge about ourselves, and on the other, through that self-same undertaking, undermining the very basis for such knowledge. For Foucault, this fundamental paradox is thus a product of its formulation. It is an artefact of modern thinking that is self-defeating. It is rendered through its non-rendering: it is the 'missing' subject – the 'observed observer' in Velázquez's painting – that can only be depicted by its absence. And it is this paradoxical, 'objectified' subject that, Foucault suggests, is also the wrongly-conceived premise of all distinctively modern human sciences such as biology, psychiatry, and political economics.

Once again, we can observe a similarity between Foucault's critique of the 'analytic doubles' intrinsic to modern epistemology – the prescribed notion of an '[i]dentity separated from itself by a distance which, in one sense is interior to it' – and Elias's critique of such notions as presenting an image of humans as *homo clausus*. Like Foucault, Elias sought to circumvent this basic problem of modern epistemology – the fabled 'I' without a 'we', irretrievably lost in the dilemma of *'how can I know' when my knowledge of the world 'out there' is governed by my simultaneous involvement within it* – through rejecting its very premises. In Elias's case, this involved reformulating the problem as one which pertains to human figurations as *homines aperti*, and to the conditions under which certain kinds of knowledge might develop. This is a problem that Elias discussed at length in the chapters subsequent to his analysis of *Las Meninas* in the Introduction to *Involvement and Detachment* (see also Chapter 5 in the present book).

Ultimately, however, the analyses of *Las Meninas* presented by the two authors proceed in quite different directions. Foucault uses the example to lead into what he called an 'archaeology' of changing epistemic regimes – the shifting power/knowledge conditions for accepted 'truth'. Elias, by contrast, employed the analysis, firstly, to examine shifting 'we-I' balances, and secondly, to consider the changing figurational conditions, especially the changing power-balances, for differential ratios of involvement and detachment. Importantly, and unlike Foucault, Elias did not entirely reject the possibility of 'positive' knowledge being derived from 'human sciences', though, of course, he would not have conceived the issue precisely in these terms. Indeed, Elias's ultimate aim was to lay the foundations within sociology for the inter-generational development of a social fund of knowledge about human figurations which might help to avert the recurrent crises – the conflicts, privations, injustices, brutality, and more general causes of human suffering – that are characteristic, to a greater or lesser extent, of societies which possess at different developmental levels different control chances over the interlocking relationships of which they are comprised. As we have seen, in this respect Elias's position presents us with the possibility of the human generation of more autonomous knowledge, albeit under specific figurational conditions and through a detour *via* detachment.

Foucault, by contrast, understood the quest for 'positivity' in human scientific knowledge to be a chimera. As he saw it, it was ultimately the expression of, and disciplinary vehicle for, a power/knowledge complex which *produces* a 'docile' modern subject. Foucault developed as an alternative to positivism/empiricism an 'archaeological' – and subsequently a Nietzsche-derived 'genealogical' – method as a kind of 'discourse about discourses' (Foucault 1969: 205) in which his express intention was precisely not to elevate one account of scientific knowledge over and above that which it takes as its subject matter. In this way, Foucault sought to part company from the likes of Althusser (1969) who, in the final analysis, presented his own critical insights, firstly, as the only source of 'true knowing', and secondly, as always in opposition to 'ideological' accounts of social reality produced by 'state apparatuses' that are expressive of class interests. In fact (and again, the influence of Nietzsche can be observed here), Foucault more fundamentally disavowed any forms of 'absolute truth' or totalising explanation and metanarrative more fundamentally since, from his perspective, all knowledge is partial: all is expressive of a particular 'order of things', of particular interests, of particular historical periods, of particular social groups – everything is inevitably the medium and outcome of particular sets of power relationships which govern the limits of discursive and scientific possibility. This is similar to the critique of 'historicism' developed by Mannheim in the early 1920s. Indeed, as we have seen, for Foucault the very notion of 'absolute truth' is predicated upon a fictional human subject – the autonomous knower entirely devoid of epistemic finitude – which itself is little more than an artefact of the 'modern sciences of man'. However, in rejecting the truth/ideology opposition and the notion of 'absolute truth', Foucault sought equally to avoid abject epistemic relativism. He did so, in part, by rejecting the enterprise of 'epistemology' itself.

In pursuing what he termed the 'archaeology' and 'genealogy' of knowledge, Foucault sought to replace the 'modern' epistemological question of 'what constitutes valid knowledge?' with questions about the 'effects' and 'consequences' of particular forms of power/knowledge and discursive practice. In a manner in some ways reminiscent of W. I. and Dorothy Thomas's (Thomas and Thomas 1929: 572) earlier cited definitive statement that 'If men define situations as real, they are real in their consequences', Foucault sought effectively to move away from the thorny issues involved in the arbitration of truth claims, and in debates about what is 'real' and what 'illusory'. Instead, he explored the power effects of particular nexuses of seeing, saying, and doing which, according to his approach, are inevitably expressive of social power (Layder 2006). For Foucault, moreover, it was precisely the process by which some truth claims came to be attributed with a privileged legitimacy status relative to others – including those within the field of sociology and other human sciences – that is the proper concern for archaeological and genealogical analyses. So, for example, he would have been less interested in the question of whether notions of addiction as a 'disease' are 'valid' or 'true', and more concerned with the discursive and epistemic conditions under which they come to be *accepted* as 'true', and, furthermore, how such ideas might be drawn upon in therapeutic encounters to *produce* a 'clinically addicted subject' with all the associated 'power effects'. For Foucault, then, questions of 'truth' are better conceived and approached as effectively questions about legitimisation contests concerning the shifting configuration of 'normalising' discourses that consist within a particular historical set of knowledge conditions or, to use his term, *epistème*.[61]

Foucault's approach to these issues smacks once again of, to reinvoke the formulation we adopted earlier in this chapter, a sentiment of 'relativistic egalitarianism'. Indeed, in seemingly positing that all expressions of knowledge are equipotent discourses, Foucault ostensibly shared with the 'strong programme' in sociological studies of science something akin to a 'symmetry principle'. His position was definitely not to suggest that his analytical disciplines provide a basis for a 'true' or 'liberating' account of the world. Indeed, Foucault's work is perhaps at its most powerful and insightful in exposing the fallacy of any such undertaking. But in rejecting the notion of absolute truth and in recognising the inevitably partial character of knowledge, Foucault's alternative strategy – of exploring what comes to count as knowledge and its power effects – leaves the abyss of epistemic relativism that he sidestepped firmly in place. To continue with the arguments from previous chapters, in the techniques of archaeology and genealogy, Foucault provided only a means for examining the 'value-congruence' of knowledge – *via* reconstructing the legitimating trajectories of particular forms of discourse – but provided no basis for determining the object-adequacy or reality-congruence of any supposed or postulated item of knowledge. Indeed, such an undertaking would, for Foucault, once again inevitably entail the production of yet another discourse which, in turn, would serve to 'normalise' and 'regulate' particular ways of understanding and 'being in the world'. It would also have its own particular power effects. Rather, as Smith (1999) astutely observed, Foucault's position is ultimately that the only responses, once the dynamics of a 'disciplinary society' are properly understood, '… are either direct political attack upon its structures or radical action to subvert the consciousness of the self it imposes upon us … [including] the pursuit of limit-experiences through various forms of experimentation with the bodily senses' (1999: 82).

It is evident that Foucault's renunciation of epistemology, the humanist, 'centred' autonomous subject, and the truth/ideology binary are each, at least in part, related to a more fundamental rejection of utopian thinking and his tacit acceptance of the diffuse ubiquity of '… the fact of domination… and its brutality' (cited in Lukes 1974: 231). The inspiration for this is, once again, Nietzschean (Kilminster 1998: 88). Similarly, Foucault's advocacy of subverting consciousness through limit-experiences can be seen as relating to a Nietzschean or Heideggerian aspiration to achieve more 'direct experience of the "depths of being"' (Smith 1999: 82). We agree with Kilminster (1998) on this issue that, while Foucault positioned his approach as distinct and separate from philosophies of knowledge – particularly through the invention of 'archaeology' and 'genealogy' as analytical alternatives to epistemology – it ultimately did not mark as fundamental a break from these as he claimed.

Despite its at times 'dazzling conceptual artistry' (Kilminster 1998: 85), Foucault's work remains dependent on much of the terminology and assumptions of the philosophy that was its point of departure. The concept of *epistème* is a case in point. Its Kantian underpinnings are particularly evident when Foucault defines the term as the 'historical *a priori*' (1966: 157). As we suggested earlier, the concept of *episteme* refers to a kind of axiomatic backdrop which contains certain guidelines for what can be thought or said, what comes to count as knowledge and what does not, and which orders both the limits to and the possibility for certain forms of 'truth'. An *episteme* is not so much a totality, or monolithic set of discourses. Rather it defines the relationships between discourses. As such, it involves a shifting set of *intersections*, a configuration (Kilminster 1998: 87). As Kilminster puts it:

> Each discursive formation has its own rules, its own unity, which defines the 'mode of being' of objects and *enables them to appear* and be recognised as objects. In other words, in typical Kantian fashion, any unity or regularity in the world does not reside in the object, but rather is shaped by the *a priori* conditions, in this case discourses. For example, for Foucault mental illness in the nineteenth century *was* all that was said in all the statements that made up the discourse. It was, and still is, the interplay of the rules of the discourse that make it possible for the object of mental illness to appear at all. (1998: 87)

The adoption of a re-worked Kantian *a priori* thus seems to lead Foucault on the road towards nominalism. And yet, in many important ways, Foucault's work arguably *does* mark an important departure from the philosophy it was predicated upon. As we have seen, Foucault shared with Elias a concern with the historical emergence of the particular forms of subjectivity that much philosophy takes as its starting point. Indeed, Smith goes so far as to suggest that, in their respective accounts in *The History of Sexuality* and *On The Process of Civilisation*, Foucault and Elias have provided a kind of 'unwitting collaboration' which presents a critical analysis of the transformation of 'perceptions of selfhood and society along with standards of behaviour with respect to bodily functions and the management of feelings' from the 'pre-Socratic to the post-Kantian eras' (Smith 1999: 81).

There are, however, significant differences between Foucault's and Elias's approaches to historical analysis. A device used by Foucault throughout his work, but perhaps most notably in the opening sections of *Discipline and Punish*, consisted of contrasting the dramatic 'ruptures' between a previous order and a succeeding one. In this sense, we can observe a greater emphasis by Foucault than Elias on historical/epistemic discontinuity. This tendency is not accidental. Foucault used such dramatic contrasts as a means of 'making strange' and undermining the supposed legitimacy of the prevailing discourses of the present. It is also part and parcel of a more fundamental rejection of grand theory, in particular of evolutionary accounts of social development such as those provided by Spencer, Comte, and Marx (Layder 2006: 129). To return once more to an argument from preceding chapters, Foucault's emphasis on historical/epistemic discontinuity as a reaction to the grand narratives of the Enlightenment involves in many ways the substitution of one problematic set of assumptions for another. For Elias, the assumption of either inevitable growth or inevitable rupture ought to be jettisoned in favour of investigations into the shifting ratio between continuity and discontinuity in the development of particular social fields (see again the arguments presented in Chapter 5).

In this respect, we can locate Foucault's work within the primarily philosophical, 'epistemological break' tradition exemplified by writers such as Gaston Bachelard and his pupil, Georges Canguilem – both of whom were explicitly cited by Foucault. As we have seen, Elias's work can be seen, by contrast, as having arisen out of a sociological tradition exemplified by Comte (against whom writers such as Bachelard and Canguilem directly reacted) and which places a greater emphasis on historical continuity. In Elias's case, however, it is a question, not of 'continual progress', but of the theoretical-empirical determinability of the balance between 'continuity' and 'discontinuity'.[62] Such differences in intellectual lineage present considerable difficulties to those who wish to engage in a comparison of these authors' works. As we have aimed to stress throughout this book, Elias was fastidiously concerned with the clarity, precision, and reality-congruence of the technical language that he used. He saw it as necessary to depart from philosophical precepts and language in order to develop a more properly sociological orientation. This involved avoiding reification; developing processual and relational conceptual formulations; and in particular adopting forms of language which are attuned to pluralities of human beings, not '*the* individual' as a static and isolated abstraction. From a figurational perspective, Foucault's language is replete with *homo clausus* formulations and reifications. The concept of power is a particular case in point. It is rendered in Foucault's writing as a self-consisting entity that 'possesses' and exercises intentions and plans. This can be seen, for example, in formulations where 'power' is held by Foucault to 'establish a network in which it freely circulates', 'installs itself and produces its real effects', 'surmounts the rules of right' and 'extends itself beyond them' (cited in Kilminster 1998: 88). That said, such formulations are at odds with Foucault's more general understanding of power as relational, multiple, diffuse and without 'essence'.

It could be argued that it is unfair to criticise Foucault on grounds such as these since his intellectual lineage afforded him a degree of licence for what is, in places, a kind of critical conceptual poetry. He had his own reasons for avoiding the adoption of a scientific (perhaps more properly 'scientistic') lexicon. Equally, however, this 'poetic' tendency is such that, at times, it presents an obstacle to the precision and conceptual utility of his ideas. In addition, Foucault's tendency to declare what his work is *not* – the manifold qualifications and provisos that often precede his key arguments – sometimes lends to it a degree of 'philosophical awkwardness' (Kilminster 1998: 84). By equal measure, however, we can see how, from a Foucauldian perspective, Elias's writing takes on all the rhetorical force of a science – its tight, precise, detached formulations render a world where fantasy and imagination are little more than mythology, and where Freudian formulations are unapologetically adopted. Indeed, in an imaginary dialogue between Elias and Foucault, we might find Elias challenging Foucault to place the discourse of philosophy itself on Foucault's analytical operating table. Likewise, we might observe Foucault challenging Elias to undertake a sociogenetic examination of the Freudian 'repressive hypothesis' – as manifest, for example, in the notion of libidinous 'animalic' aspects of the self and their 'restraint' – and to consider the 'power effects' of this notion in the production of the fabled 'modern subject'.

In a spirit of openness, we shall avoid seeking here a final resolution to our fictional dispute (though, of course, we hope to have answered many of the imaginary charges against Elias in this and preceding chapters)! It is worth adding in this regard that, at the time of our writing, there appears to have been an increasing amount of shared interest in dialogue between Eliasian and Foucauldian scholars. For example, there has recently taken place a well-attended conference entitled 'Care or control of the self' at the University of Hamburg in 2008.[63] There is also a special edition of the journal *Foucault Studies* devoted to a comparison of the work of the two authors, published in 2010.

## Elias and Bourdieu

As we sought to demonstrate above, while an important hurdle to a conceptual comparison of the work of Elias and Foucault is constituted by the differences in language and intellectual orientation of the two men, this is considerably less the case for Elias and another of his contemporaries, Pierre Bourdieu. Indeed, Bourdieu's self-conscious adoption of relational concepts, his explicit identification with the enterprise of developing a 'scientific' sociology, and his rejection of dualistic theorising, all present a promising source of potential common ground with Elias. Unlike Foucault and perhaps to a lesser degree, Giddens, Bourdieu stands apart as one of the few key sociologists of the twentieth century to have engaged seriously with Elias's work. It is perhaps not insignificant that both Bourdieu and Elias wrote on a range of topics not normally addressed by major sociological theorists. These include: sport, art, leisure, taste, and quotidian aspects of social life such as eating habits, manners, and standards of dress. Importantly, both authors were simultaneously researchers and theoreticians; both developed concepts and more general theoretical models in relation to empirically embedded and grounded study; both lamented the divorce of theory from research; and both shared the aim of, to use a phrase of Bourdieu's that we cited in the Introduction, '... preventing people from being able to utter all kinds of nonsense about the social world' (Bourdieu and Wacquant 1992: 53).

In addition to a substantial number of citations of Elias in some of his (Bourdieu's) major studies, notably *Distinction*, *In Other Words*, and *An Invitation to Reflexive Sociology*, Bourdieu frequently expressed his admiration for and intellectual sympathy with Elias in interviews and public workshops. However, Bourdieu tended to depict Elias more as a 'fellow traveller' than as a founding influence on his own ideas. Bourdieu suggested, for example, that commonalities in the fundamental principles of his and Elias's sociology derived from the shared intellectual heritage of Weber, Durkheim, and, with regard to their common stress upon relational concepts, Ernst Cassirer (Bourdieu and Wacquant 1992: 92; 97). The degree of direct influence of Elias's sociology on that of Bourdieu is more difficult to determine. It is notable that, while the term *habitus* is generally attributed to Bourdieu, Elias employed the concept extensively in the original (1939) German version of *On the Process of Civilisation*. The term was rather problematically translated as 'psychological makeup' in the first English version, published in 1969. More importantly, however, while a number of other key thinkers – Weber, Durkheim, Husserl, and Mauss among them (Bourdieu 1990: 12) – also employed the term prior to Bourdieu, they did so arguably without the centrality and level of theoretico-empirical articulation of the concept found in the work of Elias and subsequently Bourdieu. A number of secondary commentators have identified what they consider to be a clear line of influence from Elias to Bourdieu in respect of the concept of habitus (see, for example, Pickel 2005). However, whether or not Elias was a significant influence on Bourdieu, there are definite similarities between the work of the two scholars.

As we mentioned above, in a manner similar to that of Elias, Bourdieu opposed 'theorising' as an enterprise separate from researching. In an interview with Loïc Wacquant (Wacquant 1989: 50), he emphatically stated that:

> I never 'theorize', if by that we mean engage in the kind of conceptual gobbledygook (*laïus*) that is good for textbooks and which, through an extraordinary misconstrual of the logic of science, passes for theory in much of Anglo-American social science. I never set out to 'do theory' or to 'construct a theory' *per se*... it is a complete misapprehension of my project to believe that I am attempting some kind of 'synthesis of classical theory' *à la* Parsons. There is no doubt a theory in my work, or better, a set of *thinking tools* visible through the results they yield, but it is not built as such.

In his introductory text on Bourdieu, Richard Jenkins (2002) argues that Bourdieu's statements concerning 'theorising' in the above passage are rather too 'modest', and do not square easily with his use of the term 'theory' to describe his work elsewhere – examples include *Outline of a Theory of Practice*; 'Elements for a Theory of the Political Field', etc. Nor do they fit with the more general intellectual project that Bourdieu's work constitutes. According to Jenkins, it '... amounts to nothing less than an attempt to construct a theory of social practice and society' (Jenkins 2002: 67). In particular, Jenkins takes issue with Bourdieu's proclamation that theory '... is a temporary construct which takes shape for and by empirical work' (Bourdieu in Wacquant 1989: 50). For Jenkins, it is unequivocally *not* the case in Bourdieu's work that theory is 'subordinate' or secondary to empirical research since 'Bourdieu has developed a body of *social theory* which is worthy of detailed discussion in its own right' (Jenkins 2002: 67; our emphasis).

However, this misses an important aspect of Bourdieu's, and by comparison Elias's, overall orientation towards sociology. Bourdieu shared with Elias an approach to sociology that entailed the conscious and consistent interweaving of the 'empirical' and the 'rational' 'theoretical' components of sociological inquiry. Like Elias, Bourdieu was centrally concerned with avoiding the extremes of reification and determinism on the one hand, and reductionism and voluntarism on the other. Both authors understood that a key means by which it becomes possible to move beyond the selection between such static logical extremes resides in the development of a different vehicle for sociology, one which, in a manner similar to that of the physical sciences, effectively dissolves the conventional distinction between 'theory' and 'research', and in which general conceptual models take form gradually and inextricably in conjunction with – indeed as an integral component of – substantive investigations. Thus, in both Elias's and Bourdieu's work, 'grand theory' of the type presented in the programmatic statements of Parsons or the elaborate social ontology of Giddens, is very largely absent. And yet – and to this extent we agree with Jenkins – each author does present a coherent body of sociological insights, concepts, and observations which have profound implications for debates within theoretical sociology, and which might indeed involve a synthesis of classical and modern ideas, whether or not they were designed or 'constructed' as such.

Notwithstanding the previous point, what both Bourdieu and Elias opposed is the fetishistic treatment of 'theory' as an enterprise in and of itself – as a kind of professional specialism which can be undertaken largely in isolation from empirical research. In this respect, Jenkins's comments are rather more problematic. Bourdieu explicitly opposed the abstract discussions of 'social theory' involving the '... endless and unassailable "conceptual melting pots" of neologisms, refurbished categories, and pseudo-theorems, generally closed by a call for further research or empirical application, preferably by others' (Bourdieu in Wacquant 1989: 50). To this end, Bourdieu developed the distinction between 'theoretical theory' and 'scientific theory'.[64] In 'theoretical theory', he argued, theoreticians treat theory as a substitute for research. In that context, 'theory' as such invariably takes the form of sterile, abstract polemics. It becomes a self-perpetuating and ultimately 'vacuous meta-discourse around concepts treated as intellectual totems' (1989: 50). Scientific theory, by contrast, '... emerges from a programme of perception and of action – a scientific habitus if you wish – which is disclosed only in the empirical work which actualises it' (1989: 50). Within sociology, Bourdieu argues, 'theoretical theory', 'theory without object' is, *via* a professionally-instilled separation, practically divorced from research which frequently involves 'science without a scientist' as in surveys of public opinion and the 'scientific monster' of 'methodology' (1989: 51). He states:

> This opposition between the pure theory of the *lector* devoted to the hermeneutic cult of the scriptures of the founding fathers (if not his own writings), on the one hand, and survey research and methodology on the other is an entirely *social* opposition. It is inscribed in the institutional and mental structures of the sociological profession, rooted in the academic distribution of resources, positions, and competencies, as when whole schools (for example, conversation analysis or status attainment research) are based almost entirely on one particular method, and reinforced by the political demand for instruments of rationalisation of social domination – and it must be rejected. (Bourdieu in Wacquant 1989: 51)

Similar arguments pertaining to the divorce of theory from research have been developed in a number of seminal treatises (see for example, Merton 1957; Mills 1959; Glaser and Strauss 1967; Blumer 1969; Goudsblom 1977). Indeed, Bourdieu directly invokes Glaser and Strauss's image of theoretical theorists as 'theoretical capitalists' (though Bourdieu preferred the term 'rentiers') who, after furnishing grand classificatory schemes, set 'proletarian researchers' to work testing and operationalising such honoured logical hypotheses – a depiction which, as Goudsblom (1977: 102) observes, aptly captures the flavour of Etzioni's preface to a 600 page theoretical treatise which contains the statement: 'The power of the propositions produced by this theory have [sic] to be tested in empirical research and social action' (Etzioni 1968: Goudsblom 1977: 102). As Bourdieu implies in the passage cited above, there is an inherent elitism, a sociogenetic power differential both to this separation of theory and research, and to the specialist linguistic obfuscation that often accompanies the practice of theoretical theory. In the same way, he suggests, the prevailing distrust of the scientific status of sociology stems from reasons which are considerably more 'social than epistemological' (1989: 52). For Bourdieu – and again we can observe some important similarities with Elias in this connection – in order to bypass such problems, it is necessary to depart in two key ways from what became, in the mid-twentieth century, conventional sociology: firstly by developing an alternative sociological *practice* and *method*; and secondly, by deploying a radical 'epistemic reflexivity' (Bourdieu and Wacquant 1992: 48). Let us consider each undertaking in turn.

With regard to statements concerning his sociological 'practice' or 'method', Bourdieu was, on the whole, considerably more explicit and didactic than Elias. Bourdieu referred to his distinctive approach as one of 'social praxeology' (Bourdieu and Wacquant 1992: 10–11). As we have seen, like Elias, this practice and method entailed at the most fundamental level a '*logic of research* which is... *inseparably* empirical and theoretical' (Bourdieu in Wacquant 1989: 50).[65] Also, in a manner again comparable to that of Elias, Bourdieu's practice involved addressing perennial issues, debates, controversies, and philosophical dilemmas by reframing and in some cases circumventing certain basic 'epistemological' and 'ontological' problems through revisiting the manner of their formulation. A comparison can also be drawn between Elias's image of 'steering the sociological vessel' between the 'Scylla of philosophical absolutism and the Charybdis of sociological relativism' (Elias 1971b: 358) and the sociological strategy developed by Bourdieu. As Wacquant proposes, Bourdieu's approach harnesses the 'epistemic virtues' of, on the one hand, an empiricist *social physics* which apprehends social reality from the 'outside' as a set of objective structures, and which seeks to uncover the 'determinant relations' of social existence; and on the other hand, the lens of *social phenomenology* in which society is understood to be 'produced', continually 'made' and 'remade', saturated with meanings and representations, and as such, approached from the 'inside' through the 'life-worlds' of those who constitute it (Bourdieu and Wacquant 1992: 8–9).

For Bourdieu, the basic problem of sociological knowledge is that '[s]ocial facts are objects which are also the object of knowledge within reality itself because human beings make meaningful the world which makes them' (Bourdieu and Wacquant 1992: 7). In many ways, this is a parallel of the problem that Foucault and Elias addressed in their analyses of *Las Meninas*. The principal danger with the *social physics* approach, from Bourdieu's perspective, is the slippage from model to reality by means of the reification of institutions and other structural regularities as 'agents' which 'act', leading social reality to be conceptually reduced to the operation and execution of a model that is, paradoxically, intellectually constructed through methodically ignoring the experiences people have of 'it' (Bourdieu and Wacquant 1992: 7). Conversely, *social phenomenology* provides no means of accounting for the resilience of certain social regularities, the 'objective configurations' that individual strategies and acts of classification produce and reproduce (Bourdieu and Wacquant 1992: 7). Thus, to overcome the limitations and seize upon the virtues of each, in Bourdieu's *social praxeology* elements of structuralism and constructivism are combined as different analytical phases into a kind of 'genetic structuralism' (Bourdieu 1990: 14) through the blending and interweaving of considerations of 'class' and 'classifications', 'positions' and 'dispositions', and so forth. As Wacquant explains it:

> First, we push aside mundane representations to construct the objective structures (spaces of *positions*), the distribution of socially efficient resources that define the external constraints bearing on interactions and representations. Second, we reintroduce the immediate, lived experience of agents in order to explicate the categories of perception and appreciation (*dispositions*) that structure their action from the inside. It should be stressed that, although the two moments of analysis are equally necessary, they are not equal: epistemological priority is granted to objectivist rupture over subjectivist understanding. (Bourdieu and Wacquant 1992: 10–11)

The nod here to Bachelard – towards 'objectivist rupture' – and indeed, the sharp delineation between 'objectivist rupture' and 'subjectivist understanding', 'external constraints' and 'interactions', and 'positions' and 'dispositions', mark significant differences between the intellectual orientations of Bourdieu and Elias. We shall return to them shortly. For the moment, it is sufficient to note that this passage has something of the appearance of the self-same 'theoretical theory' that Bourdieu wished to avoid. Indeed, Wacquant's depiction of Bourdieu's work as involving a fusion of elements of structuralism and phenomenology implies that, *pace* Bourdieu's earlier cited comments, it involves precisely the kind of 'classical synthesis' and conceptual elaboration that Bourdieu took as his point of departure. However, the passage was written (by Wacquant) as part of a more general exegesis of Bourdieu's approach in *An Invitation to Reflexive Sociology*. It is something of a paradox that – just as we have done in the present book in relation to Elias's sociology – the very process of conceptual exposition and discussion necessitates, to varying degrees, the splitting off of 'theory' from 'research': the extraction of an abstracted theoretical model from the more general work of which it forms an integral part. And yet a key tenet of the approach thus discussed involves laying stress upon the necessary and fundamental integration of theory and research. It is perhaps, then, not coincidental that Bourdieu left it to Wacquant to write the introduction to his (Bourdieu's) approach in *An Invitation to Reflexive Sociology*. Elias's resistance to secondary introductions to his work is also perhaps easier to understand in this light.

That said, Wacquant was describing, albeit rather abstractly, a sociological practice in which both theory and research are combined, first through the development of concepts aimed at establishing a 'theoretical stance, a principle of methodological choice' as part and parcel of the research process, and subsequently the '*ex post*' systematisation of ideas whereby concepts are gradually tried, tested, and selected according to their utility and capacity to 'bear fruit' within an on-going programme of research (Bourdieu in Wacquant 1989: 51). The 'trick' to Bourdieu's sociological practice is, he suggests, to combine '… immense theoretical ambition with extreme empirical modesty': to treat precise and seemingly mundane 'objects' of study in a manner which, nonetheless, permits an engagement with 'high theoretical stakes' (Bourdieu in Wacquant 1989: 51). The 'habits' of Bourdieu's sociology are all the more interesting in the context of the notion of 'intellectual modesty' advocated by Pels that we discussed earlier in this chapter. Like Elias, Bourdieu's intellectual humility did not extend so much to his intentions regarding the development of a scientific sociology, as to the substantive concerns of his work. Again, we might observe the commonalities shared by Elias and Bourdieu in respect of their focus upon topics not normally treated as worthy of 'grand theory' – sport, leisure, the arts, manners, etiquette, etc. – as Bourdieu puts it: '… the power of a mode of thinking never manifests itself more clearly than in its capacity to constitute socially insignificant objects into scientific objects … or … to approach a majorly socially significant object in an unexpected manner' (1989: 51). In these key respects, then, the sociological practice of Bourdieu and Elias shares some remarkable similarities.

That said, on the face of it, Bourdieu's concept of 'epistemic reflexivity' would appear to point towards a more substantial difference between the work of the two authors. A simple reading of the term smacks of the classical epistemological invitation to engage in cognitive self-reflection, or 'navel gazing': to consider time and again how our knowledge of the world 'out there' might reflect only what's 'in here' – how it may be little more than a reflection of our own 'subjective' experiences and modes of representation. In previous chapters, we have discussed at some length Elias's objections to this way of posing problems about knowledge. However, as Wacquant argues, Bourdieu's term actually points towards a sociological practice which permits the historicisation of scientific rationality without dissolving it. It allows, in short, for a reconciliation of 'modernist certainty' and 'postmodernist relativism' (Bourdieu and Wacquant 1992: 47). Indeed, Wacquant suggests that, 'Far from encouraging narcissism and solipsism, epistemic reflexivity invites intellectuals to recognize and to work to neutralize the specific determinisms to which their innermost thoughts are subjected...' (Bourdieu and Wacquant 1992: 46). Bourdieu thus maintains a commitment to the desirability and possibility of scientific knowledge *à la* Habermas on the one hand, whilst at the same time recognising the social contingency of such knowledge. On the other hand, together with the argument that knowledge categorisations are '... instruments of (symbolic) power possessing a constitutive efficacy', he stresses that knowledge has 'power effects' of the kinds discussed by Derrida and Foucault (Bourdieu and Wacquant 1992: 46). As we have sought to show throughout this book, for Elias, though he did not use the term, such 'reflexivity' was conceived more in terms of an awareness of, and orientation towards, seeking to understand the long-term development of human figurations and the different ways in which knowledge of the social world is tied to this development. He also sought to explore such issues as the position of sociological knowledge relative to that of other sciences, the development of the 'triad of basic controls', and more generally, problems of involvement and detachment. For Bourdieu, 'reflexivity' pertains more specifically to the social 'field' of academia, and involves an awareness of the peculiarly political implications of sociological knowledge. It is in respect of the latter, in particular, that we find the most significant differences between the two authors.

For Bourdieu, sociology is an eminently political and moral science. While he concurs with Elias that sociologists should strive to become 'destroyers of myths' (Bourdieu and Wacquant 1992: 49), Bourdieu maintains that the very process of myth-destroying has moral and political implications. Sociologists, Bourdieu argues, are centrally concerned with – and embroiled within – an academic social field involving power struggles over symbolic domination. As such, there can be no such thing as a 'disinterested' or 'neutral' sociology.

It can never reach the 'uncontroversial status' of the natural sciences (Bourdieu and Wacquant 1992: 50). Bourdieu accordingly suggests of the social sciences that:

> The idea of a neutral science is a fiction, and an interested fiction, which enables one to pass as scientific a neutralised and euphemised form of the dominant representation of the social world that is particularly efficacious symbolically because it is partially misrecognisable. By uncovering the social mechanisms which ensure the maintenance of the established order and whose properly symbolic efficacy rests on the misrecognition of their logic and effects, *social science necessarily takes sides in political struggles*'. (Bourdieu and Wacquant 1992: 51)

This is a problem to which Elias arguably paid less attention than Bourdieu. That is, according to Bourdieu, through the very character of their subject matter, sociologists are involved in a science which has *inevitable* political ramifications. Elias's work is no exception in this regard. His stress upon conceiving the social universe in terms of pluralities of open, bonded, figurations, not isolated individuals, is a direct counter to the earlier-cited neo-liberal mantra uttered by Margaret Thatcher in 1987 that there is 'no such thing as society'. Indeed, Elias's work as a whole might be understood as constituting a sustained attack on the myth of the 'autonomous individual' or 'self-made man' (to use the colloquial and sexist formulation). Similarly, Elias's emphasis on understanding 'economic' activity as an aspect of human relationships effectively 'dispels' the myth of the 'market' as a kind of 'god' which has its own agency; its own 'natural' 'equilibrium' – and that, like water, it will always find its own level. For Elias, markets are not 'gods' to which we must offer 'sacrifices' in order for them to be appeased. In this sense, Elias's ideas, while not formulated as political doctrines, nonetheless have a profoundly political relevance.

For Bourdieu, advances in the field of social scientific knowledge towards greater autonomy do not go hand in hand with greater 'political neutrality'. If anything, in his view, the more 'scientific' that sociological knowledge becomes, the more its political significance increases, if only in its capacity to act as a 'shield' against '... forms of mystification and symbolic domination that routinely prevent us from becoming genuine political agents' (Bourdieu and Wacquant 1992: 51). That is to say, particular accounts of the social world are advanced and resisted in the legitimation struggles between different social groups. As such, inaccurate models of the social universe might not be simply erroneous forms of knowledge, but deliberate attempts, deployed in power struggles within asymmetrical human figurations, to mask or obfuscate an oppressive social order.

It would appear, then, that their views on the political status of sociology mark a clear separation between the work of Elias and Bourdieu. Van Krieken (1998) has argued as much, suggesting that it is in this key respect that Elias's sociology of knowledge remains one of the most problematic aspects of his overall body of work (1998: 83). Van Krieken concludes that, in contrast to Bourdieu and scholars who argue similarly, Elias has: '... an essentially Weberian position on scientific "value freedom"' (1998: 82). And in relation to his emphasis upon 'detachment' concerning '... the politics and social context of sociological theory and research', Elias's approach affords us, says Van Krieken, '... very little purchase on either the rough and tumble of social scientific practice, or the impact and effects on social life of sociological knowledge itself' (1998: 82).

However, once again, Elias's position is rather more complex than it might at first appear. As we have endeavoured to demonstrate in various sections of this book, *pace* the arguments of van Krieken, Elias shared with Bourdieu an objection to the notion of a 'watertight separation between fact and value' (Bourdieu and Wacquant 1992: 48). He proposed, directly *contra* Weber, that the notion of absolute 'detachment' or absolute 'value freedom' is a chimera. He maintained, instead, that sociologists should consider such issues in terms of the *different* ways in which knowledge about the world is tied to the structure, values, and interests of different social groups. To put it simply, it is not just a question of whether or not knowledge is value-laden, but a question of the *degree* to which and the *ways* in which it is value-laden. It is also a question of *which values?* and *whose values?* Do, for example, such values stem from a commitment to understanding the world as it *is*, or more from understanding the world as it is believed that *it ought to be*, or indeed, *ought not to be?* Thus, for Elias, questions concerning value congruence must necessarily be considered in conjunction with questions about reality congruence. The representation in the passage from Bourdieu cited above of an absolute division between a 'completely detached', 'value free', 'disinterested' social science on the one hand and a highly involved political sociology on the other is, in this sense, problematic. The notion of degrees of 'involvement' and 'detachment' advanced by Elias as opposed to such dichotomous polarities as 'true' and 'false', 'objective' and 'subjective', 'neutral' and 'interested', is expressly intended to contribute to a movement beyond such oppositions. That is the case because they make the problem to which they pertain intractable through steering thinking away from conceiving of *degrees* of approximation, and *degrees* of agreement between 'understandings of the world' and 'the world thus'. Indeed, the notion of an 'absolute truth' that is masked by an equally absolute 'ideology' that is brought to mind by Bourdieu's images of the 'myths' that 'cloak the exercise of power' (Bourdieu and Wacquant 1992: 49) paradoxically reintroduces a pointed distinction between 'the exercise of power', 'the world as it really is' – 'facts', and 'the world as we are compelled to see it', the 'cloak of mythology' – and 'values'. Such notions stand in contrast to a consideration of how, as we have discussed, even highly-involved 'ideological knowledge' may have an albeit limited degree of reality congruence *as well as* a high degree of value congruence, and of how investigations of one form of approximation without the other inevitably steer us back to the model of a clear-cut separation between 'reality' and 'fantasy', and ultimately, 'fact' and 'value'.

Where van Krieken principally goes wrong, in our view, is in his treatment of the concept of 'detachment' in Elias's work as a *substance* rather than an aspect of a *relationship*. Detachment, Elias argued, must always be understood *in relation to* involvement. It was only van Krieken's artificial divorce of the concept of 'detachment' in this manner that allowed it to be treated as effectively synonymous with the notion of 'value freedom'. It is also misleading to suggest, as van Krieken does, that Elias equated 'detachment' with political neutrality. As Goudsblom expressed it in his funeral oration for Elias in *Theory Culture and Society* in 1990, while Elias claimed that he had worked, 'not to please any power', his sociological insights, notwithstanding this aim, are nonetheless potentially valuable as political tools. It is useful in this connection to draw a distinction (though, of course, not a cast-iron one) between political *incursions* into scientific knowledge, and the political *significance* and *ramifications* of such knowledge.[66] Employing this distinction, it is arguable that Elias's concept of 'detours *via* detachment' stresses precisely the *political significance* of sociological knowledge, indeed, of all scientific knowledge. For Elias, an *orchestrated* political role for sociology is perhaps some way off. It might be progressively realised in tandem with the development of a relatively stable stock of more reliable reality congruent sociological knowledge. Nonetheless, the potential for sociological knowledge to have political utility, or perhaps better, to serve as a basis for systematic interventions in the sphere of human figurations, is of paramount importance. For Elias, it is *the raison d'être* of sociological knowledge to provide a more adequate and secure basis for such interventions so as to secure more intended relative to unintended consequences in the struggle against social injustice, the spread and perpetuation of human suffering, the recurrence of social catastrophes including wars, famines, and ultimately the destruction of the planet. Of course, the problem of 'which interventions' and 'whose control of whom?' (van Krieken 1998: 82) – that is, of the 'abuse' of social scientific knowledge, remains pertinent. For both Elias and Bourdieu, such a concern points all the more sharply to the need to establish greater scientific autonomy within the social scientific field. As Bourdieu argued:

> There is in history what we may, after Elias, call a *process of scientific civilisation*, whose historical conditions are given with the constitution of relatively autonomous fields within which all moves are not allowed, in which there are immanent regularities, implicit principles, and explicit rules of inclusion and exclusion, and admission rights which are being continually raised. (Bourdieu and Wacquant 1992: 189)

In other words, Bourdieu, like Elias, stressed the need for the development in sociology of institutional safeguards to ensure higher degrees of professional autonomy and to maintain a high degree of control over the knowledge thus produced. Bourdieu, again like Elias, was concerned to guard against the incursion of non-scientific political agencies into sociological research.

Bourdieu envisaged sociology as becoming a discipline in which scientific knowledge is progressively established not so much through the elaboration of ethical norms or methodological rules, but in the scientific competition between different accounts of the social universe. Thus, for Bourdieu, 'genuine intellectuals' are those who have been able to achieve a degree of independence from 'temporal powers', a degree of autonomy from the interventions of political and economic authorities (Bourdieu and Wacquant 1992: 56). Like Elias, Bourdieu stressed the importance of simultaneously maintaining a 'critical detachment *and* involvement' (1992: 55). The key point for Bourdieu was to recognise that, while science is a 'political activity' in the sense that the knowledge it produces has political ramifications, it is not '… *merely* a politics and therefore incapable of yielding universally valid truths' (1992: 47). For Bourdieu, scientific knowledge is paradoxical in that it can 'escape history' in the sense of gaining a degree of autonomy from historical specificity, but only under certain conditions. These conditions in particular are those in which safeguards for 'the institutional bases of rational thought' are continuously produced and reproduced (1992: 48). As such: 'To conflate the politics of science (knowledge) with that of society (power) is to make short shrift of the historically instituted autonomy of the scientific field and to throw the baby of sociology out with the bathwater of positivism' (Bourdieu and Wacquant 1992: 47–48).

Thus far we have found rather more in the way of agreement than disagreement between Bourdieu and Elias. However, there are indeed important differences between the two. The most significant of these, as we have alluded to above, relates to the residual structuralist and Kantian elements which arguably remain embedded in Bourdieu's approach. As Layder (2006: 194) astutely observed, a key difference between Bourdieu and Giddens (and Elias by extension) is that Bourdieu ultimately maintains the notion of an 'objective world' which is distinct from the world of 'situated behaviour': that there are 'generative mechanisms' which stand as separate from the observable realm of 'situated interaction', with 'habitus' acting as a kind of conduit which conjoins these. This is not to suggest that Bourdieu adheres to a simple, mechanistic determinism, but rather that, for him, there are aspects of the social universe beyond the level of social 'encounters'. For example, Bourdieu wrote:

> It is good to recall, against certain mechanistic visions of action, that social agents construct social reality, individually and also collectively. We must be careful not to forget, as the interactionists and ethnomethodologists often do, that they have not constructed the categories they put to work in this work of construction. (Bourdieu 1989: 47)

In a classical Kantian sense, then, there is something 'prior' to action, in this case, 'categories'. They are more enduring than the products of social agents. It is as if such categories could be understood as not themselves the 'products' of human 'figurations'. Indeed, while Bourdieu's use of the term 'social field' looks, superficially, like a rough equivalent to Elias's use of the term figuration, there are considerable differences between the two concepts. Most importantly, Elias's concept of figurations defines the (diachronic) structure of relations between *people*. For Bourdieu, by contrast, the concept of a social field implies the structure of relations between *positions* in a manner similar to Bhaskar's (1989) notion of a 'position-practice system' (Vandenberghe 1999: 22). Bourdieu's approach stems from an essentially realist social ontology wherein a sharp delineation is drawn between 'things in themselves' *as opposed* to things as they are apprehended by the senses *via* their phenomenal characteristics. But critically it also involves the clear possibility of *things in themselves* operating without observable consequences. As such, the observable structural regularities of 'fields of positions' are understood to be *expressive of a priori* governing conditions or 'noumenal' structures (*à la* Bachelard); 'generative mechanisms' (*à la* Harré); or 'tendencies and causal powers' (*à la* Bhaskar). As the latter explained it:

> If science is to be rendered intelligible, the world must be seen as one of persisting things, of differing degrees of structure and complexity, to which powers and tendencies are ascribed; it cannot be reconstructed as a world of atomistic events apprehended in sense-experience... Generative mechanisms, I have argued, must be analysed as the ways of acting of things; and their operations must be understood in terms of the exercise of tendencies and causal powers. (Bhaskar 1978: 184)

Elias's insistence that social figurations consist of the relationships between human beings, marks him out from this perspective as an unreformed empiricist. It would seem that Elias is only concerned with the *prima facie* characteristics of the social world, and as such, is unable to apprehend 'deeper' aspects of reality that cannot be 'observed'. But, of course, this would be a rather too simplistic reading of his position. For Elias, different aspects of social reality, different planes of the social universe, exist not as 'distinct realms', but as *different levels of integration* and *different levels of structural complexity*. To provide a basic example: as a social figuration becomes more complex, it may well become increasingly 'opaque' to the people who comprise it. Accordingly, it is impossible for them to 'see' or 'apprehend' it in any simple or direct sense. Thus 'structures' might be considered to be 'deep' in the sense that they involve levels of complexity that cannot be directly apprehended by the senses, or directly 'observed'. Nonetheless, this by no means obviates the possibility that they can be understood, over time, through the systematic interweaving of theory and enquiry by interdependent generations of scholars.[67] The conceptual 'partitioning' of social reality into ontologically discrete spheres which then sit 'in relation' to one another, bridged by the concept of 'habitus', is, for Elias, restricted in its utility for serving as an orientation towards social reality. It presents a sociological schema which is only in part 'relational'.

It sits, to use Depelteau's (2008) 'classification' of Bourdieu's model, somewhere between a 'deterministic' and a radically 'relational' position, as a kind of 'co-deterministic' halfway house. The net outcome of such a position appears, moreover, to involve, to the degree that Vandenberghe's (1999) analysis of Bourdieu's position is accurate, the pursuit of questions which range from a resurrected epistemological 'how can I know the world out there?', in the form of 'how do we know that those transfactual structures exist?', through to a 'great man' view of scientific knowledge apparent in such questions as: 'Who has accorded primacy of the unobservable over the observable? Who speaks for those structures? Who speaks in their name?' (Vandenberghe 1999: 35). Elias's reservations concerning the premises and fruitfulness of such questions have been discussed by us at length in the preceding two chapters.

There are, then, elements of Bourdieu's approach which ultimately return his thinking to some of the classical philosophical dilemmas that Elias (and to an extent Bourdieu himself) sought to escape. Nonetheless, as we hope to have shown, perhaps more than any other theorist, there is much in Bourdieu's work that is compatible with the work of Elias. Bourdieu's work also provides a useful consideration of some areas that were neglected by Elias, in particular the political role of sociology, plus his extensive discussion of the *practice* and *reflexivity* of sociologists. In many ways, to answer the critique of Elias presented by Rojek (1986), Bourdieu provides more than Elias in the way of a 'drill', a model of sociological practice in terms of which individual researchers might be able to negotiate the problems of cross-fertilising theory and research, and of blending and balancing their involvement and detachment in sociological inquiry.

We now turn to the conclusion of this book by considering the prospects for the realisation of Elias's great hope: that he would have made a contribution to the beginnings of a more general reorientation of sociology – as we have called it, a 'relational turn'.

# Conclusion

## A relational 'turn'? The future prospects of figurational sociology

It is probably fair to say that sociology at the moment is characterised by the dominance of a culture of discussion and critique over a culture of testing and research. Such a situation seems to have come about largely in conjunction with the rise to prominence of social – as opposed to sociological – theory (Mouzelis 1995) and the various strands of what have come to be known as 'cultural studies'. As we have seen, Elias was in favour of discussion and critique but he always insisted that they should go hand in hand with research and 'testing'. Institutional pressures for sociologists to be 'research active' appear, by and large, to have done little to rectify this state of affairs.

In the UK at the time of writing, for example, the periodic government research audit called the Research Excellence Framework (REF) (formerly the Research Assessment Exercise) has arguably broadened the divide between theory and research within academic sociology. In this review, a panel of subject experts (key academics from leading institutions) assess the output both of individual academics and of the departments to which they belong. Individuals and departments are awarded between one and four stars according to the perceived quality of their published outputs, the research grants they have been awarded, and various other 'indices of esteem'. The REF is the spearhead of a set of competitive pressures faced by sociologists and other academics in the UK compelling them to seek to be published in the 'right journals', to get funding from the 'right' funding councils, to publish books with the 'right' publishing houses, and so forth. Much has been written about the implications of the RAE/REF, but suffice it to say that books like Marx's *Kapital*, Durkheim's *The Division of Labour*, Weber's *The Protestant Ethic*, or indeed, Elias's *On The Process of Civilisation*, would have been difficult, perhaps impossible, to produce within the competitive dynamics of what we might call the REF/RAE climate. In a similar manner, scholars from other disciplines, including the astronomer Copernicus (to whom we have referred to on more than one occasion in this book) and, as another instance, the progenitor of modern mathematical logic, Friedrich Gottlob Frege, would have been equally disadvantaged (Gillies 2006).

This prevailing set of competitive social dynamics seems, with a few notable exceptions, to have compounded a more general tendency for sociologists to focus on highly specialised social issues, over short time-spans, and to neglect long-term social processes, and associated broader overarching questions about human societies – a characteristic neatly encapsulated in the title of Elias's (1983a) article, 'The retreat of sociologists into the present'. Comparative and developmental sociological research involves relatively long planning or 'lead-times', the requirement for sustained levels of continuous funding and support, and the need to look beyond the immediate social issues of the present – demands which do not sit well with the timeframes of the REF/RAE climate, or with the growing requirement for research to have clearly identifiable 'pay-offs' or 'impacts' for specific 'user groups'. Paradoxically, as Elias has suggested, it is arguably only through an engagement with such longer-term processes and frames of reference, and only through a relatively high degree of detachment from immediate social pressures and the demands of specific 'user groups', that sociologists will be able to begin to develop knowledge with sufficient reality-congruence to form the basis for interventions in the sphere of human figurations since the latter have a lower level of intended relative to unintended consequences than is the case in the physical and biological sciences. For Elias, although he never used the term, the envisaged key 'user group' for sociological knowledge would have been 'humanity as a whole' or all the interdependent participants in given sets of figurational dynamics. However, these premises are considerably at odds with dominant trends in contemporary sociology, perhaps especially in the United Kingdom.

It is difficult to say anything specific about the current state of British sociology, let alone sociology more generally, without engaging in sweeping over-generalisations. Indeed, perhaps the least contentious point to make is that British sociology, as is indicative of the more general sociological crisis we have discussed throughout this book, is currently marked by a great deal of paradigmatic heterogeneity, diversity of interests, and inter-school tensions. It is perhaps also not so controversial to claim that, at its current stage of development, sociology in Britain has no clearly distinct boundaries from the disciplines of cultural studies and philosophy. In tandem with the broad tendency that we noted earlier for sociological research to neglect long-term processes and focus on highly specialised fields of investigation, there is also a tendency towards a preoccupation with the cultural sphere and the reading of its (inter-) textuality – a tendency which has involved '... endless terminological disputes and esoteric debates about the disappearance of reality' (Rojek and Turner 2000: 639). As Rojek and Turner suggested (2000: 640), in the context of a general funding shortage in the social sciences, current trends in academic publishing, and the REF/RAE environment, academic sociologists are rewarded '... for exegesis and penalise[d for] long-term qualitative and quantitative work'. Under such conditions, the sophisticated theoretical insights of specialists in 'decorative social theory' are used not so much to 'guide', but to adorn, embellish, and otherwise lend ostensible veracity to such funded empirical studies.

To formulate the problem provocatively: in much sociological research, theory is rather more 'tasted' than 'tested'.

Of course, large-scale sociological research still takes place, and some of it is indeed historical and comparative. And not all sociology is pre-occupied with questions of inter-textuality and the supposed 'disappearance of reality'. Nonetheless, it is perhaps not inaccurate to suggest that the tendencies observed above have become pervasive, and have come to dominate many, but by no means all, debates within the field. It is perhaps rather less contentious to argue that, in its current state, there is little consensus regarding the future direction of sociology, and indeed, the overall purpose of the sociological enterprise. It is this need for a degree of consensus concerning the purpose and direction of sociology that underpins Elias's call for a climate of research and testing. In placing stress upon the 'testing' of sociological concepts and theories, Elias was not supporting a 'scientistic' view of the subject, that is, one whose practitioners seek to emulate the natural sciences and predominantly use quantitative and experimental methods. Rather, he was advocating a model of the sociological enterprise in which professional sociologists share a commitment to the generation of 'advances' in knowledge of the social world. Thus, for Elias, the notion of 'testing' necessitates the development of an intergenerational body of social scientists concerned with establishing over time and with higher degrees of certainty whether any particular models of the social universe, and in particular, ideas concerning the structure, 'direction', or even enduring characteristics of social processes, have utility in the sense of 'fitting' more with what is shown to hold in the course of subsequent research-based investigations.

However, Elias's stress on the centrality of research for the process of testing sociological knowledge is not without its critics. Indeed, the self-professed data-dependency of Elias's concepts and theories has played a part in leading his sociology sometimes to be described as 'non-explanatory, purely descriptive' (Zubaida, cited in Dunning and Mennell 2003). Working in the same direction is the fact that Elias argued against the adequacy of causal, factor and law-like explanations at the human-social level of reality. Such explanations are fitting, Elias used to argue, as far as the structurally relatively simple and relatively slowly-changing physical and chemical levels of the universe are concerned. At the more complex and rapidly-changing biological and human-social levels, by contrast, what are needed are structure-and-process concepts and models. Darwin's theory of biological evolution is one example. Elias's theory of the relations between civilising processes and state-formation is another.

Elias's insistence on the testability/refutability of concepts and theories is contradicted by a widespread judgement that holds the opposite. For example, Smith (1984) argued that the theory of civilising processes is 'irrefutable'. Such an argument was echoed by Leach, the anthropologist, two years later when he suggested that the theory is 'impervious to testing' (Leach 1986).

In 1988, Armstrong similarly wrote that Elias's theory 'is a fusion of untestable and descriptive generalisations' (1998: 317). Giulianotti even went so far in 1999 as to claim that Elias introduced the concept of 'decivilising spurts' in order 'to rebut ... counter evidence' (1999: 45). As we showed, Elias dealt with decivilising processes from the beginning. Moreover, despite such criticisms, there is a growing body of research-based investigations which have 'applied', 'tested', 'developed' and 'revised' Elias's ideas precisely in the manner that these critiques suggest is not possible. Mennell (1985; 2007) has attempted to test the theory in two main ways: firstly by means of a comparative study of the development of tastes and eating in England and France; and secondly by means of a comprehensive study of the American civilising process. Similarly, Elias and Dunning (1966; 1971c; 1986; 2008) attempted a limited test of the theory by reference to leisure and sport. Other tests have been carried out by Goudsblom (1992) regarding fire; Hughes (2003) regarding smoking; Spierenburg (2008) regarding murder; Wouters (1977, 1986, 2004, 2007) regarding 'informalisation'; Waddington (2000) and Waddington and Murphy (1992) regarding sport and drugs; Maguire (1999; 2005) regarding sport and globalisation; Sheard (2004) and Sheard and Murphy (2008) regarding boxing; Dunning and Sheard (1979; 2000) regarding rugby, and Malcolm (1997, 1999, 2000, 2012) regarding cricket, to name but a few.

Further tests of Elias's theory will have to draw a distinction between at least two aspects: his conclusions regarding the overall directions of European civilising processes and his conclusions regarding their socio- and psycho-genesis. As to the question of directions, Elias's theory would be successfully refuted if it could be shown empirically that the *overall* trend of European development in the time-frame he considered – roughly from the Middle Ages to the period after the First World War – was not in a civilising direction in England and France. (As we saw in previous chapters, he began to trace the more or less simultaneous decivilising development of Germany in *On the Process of Civilisation* (2012b), and took the analysis considerably further in *The Germans* (1996).) Decivilising developments since that time – for example, of the kind shown in trends of violent crime throughout the West since 1960 (Spierenburg and Body-Gendrot 2007; Pinker 2011) – would not refute the theory or require it to be substantially revised unless it could be shown that they had occurred as a result of changes that Elias's theorisation would lead one to expect to produce consequences of a predominantly civilising kind. In other words, demonstration of the occurrence in Western Europe of greater or lesser long-lasting decivilising changes during and after the Second World War would not, *ipso facto*, constitute a refutation of Elias.

This discussion of Elias's and other figurational sociologists' analyses of decivilising as well as 'civilising' processes brings us to the second aspect. In order to test Elias's theorisation of the socio- and psychogenesis of European civilising processes further than has been accomplished so far, attention will have to be paid to how Elias theorised the complex interrelationships and interactions between, on the one hand, *social structural* developments such as state-formation, pacification under state-control, growing trade, growing wealth and the monetarisation of social relations, the lengthening of interdependency chains and functional democratisation, and on the other hand, normative, behavioural, and personality developments at the levels of manners and habitus. Attention will have to be paid in these regards to the balance of similarities and differences in the developmental paths of culture areas, nations, classes, regions, ethnic minorities, males and females, etc. In short, the aim should always be to push the frontiers of knowledge and understanding beyond what was bequeathed by Elias. This should involve investigating hitherto unexplored geographical, cultural, and problem areas and the development of new concepts and explanatory propositions. Goudsblom's (1995) study of fire and what he calls 'the anthroposphere' are examples.

As a result of such applications and empirical assessments of Elias's ideas, a number of criticisms of his work have been advanced, sometimes by those who worked closely with him. For example, Dunning began to develop a criticism of Elias as early as 1969 when he suggested that greater attention should have been paid in their essays, 'The Quest for Excitement in Leisure' and 'Leisure in the Sparetime Spectrum' (both reprinted in Elias and Dunning 1986; second edition, 2008) to questions of identity and identification because ego-involvement and meaningful identifications are preconditions for the full arousal of excitement in the context of sport and leisure events. More particularly, for emotional arousal, for 'the gears of one's passions to be engaged', one *has to care*, to be *involved* (see Dunning 1999). Later, Dunning suggested that, in *On The Process of Civilisation*, Elias operated with a concept of violence that is too general and that he failed to recognise that implicit in his work is the idea of a continuum running from highly affect-charged or expressive violence at one pole to violence of a cooler, more rational and instrumental kind at the other (Dunning 1986; 2008). In his *Sport Matters*, Dunning is also critical of Elias's discussion of sport and leisure activities as counters to 'stress tensions', arguing that Elias and he had deliberately shelved that thorny issue in their joint work (Dunning 1999). Finally, in their essay 'On the Balance Between 'Civilising' and 'Decivilising' Trends in the Social Development of Western Europe: Elias on Germany, Nazism and the Holocaust' (1998), Mennell and Dunning agreed with the judgement of Austrian figurational sociologist, Helmut Kuzmics, when he suggested of Elias's study of the Germans that: 'In some respects, Elias's interpretation seems to be biased – Prusso-centric '*kleindeutsch*' and Protestant' (Kuzmics 1994: 11,12). Mennell and Dunning added:

> Such a judgement is plausible and worthy of further research. It might help to explain such lacunae in Elias's work as his failure to seek an explanation for such facts as that the Nazi Party originated primarily in Munich and that its leader was

an Austrian. The plausibility of Kuzmics's judgement is, in our opinion, reinforced by the fact that it is based on a thorough understanding and appreciation of Elias's contribution and a thorough knowledge of German history, social development and the relevant sources. It grows, that is, out of original research and is not expressive of an essentially philosophical/ideological 'quick-fix'... (Dunning and Mennell 1998: 354)

In relation to Elias's specific work on civilising processes, established-outsider relations, violence, etc. at least, it is manifestly the case that his ideas can be revised, refined, and sometimes rejected through research-based investigations. However, what of Elias's much broader vision of sociology as a whole committed to the establishment, revision and building-up of a central corpus of knowledge – the 'inter-generational' sociological enterprise discussed above? Loyal and Quilley (Loyal and Quilley 2004; Quilley and Loyal 2005) have argued that Elias's work itself might constitute a partial foundation for the development of a 'cumulative science of social processes' – a 'central theory' for sociology more generally. It is worth quoting their arguments at length. They wrote:

In our view, it is time to review the sociological contributions of the twentieth century, with a view to identifying the beginnings of a cumulative science of social processes. The unifying features of [such a] project would be six-fold:

1. A commitment to the idea of sociology as a science, in the sense identified earlier.
2. An epistemological recognition of the relationship between the various biological and social planes of integration inevitably involved in all areas of human science.
3. The explicit recognition of both the differences and interactions between evolutionary, developmental and historical processes.
4. A commitment to theoretically informed empirical studies, framed in such a way as to permit cross-fertilisation, comparison, testing, reformulation, elimination and revision of competing hypotheses about connections between events and processes in the social world.
5. In the conduct of research – an orientation towards greater detachment and the progressive/cumulative establishment of institutional checks and balances and the fostering of greater secondary involvement and less directly 'political' and/or normative engagement.
And (somewhat paradoxically),
6. In relation to the longer-term explanatory significance of sociological knowledge, the commitment to more realistic social, economic and political-regulatory interventions drawing upon a more reality-congruent stock of social scientific knowledge.

Quilley and Loyal (2005: 848-849)

A particular strength of Loyal and Quilley's sociological manifesto as outlined in the passage above is that, while it effectively distils many of the key principles of Elias's approach, it does so in a manner that leaves the metaphorical 'door open' to a range of complementary perspectives. The prospects for such a model to become established within the discipline are, of course, more open to question. It is rather unlikely that sociologists, at least in the current climate, will come to rally around a single approach in the manner implied by the notion of a 'central theory'. This is the case not least because such an undertaking falls foul of the prevailing '*habits of good sociology*' discussed in the previous chapter. Moreover, sociology as an academic field has been characterised over the past few decades by repeated 'ground-clearing' exercises, perhaps most notably Gouldner's *The Coming Crisis*, or attempts at presenting a unified perspective, notably Giddens's *The Constitution of Society*, which have, for reasons we have discussed in various parts of this book, yielded little in the way of paradigmatic conciliation or resolution (on this, see Kilminster (1998)).

Nonetheless, it is perhaps not so unrealistic to anticipate a future in which the 'decorative turn' in sociology might be displaced by a 'relational turn' (see, for example, Emirbayer 1997), and where the beginnings of a common sociological enterprise of the type envisaged by Elias might come to be established: a future in which some provisional agreement, particularly a commitment to a culture of research and testing, and to cumulative developments in the fund of knowledge about the social universe, may be established. Whether such an enterprise is based upon the work of Elias, or any other sociologist who shares a commitment to the key principles we have discussed in this chapter, is in many respects immaterial. A 'central theory' as we envisage it would not be a final, finished, all-encompassing paradigm which 'finally wins the day' as the cornerstone for all sociology, becoming a *sine qua non* before the discipline can proceed. Rather, it would emerge *via* a gradual, probably non-linear process which would be marked at an early stage by the establishment of a common set of objectives and basic principles. As we hope to have shown in this book, the work of Elias provides a particularly promising basis for such a transformation of sociology.

# Notes

1 Elias's understanding of the term 'scientific', and indeed, the model of 'science' that he advocated are discussed in some detail in the chapters that follow. We have placed the word in inverted commas simply to acknowledge at this stage in the book that considerable debate surrounds the usage of this term.
2 In this sense, our own usage of the term 'sociological crisis' comes close to Thomas Kuhn's description of a 'paradigmatic crisis'. However, where Kuhn envisaged such a crisis as a phase of paradigmatic fragmentation sandwiched between periods of 'normal science', we view the crisis as rather more fundamental. In Kuhn's sense, there has never been anything approaching 'normal science' in the discipline of sociology. Equally, however, we do not subscribe to the notion that sociology is 'pre-paradigmatic', in the sense that Richard Rorty (1979) used this term. That is, we do not consider sociology to be an enterprise that will mature into a predictive science along the contours of the natural sciences of the present day. Nonetheless, as we shall discuss, *pace* the arguments of, for example, Flyberg (2001), we maintain the notion that sociology can become more 'scientific', partly because of the specific meanings we have in mind in using that term, in particular our understanding that while 'social science' and 'natural sciences' are distinct enterprises, a theoretical-empirical analysis of the development of natural scientific knowledge serves as a useful basis for understanding the figurational conditions under which social scientific knowledge might come to 'develop'. How it might develop, or perhaps better, how it 'needs' to develop, are central to our discussions throughout this book.
3 A not dissimilar dissatisfaction with the ways in which sociology was developing was expressed in 1997 by the anthropologist, Peter Worsley, formerly Professor of Sociology at the University of Manchester. It appeared in an interview published in *Network*, the newsletter of the British Sociological Association. In it, Worsley argued: 'My interests have always been wider than those associated with a particular society like Britain, or even with a particular type of society, however important, like industrial society. I have been interested in the variety of humankind, and with supra- as well as national relationships. I don't find much of it in *Sociology*, for example. A friend who has an interest in Third World development recently told me that he hadn't found a single article on the subject for a very long time in the pages of *Sociology*. When I published a book called *The Three Worlds* in 1984, which got excellent reviews across the world, *Sociology* didn't even review it. So people like me, with these types of interest, are getting turned off by *Sociology*... I must say, I do feel terribly alienated. You know, whatever the epoch in the intellectual world generally one spends time, not developing positive theories, but combatting bad stuff... One spends time picking holes in others. I'm fed up with that... I grew up in an epoch where the major paradigms were functionalism and Marxism. Functionalism is dead and Marxism is dead, as effective forces that is. Ranging from Althusserianism (which is also dead) to post-modernism, which I think is fairly dead now, the subsequent changes in intellectual paradigmatic fashion just don't turn me on at all. This may all sound very negative, but the nature of change, or the rate of demise, of paradigmatic systems is expressive of some kind of malaise. People are desperately trying to put in place some kind of paradigm which can be permanent but they

are all failing at an increasingly rapid rate' (Worsley 1997: 7, 8). Worsley's observations echo those of Gouldner to the extent that they each suggest that sociologists have become trapped in a worsening negative feedback cycle of what Elias, following American anthropologist, Gregory Bateson, called a 'double-bind figuration' or a deteriorating 'double-bind trap'.

4  The term 'revolutions' can be understood as referring to changes that are short-term and immediate, hence our use of inverted commas in introducing these terms. Elias preferred in this connection to use the process suffix '-isation' in order to indicate that long-term processes are involved. His preferred usages were, for example, 'scientisation' and, more commonly, 'industrialisation' and 'democratisation', etc.

5  Former Leicester, later Cambridge and currently Oxford sociologist, John H. Goldthorpe, is one of the staunchest advocates of statistical methods in contemporary British sociology. See his (2000) *On Sociology: Numbers, Narratives, and the Integration of Research and Theory* (Oxford: OUP). Among the more idiosyncratic features of this book is the fact that, in it, Goldthorpe traces the origins of sociology to Quetelet rather than Comte, failing to see the importance in this connection, not only of Comte's contributions but also of the need for a relational approach which brings out the partly independent, partly interdependent contributions of these two pioneering figures.

6  Central among them were figures such as Talcott Parsons, Robert K. Merton, A.R. Radcliffe-Brown and P. Lazarsfeld.

7  It is clear that Mertonian functionalism did not encounter these difficulties to the same extent except, perhaps, in relation to power.

8  See, above all, Giddens's (1986) *The Constitution of Society* (Cambridge: Polity).

9  It is beyond the scope of our discussion here properly to qualify this line of argument. Generalisations, even in the broadest sense, about the disciplines of psychology and economics are bound to be rather too simplistic; indeed, there are branches of both disciplines that share considerable overlap with sociology. Nor do we mean to suggest that either economics or psychology offers an exemplary model for cumulative knowledge development, and at that, one that it would be desirable for sociology to emulate. Events since the global economic 'crisis' of 2008 in particular have, for example, called into question not just core assumptions made by many economic theorists, but the very institutional practice of economics itself. Even from within the discipline, leading economists such as Ha-Joon Chang have called for a fundamental shift in economic thinking, particularly with regard to the 'myth' of the free market and its associated premises (Chang 2010). Chang goes so far as to suggest that the complex financial instruments developed as a result of a sustained programme of economic research are demonstrably dangerous and deleterious to human lives, and as such should be altogether outlawed unless they can be shown to be of unquestionable social benefit for those whom they affect (Chang 2010). Rather, our arguments here involve drawing a contrast between the disciplines of sociology, psychology, and economics in terms of the degree to which each has been successful in establishing a centralised academic consciousness and shared sense of intellectual endeavour. Whilst, as mentioned above, the dangers of a simple paradigmatic consensus are arguably *demonstrated* through some of the practices of contemporary psychology and economics, as we shall argue, we do not agree that this means that sharing a collective sense of endeavour, a commitment to specific professional standards, and a common programme of theory and research are in themselves necessarily problematic. It will depend, of course, on the *character* of such an

endeavour, such standards, such a programme, and, indeed, upon the relationship between these various elements at the core of the discipline.

10  Notwithstanding the affinities in Freud's and Elias's core foci, it would be wrong to depict Elias as in any simple sense a 'closet Freudian'. He certainly incorporated a number of Freud's ideas and concepts into his thinking. For example, he used such Freudian terms as 'id', 'ego' and 'super-ego', 'drives', 'libido', 'unconscious' and 'repression' (in his earliest work), especially in his discussions of the sorts of psychological changes that take place in the course of social or individual 'civilising processes'. Yet Elias never accepted Freud's ideas entirely or uncritically. As Mennell (1998) has argued, he (Elias) accused Freud of having an ahistorical view of human psychology, charging him and his followers with adhering to the view that people have always had the same balance between conscious and unconscious mental functions as were visible and detectable in his (Freud's) own times. In Britain, we refer in this connection to the 'Victorian' personality type. As we shall see in greater detail later, it was Elias's contention that the emergent division between conscious and unconscious mental functions is just one result, albeit an important one, of a long-term process in which sociogenetic drive-controls become firmly implanted in the majority of 'normal' contemporary humans. What is important, as Elias puts is, is: 'always *the relationship* between [the] various sets of psychological functions, partly conflicting and partly cooperating in the way [human individuals steer themselves]. It is they, these relationships *within* [people] between the drives and affects controlled and the built-in controlling agencies, whose structure changes in the course of [a] civilizing process, in accordance with the changing structure of relationships *between* individual human beings in society at large' (Elias cited in Mennell 1998: 100–101).

11  'Neo-colonial' is, in our view, a more accurate term than 'post-colonial' because it cannot be construed as implying that the dominance-subordination relations of the old colonial era have either entirely disappeared or changed significantly in an equalising direction. It is rather the case that they have altered, becoming less direct and operating through organisations such as the International Monetary Fund and multi-national corporations.

12  The philosophy of 'ideal forms' was originally an approach used by Plato who claimed he had inherited it from Socrates. See, for example, his (Plato's) *The Republic*. Hegel transformed it by making it historical and 'dialectical' and it was later further transformed by Marx who made it 'materialist' in opposition to the idealism of Hegel.

13  Elias's grounding in Latin and Greek proved to be of great use when he and Dunning were working on their essay, 'The quest for excitement in unexciting societies' in 1966. The idea of the centrality of excitement or 'emotional arousal' in sport and leisure came to them when, partly as a research exercise and partly for pleasure, they jointly watched most of the televised matches in the 1966 World Cup Finals which were played in England. In that context, they were able to observe the emotional arousal of players and spectators as well as of themselves. 'Aristotle wrote about this in his discussion of theatre in *The Poetics*', said Elias. 'He called it "catharsis". Augustine wrote about it, too, in his *Confessions*. "Go and get the translations out of the library, Eric; read them and tell me what they say"'. Dunning did this – it was their usual way of working – and Elias said in relation specifically to Aristotle's *Poetics*, 'I don't trust the translation. It's bowdlerised. Present-day people evidently cannot see the similarity of "cleansing your soul" at the theatre and cleansing your bowels through defecating. That's what Aristotle meant by "catharsis"'!

14  Elias related these words to Dunning in the early 1960s. Part of the stimulus was provided by the media coverage at that time of the trial of the Nazi war criminal, Adolf Eichmann, in Jerusalem.
15  Chang's arguments here also point to a further complexity related to Elias's model of 'reality congruence', one that we discuss in later sections. As Chang notes, economists '... supplied arguments that insist that all those economic outcomes that many people find objectionable in this world – such as rising inequality, sky-high executive salaries, or extreme poverty in poor countries – are really inevitable, given (selfish and rational) human nature and the need to reward people according to their productive contributions' (2010: 248). We might view the economists' tendencies in this respect to be simply the misguided recommendations of academics and practitioners who, with all good intentions, placed their faith in a deeply flawed economic meta theory. But there is, of course, another possibility: namely, that those in question consciously propagated a series of mythological economic precepts, not out of a belief in their accuracy as 'maps of the financial and economic world', but in the knowledge that the perpetuation of such ideas served as a means to justify their (the economists') own gains and the corresponding 'losses' of others: the vast inequalities that indeed such gains were in fact predicated upon. This, of course, raises a broader set of issues about the basis of neo-liberal thinking; the precipitation of 'academic discourse' into 'lay discourse'; the more general relationship between the academy and the business practitioner community; and the slippage from 'ideas' to 'ideology' that was a central concern of Elias's sociology of knowledge.
16  Ilse Seglow, an actress who wrote her dissertation on the theatre, became a leading group psychoanalyst in London. Her son, Peter, became a Sociology Lecturer at Brunel University.
17  Elias took Dunning to the Reading Room in the mid-1960s to look up work on cricket. At the end of the day, Dunning had meticulously collected detailed material from one book, whilst Elias had collected valuable data from some six or seven historical sources. 'How do you do it, Norbert?' asked Dunning. 'You have to follow your nose', replied Elias. 'It's a form of hunt'. From that point on, Dunning started to 'follow his nose' as well and his academic productivity increased by leaps and bounds.
18  Originally published with the title, 'Studies in the Genesis of the Naval Profession: I, Gentlemen and Tarpaulins', *British Journal of Sociology*, 1: 4 (1950), subsequently published as Chapter 1 of Elias (2007) *The Genesis of the Naval Profession*, Rene Moelker and Stephen Mennell (*eds*) (Dublin: UCD Press).
19  Elias's 1941 letter to his parents was brought to our attention and made available to us by Marc Joly. See his (2010) 'Dynamique de champ et "evenements". Le project intellectuel de Norbert Elias (1930–1945)', *Vingtième Siècle*, 106: 91.
20  It was also kept alive in British anthropology by A. R. Radcliffe-Brown and E. E. Evans-Pritchard and, in the United States, by Leslie White.
21  Elias refused to speak and write of social 'evolution' among other reasons because, unlike their biological counterparts, social developments are reversible.
22  That is to say Dunning, Patrick Murphy and Ivan Waddington.
23  The late Ronald Meek, one of the Professors of Economics at Leicester in those days, complained that the sociologists were 'stealing' their students by teaching about subjects like suicide and sex.
24  In 1964, Anthony Giddens urged Dunning to read Peter Blau's *Exchange and Power in Social Life* (1964) because, he (Giddens) said, in it, Blau had successfully resolved the agency-structure dilemma by bringing issues of power and conflict

into the equation. On reading the book, Dunning came to the conclusion that, whilst Blau may have successfully dealt with power and conflict at the micro-social level, his attempt at reconciling this with macro-level phenomena was based on consensualist ideas similar to those of Talcott Parsons.
25 Dunning was involved in long and heated discussions of *The Poverty of Historicism* with Elias and Percy Cohen in 1961, Elias and John H. Goldthorpe in 1964. It was these, more than anything else that provided the stimulus for his writing. See, for example, his (1977) paper, *In Defence of Developmental Sociology*.
26 The 'Donald' referred to here was Donald Macrae, who was then a Lecturer at the London School of Economics, subsequently to become Professor Emeritus.
27 A comprehensive set of notes on this course as given in the 1961–62 academic year, the last year in which Elias gave it, were written up by Michael Levin, a Leicester first year undergraduate and subsequently Senior Lecturer in Politics at Goldsmiths College, University of London. These notes are available from the Norbert Elias Foundation.
28 For a discussion of this phase of Elias's career, see Goodwin and Hughes (2011).
29 While Elias was indeed sceptical about some currents of British anthropology, he was by no means dismissive of anthropology *per se*. Indeed, he was sympathetic with 'anthropologie' in the French tradition, particularly that of, for example, Lévy-Bruhl, Mauss, van Gennep, etc. – writers who shared with Elias a broader conception of the human condition or human predicament. Elias's comments on Thurnwald and primitive art (Elias 1929) also show a clear sympathy with a conception of human science as the 'science of man', irrespective of historical period or 'social type'.
30 This latter point is best elaborated on in Elias's own words. He wrote: '[The] opportunity to distance oneself from the dominant, and especially the nationalistic ideologies of the established group, practically always associated even in Wilhelmine Germany and more strongly in the Weimar Republic – as in other countries as well – with belligerent slogans against the Jews, was, of course, only one of the peculiar experiences that came one's way when growing up in a widely stigmatised outsider group. Later one found oneself facing the question: what was it that bound one to the tradition of a group whose most obvious distinguishing feature was the peculiarity of their religion, if one's own beliefs had been completely secularised? Only very gradually, and in conjunction with my sociological insight, did I realise that the social peculiarity brought about by a person's origin, above all the fact of growing up within a stigmatised outsider group, has *per se*, a strong, shaping influence on the mentality of the young person concerned. And the special religion, even though increasingly secularised probably continued to act as a peculiarity of his cultural tradition for some time. It manifested itself, for example, in what I referred to provisionally for my own purposes as the society-specific features of conscience-formation. I suspected – and it was really no more than a conjecture – that in the Jewish tradition the sense of the sinfulness of human beings, and thus the tabooing of their animal impulses, especially sexuality, is less oppressive, and that differences of this kind are maintained, given social continuity, despite increasing secularisation. The same applies to the taste for emotively charged metaphysical religious assumptions; they remain alien to me. I have sometimes played with the supposition that my own ability in breaching the dominant taboos, to perceive the changing ways in which civilisation deals with elementary impulses may be linked to such a peculiarity of conscience-formation' (Elias 1994: 129).

31 Sennett (2003), for example, provides a discussion of Elias's work on civilising processes after briefly reviewing Castiglione's *Book of the Courtier* (1528) and Della Casa's *Galateo* (1558). He writes: 'A grander connection between civility past and present appears in the writings of the sociologist Norbert Elias. His great book, *The Civilizing Process*, argues that courtesy marked a great sea-change in European civilization. Elias was convinced that social behaviour in the courts of the sixteenth and seventeenth centuries laid the foundations for what we today call "courtesy", behaviour which is non-aggressive and respectful in character, courtly behaviour which became the model in the eighteenth and nineteenth centuries for the bourgeoisie. The key to this change lay in bodily self-control...' (Sennett 2003: 118). This is a partly accurate summary of what Elias wrote. His argument, as we have shown before, was that 'courtesy', 'civility', and 'civilisation' formed a series marking the successive dominance of courts, towns, and nation-states in the emergent dominance patterns of the people of Western Europe. However, Sennett arguably goes astray when he suggests that: 'Though Elias was Jewish, his text presents a very Protestant account of civility. Shame about oneself serves to restrain criminal aggression... But is shame the single driver of this effort? Is fear of losing control really what makes us civilized? Elias underplays the pleasurable aspects of civility, and he turns a blind eye to its cooperative character... Civility, more than a personality trait, is an exchange in which both parties make one another feel good about the encounter... It is a win-win exchange' (pp. 119–120). We shall provide a fuller discussion of Elias's theory of civilising processes in the chapters that follow. However, for the moment, it is worth noting that Elias was at pains to avoid passing normative judgements about civilising standards – whether an exchange is, to follow Sennett's language, 'win-win', 'win-lose', or even 'lose-lose', in terms of whether the 'parties' involved in such an 'exchange' 'felt good' is anything but an inevitability. It would be worth exploring more concretely what Sennett means by 'feeling good' in this context, and, moreover the social conditions under which this structure of feeling becomes possible, and even, to the degree that Sennett is correct, commonplace. Perhaps Sennett is referring here to how 'polite exchanges' can leave people feeling satisfied in relation to a specific set of social 'needs', particularly the need for 'mutual respect'? It is precisely Elias's point to explore how such 'needs' are themselves historically emergent and are, if anything, a counterpart to, say, a fear of shame, rather than an altogether separate, independent, and alternative 'driver' of 'what makes us civilized'.

32 Many of our 'cavils' at Pinker's work relate to minor factual errors in *The Better Angels of Our Nature*. For example, Breslau where Elias was born, is now Wrocław in Poland (pronounced 'vrotswav'), not 'Wroctaw' as Pinker has it (page 59) – the 'l with stroke' character (ł) is, orthographically speaking, a 'w' sound in Polish, not a 't'. Moreover, Elias studied philosophy and medicine at the University of Breslau when Breslau was still a German town, not sociology and the history of science. He switched from philosophy to sociology after quarrelling with his supervisor, Richard Hönigswald. When the Nazis came to power in 1933, Elias did not immediately flee from Germany to England but, instead, spent two years in France where he tried to make a living with two German communist friends, making and selling children's toys. Norbert was the salesman, not the toy-maker (this is another factual mistake in Pinker's account of Elias's biography). Elias certainly lost both his parents in the Holocaust. However, his father died while they were both still in Breslau, and only his mother died in a death camp. Similarly, the historian J.S. Cockburn did not, as Pinker puts it, compile time-series data on 'the town' of Kent between 1560 and 1985. Kent is

a county, not a town. Perhaps more substantially, Pinker repeatedly capitalises 'Civilising Process' and always used the term in its singular form. Elias himself moved increasingly away from such formulations as, with the passage of time, he gained greater control over his data and analyses. You can use the terms 'civilisation' and 'civilised' in relation to particular individuals, he used to argue, or in relation to humanity as a whole. One can also use them in relation to countries, classes or ethnic groups, etc. 'Social processes are like symphonies', he once said in a lecture that Eric Dunning attended. That is, they are complex admixtures of rising and falling themes. 'Civilising processes are examples'. They are admixtures with their opposites, 'decivilising' processes and according to Pinker, 're-civilising' processes, too. Pinker provides an excellent example of a 'decivilising' process in his discussion of the thirty-year long period of increasing violence documented as having occurred in the USA and Western Europe in the 1960s, 70s and 80s, followed by a set of twenty-year long 're-civilising' processes in the 1990s and 2000s. Elias never used the term 're-civilising' process(es) himself, though it is likely that he would have approved of it. Finally, at a rather more substantive level, Pinker neglects to explain sociologically the broad stages of social development through which the major societies of Western Europe passed on their way from feudalism to modernity in the eleventh and twelfth to the eighteenth, nineteenth, and twentieth centuries. These were, more particularly, a stage of monarchical absolutism which was weakest in England, strongest in France, and characterised in the German case by a high degree of fragmentation, except in the cases of Prussia and Austria. Each of these stages was noted and named by Elias. The stage of 'courtisation' (*Verhöflichung*, rule from royal courts) came first; that of 'civility' (rule from royal courts and urban centres) came second; and 'civilisation' (world dominance by Europe and the USA) came third.

33 One of Elias's teaching aids in the 1950s and 1960s was a book of photographs of the French comedian, Fernandel, a man with an exceptionally mobile face. Older readers may remember him in a TV commercial for the French alcoholic drink Dubonnet, in the 1970s. Elias also gave a public lecture on laughter at the University of Leicester in the 1950s. It was to the staff forum, the 'Haldane Society' which no longer exists. Michael Schröter has translated Elias's originally English lecture notes into German in an essay entitled 'Wer lacht kann nicht beissen' ('S/he who laughs cannot bite').

34 Dunning remembers bumping into Elias on the Leicester campus on his (Elias's) return from one of his earliest trips to Amsterdam when he said: 'Eric my dear, I think we should abandon the prefix "con" because one is unnecessarily saying "with" twice if one speaks or writes of the "configurations" that human beings form with one another'. It was in this way that the concept of figurations was born.

35 These time periods are brief compared with the physical evolution of the universe and biological evolution.

36 As we discuss in various sections of this book, this is consistent with Elias's view of social funds of knowledge as intergenerational and collective. Knowledge-accumulation, he suggested, is like a relay race with one generation passing the 'baton' or 'torch' onto the next. He did not, of course, ignore the fact that, in relay races, the baton is sometimes dropped, i.e. knowledge is sometimes lost as well as gained.

37 See Stephen Mennell's highly original application of Eliasian ideas to the understanding of the history and social development of the United States in his (2007) *The American Civilizing Process* (Cambridge: Polity).

38 Elias at first followed the traditional usage of 'man' and 'men' in this connection, but adopted the gender-neutral terms 'person' and 'people' in the 1970s. See his note in *Involvement and Detachment* (Dublin: UCD Press (2007a), Collected Works, vol. 8), p109.
39 According to Elias, an example of the persistent strength of ascriptive ties in Germany is provided by the fact that, in the Nazi period, people were required to provide proof of a certain number of 'Aryan' ancestors in order to establish that they were not Jews. See his (1996) *The Germans*.
40 In his *Mozart: the Sociology of a Genius*, Elias shows how the Germans and Austrians developed a humour surrounding farting and defecation which would have been found repulsive by a majority of Frenchmen and Englishmen at the time. He also pinpointed the apparent anomaly posed by the beauty of Mozart's music and the frequency of 'toilet humour' in his and his father's letters to one another.
41 Elias (2000: 43) acknowledges that it did not figure centrally among the slogans of the French Revolution.
42 This is similar to biological evolution in which, even though homin*oid* species such as Australopithecus, Neanderthalers and other early homin*ids* such as Peking man and Java man may have become extinct, other hominoids such as apes and humans continue to coexist.
43 Elias explicitly discusses Freud's concept of the superego on pp. 408–410 of *On the Process of Civilisation* (2000).
44 It was common practice at this time for upper class people to dip their hands into a common bowl of water before meals.
45 On this, see again Stephen Mennell's insightful (2007) *The American Civilizing Process* (Cambridge: Polity).
46 See his (1985) *The Nation State and Violence* (Cambridge: Polity).
47 This is suggested by his use of the terms centripetal and centrifugal pressures. The psychologist Kurt Lewin was among the first protagonists of 'field theory'. Elias lectured Dunning and his fellow undergraduates on this subject in the 1950s and he (Elias) and Dunning had the work of Lewin consciously in mind when they wrote their essay, 'The Dynamics of Sport Groups with Special Reference to Football' in 1966.
48 The Romans left Britain in 410 AD as part of the shift of the balance of power in their empire from West to East, more particularly from Rome to Constantinople (now Istanbul) which came to form the ruling centre of the Byzantine Empire.
49 When Dunning asked Elias in the 1960s whether there was anything in *Über den Prozess der Zivilisation* that he now found fault with and would change, he replied that his use of this pair of concepts was perhaps too mechanistic.
50 It is arguable that in his later work, particularly *Das Kapital*, Marx moved away from this position to a considerable degree.
51 Perhaps significantly, neither Lakatos nor Kuhn neatly conforms to the disciplinary labels ascribed to them by Elias here. Lakatos achieved a PhD in mathematics, physics and philosophy; likewise, Kuhn's initial academic training was in the field of physics.
52 It is in this connection that we can see the imprint of Mannheim's model of the sociology of knowledge on Elias's thinking. For example, in his *Ideology and Utopia* Mannheim expresses a position similar to Elias's in a number of important respects: 'The sociology of knowledge should seek to investigate the conditions under which problems and disciplines come into being and pass away. The sociologist in the long run must be able to do better than to attribute the emergence and solutions of problems of a given time and place to the mere

existence of certain talented individuals. The existence of and the complex interrelationship between the problems of a given time and place must be viewed and understood against the background of the structure of the society in which they occur, although this may not always give us an understanding of every detail. The isolated thinker may have the impression that his crucial ideas occurred to him personally, independent of his social setting… Sociology, however, cannot be content with understanding immediate problems and events emerging from this myopic perspective which obscures every significant relationship. These seemingly isolated and discrete facts must be comprehended in the ever-present but constantly changing configurations of experience in which they actually are lived' (Mannheim 1997 (1936): 97).

53  That said, research on the brain by neuroscientists such as Joseph Ledoux (1996) and António Damásio, among others, suggests that lower parts of the brain, e.g. parts of the limbic system, principally the amygdala, can at times 'hijack' higher level functioning.

54  Becker bases this archetypal trajectory on the research of Driscoll (1971). He notes that there is no inevitable or simple relationship between homosexuality, transvestism, and transexuality, but the trajectory nonetheless describes a pattern observed in Driscoll's study. Becker also uses this example to illustrate a point about 'sense making' – that if any particular behaviour appears to the researcher to be bizarre or unintelligible, it probably indicates that we do not know enough about it. In such cases, it is better to assume that it makes some kind of sense to those engaged in the behaviour and, indeed, to seek to elucidate the process by which it has come to 'make sense' (1998: 28).

55  Such a code perhaps finds its clearest intellectual expression in the methodological relativism developed by advocates of the 'strong programme' in sociological studies of scientific knowledge; in particular, in relation to the 'symmetry principle' (see, for example, the work of writers such as Barry Barnes (Barnes and Bloor 1986), David Bloor (1991), and the associated 'Edinburgh school'). The principle, which takes as a methodological premise, the effective rejection of any engagement with the 'reality congruence' of scientific knowledge in accounting for the success or otherwise of competing 'truth claims', has been extensively and convincingly contested, perhaps most notably by Sokal and Bricmont (1998), and as part of the now infamous 'Sokal Affair'.

56  For example, the British Sociological Association's guidance on the use of language relating to race and ethnicity (BSA 2005) contains an entry on 'civilised/civilisation' which reads: 'This term can still carry racist overtones that derive from a colonialist perception of the world. It is often associated with Social Darwinist thought and is full of implicit value judgements and ignorance of the history of the non-industrialised world. However, in some cases, such as the work of Norbert Elias, civilisation takes on a different meaning without racist overtones'.

57  Elias's arguments concerning violent and 'animalic' aspects of human behaviour becoming pushed 'behind the scenes' are complex and nuanced. A case in point pertains to the shifting 'visibility' of death in tandem with civilising processes. As Stanley and Wise (2011) have observed, Elias's position, particularly as it is outlined in his *The Loneliness of the Dying*, is considerably more sophisticated than the now orthodox notion that death has become entirely sequestrated from 'private' domestic settings into, increasingly, 'public' institutions such as hospitals, nursing homes, hospices, etc. Stanley and Wise applaud Elias's commitment to analysing long-term trends in the visibility and social organisation of death in a manner which is simultaneously theoretical and empirical, and, most

importantly, historically grounded. Elias's approach elucidates a more complex set of sometimes contradictory processes than is suggested by the 'juggernaut of sequestration' (Stanley and Wise 2011: 948) involving both a degree of sequestration and a persisting significance of domestic figurations.

58 Two of these years were spent by Giddens as Visiting Professor in Canada and the USA.
59 Elias distanced himself from Mannheim in his *Reflections on a Life* (1994). However, Dunning has a clear memory of him discussing Simmel at length, and in a positive manner, with the Simmel scholar Kurt Wolff and Ilse Seglow in Bielefeld in the mid 1980s.
60 The Elias Foundation arranged and paid for annual conferences in the 1980s, and Foucault was an eagerly awaited speaker at the 1987 event in Bielefeld. It was a great disappointment to Elias and virtually everyone in attendance that Foucault failed to turn up. As we learned, during the conference, he had died of AIDS.
61 Foucault defined the concept as follows: 'I would define the episteme retrospectively as the strategic apparatus which permits of separating out from among all the statements which are possible those that will be acceptable within, I won't say a scientific theory, but a field of scientificity, and which it is possible to say are true or false. The episteme is the "apparatus" which makes possible the separation, not of the true from the false, but of what may from what may not be characterised as scientific' (1980: 197).
62 See the preceding chapter for a discussion of Elias's contrasting position to those of Bachelard, Foucault, and Kuhn on this issue.
63 The conference was organised by Andrea Bührmann and Stefanie Ernst; see http://www.wiso.uni-hamburg.de/index.php?id=5893
64 Bourdieu's distinction here straddles similar, but not identical, axes to those of Mouzelis (1995) between 'social theory' and 'sociological theory'; and Althusser between theory as 'thought-abstract' and theory as 'thought-concrete' (Althusser 1969).
65 Elias would have rejected the notion that research has an intrinsic 'logic'. The term has philosophically idealist connotations and as such plays down, amongst other things, the important part played by serendipity in scientific research.
66 In adopting this distinction, we are also intending to include under the heading of the 'political ramifications' of sociological knowledge something akin to Foucault's notion of the 'power effects' of knowledge. For example, the publication of Freud's work, and in particular, the cross-over into lay understandings of his ideas concerning the centrality to the human psyche of the repression of libidinal impulses, had demonstrably important 'political ramifications' or 'power effects'. Put simply, Freudian understandings of 'the self' arguably came to inform 'self-experiences' in important ways. That is to say, for some people, Freudian understandings came to 'frame' and to 'mediate' self-experience through informing their manner of 'self-reflection'; through providing a conceptual vocabulary with which to think, and articulate such thoughts, about themselves; through providing a mode of self-analysis; and through influencing how people seek to apprehend and address their 'psychic' problems, including the very classification of such problems. We are using this example to acknowledge an inevitable 'balance' between the fundamentally inter-related scientific endeavours of 'understanding' and 'changing' the social world.
67 Elias might have agreed with the notion that there are some aspects of social reality that are beyond the reach of 'observation', but only in the sense that the current fund of knowledge in the human sciences may be insufficient to allow for

certain aspects of the social world to be apprehended. Indeed, as we have shown, Elias considered our present-day knowledge of human figurations to be at best, at a very early stage of development and articulation. But equally, he would not have considered the 'invisibility' or 'unobservability' of such aspects of social reality as a logical inevitability, nor as an essential characteristic of their 'form' or 'substance'. It would, we think, be congruent with Elias's position to suggest that developments in the knowledge pertaining to any particular scientific field might render observable that which previously resided beyond the ken of scientific observers. For example, the development of an accurate map of the human genome would not have been possible without an antecedent understanding of hybrid cell mapping, the chromosomal basis of heredity, the structure of DNA, and biochemical genetics more generally.

# Bibliography

## A

Adorno, T. W. (1973) *Negative Dialectics*. Trans. E. B. Ashton. London: Routledge.
Alatas, S. H. (2006) 'The autonomous, the universal and the future of sociology'. *Current Sociology* 54(1): 7–23.
Althusser, L. (1969) *For Marx*. London: New Left Books.
Andreski, S. (1974) (ed.) *The Essential Comte*. Trans. M. Clarke. London: Croon Helm.
Apel, K. (1980) *Towards a Transformation of Philosophy*. Trans. G. Adey and D. Frisby. London: Routledge & Kegan Paul.
Aristotle (2006) *Poetics*. Trans. J. Sachs. Newburyport, MA: Focus Publications/Pullins Press.
Armstrong, G. (1998) *Football Hooligans: Knowing the Score*. Oxford: Berg.
Augustine (2008) *The Confessions*. Trans. H. Chadwick. Oxford: Oxford University Press.

## B

Bachelard, G. (2002) *The Formation of the Scientific Mind. A Contribution to a Psychoanalysis of Objective Knowledge*. Trans. M. M. Jones of the (1938) original French *La formation de l'esprit scientifique. Contribution à une psychanalyse de la connaissance*. Manchester: Clinamen Press.
Barnes, B. and Bloor, D. (1986) *Scientific Knowledge: A Sociological Analysis*. Chicago: University of Chicago Press.
Bateson, G., Jackson, D., Haley, J. and J. Weakland (2000) [1956] 'Toward a Theory of Schizophrenia' in Bateson, G. *Steps to an Ecology of Mind: Collected Essays in Anthropology, Psychiatry, Evolution, and Epistemology*. Chicago: University of Chicago Press.
Bauman, Z. (1979) 'The phenomenon of Norbert Elias'. *Sociology* 13: 117–125.
Becker, H. S. (1998) *Tricks of the Trade: How to Think About Your Research While You're Doing it*. Chicago: University of Chicago Press.
Blok, A. (1982) 'Primitief en geciviliseerd'. *Sociologisch Gids* 29(3–4): 197–209.
Bhaskar, R. (1978) *A Realist Theory of Science*. Hemel Hempstead: Harvester Wheatsheaf.
Bhaskar, R. (1989) *The Possibility of Naturalism. A Philosophical Critique of the Contemporary Human Sciences*. Hemel Hempstead: Harvester Wheatsheaf.
Blau, P. (1964) *Exchange and Power in Social Life*. New York: Wiley and Sons.
Bloor, D. (1991) *Knowledge and Social Imagery*. Second Edition. Chicago: University of Chicago Press.
Bocock, R. (2002) *Sigmund Freud*. Routledge Key Sociologists Series. Revised Edition. London and New York: Routledge.
Bott E. (1957) *Family and Social Network. Roles, Norms and External Relationships in Ordinary Urban Families*. London: Tavistock Publications.
Bourdieu, P. (1984) [1979] *Distinction: A Social Critique of the Judgement of Taste*. London: Routledge and Kegan Paul.
Bourdieu, P. (1990) *The Logic of Practice*. London: Routledge.

Bourdieu, P. and Wacquant, L. (1992) *An Invitation to Reflexive Sociology*. Chicago: University of Chicago Press.
Brown, R. (1977) Unpublished letter to Norbert Elias. Deutsches Literaturarchiv, Marbach Am Neckar, Germany. 11 June 1977.
Bryant, C. and Jary, D. (eds). (1991) *Giddens's Theory of Structuration: A Critical Appreciation*. London: Routledge.
Bryant, C. and Jary, D. (eds). (1997) *Anthony Giddens: Critical Assessments*. London: Routledge.
Bryson, B. (2004) *A Short History of Nearly Everything*. London: Black Swan.

## C

Callinicos, A. (1985) 'Anthony Giddens: a contemporary critique'. *Theory and Society* 14: 133–66.
Chang, H. J. (2010) *23 Things They Don't Tell You About Capitalism*. London: Allen Lane.
Childe, V. G. (1952) [1928] *New Light on the Most Ancient East*. Rev. ed. New York: Praeger.
Childe, V. G. (1958) [1936] *The Dawn of European Civlization*. 6$^{th}$ Ed. New York: Knopf.
Comte, A. (1830–1842) *Cours de Philosophie Positive*.
Coser, L. A. (1971) *Masters of Sociological Thought: Ideas in Social and Historical Context*. New York and Chicago: Harcourt Brace Jovanovich.

## D

Dahrendorf, R. (1959) *Class and Class Conflict in Industrial Society*. Stanford, AC: Stanford University Press.
Della Casa (1558; 1609) *Galateo*.
Depelteau, F. (2008) 'Relational thinking: a critique of co-deterministic theories of structure and agency'. *Sociological Theory* 26(1): 51–73.
Dreyfus, H. and Rabinow, P. (1982) *Michel Foucault: Beyond Structuralism and Hermeneutics*. Chicago: University of Chicago Press.
Driscoll, J. P. (1971) 'Transsexuals'. *Transaction*, March/April: 28–37.
Dunne, S. (2009) 'The politics of Figurational Sociology'. *Sociological Review* 57(1): 28–57.
Dunning, E. (1977) 'In defence of developmental sociology: a critique of Popper's *Poverty of Historicism* with special reference to the theory of Auguste Comte'. *Amsterdams Sociologisch Tijdschrift* 4(3): 327–349.
Dunning, E. (1999) *Sport Matters: Sociological Studies of Sport, Violence and Civilisation*. London: Routledge.
Dunning, E. and Sheard, K. (2008) [1979] *Barbarians, Gentlemen and Players: a Sociological Study of the Development of Rugby Football* (2$^{nd}$ edition). London: Routledge.
Dunning, E. and Mennell, S. (1998) 'On the Balance Between 'Civilising' and 'Decivilising' Trends in the Social Development of Western Europe; Elias on Germany, Nazism and the Holocaust' *British Journal of Sociology* 49(3): 339–357.
Dunning, E. and Mennell, S. (eds) (2003) Norbert Elias. *Sage Masters in Modern Social Thought Series*. London: Sage.
Durkheim, E. (1982) *The Rules of Sociological Method*. Ed. S. Lukes; Trans. W. D. Halls. New York: Free Press.

# E

Elias, N. (1924) 'Idea and individual: a contribution to the philosophy of history', (Dr Phil. thesis, Universität Breslau), trans Edmund Jephcott in *Early Writings*. Dublin: UCD Press, 2006 (Collected Works. vol. 1), pp. 23–54.

Elias, N. (1929) 'On primitive art', trans. J. Goudsblom and S. Mennell, in *Early Writings*. Dublin: UCD Press (Collected Works, vol. 1), pp. 71–6. (First published in German, 1929.)

Elias, N. (1935a) 'The kitsch style and the age of kitsch', trans. Edmund Jephcott, in R. Kilminster (ed.) *Early Writings*. Dublin: UCD Press, 2006 (Collected Works, vol. 1), pp. 85–96.

Elias, N. (1935b) 'The expulsion of the Huguenots from France', trans. Edmund Jephcott, in R. Kilminster (ed.) *Early Writings*. Dublin: UCD Press, 2006 (Collected Works, vol. 1), pp. 97–104.

Elias, N. (1936; 1939), *Über den Progress der Zivilisation*. (2 vols.) Basel: Haus zum Falken.

Elias, N. (1950) 'Studies in the genesis of the naval profession'. *British Journal of Sociology* 1(4): 291–309, included, as 'Gentlemen and Tarpaulins', in: Essays II: On Civilising Processes, State Formation and National Identity. Dublin: UCD Press, 2008 (Collected Works, vol. 15), pp. 170–95; and in The Genesis of the Naval Profession, René Moelker and Stephen Mennell (eds). Dublin: UCD Press, 2007, pp. 27–51.

Elias, N. (1956) 'Problems of involvement and detachment'. *British Journal of Sociology* 7(3): 226–52, reprinted in Involvement and Detachment, Dublin: UCD Press, 2007 (Collected Works, vol. 8), pp. 68–104.

Elias, N. (1961) Application to post of Chair at the University of Ghana. Unpublished correspondence obtained from *The Norbert Elias Foundation Archive*, Marbach am Neckar, Germany.

Elias, N. (1970a) Introduction to African Art from the Collection of Norbert Elias. Exhibition Catalogue. Leicester: City of Leicester Art Gallery, reprinted as 'African art' in Essays III: On Sociology and the Humanities. Dublin: UCD Press, 2009 (Collected Works, vol. 16), pp. 201–8.

Elias, N. (1970b) 'Stages of African art, social and visual, in Essays III: On Sociology and the Humanities. Dublin: UCD Press, 2009 (Collected Works, vol. 16), pp. 209–32.

Elias, N. (1971a) 'Sociology of knowledge: new perspectives. Part 1'. *Sociology*, 5(2): 149–168, reprinted in Essays I: On the Sociology of Knowledge and the Sciences. Dublin: UCD Press, 2009 (Collected Works, vol. 14), pp. 1–41.

Elias, N. (1971b) 'Sociology of knowledge: new perspectives. Part 2'. *Sociology*, 5(3): 355–70, reprinted in Essays I: On the Sociology of Knowledge and the Sciences. Dublin: UCD Press, 2009 (Collected Works, vol. 14), pp. 1–41.

Elias, N. (1971c), 'The Genesis of Sport as a Sociological Problem, Part 1', in Elias and Dunning, Quest for Excitement. Dublin: UCD Press, 2008 (Collected Works, vol. 7), pp. 107–33 (first published in Eric Dunning (ed.) *The Sociology of Sport: a Selection of Readings*. London: Frank Cass, 1971).

Elias, N. (1972) 'Theory of science and history of science: comments on a recent discussion'. Economy and Society 1(2): 117–133, reprinted in Essays I: On the Sociology of Knowledge and the Sciences. Dublin: UCD Press, 2009 (Collected Works, vol 14), pp. 85–101.

Elias, N. (1974) 'The Sciences: Towards a Theory', in Richard Whitely (ed.) Sociological Processes of Scientific Development. London: Routledge and Kegan Paul., pp. 21–42, reprinted in Essays I: On the Sociology of Knowledge and the Sciences, Dublin: UCD Press, 2009 (Collected Works, vol. 14), pp. 66–84.

Elias, N. (1978) [1970] *What is Sociology?* London: Hutchinson.
Elias, N. (1982) 'Scientific establishments', in Essays I: On the Sociology of Knowledge and the Sciences. Dublin: UCD Press, 2009 (Collected Works, vol. 14), pp. 107–60 (First published in Elias, N., Whitley, R. and H. G. Martins (eds). Scientific Establishments and Hierarchies. Dordrecht: Reidel, 1982, pp. 3–69.)
Elias, N. (1983) *The Court Society*. Oxford: Blackwell. First German edn, Die höfische Gesellschaft, 1969).
Elias, N. (1983a) 'The retreat of sociologists into the present', in Essays III: On Sociology and the Humanities. Dublin: UCD Press, 2009 (Collected Works, vol. 16), pp. 107–26. (First published in German, 1983, and in English in Theory, Culture and Society 4(2–3) 1987: 223–47).
Elias, N. (1983b) 'What is the role of scientific and literary utopias for the future?', in Essays I: On the Sociology of Knowledge and the Sciences. Dublin: UCD Press, 2009 (Collected Works, vol. 14), pp. 269–87. (First published in Limits to the Future. Wassenaar: NIAS,1983, pp. 60–80.)
Elias, N. (1985) Human conditio: observations on the development of humanity on the fortieth anniversary of the end of a war (8 May 1985), in *The Loneliness of the Dying and Humana Conditio*. Dublin: UCD Press, 2010 (Collected Works, vol. 6), pp.77–170. (First published in German, 1985)
Elias, N. (1987a) *Involvement and Detachment*. Michael Schröter (ed.). Trans. Edmund Jephcott. Oxford: Blackwell.
Elias, N. (1987b) *Los der Menschen: Gedichte/Nachdichtungen*. Frankfurt: Suhrkamp.
Elias, N. (1987c) 'On human beings and their emotions'. Theory Culture and Society 4(2): 339–361 in Essays III: On Sociology and the Humanities. Dublin: UCD Press (Collected Works, vol. 16), pp. 141–58.
Elias, N. (1991a) *Time: an Essay*. London: Routledge.
Elias, N. (1991b) *The Symbol Theory*. London: Sage.
Elias, N. (1993) *Mozart: Portrait of a Genius*. Cambridge: Polity Press.
Elias, N. (1994) *Reflections on a Life*. Cambridge: Polity Press.
Elias, N. (1996) *The Germans: Power Struggles and the Development of Habitus in the Nineteenth and Twentieth Centuries*. Cambridge: Polity Press.
Elias, N. (1997) 'Towards a theory of social processes'. *British Journal of Sociology* 48(3): 355–383 in Essays III: On Sociology and the Humanities. Dublin: UCD Press, 2009 (Collected Works, vol. 16), pp. 9–39.
Elias, N. (2000) [1939] *The Civilising Process*. (Single volume edition.) Oxford: Blackwell.
Elias, N. (2001) , 'On the Sociology of German Anti-Semitism', trans. Eric Dunning, Stephen Mennell and Hermann Korte, in Early Writings. Dublin: UCD Press (Collected Works, vol. 1), pp. 77–84. (First published in German, 1929; translation first published in Journal of Classical Sociology, 2001, 1(2): 219–225.)
Elias, N. (2006a) *Early Writings*. Edited by Richard Kilminster. Dublin: UCD Press. (Collected Works, vol. 1).
Elias, N. (2006b) *The Court Society*. Edited by Stephen Mennell. Dublin: UCD Press. (Collected Works, vol. 3).
Elias, N. (2007a) *Involvement and Detachment*. Edited by Stephen Quilley. Dublin: UCD Press. (Collected Works, vol. 8).
Elias, N. (2007b) *An Essay on Time*. Edited by Steven Loyal and Stephen Mennell. Dublin: UCD Press. (Collected Works, vol. 9).
Elias, N. (2007c) *The Genesis of the Naval Profession*. Edited by René Moelker and Stephen Mennell. Dublin: UCD Press. (Supplementary volume to the Collected Works).

Elias, N. (2008) *Essays II: On Civilising Processes, State Formation and National Identity*. Edited by Richard Kilminster and Stephen Mennell. Dublin: UCD Press. (Collected Works, vol. 15).

Elias, N. (2009) 'The changing balance of power between the sexes – a process-sociological study: the example of the ancient Roman state', in Essays III: On Sociology and the Humanities. Dublin: UCD Press (Collected Works, vol. 16), pp. 240–65. (First published in Theory, Culture and Society 4(2–3) 1987: 287–316.)

Elias, N. (2009a) *Essays I: On the Sociology of Knowledge and the Science*. Edited by Richard Kilminster and Stephen Mennell. Dublin: UCD Press (Collected Works, vol. 14).

Elias, N. (2009b) Essays III: On Sociology and the Humanities. Edited by Richard Kilminster and Stephen Mennell. Dublin: UCD Press (Collected Works, vol. 16).

Elias, N. (2009c) 'The creed of a nominalist: observations on Popper's The Logic of Scientific Discovery', Essays I: On the Sociology of Knowledge and the Sciences. Dublin: UCD Press (Collected Works, vol. 14), pp. 161–191.

Elias, N. (2010a) *The Loneliness of the Dying and Humana Conditio*. Edited by Alan and Brigitte Scott. Dublin: UCD Press. (Collected Works, vol. 6).

Elias, N. (2010b) *The Society of Individuals*. Edited by Robert van Krieken. Dublin: UCD Press. (Collected Works, vol. 10).

Elias, N. (2010c) *Mozart, and Other Essays on Courtly Culture*. Edited by Eric Baker and Stephen Mennell. Dublin: UCD Press. (Collected Works, vol. 12).

Elias, N. (2011) *The Symbol Theory*. Edited by Richard Kilminster. Dublin: UCD Press. (Collected Works, vol. 13).

Elias, N. (2012a) *On the Process of Civilisation*. Edited by Stephen Mennell, Eric Dunning, Johan Goudsblom and Richard Kilminster. Dublin: UCD Press. (Collected Works, vol. 3). (First published in German (1939) *Über den Process der Zivilisation*. (2 vols). Basel: Hans zum Falken; earlier English editions published by Blackwell (2 vols) 1994 and 2000 (both in one vol.)).

Elias, N. (2012b) *What is Sociology?* Edited by Artur Bogner, Katie Liston and Stephen Mennell. Dublin: UCD Press. (Collected Works, vol. 5).

Elias, N. and Dunning, E. (1966) 'Dynamics of sport groups with special reference to football', in Quest for Excitement. Dublin: UCD Press, 2008 (Collected Works, vol. 7), pp. 189–202. (First published in *British Journal of Sociology* 17(4) 1966: 388–402.)

Elias, N. and Dunning, E. (1971) 'Folk football in medieval and early modern Britain', Quest for Excitement. Dublin: UCD Press, 2008 (Collected Works, vol. 7), pp. 174–88. (First published in Eric Dunning (ed.), *The Sociology of Sport*. London: Frank Cass, 1971, pp. 116-32.)

Elias, N. and Dunning, E. (1986) *Quest for Excitement: Sport and Leisure in the Civilising Process*, 1st edition. Oxford: Blackwell.

Elias, N. and Dunning, E. (2008) [1986] *Quest for Excitement: Sport and Leisure in the Civilising Process*, 2nd edition; revised and enlarged. Dublin: UCD Press (Collected Works, vol. 7).

Elias, N. and Dunning, E. (2008) *Quest for Excitement*. Edited by Eric Dunning. Dublin: UCD Press. (Collected Works, vol. 7).

Elias, N. and Scotson, J. (1994) [1965] *The Established and the Outsiders*. London: Frank Cass. Reprinted with a new Introduction by Elias in 1994. London: Sage.

Elias, N. and Scotson, J. (2008) *The Established and the Outsiders*. Edited by Cas Wouters. Dublin: UCD Press. (Collected Works, vol. 4).

Emirbayer, M. (1997) 'Manifesto for a relational sociology'. *The American Journal of Sociology* 103(2): 281–317.

Erasmus of Rotterdam (1530) *De Civilitate Morum Puerilium*.
Erasmus of Rotterdam (1518) *Colloquies*.
Evans, R. (2003) *The Coming of the Third Reich*. London: Allen Lane.
Evans-Pritchard, E. (1940) *The Nuer: A Description of the Modes of Livelihood and Political Institutions of a Neolithic People*. Oxford: Clarendon Press.

## F

Flyberg, B. (2001) *Making Social Science Matter: Why Social Inquiry Fails and How it can Succeed Again*. Cambridge: CUP.
Foer, J. (2011) *Moonwalking with Einstein: The Art and Science of Remembering Everything*. New York: Penguin Press.
Foucault, M. (2002) [1966] *The Order of Things: An Archaeology of the Human Sciences*. 2nd ed. London Routledge.
Foucault, M. (1974) [1969] *The Archaeology of Knowledge*. Trans. A. M. Sherridan Smith. London: Tavistock.
Foucault, M. (1980) *Power/Knowledge: Selected Interviews and Other Writings*. Ed. C. Gordon. London: Harvester.
Freud, S. (1930) *Civilisation and its Discontents*. London: Hogarth Press.
Friedman, M. (2003) 'Kuhn and logical empiricism', chapter 1 in Nickles, T. (ed.) *Thomas Kuhn*. Cambridge: Cambridge University Press.
Fulbook, M. (ed.) (2007) *Uncivilising Processes? Excess and Transgression in German Society and Culture: Perspectives Debating with Norbert Elias*. Amsterdam: Rodopi.

## G

Garfinkel, H. (1967) *Studies in Ethnomethodology*. Engelwood Cliffs, New Jersey: Prentice-Hall.
Gates, W. (1967) 'The spread of Ibn Kaldun's ideas on climate and culture'. *Journal of the History of Ideas* 28(3): 415–422.
Giddens, A. (1984) *The Constitution of Society*. Cambridge: Polity.
Giddens, A. (1987) *The Nation-State and Violence. Volume II of a Contemporary Critique of Historical Materialism*. California: University of California Press.
Giddens, A. and G. Mackenzie (1982) *Social Class and the Division of Labour: Essays in Honour of Ilya Neustadt*. Cambridge: Cambridge University Press.
Gillies, D. (2006) 'Why research assessment exercises are a bad thing'. Post-Autistic Economics Review, 37: 2–9.
Ginsberg, M. (1934) *Sociology*. New York: Henry Holt & Co.
Giulianotti, R. (2005) *Sport: A Critical Sociology*. Oxford: Polity Press.
Glaser, B. and Strauss, A. (1967) The Discovery of Grounded Theory: Strategies for Qualitative Research. Chicago: Aldine Publishing Company.
Gleichmann, P., Goudsblom, J. and Korte, H. (eds). *Human Figurations: Essays for/ Aufsätze für Norbert Elias*. Amsterdam: Stichting Amsterdam Sociologisch Tijdschrift.
Goldenweiser, A. (1935) 'Social Evolution' *Encyclopaedia of the Social Sciences*. Vol. 5, 656ff.
Goldthorpe, J. H. (2000) *On Sociology: Numbers, Narratives, and the Integration of Research and Theory*. Oxford: OUP.
Goodwin, J. and O'Connor, H. (2002) '"They had horrible wallpaper": representations of respondents and the interview process in interviewer notes'. *CLMS Working*

*Paper Series*, no. 39. Leicester: Centre for Labour Market Studies, University of Leicester. https://lra.le.ac.uk/bitstream/2381/8522/1/working_paper39.pdf
Goodwin, J. and O'Connor, H. (2006) 'Norbert Elias and the lost Young Worker project'. *Journal of Youth Studies* 9(2): 159–173.
Goodwin, J. and Hughes, J. (2011) 'Ilya Neustadt, Norbert Elias, and the Leicester Department: Informal Sources and the History of Sociology in Britain', *British Journal of Sociology* 62(4): 677–695.
Goody, J. (2002) 'Elias and the anthropological tradition'. *Anthropological Theory* 2(4): 401–412.
Goudsblom, J. (1977) *Sociology in the Balance*. Oxford: Blackwell.
Goudsblom, J. (1992) *Fire and Civilization*. London: Penguin.
Goudsblom, J. (1995) 'Elias and Cassirer, sociology and philosophy'. *Theory, Culture and Society* (12): 121–6.
Gouldner, A. (1970) *The Coming Crisis in Western Sociology*. New York: Basic Books.

# H

Hackeschmidt, J. (1997) '"Die Kulturkraft des Kreises": Norbert Elias und die zionistische Jugendbewegung 1918–1925', paper presented at the *Norbert Elias Centenary Conference*, Zentrum für interdisziplinäre Forschung, University of Bielefeld, Germany, 20–22 June 1997.
Halsey, A. H. (2004) *A History of Sociology in Britain*. Oxford: Oxford University Press.
Hargreaves, J. (1992) 'Sex, Gender and the Body in Sport: Has there been a Civilising Process?' in E. Dunning and C. Rojek (eds). *Sport and Leisure in the Civilising Process: Critique and Counter-Critique*. London: Macmillan.
Hargreaves, J. (1994) *Sporting Females: Critical Issues in the History and Sociology of Women's Sports*. London: Routledge.
Hayek, H. F. (1944) *The Road to Serfdom*. London: Rouledge and Kegan Paul.
Hobsbawm, E. (2002) *Interesting Times: a Twentieth Century Life*. London: Abacus.
Horowitz, I. L. (1966) *Three Worlds of Development: The Theory and Practice of International Stratification*. New York: Oxford University Press.
Hughes, J. (2003) *Learning to Smoke: Tobacco Use in the West*. Chicago: University of Chicago Press.

# J

Johnson, E. A. and Monkkonen, E. (1997) *The Civilisation of Crime: Violence in Town and Country Since the Middle Ages*. Urbana: University of Illinois Press.
Joly, M. (2010) 'Dynamique de champ et "evenements". Le project intellectuel de Norbert Elias (1930–1945)' *Vingtième Siècle* 106: 91.

# K

Khaldun, I. (1958) *The Muqaddimah*. Translation by Franz Rosenthal. London: Routledge and Kegan Paul.
Kilminster, R. (1991) 'Structuration theory as a world-view', chapter 4 of Bryant, C. and Jary, D. (eds). *Giddens's Theory of Structuration: A Critical Appreciation*. London: Routledge.
Kilminster, R. (1998) *The Sociological Revolution: From the Enlightenment to the Global Age*. London: Routledge.

Kilminster, R. (2004) 'From distance to detachment: knowledge and self-knowledge in Elias's theory of involvement and detachment', chapter 2 in Loyal, S. and S. Quilley (eds). *The Sociology of Norbert Elias*. Cambridge: Cambridge University Press.

Kilminster, R. (2007) *Norbert Elias: Post-Philosophical Sociology*. London: Routledge.

Kilminster, R. and Wouters, C. (1995) 'From philosophy to sociology: Elias and the neo-Kantians'. *Theory, Culture and Society* 12(3): 81–120.

Kilminster, R. (2011) 'Norbert Elias's post-philosophical sociology: from "critique" to relative detachment', in Stephen Mennell and Norman Gabriel (eds) Norbert Elias and Figurational Research: Processual Thinking in Sociology. Sociological Review Monograph Series. Oxford: Wiley-Blackwell.

Kuhn, T. (1962) *The Structure of Scientific Revolutions*. Chicago: University of Chicago Press.

Kuipers, G. (2006) *Good Humour, Bad Taste. A Sociology of the Joke*. Berlin/New York: Mouton de Gruyter.

Kuzmics, H. (1994) 'State-formation, economic development and civilization in North-Western and Central Europe: a comparison of long-term civilizing processes in Austria and England', unpublished paper given at the World Congress of Sociology, Bielefeld.

## L

Layder, D. (1990) *The Realist Image in Social Science*. London: Macmillan.

Layder, D. (1994) *Understanding Social Theory*. London: Sage.

Layder, D. (2006) *Understanding Social Theory*. 2$^{nd}$ Revised Edition. London: Sage.

Leach, E. R. (1986) 'Violence', *London Review of Books*, 23 October.

Lewin, K. (1952) *Field Theory in Social Science: Selected Theoretical Papers*. Edited by D. Cartwright. London: Tavistock.

Lewis, O. (1951) *Life in a Mexican Village: Tepoztlán Restudied*. Urbana: University of Illinois Press.

Lewis, W. A. (1954) 'Economic Development with Unlimited Supplies of Labour'. The Manchester School, 22 (2): 139–191.

Lockyer, S. and Pickering, M. (2005) (eds). *Beyond a Joke: The Limits of Humour*. Basingstoke: Palgrave.

Loyal, S and Quilley, S. (2004) 'Towards a "central theory": the scope and relevance of the sociology of Norbert Elias', chapter 1 of Loyal, S. and S. Quilley (eds). *The Sociology of Norbert Elias*. Cambridge: Cambridge University Press.

Lukes, S. (1974) *Power: A Radical View*. London: Macmillan Press.

## M

Maguire, J. (1999) *Global Sport: Identities, Societies, Civilizations*. Cambridge: Polity.

Maguire, J. (2005) *Sport and Leisure in Social Thought*. London: Routledge.

Malcolm, D. (1997) 'Stacking in Cricket: A Figurational Sociological Reappraisal of Centrality'. *Sociology of Sport Journal* 14(3): 263–82.

Malcolm, D. (1999) 'Cricket Spectator Disorder: Myths and Historical Evidence', *Sports Historian* 19(1): 16–37.

Malcolm, D. (2000) 'Football Business and Football Communities in the Twenty-First Century', *Soccer and Society* (3): 102–13.

Malcolm, D. and Waddington, I. (eds). (2008) *Matters of Sport: Essays in Honour of Eric Dunning*. London: Routledge.

Mannheim, K. (1997) [1936] *Ideology and Utopia: Collected Works of Karl Mannheim, Volume One*. London: Routledge.
Marx, K. (1953) *Das Kapital*, new edition, Berlin.
Marx, K. and Engels, F. (1942) *Collected Works*, 2 vols.
McNeill, J.R. and McNeil, W.H. (2003) *The Human Web: a Bird's Eye View of World History*, New York and London, W.W. Norton.
Maso, B. (1995) 'Elias and the Neo-Kantians: Intellectual Backgrounds of *The Civilising Process*', *Theory, Culture and Society* 12: 43–70.
Ménétra, J. L. (1986) *Journal of My Life*. Ed. D. Roche, trans. A. Goldhammer. New York: Columbia University Press.
Mennell, S. (1983) *On Social Democratic Ideology*. London: The Tawney Society.
Mennell, S. (1985) *All Manners of Food: Eating and Taste in England and France from the Middle Ages to the Present*. Oxford: Blackwell.
Mennell, S. (1998) *Norbert Elias: an Introduction*, Dublin: UCD Press.
Mennell, S. (2006) 'Elias and the counter-ego: personal recollections'. History of the Human Sciences 19(2): 73–91.
Mennell, S. (2007) *The American Civilising Process*. Cambridge: Polity.
Merton, R. K. (1936) 'The unanticipated consequences of purposive social action', *American Sociological Review* 1(16): 894–904.
Merton, R. K. (1957) *Social Theory and Social Structure*. New York: Free Press.
Mills, C. W. (2000) [1959] *The Sociological Imagination*. 40th Anniversary edition. Oxford: Oxford University Press.
Mouzelis, N. (1993) *Back to Sociological Theory*. Basingstoke: Palgrave.
Murphy, P. (2008) 'Boxing blind: unplanned processes in the development of modern boxing', in D. Malcolm and I. Waddington (eds). *Matters of Sport: Essays in Honour of Eric Dunning*. Abingdon: Routledge.
Murphy, P., Sheard, K. and Waddington, I. (2000) 'Figurational Sociology and its Application to Sport' in J. Coakley and E. Dunning (eds). *Handbook of Sports Studies*. London: Sage.

# N

Neustadt, I. (1952) Unpublished letter to Norbert Elias. Deutsches Literaturarchiv, Marbach Am Neckar, Germany. 20 October 1952.

# O

Ogburn, W. F. (1922) *Social Change*. New York: H. W. Huebsch.

# P

Parsons, T. (1937) *The Structure of Social Action*. New York: McGraw-Hill.
Parsons, T. (1951) *The Social System*. Glencoe Ill. Free Press.
Pels, D. (1991) 'Elias and the politics of theory', *Theory, Culture and Society* 8: 177–183.
Pickel, A. (2005) 'The habitus process: a biopsychosocial conception', *Journal for the Theory of Social Behaviour* 35(4): 437–461.
Pinker, S. (2011) *The Better Angels of Our Nature: Why Violence Has Declined*. London: Allen Lane.
Popper, K. (1957) *The Poverty of Historicism*. London: Routledge and Kegan Paul.
Popper, K. (1959) *The Logic of Scientific Discovery*. London: Routledge and Kegan Paul.

## Q

Quilley, S. and Loyal, S. (2005) 'Eliasian sociology as a "central theory" for the social sciences', *Current Sociology* 53(5): 807–828.

## R

Redfield, R. (1930) *Tepoztlán, A Mexican Village: A Study of Folk Life*. Chicago: University of Chicago Press.
Rojek, C. (1986) 'Problems of involvement and detachment in the writings of Norbert Elias', *British Journal of Sociology* 37(4): 584–596.
Rojek, C. and Turner, B. (2000) 'Decorative sociology: towards a critique of the cultural turn', *Sociological Review* 48(4): 629–648.
Rorty, R. (1979) *Philosophy and the Mirror of Nature*. Princeton New Jersey: Princeton University Press.
Rostow, W. W. (1960) *The Stages of Economic Growth: A Non-Communist Manifesto*. Cambridge: Cambridge University Press.
Russell, B. (1998) [1948] 'Postulates of scientific inference' in J. G. Slater (ed.) *The Collected Papers of Bertrand Russell*. London: Routledge.
Russell, Steven (1997) Jewish Identity and Civilising Processes. Basingstoke: Macmillan.

## S

Said, E. (1978) *Orientalism*. London: Penguin.
Salumets, T. (ed.) (2001) *Norbert Elias and Human Interdependencies*. Montreal: McGill-Queen's University Press.
Scheff, T. J. (2001) 'Unpacking the civilizing process: interdependence and shame', chapter 5 of T. Salumets (ed.) (2001) *Norbert Elias and Human Interdependencies*. Montreal: McGill-Queen's University Press.
Sennett, R. (2003) Respect: the formation of Character in a World of Inequality. London: Penguin Allen Lane.
Sheard, K. (2004) 'Boxing in the Western Civilising Process' in Dunning, Eric, Malcolm, Dominic, and Waddington, Ivan (eds). *Sport Histories: Figurational Studies of the Development of Modern Sports*, London and New York, Routledge, pp. 14–30.
Sheard, K. and Murphy, P. (2008) 'Boxing blind: unplanned processes in the development of modern boxing', chapter 4 in Malcolm, D. and Waddington, I. (eds). (2008) *Matters of Sport: Essays in Honour of Eric Dunning*. London: Routledge.
Sheard, K. and Dunning, E. (1973) 'The rugby football club as a type of male preserve: some sociological notes'. *International Review of Sport Sociology* 5(3): 5–24.
Simmel, G. (1964) [1908] 'Quantitative aspects of the group', in Wolff, K. H. *The Sociology of Georg Simmel*. New York: Free Press.
Smith, D. (1984) 'Norbert Elias – established or outsider?', *Sociological Review* 32: 367–89.
Smith, D. (1991) *The Rise of Historical Sociology*. Cambridge: Polity.
Smith, D. (2001) *Norbert Elias and Modern Social Theory*. London: Sage.
Sokal, A. and Bricmont, J. (1998) *Intellectual Impostures*. London: Profile Books.
Spierenburg, P. (2008) *A History of Murder: Personal Violence in Europe from the Middle Ages to the Present*. Cambridge: Polity Press.
Stanley, L. and Wise, S. (2011) 'The domestication of death: the sequestration thesis and domestic figuration', *Sociology* 45(6): 947–962.

Spierenburg, P. and Body-Gendrot, S. (eds). (2007) *Violence in Europe: Historical and Contemporary Perspectives*. New York: Springer.

## T

Thomas, W. I. and Thomas, D. S. (1929) *The Child in America: Behavior Problems and Programs*. New York: Alfred A. Knopf. 2nd Edition.

Thurnwald, R. (1932) *Die Aufänge der Kunst. (The Beginnings of Art.)*

## U

Urry, J. (1990) *The Tourist Gaze: Leisure and Travel in Contemporary Societies*. London: Sage.

## V

Vandenberghe, F. (1999) '"The real is relational": an epistemological analysis of Pierre Bourdieu's generative structuralism' *Sociological Theory* 17(1): 32–67.

Van Krieken, R. (1998) *Norbert Elias*. New York and London, Sage.

## W

Wacquant, L. (1989) 'Toward a reflexive sociology: a workshop with Pierre Bourdieu', *Sociological Theory* 7(1): 26–63.

Waddington, I. (2000) *Sport, Health and Drugs: A Critical Sociological Perspective*. London: Routledge.

Waddington, I. and Murphy, P. (1992) 'Drugs, sport and ideologies'. In E. Dunning and Rojek, C. (eds). *Sport and Leisure in the Civilizing Process*. Basingstoke, Macmillan.

Watson, J. (2001) [1968] *The Double Helix: A Personal Account of the Discovery of the Structure of DNA*. Rep. Austin, Texas: Touchstone.

Weber, M. (1956) [1930] *The Protestant Ethic and the Spirit of Capitalism*. London: Allen and Unwin.

Weber, M. (1944) 'Max Weber on Bureaucratization in 1909' in J.P. Mayer, 1909/1944, *Max Weber and German Politics*, London: Faber & Faber.

Weber, M. (1946) [1918] in Hans Gerth and C. Wright Mills (eds). *From Max Weber*, New York, Oxford University Press.

Williams, J. (1991) 'Having an away day: English football spectators and the hooligan debate' in, J. Williams and S. Wagg (eds). *British Football and Social Change: Getting into Europe*. Leicester: Leicester University Press.

Wilson, B. (1977) 'A tribute to Elias'. *New Society*, 7th July 1977, pp. 15–16.

Winch, P. (1958) *The Idea of a Social Science*. London: Routledge and Kegan Paul.

Winnicott, D. W. (1965) *The Family and Individual Development*. London: Tavistock Publications.

Wittfogel, K. A. (1957) *Oriental Despotism: A Comparative Study of Total Power*. New Haven: Yale University Press.

Worsley, P. (1997) 'Catching up with Peter Worsley'. Interview by Liam Murphy, *Network: Newsletter of the British Sociological Association*, no. 67, March 1997: 7–8.

Wouters, C. (1977) 'Informalization and the civilizing process' in P. R. Gleichmann, J. Goudsblom, H. Korte, *Human Figurations*. Amsterdam. pp. 437–455.

Wouters, C. (1986) 'Formalization and informalization: changing tension balances in civilising processes'. *Theory, Culture and Society* 3(2): 1–18.
Wouters, C. (2004) *Sex and Manners: Female Emancipation in the West 1890–2000*. London: Sage.
Wouters, C. (2007) *Informalization: Manners and Emotions Since 1890*. London: Sage.

# Index

a prioris, 12, 29, 185, 186, 199
actor-network theory, 7
Adorno, Theodor, 13, 24, 39, 137, 138, 160
aggression, 94, 96, 213n
Alatas, Syed Hussain, 139
Albrow, Martin, 31
Alexander, Jeffrey, 8
Allen, Sheila, 31
Althusser, Louis, 57, 183, 208n, 217n
Andreski, Stanislav, 139
anomie, 177
anticipatory motif, 48, 159–160
Aristotle, 33, 210n
Armstrong, Gary, 103, 204
Ashton, David, 31, 32
Ashworth, Clive, 31
Atkinson, Michael, 42
Attalides, Mike, 31
Augustine, 210n

Bachelard, Gaston, 126, 127, 187, 192, 199, 217n
Baker, Tanya, 169
Banks, Olive, 31
Barnes, Barry, 216n
Barnett, Anthony, 31
Bateson, Gregory, 142, 209n
Baudrillard, Jean, 6
Bauman, Zygmunt, 13, 41, 103, 160
Becker, Howard S., 149, 216n
Bendix, Reinhard, 65
Berger, Peter, 81
Bernstein, Basil, 174
Bettelheim, Bruno, 11
Bhaskar, Roy, 199
billiard ball model of causation, 35
bird's eye view of human history, 33–5
*Blau Weiss Bund* (Blue-White League), 19–20
Bloch, Ernst, 170
Blok, Anton, 38, 117
Bloor, David, 216n
Boas, Franz, 118, 120: Boasianism, 120
Bocock, Robert, 137

bodily functions, 86, 88, 89, 90–2, 95, 210, 215
Bott, Elizabeth, 177
Bouglé, Célestin, 30
Bourdieu, Pierre, 8, 10, 16, 98, 172, 188–200, 217n
boxing, 204
Bricmont, Jean, 10, 216n
British Sociological Association, 27, 208n, 216n
Brown, Richard, 31, 32
Bryant, Chris, 31, 173
Bührmann, Andrea, 217n
Burgess, Ernest, 43

Callinicos, Alex, 177
Canguilem, Georges, 187
Cannon, Walter Bradford, 30
Cassirer, Ernst, 112, 189
catharsis, 210n
central theory, *see* Elias, Norbert: central theory
centralisation, 98, 106, 110, 166: Chinese form, 110
Chang, Ha-Joon, 23, 209n, 211n
chicken and egg conundrum (*see also* processes: primacy of process), 114–6, 148
Childe, Vere Gordon, 35, 3
citizenship, 103
civilisation: culture and civilisation, 11, 27, 82–5, 87, 171–2; civilised/primitive distinction, 38, 82, 118, 168–9; civilised/uncivilised distinction, 78, 87; and courtesy/civility, 81, 85, 87–9, 96, 102, 213; as enduring terminological obstacle, 171–2; zero-point, lack of, 94, 168
civilising processes (*see also* decivilising processes), 2, 25, 33, 39, 42, 43, 47, 52, 86–111, 141: American, 204, 214n, 215n; as 'blind' and largely unplanned, 21, 46–7, 143, 152–6, 166; British, 104–8

civilising processes (*Continued*)
and childhood, 92–3, 96; and crime, 42–4, 171, 204, 213–4n; as 'curved', 121; critiques of, 46–8, 59–60, 103–4, 153–4, 167, 168–9, 171–2, 203–6; and detachment, 46–9, 157–8; as Eurocentric, 33, 81, 103, 108–111; European, 81, 121, 204; French, 104–8; Germany's *Sonderweg* (special path), 82, 84–5, 105–8, 166, 171; and knowledge, 47–8, 143, 197–8; as a middle-class 'weapon' 87; as multi-linear (not unilinear), 41, 98, 103, 104, 117, 120, 121, 122–3, 129, 166; and sex, 93–4; as specific transformations of behaviour, 85–92; 'spurts' and 'counter-spurts', 78, 88, 108, 121, 143, 204; and state formation, 97–103; testing, 204–6; and 'un-civilising' processes (*see also* decivilising processes), 165

climate change, 4, 137, 144, 145
*cogito*, Cartesian 181
Cohen, Percy, 31, 32, 36, 169, 173, 212n
Cold War, 6
comedy, 52
Comte, Auguste, 4, 5, 7, 8, 17, 30, 33, 34, 35, 36, 42, 112, 113, 123, 129, 139, 142, 146, 166, 175, 186, 187, 209n: law of three stages, 113, 139
continuity/discontinuity, 2, 126–7, 186
Copernicus, Nicolaus, 14, 73, 74, 75, 143, 157, 201
Coser, Lewis, 41
courtisation, 51, 102, 214n
Crick, Francis, 152
crises: economic, 4, 23–4, 209–210n; human, 1–2; human and sociological as 'twin', 1; sociological, 1, 2–10, 15, 17, 202, 208n
critical theory, 14–16, 24, 137–8, 182
culture, *see* civilisation: culture and civilisation

Dahrendorf, Ralf, 5
Damasio, Antonio, 216n
Dandeker, Chris, 31

Darwin, Charles, 14, 33, 73, 74, 203, 216n: Darwinism, 120
De Gaulle, Charles, 6
death, 77, 216–7n
decivilising processes (*see also* civilising processes), 2, 39, 88, 98, 108, 120, 122, 204, 205, 214n: 'breakdowns' of civilisation, 22, 85, 98, 166
decorative turn, 129, 202, 207
deductivism/inductivism dualism, 124, 130, 133
Depelteau, Francois, 200
Derrida, Jacques, 6, 194
detachment, *see* involvement and detachment
determinism, 46, 57, 81, 190, 198, 200; co-determinism, 200
development, concept of, 116–123: diachronic structures/*Gestalten*, 14, 121, 131, 150, 152, 199; as a 'taboo', 118; developmental agnosticism, 117; and 'progress', 33, 103–4, 117, 118–120, 122–5, 170; social versus biological, 120–1
DNA, 54, 152, 218n
Donnelly, Peter, 42
DSIR (Department of Scientific and Industrial Research), 150
Duncan, Peter, 169
Dunne, Stephen, 46–48
Dunning, Eric, 13, 17, 24, 27, 32, 34, 38, 39, 40, 42, 45, 47, 50, 54, 58, 79, 137, 158, 166, 173, 175, 178, 203, 204, 205, 201n, 211n, 212n, 214n, 215n, 217n
Durkheim, Emile, 4, 7, 9, 17, 30, 33, 34, 35, 36, 43, 53, 58, 121, 174, 176, 177, 189, 201

economic reductionism, 60–1, 62: 'economistic' thinking 35, 61, 96
Eichendorff, Joseph Freiherr, 18
Einstein, Albert, 69, 127, 141
Eldridge, John, 31
Elias, Hermann (father), 18, 22
Elias, Norbert: Aachen, 39; Amalfi Prize, 39; Amsterdam 1975–1978, 18, 25, 38, 39; and anthropology, 36–8, 117, 120, 168–170; on

anti-Semitism, 20; Bielefeld 1978–1984, 38, 217n; biography and his sociology, 39–40; Bochum, 39; Breslau (Wrocław), 18; at British Museum, 25, 211n; and crime historians, 42–4, 171; central theory, 76–7, 207; criticised as progress theorist, 27–8, 33, 36, 38, 103–4, 117, 122–3, 129–130, 163, 171–2; counter-ego, 162; *Die Ballade vom armen Jakob* (*The Ballad of Poor Jacob*) – Elias-authored opera, 26; doctoral thesis, 29; attachment to *Ecole Normale Supérieure*, 30; education, 18, 28–9; enigmatic status, 17, 31, 42, 44–9; England, 25, 30; and ethnocentrism, 33, 110; experiences as a Jew, 18, 19–20, 39–40; experiences as a soldier in the Kaiser's army, 18, 19; as 'export manager', 21; first-year course at Leicester, 31–2; Frankfurt 1930–1933, 24, 30; and 'Frankfurt School', 24, 137, 138; Freudianism, 210n, 215n; *Habilitationsschrift*, 25, 29, 30, 54; and Hans Gerth, 30; on history, 71–3, 152; and the human condition, 51; Ghana 1962–1964, 36–7, 168, 169; increasing influence, 41–2, 163–4; internship on the Isle of Man, 26; on Kitsch style, 30; at London School of Economics, 25–6; Konstanz, 39; Leicester 1954–1962, 26, 28, 30, 31–8, 59, 68, 79, 169, 173, 212n; London 1935–1954, 26; and organisational studies, 163; and Karl Mannheim, 24, 25, 29–30; migration, 25; as 'naïve empiricist', 45, 129, 132, 134; methodology, 138, 147–152, 175; and Ilya Neustadt, 30, 31, 33, 35, 79, 169, 172, 174; as 'optimistic realist', 15; as outsider, 43–5; parents, 18, 19, 22, 39; and Talcott Parsons, 76–7; as post-philosophical, 74, 147; primal contest model, 177; as radical sociologist, 73–75, 115, 136; radicalism (political), 19, 79; Paris 1933–34, 25, 30; and the sociological crisis, 4; and the sociology of the body, 39, 41, 42; and the sociology of consumption, 41; and the sociology of emotions, 39, 41, 42; and the sociology of leisure, 42, 45, 77, 109, 146, 188, 204, 205, 210n; and the sociology of sport, 13, 32, 39, 42, 45, 54, 77, 109, 131, 146, 188, 204, 205, 210n, 215n; Elias's sociological practice (*see also* figurational sociology), 2, 49, 121, 147, 174, 194, 200; technical language, 187; *Theory, Culture & Society* special issue, 39, 197; University of Warwick, 38; Weimar Germany, 21–22; and 'Young Worker' project, 32, 150–1, 153; as Zionist, 19, 46

Elias, Sophie (mother), 18, 22
Eliasians, *see* figurational sociology: 'figurationalists'
Emirbayer, Mustafa, 207
emotions, 41, 42, 51, 61, 76, 86, 89, 93–5, 97, 136, 140, 142, 145, 163, 169, 178, 205, 210n
empiricism, 5, 9, 36, 45, 109, 123, 125, 128, 129, 132, 134, 139, 192, 199: abstract, 138; empiricism/ rationalism split, 130
Enlightenment, 7, 45, 46, 118, 129–130, 148, 186
epistemology, 112, 115, 130, 137, 138, 147, 148, 183, 184, 185
Erasmus, Desiderius (of Rotterdam), 86, 92, 157
Ernst, Stephanie, 217n
ESRC (Economic and Social Research Council), 150
established and outsiders, *see* figurations: established and outsider figurations
ethnomethodology, 7, 198
Etzioni, Amitai, 191
eugenics, 33, 120
Eurocentricism, *see* civilising processes: as eurocentric

Evans-Pritchard, Sir Edward Evan, 37, 169, 211n
Evans, Richard, 21
evolution, 14, 27, 29, 32, 33, 35, 45, 50, 72, 73, 74, 75, 103, 109, 116, 117, 140, 168, 203, 206, 211, 214, 215n: evolutionism, 118, 120, 122, 170, 174

feminism, 5, 7, 8
Field, David, 31
figurational sociology 2, 7, 8, 16, 17, 19, 35, 46, 48, 49, 144, 163, 165, 173; basic concepts, 50–75; as difficult to practice, 49; 'figurationalists', 17, 32, 163–4, 188; future prospects, 201–218; politics of (*see also* involvement: and detachment; involvement: detour *via* detachment; involvement: secondary), 45, 46–7, 79–80, 163–4, 196–198; as radically processual and relational, 50; as simultaneously theoretical and empirical, 49, 69, 147, 152, 189–190, 199, 208n, 216n
figurations: as an alternative to structure/agency dualism, 53, 155–6; change in (*see also* continuity/discontinuity), 72; compared to concepts such as 'society' and 'institutions', 52, 54, 57–9, 155–6; and configurations, 54, 214n; as dance, 53; defined, 52–6, 155–6; and 'division of labour', 60; double-bind, 2, 47, 142, 145, 209n; established and outsider figurations, 63–8, 147, 153, 206; and *homo clausus/homines aperti*, 52; as opaque, 199; origins of the term, 54, 214n; and social order, 62–3; as survival units, 62, 97; as 'webs of interdependence', 58
fire, 109, 204, 205
First World War, 18, 19, 20, 39, 85, 106
*Fisherman in the Maelstrom, The*, 157
Fleming, Alexander, 152
Fletcher, Jonathan, 1, 59, 60
Flyberg, Bent, 208n
Foer, Joshua, 29

football, 47, 54, 131, 146, 158, 215: football hooliganism, 47, 146
Foucault, Michel, 6, 7, 16, 172, 178–188, 192, 194, 217n
Franklin, Rosalind, 152
Frege, Friedrich Gottlob, 201
Freud, Sigmund, 10, 11, 30, 44, 73, 74, 75, 80, 88,146, 187, 188, 210n, 217n
Friedman, Milton, 23
Fromm, Erich, 19, 79, 80
Fulbrook, Mary, 165–167
Fulcher, James, 31
functional democratisation, 61, 67, 76, 205, 219
functionalism, 5, 7, 34, 60, 62, 208, 209: concept of 'function', 62; neo-functionalism, 8

Gál, Hans, 26
Galen, Aelius (of Pergamon), 2
Gane, Mike, 31
Gerth, Hans, 24, 30
Giddens, Anthony, 8, 14, 16, 31, 32, 41, 68, 69, 96, 103, 169, 172–8, 188, 190, 198, 207, 209n, 211n, 215n, 217n
Ginsberg, Morris, 25, 27, 28, 121
Giulianotti, Richard, 103, 204
Glaser, Barney, 191
Goebbels, Josef, 61
Goebbels, Magda, 61
Goethe, Johann Wolfgang, 18
Goldsmiths College London, 212
Goldthorpe, John, 31, 32, 36, 143, 209n, 212n
Goodwin, John, 31, 150, 212n
Goody, Jack, 37, 103, 117, 168–9
Goudsblom, Johan, 1, 2, 32, 73, 74, 112, 143, 191, 197, 204, 205
Gouldner, Alvin, 3–5, 207, 209n

Habermas, Jürgen, 8, 13, 41, 160, 194
habitus, 76, 78, 79, 81, 86, 88, 95, 97, 101, 104, 167, 178, 189–190, 198, 199, 205
Hall, Stuart, 4
Halsey, Albert Henry ('Chelly'), 27
Hanawalt, Barbara, 43
Harré, Horace Romano ('Rom'), 199

Hayek, Friedrich, 56
Hegel, Georg Wilhelm Friedrich, 12, 113, 114, 141, 210n: dialectics, 114, 210n; notion of 'spirit', 112–3
Heidegger, Martin, 68, 69, 185
Heine, Heinrich, 18
Heinemann, Klaus, 42
hermeneutics, 182
Hippocrates, (of Kos), 2
Hirst, Paul, 31
Hitler, Adolf, 20, 22, 47, 107, 108, 117, 118, 153, 156
Hobhouse, Leonard Trelawny, 27, 28, 33, 34, 35, 36
Hobsbawm, E, 26, 28
Holloway, Sydney, 31
Holy Roman Empire, 93, 99, 105–7
Homans, George, 50
*homo clausus* (closed-person model of humans): 48–9, 52, 56, 58, 75, 115, 144, 155–7, 181, 183, 187; and *homines aperti* (open, bonded, plurality model of humans), 52, 56, 58, 75, 115, 183
Hönigswald, Richard, 29, 213n
Hopkins, Keith, 31
Hopper, Earl, 31
Hughes, Jason, 17, 47, 148, 149, 204, 212n
Hurd, Geoff, 169
Hurstfield, Jennifer, 31

ideal forms, 210n
idealism, 8, 14, 74, 114, 210n
ideologies, 138–9, 145, 156, 185, 196, 211–212: truth/ideology opposition (*see also* values: bias versus neutrality; values: fact/value distinction), 184
informalisation, 6, 93, 204
Ingham, Geoffrey, 31
interdependence, 2, 39, 51–2, 56, 58, 59, 60, 61–3, 66–8, 155: versus 'independence'/'dependence', 59–60; versus interaction, 155–6; interdependency chains, 2, 65, 67, 76, 97, 101, 103, 155, 176, 177, 205; and figurations, 52, 56, 58–9, 155

involvement and detachment (*see also* values), 13–14, 130: alloys and blends of, 14, 130, 160, 196; detour *via* detachment, 13–14, 45, 131, 139–140; 151, 158–160, 180, 183, 196–7; secondary (*see also*, figurational sociology: politics of), 13, 14, 48, 131–2, 158, 160, 180, 206

Jary, David, 173
Jenkins, Richard, 189
Jewson, Nick, 31
Johnson, Eric, 42–3, 171
Johnson, Terry, 31, 169n
Joly, Marc, 1, 211n

Kant, Immanuel, 12, 18, 29, 107, 124, 131, 138, 175, 181, 185, 186, 198
Käsler, Dirk, 41
Kellner, Douglas, 6
Kelly, Mike, 31
Khaldun, Ibn, 139
Kilminster, Richard, 1, 12, 18, 19, 31, 32, 39, 73, 112, 157, 159, 160, 175, 178, 185, 186
knowledge: and civilising processes, *see* civilising process, and knowledge; expansion and contraction of, 124–8; and 'observability' of the social world, 218n; political significance and ramifications of, 197, 217n; power effects of, 184–5, 188, 217n; scientific, 6, 15, 123–8; sociology of, 1, 13, 29–30, 81–2, 112–135, 136–161, 175, 196–8, 215–6n; sociological (see also involvement: and detachment), 2, 8, 12, 45–6, 48, 128–9, 135, 136–161
Köhler, Wolfgang, 30
Korte, Hermann, 1, 19
Kristeva, Julia, 6
Kuhn, Thomas, 124, 125, 126, 127, 164, 208n, 215n, 217n
Kuipers, Giselinde, 52
*Kultur*, *see* civilisation: culture and civilisation
Kuzmics, Helmut, 1, 205–6

Lakatos, Imre, 124, 125, 128, 215n
*Las Meninas*, 179–180, 183, 192
laughing, 28, 52
Layder, Derek, 31, 132–4, 153–7, 198
Lazarsfeld, Paul, 36, 209n
Leach, Edmund, 117, 118, 203
Ledoux, Joseph, 216n
Levi-Strauss, Claude, 169
Levin, Michael, 212n
Lévy-Bruhl, Lucien, 33, 170, 175, 212n
Lewin, Kurt, 30, 98, 215n
Lewis, Oscar, 37
Lewis, William Arthur, 35
Liebknecht, Karl, 20
Lockyer, Sharon, 52
London School of Economics, 25, 26, 27, 28, 31, 43, 172, 173, 178, 212n
Louis IV, king of Western Francia (936–954), 100
Louis VI, the Fat, king of Western Francia (1108–1137), 100
Louis XIV, king of France (1643–1715), 30, 47, 104, 107, 156
Loy, John, 42
Loyal, Steven, 206
Lukacs, Georg, 40
Lukes, Steven, 185
Lüschen, Gunther, 42
Lyotard, Jean Francois, 6

MacIver, Robert, 27
Mackenzie, Gavin, 31
Macrae, Donald, 26
Maguire, Joseph, 42, 204
Malcolm, Dominic, 42, 204
Mannheim, Karl, 24, 25, 29, 30, 40, 60, 80, 98, 137, 146, 175, 184, 215n, 216n, 217n
Marcuse, Herbert, 6
Marx, Karl (*see also* critical theory; Elias, Norbert: and Frankfurt School; Marxism), 4, 6, 9, 12, 17, 21, 24, 25, 30, 33, 34, 35, 36, 64, 65, 80, 95, 96, 98, 112–115, 141, 146, 166, 174, 186, 201, 210n, 215n: and economistic determinism, 112–5; departure from Hegelian human spirit, 112–5; 'Marxburg', 24, 137
Marxism, 7, 57, 60, 208

Masaccio, 158
masculinity, 94, 147, 172
Maso, Benjo, 112
materialism, 8, 74
mathematics, 8, 18, 23, 29, 50, 83, 133, 143, 201, 215
McNeil, John, 36
McNeill, William, 36
means of ruling (*see also*, monopolies: means of ruling), 97, 99, 101, 103
Mears, Rob, 31
Ménétra, Jacques-Louis, 172
Mennell, Stephen, 1, 38, 48, 79, 117, 118, 120, 140, 162, 163, 166, 204, 205, 210n, 211n, 214n, 215n
Merton, Robert, 41, 77, 146, 191, 209n
metaphysics, 5, 13, 58, 68, 70, 113, 130, 141, 142, 160, 176, 212n
methodology (*see also*, Elias, Norbert: methodology), 112, 137, 138, 147–9, 161–2, 175, 191: fetishisation of, 133
middle range theory, 77: compared to 'central theory', 77
Mills, C. Wright, 30, 76, 77, 138, 191
modernisation, 165–6
modernism, 6, 7
modesty, 86, 88, 90, 91, 95, 164; empirical, 193; intellectual immodesty, 174
Moelker, Rene, 211
money, 66, 85, 93, 94, 95, 97–100, 102–3, 155: monetarisation, 61, 205
Monkkonen, Eric, 42–3, 171
monopolies: of power, 26, 30; of means of ruling, 100; mechanism, 98; of state control, 47, 104; taxation, 96, 97, 99–101; of violence, 22, 64, 97, 99, 101, 105
Moore, Thomas, 14
Mörike, Eduard, 28
Mouzelis, Nicos, 31, 217n
Mozart, Wolfgang Amadeus, 45, 156, 162, 215n
murder, 214
Murphy, Patrick, 31, 204, 211n

Napoleon Bonaparte, 88
*Naturvolk*, 168–9

Nazis, 13, 21, 22, 24, 30, 39, 44, 69, 108, 118, 120, 122, 137, 138, 166, 170, 211, 213, 215: Nazism, 56, 108, 205,
neo-liberalism, 4, 23–4, 56, 156, 195, 211n
Neustadt, Ilya, 30, 31, 33, 34, 35, 79, 169, 172, 173, 174
Newton, Isaac, 69, 124, 139, 141, 143
Newton, Tim, 163
nominalism, 53, 56, 74, 186
noumenal/phenomenal opposition, 199

O'Connor, Henrietta, 150
object-adequacy (*see* reality-congruence)
objectivity, *see* subjectivism: subjectivity and objectivity
Ogburn, William Fielding, 121
ontology, 7, 8, 112, 147, 175, 190, 192, 199

pacification, 76, 78, 100, 101, 103, 167, 174, 205
Park, Robert, 43
Parsons, Talcott, 5, 36, 41, 44, 62, 76, 77, 118, 140, 170, 174, 189, 190, 209n, 212n
Pauling, Linus, 152
Pels, Dick, 45, 163–164, 193
phenomenology, 182, 192–3
physics, 12, 26, 124, 127, 215; social, 4, 5, 192; quantum, 141;
Picasso, Pablo, 180
Pickel, Andreas, 189
Pickering, Michael, 52
Pinker, Steven, 43, 44, 213–214n
Plato, 210n
Poe, Edgar Allan, 157
police (*see also*, monopolies: of violence), 101, 105
politeness, 86, 88, 90, 91, 92, 213
Popper, Karl, 26, 27, 28, 32, 54, 56, 71, 132–3: critique of, 54, 71, 132–4
positivism, 5, 9, 27, 123, 128, 129, 142, 182, 183, 198
post-colonialism/neo-colonialism, 12, 210n
postmodernism, 6, 10, 117
poststructuralism, 6–7, 10

power (*see also* interdependence): balances, 2, 5, 47, 52, 58–9, 62–7, 82, 97–8, 100, 146, 163, 187–8; and functional democratisation, 61, 67–8, 76, 205; and interdependence, 66–7; as multipolar, 67; as polymorphous, 67; as relational, 66, 187
process sociology, *see* figurational sociology
processes: blind, 2, 21, 46–7, 143, 152, 153, 156, 166; 'directions' of, 45, 47, 52, 95, 97, 101, 117, 118, 121–3, 135, 214n; primacy of process, 112–6; process-reduction (*Zustandsreduktion*) (*see also*, retreat to the present), 51, 77, 121; symphonies, 214n
psychogenesis, *see* sociogenesis: and psychogenesis

Quetelet, Adolphe, 4, 5, 209n
Quilley, Stephen, 206

racism: *völkisch*, 56; scientific, 120
Radcliffe-Brown, Alfred, 37, 209n, 211n
RAE (Research Assessment Exercise), 201–2
rational choice theory, 7
realism, 53, 56, 57, 74, 180: critical, 7, 8
reality-congruence, 14, 36, 37, 132–5, 138, 139, 158, 185, 187, 202; and value congruence, 24, 131, 144, 185; versus 'truth', 132–5
Redfield, Robert, 37
REF (Research Excellence Framework), 201–2
reflexivity, 3, 148, 150, 179–181, 191, 194, 200
relational turn, 2, 207
relativism: cultural, 38, 120; epistemic, 10, 121, 128, 129, 136, 148, 164, 185; historical, 120; methodological, 216n; postmodernist, 194; relativistic egalitarianism, 164, 185; sociological, 192
religion (*see also* metaphysics), 44, 62, 95, 139, 141, 212n
retreat to the present, 46, 202

Rojek, Chris, 31, 44, 129, 159, 200, 202
Rorty, Richard, 208n
Rostow, Walt Whitman, 35
rugby, 204
rules, 104, 177, 186
Russell, Bertrand, 35
Russell, Steven, 18, 39

Said, Edward, 81
Salaman, Graeme, 31
*satisfaktionsfähigkeit*, 107–8
Scheff, Thomas, 59–60, 178
Schiller, Friedrich, 18
Schröter, Michael, 162, 214n
science (*see also*, knowledge: scientific; sociology: as a science), 7, 8, 45, 75, 123: diversification of 'the sciences', 123; neutral science as fiction, 195; possibility of, 124; scientific 'means of orientation', 2, 122–3, 129, 131, 133; scientism, 137–8, 143, 177, 203
Scotson, John, 63–4, 153
Scott, John, 31
Scylla and Charybdis, 56–7, 192
Second World War, 6, 18, 19, 25, 26, 27, 40, 44, 50, 70, 106, 162, 172, 204
Seglow, Ilse, 24, 158, 162, 211n
Seglow, Peter, 211n
self-control (*see also* civilising processes), 13, 46, 47, 59, 74, 88, 213n: self-restraint, 93, 94, 95, 143, 167, 188; balance between *Selbstzwang* (self-restraint) and *Fremdzwang* (external constraint), 167–8
shame, 41, 88, 89, 90, 91, 92, 93, 95, 178, 213n
Simmel, Georg, 30, 80, 146, 175, 177, 217n
smiling, 28, 51–2
Smith, Bonnie, 171–2
Smith, Dennis, 160, 163, 166, 167, 172, 185, 186, 203
smoking, 47–8, 77, 131, 146, 148–9, 204
social fields, 98, 187, 199; field theory, 215n
social praxeology, 191–2
social systems theory, 7
sociogenesis, 46, 80, 81, 144, 151, 156: and psychogenesis, 81, 144, 151, 156, 204

sociology: critical, 7, 11–15; decentred, 10; as destruction of myths, 46, 48, 78, 194; feminist, 7–8; fragmentation of, 9–10, 17, 42, 77; invention of the term, 4; and philosophy, 8, 10, 13, 53, 112–3, 175, 202; mores and 'habits' of, 11, 163–5, 193, 207; radical, 3; 'reflexive', 3, 7–8, 150, 188–200; as a science, 1, 7–8, 50, 45, 208n; and social control, 3; as the study of social relationships, 1; synchronic *versus* diachronic, 8
Socrates, 210n
Sokal Affair, 216n
Sokal, Alan, 10, 216n
Spierenburg, Pieter, 204
spitting, 90, 91, 92
sport, 8, 13, 32, 39, 45, 51, 54, 77, 82, 109, 131, 146, 178, 193, 205, 215
Stanley, Liz, 216n
state formation, 41, 65, 76, 80, 81, 97–103, 105–111, 146, 203, 205: as lengthening interdependency chains, 67, 97, 103, 176, 177, 205
statistics, 5, 8, 36, 43–4, 50, 150, 209
Strauss, Anselm, 191
Strauss, Leo, 19
Strinati, Dominic, 31
strong programme, 216n
structuralism, 192–3; genetic, 192
structuration theory, 7, 8, 176; critique of, 176–178
structure (*see also* figurations): duality of structure, 176–7; structure/agency dilemma, 8, 18, 39, 52, 53, 56, 74, 155, 174–178, 195, 211n; structure *and* social change, 51;
subjectivism, 14, 178: subjectivity, 186; subjectivity/objectivity dualism (*see also*, involvement and detachment), 130, 131, 132, 136, 140

table manners, 89–90, 92, 95–6
Taylor, Laurie, 31
Thatcher, Margaret, 23, 47, 56, 195
theory: and research (*see also*, figurational sociology: as simultaneously theoretical and empirical) 191; social versus

sociological, 217n; structure and process concepts, 203; testing, 9, 109, 126, 177, 191, 201, 203, 206–7; 'theoretical theory', 190, 191, 193; thought-abstract versus thought-concrete, 217n
Third Reich, 107, 118
Thomas, Dorothy, 45
Thomas, William Isaac, 45, 184
Thompson, Ken, 31
Three Worlds of Development model, 34–35
Thurnwald, Richard, 27, 212n
time, 12, 29, 68–73, 154–5, 176: and linguistic habits, 69–70, 154; past/present dualism, 156; and process, 70; and space, 176
Tönnies, Ferdinand, 43
triad of basic controls, 2, 74, 194
Turner, Bryan, 129, 202

unintended consequences, 14, 24, 47, 132, 146, 147, 197, 202
Urry, John, 178
utopias, 14–15, 20, 27, 147, 185

values, 136–147, 158, 196: bias versus neutrality, 136, 138; evaluations, heteronomous and autonomous, 47, 131, 134, 135, 137, 138, 146, 159, 164; fact/value dualism, 196; value-incursion, 131, 197, 113–4, 126, 130–1, 134–5, 196; value-freedom, 196–7
Van Eyck, Jan, 158
Van Krieken, Robert, 1, 41, 121–3, 195–7
Van Stolk, Bram, 19
Van Voss, Arend-Jan Heerma, 19

Vandenbergh, Frédéric, 199–200
Varcoe, Ian, 31
Velazquez, Diego, 156, 158, 179, 180, 181, 182
violence, 13, 18, 22, 39, 41, 43–4, 62, 77, 94–7, 101–2, 107, 108, 163, 167, 171–2, 204, 205–6, 214n, 216n
voluntarism, 46, 57, 81, 145, 190

Wacquant, Loïc, 10, 188, 189, 192, 193, 194
Waddington, Ivan, 31, 204, 211n
Wallerstein, Immanuel, 6
Walsh, David, 31
Watson, James, 152
Watson, John Broadus, 30
Watson, Rod, 31
we-I balance, 2, 181, 183
Weber, Alfred, 27, 29, 30, 40, 54, 80
Weber, Max, 4, 7, 9, 12, 17, 30, 33, 34, 35, 36, 40, 41, 53, 54, 64, 66, 80, 100, 146, 174, 178, 189, 195, 196, 201
Western triumphalism, 33, 103, 109, 118
White, Leslie, 211n
Wilson, Bryan, 31, 40
Winch, Peter, 112
Winnicott, Donald, 51
Wise, Sue, 217n
Wittfogel, Karl August, 117
Wolf, Eric, 26
Wolff, Kurt, 217n
Worsley, Peter, 169, 208n, 209n
Wouters, Cas, 1, 6, 93, 112, 204
Young Workers project, 150–1, 153

Zubaida, Sami, 31, 169, 203

www.ingramcontent.com/pod-product-compliance
Lightning Source LLC
Chambersburg PA
CBHW061440300426
44114CB00014B/1762